STAN LEE

"Hey, Fellow Ultimo-ites!

Wouldja believe we're already releasing *Ultimo* vol. 3? Time sure flies when you're having fun—and *Ultimo*'s a blast! Speaking of blasts, even though I've enjoyed helping to bring *Ultimo* to an oh-so-grateful public, I think the biggest blast of all has been tweeting, because that makes me feel like I'm talking directly to millions of my fans—well, thousands, anyway—all right, hundreds—how about we settle for dozens?

Anyway, if you can't wait to get in on the act, check out my world-famous, carefully guarded Twitter headquarters at http://twitter.com/smilinstanlee—and it's okay to tell your friends, but only if they're worthy!

So enjoy *Ultimo* (or incur my wrath!) and remember—whenever you have some time to waste and don't mind being hopelessly confused, you've got a standing invitation to tweet with me. And maybe someday we'll find out why no one ever says "You have a sitting invitation."

Excelsior!
Stan Lee

ORIGINALLY PUBLISHED IN JUMP SQUARE, NOS. 11–12, 2009; NOS. 1–2, 2010; JUMP SQUARE SECOND, VOL. 4

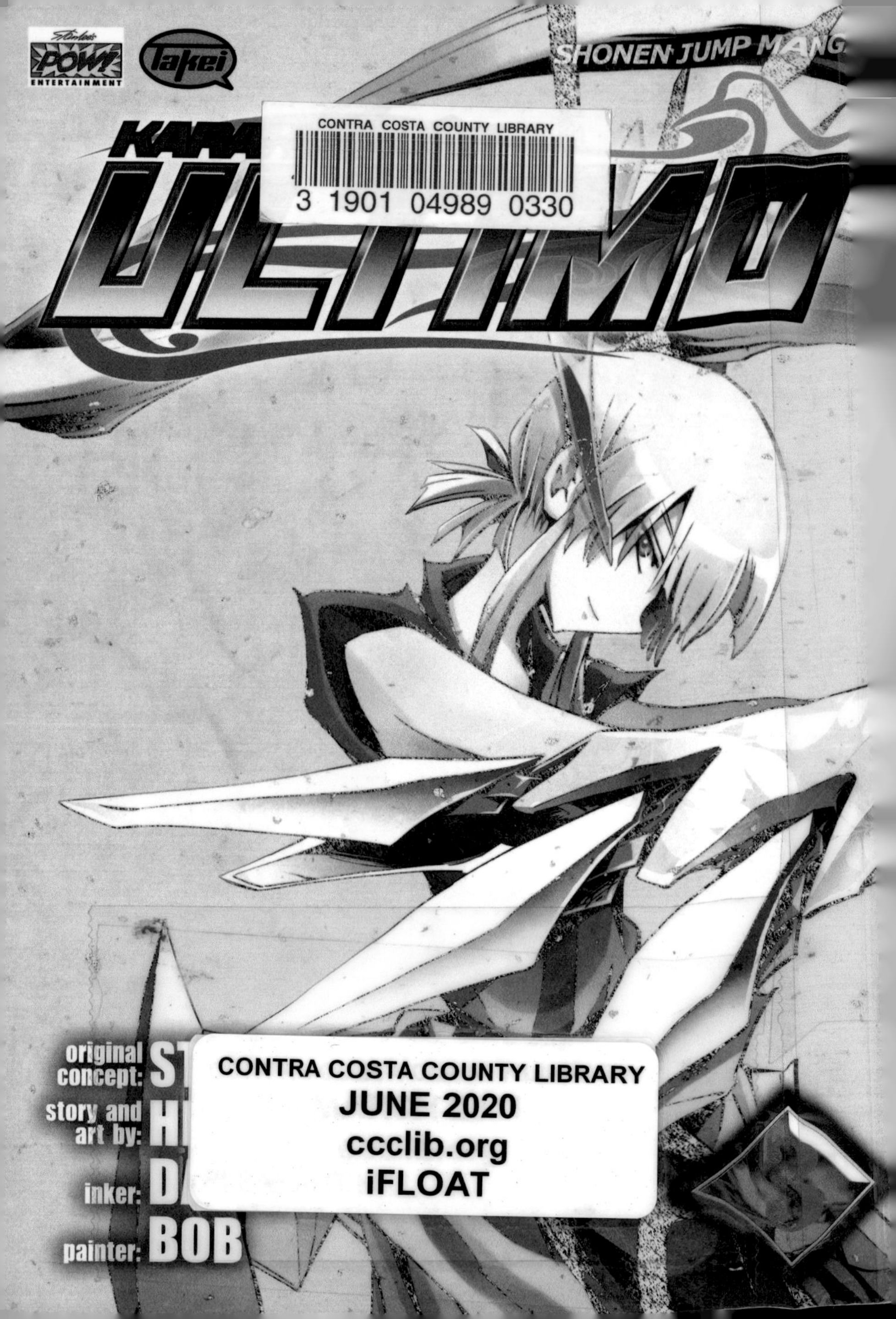
Stan Lee's
POW!
ENTERTAINMENT
Takei
SHONEN JUMP MANG
KARA
ULTIMO
original concept: ST
story and art by: H
inker: D
painter: BOB

SHONEN JUMP MANGA

KARAKURIDÔJI ULTIMO

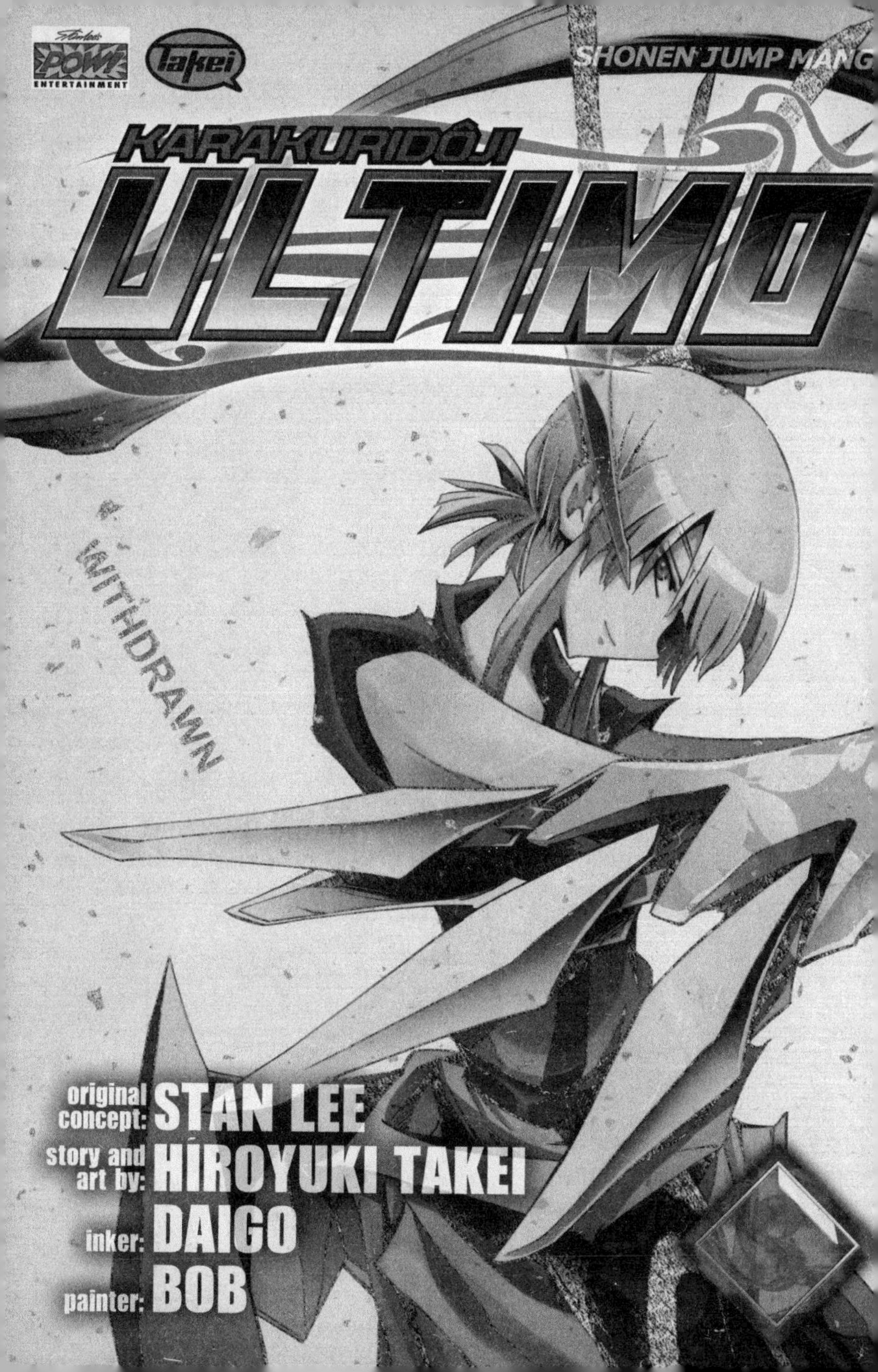

original concept: STAN LEE
story and art by: HIROYUKI TAKEI
inker: DAIGO
painter: BOB

Karakuri Dôji Ultimo

Characters

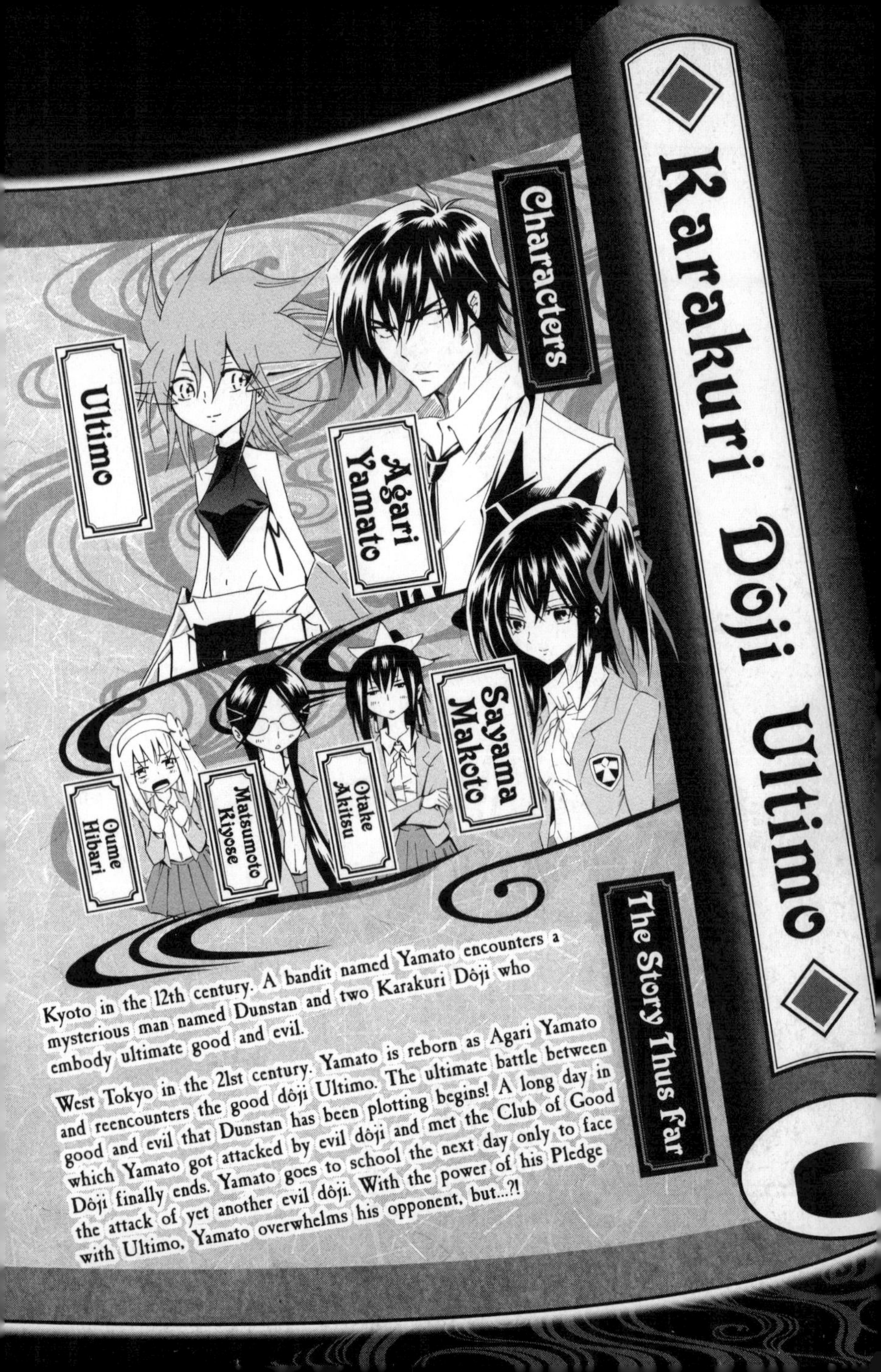
Agari Yamato
Ultimo
Sayama Makoto
Otake Akitsu
Matsumoto Kiyose
Oume Hibari

The Story Thus Far

Kyoto in the 12th century. A bandit named Yamato encounters a mysterious man named Dunstan and two Karakuri Dôji who embody ultimate good and evil.

West Tokyo in the 21st century. Yamato is reborn as Agari Yamato and reencounters the good dôji Ultimo. The ultimate battle between good and evil that Dunstan has been plotting begins! A long day in which Yamato got attacked by evil dôji and met the Club of Good Dôji finally ends. Yamato goes to school the next day only to face the attack of yet another evil dôji. With the power of his Pledge with Ultimo, Yamato overwhelms his opponent, but...?!

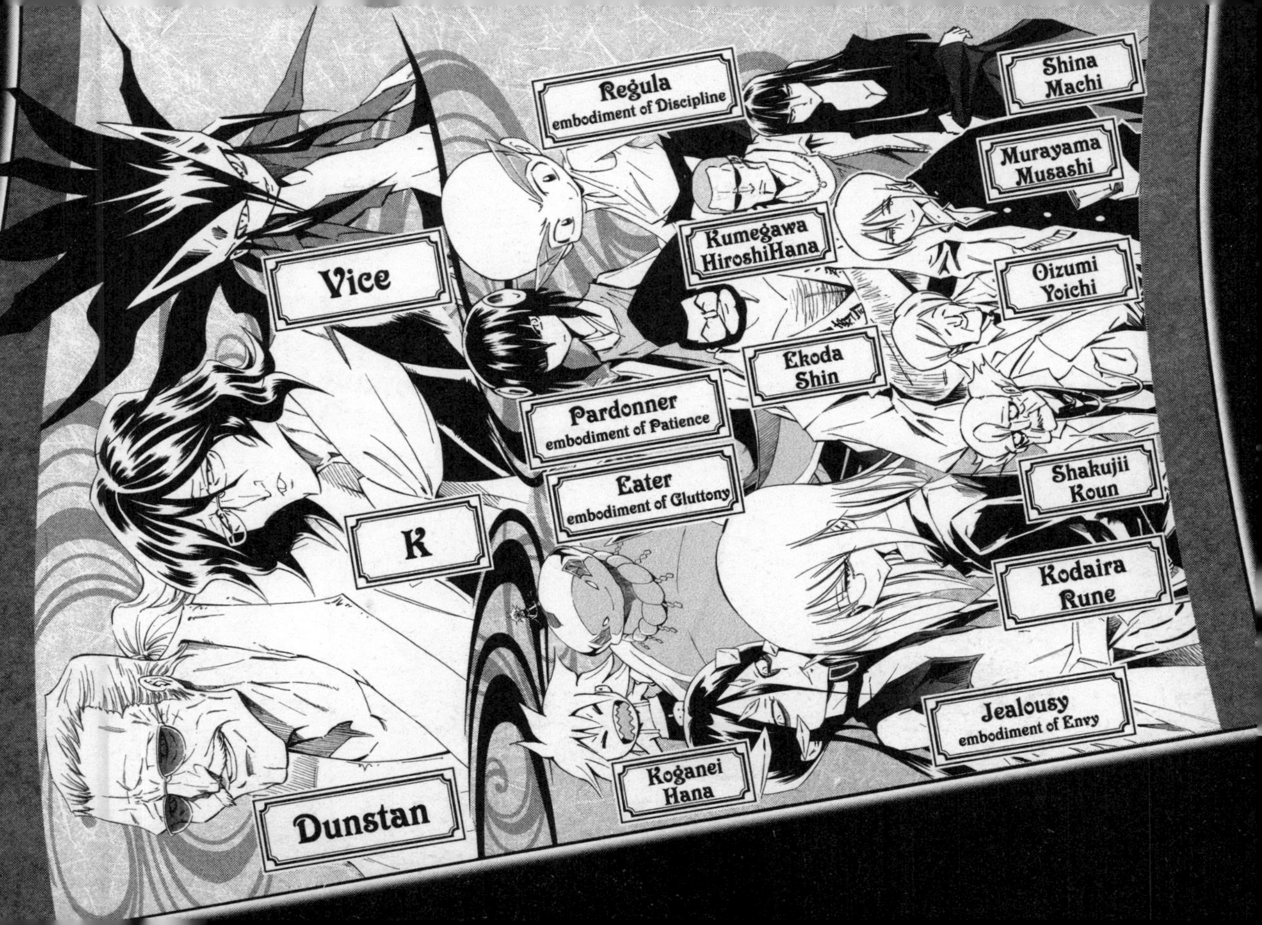
Regula
embodiment of Discipline
Shina
Machi
Murayama
Musashi
Kumegawa
HiroshiHana
Vice
Oizumi
Yoichi
Ekoda
Shin
Pardonner
embodiment of Patience
Eater
embodiment of Gluttony
Shakujii
Koun
K
Kodaira
Rune
Jealousy
embodiment of Envy
Koganei
Hana
Dunstan

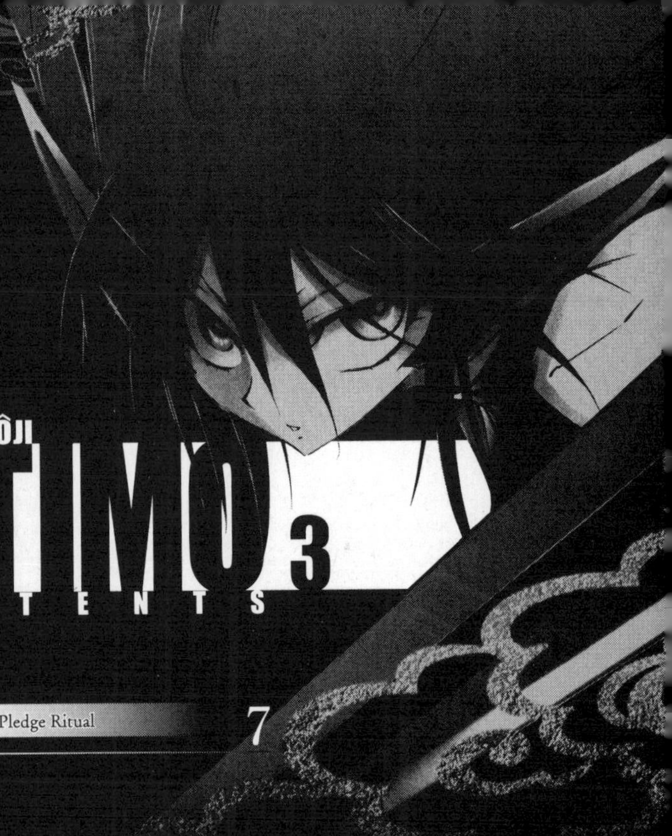

KARAKURIDÔJI

ULTIMO 3

CONTENTS

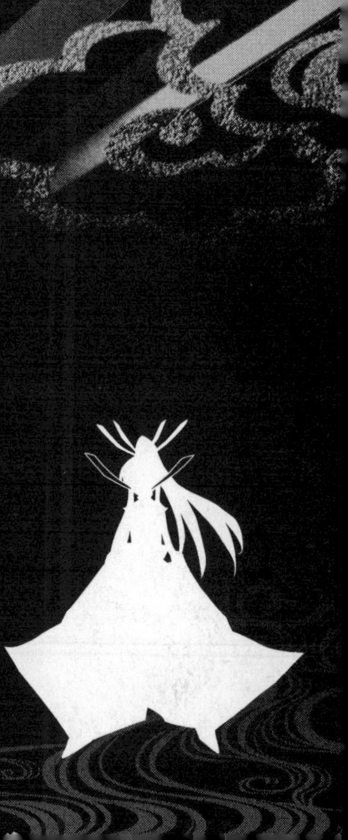

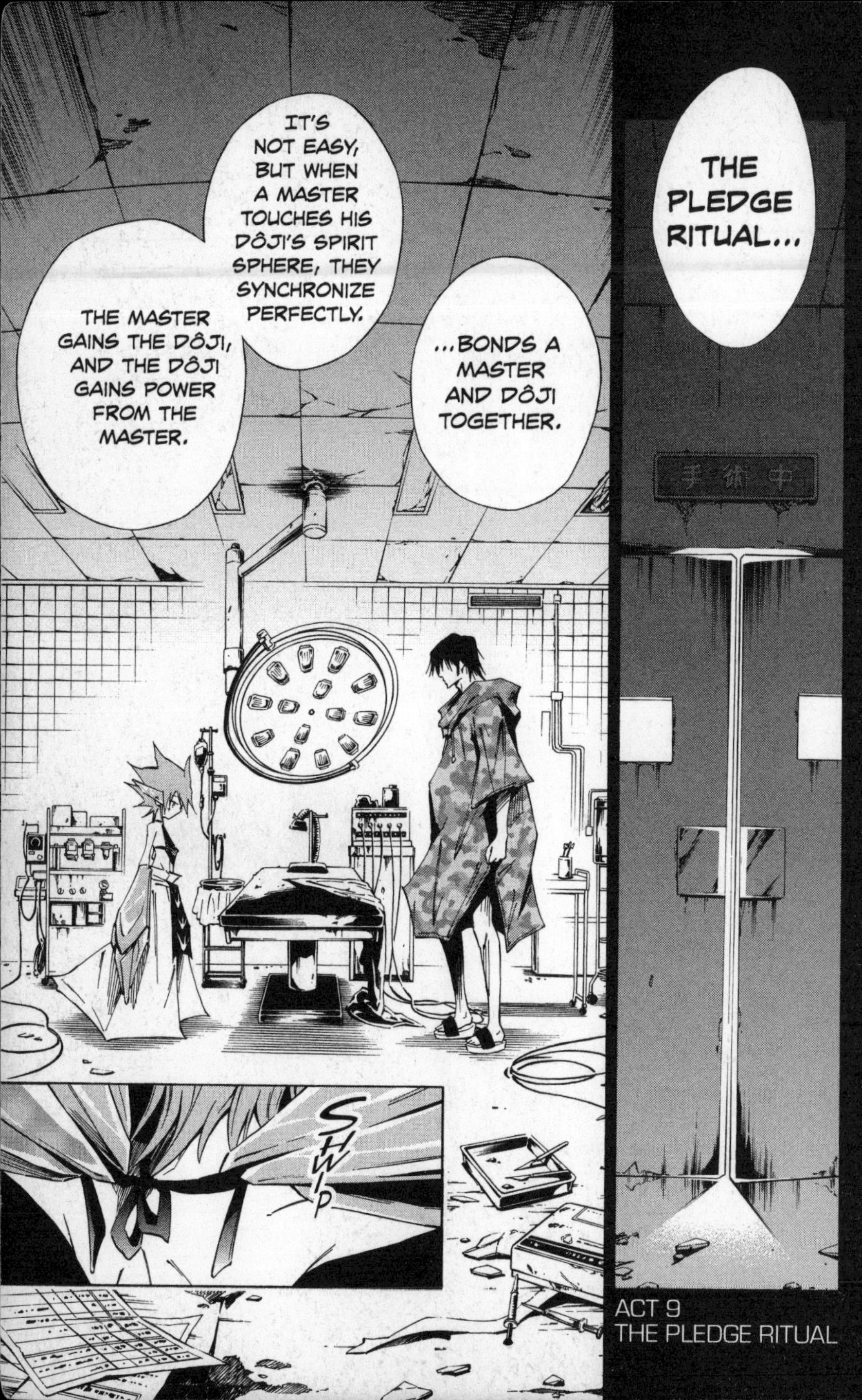
THE PLEDGE RITUAL...
手術中
...BONDS A MASTER AND DÔJI TOGETHER.
IT'S NOT EASY, BUT WHEN A MASTER TOUCHES HIS DÔJI'S SPIRIT SPHERE, THEY SYNCHRONIZE PERFECTLY.
THE MASTER GAINS THE DÔJI, AND THE DÔJI GAINS POWER FROM THE MASTER.
SHWIP

ACT 9
THE PLEDGE RITUAL

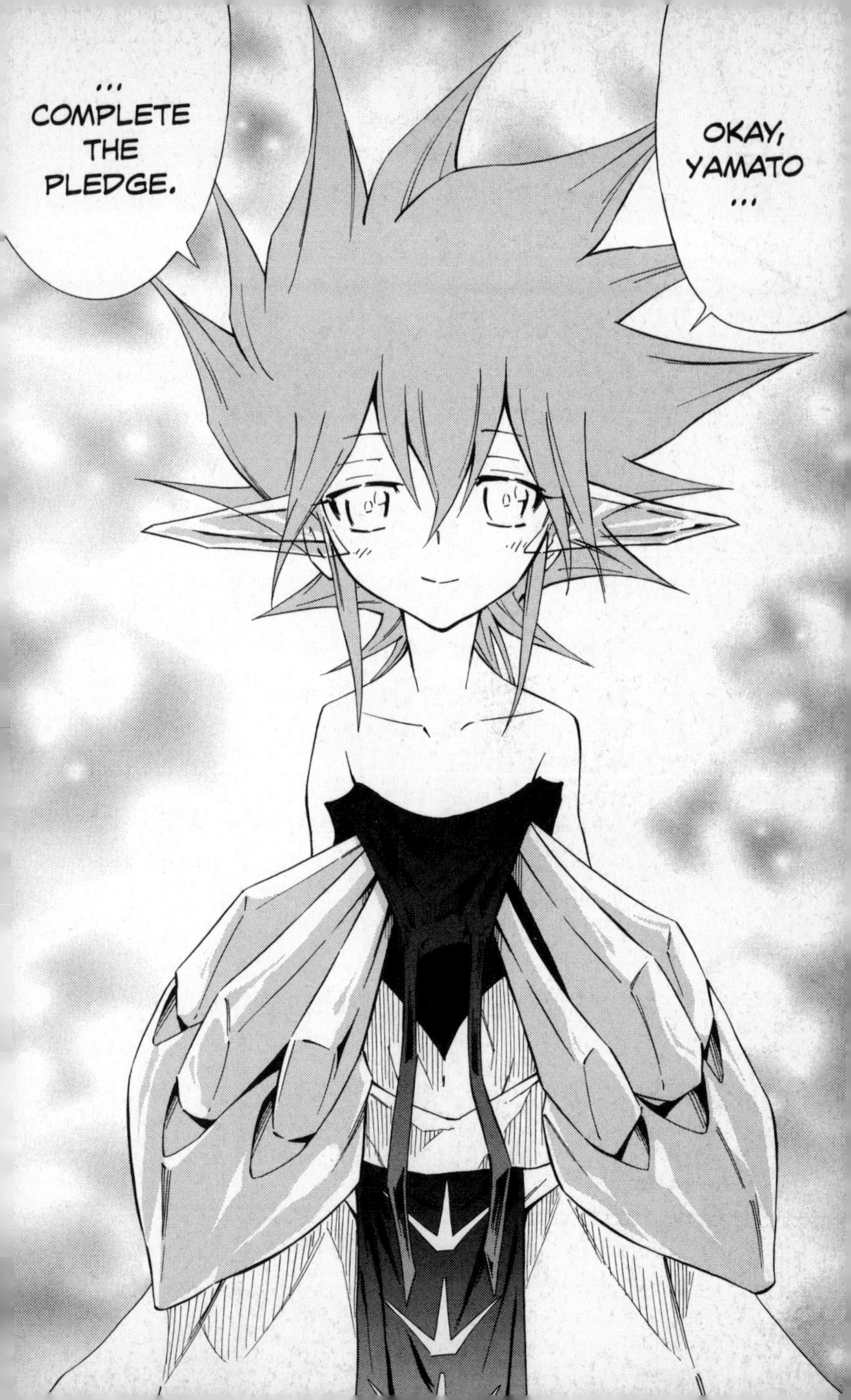
OKAY, YAMATO ...
... COMPLETE THE PLEDGE.

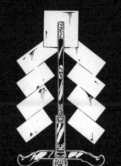

ACT 9
THE
PLEDGE
RITUAL

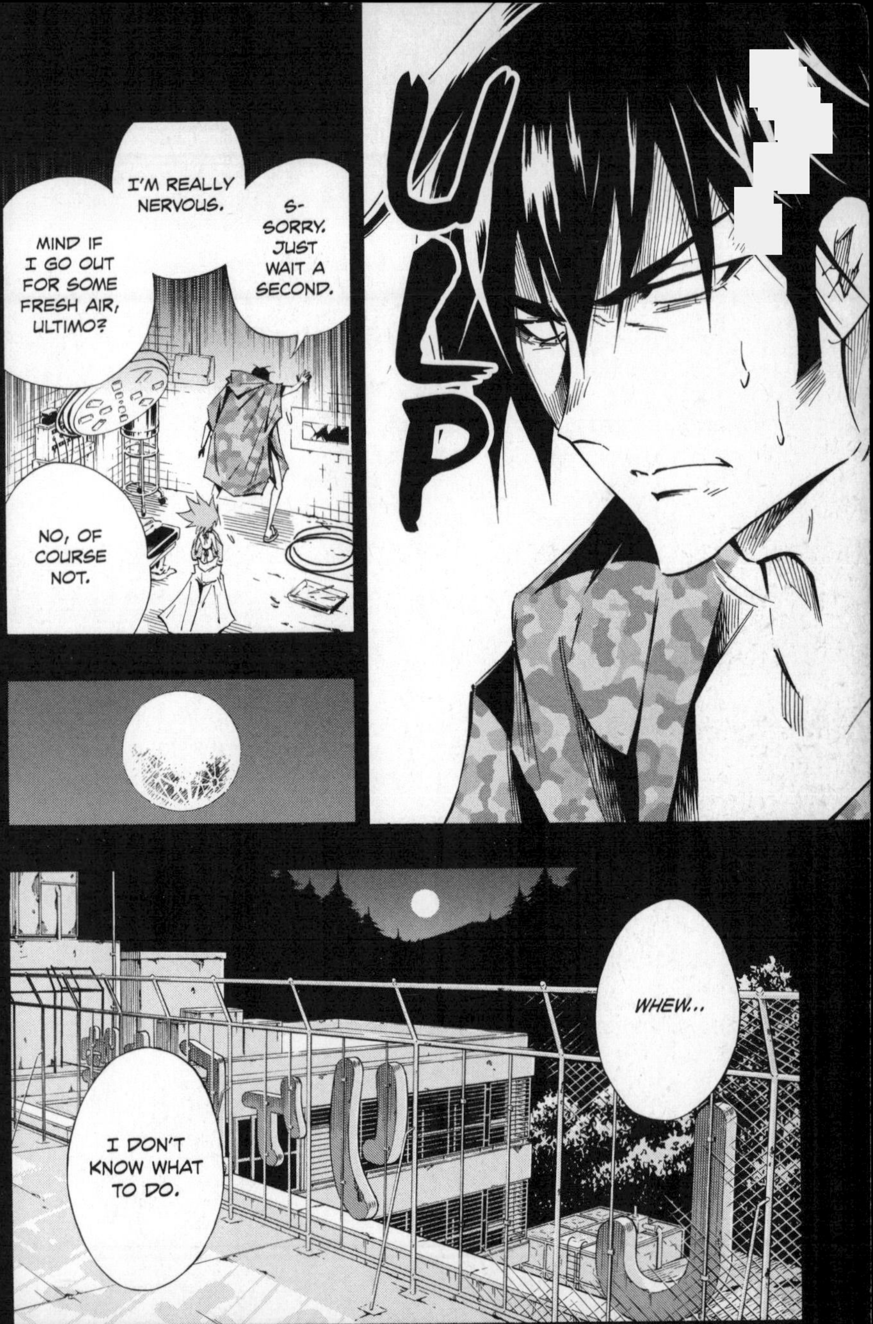
ULP
S-SORRY. JUST WAIT A SECOND.
I'M REALLY NERVOUS.
MIND IF I GO OUT FOR SOME FRESH AIR, ULTIMO?
NO, OF COURSE NOT.
WHEW...
I DON'T KNOW WHAT TO DO.

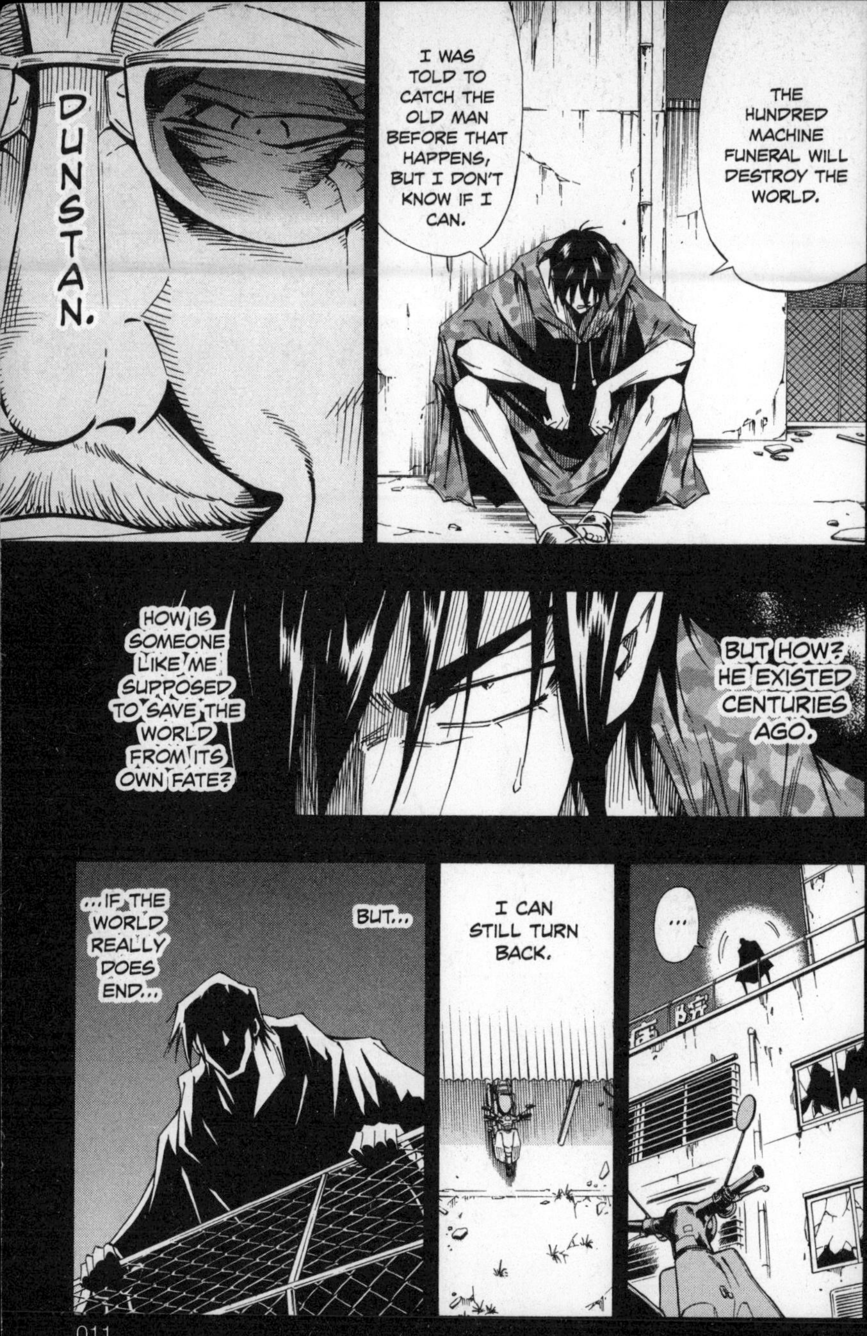
THE HUNDRED MACHINE FUNERAL WILL DESTROY THE WORLD.
I WAS TOLD TO CATCH THE OLD MAN BEFORE THAT HAPPENS, BUT I DON'T KNOW IF I CAN.
DUNSTAN.
BUT HOW? HE EXISTED CENTURIES AGO.
HOW IS SOMEONE LIKE ME SUPPOSED TO SAVE THE WORLD FROM ITS OWN FATE?
...
I CAN STILL TURN BACK.
BUT...
...IF THE WORLD REALLY DOES END...

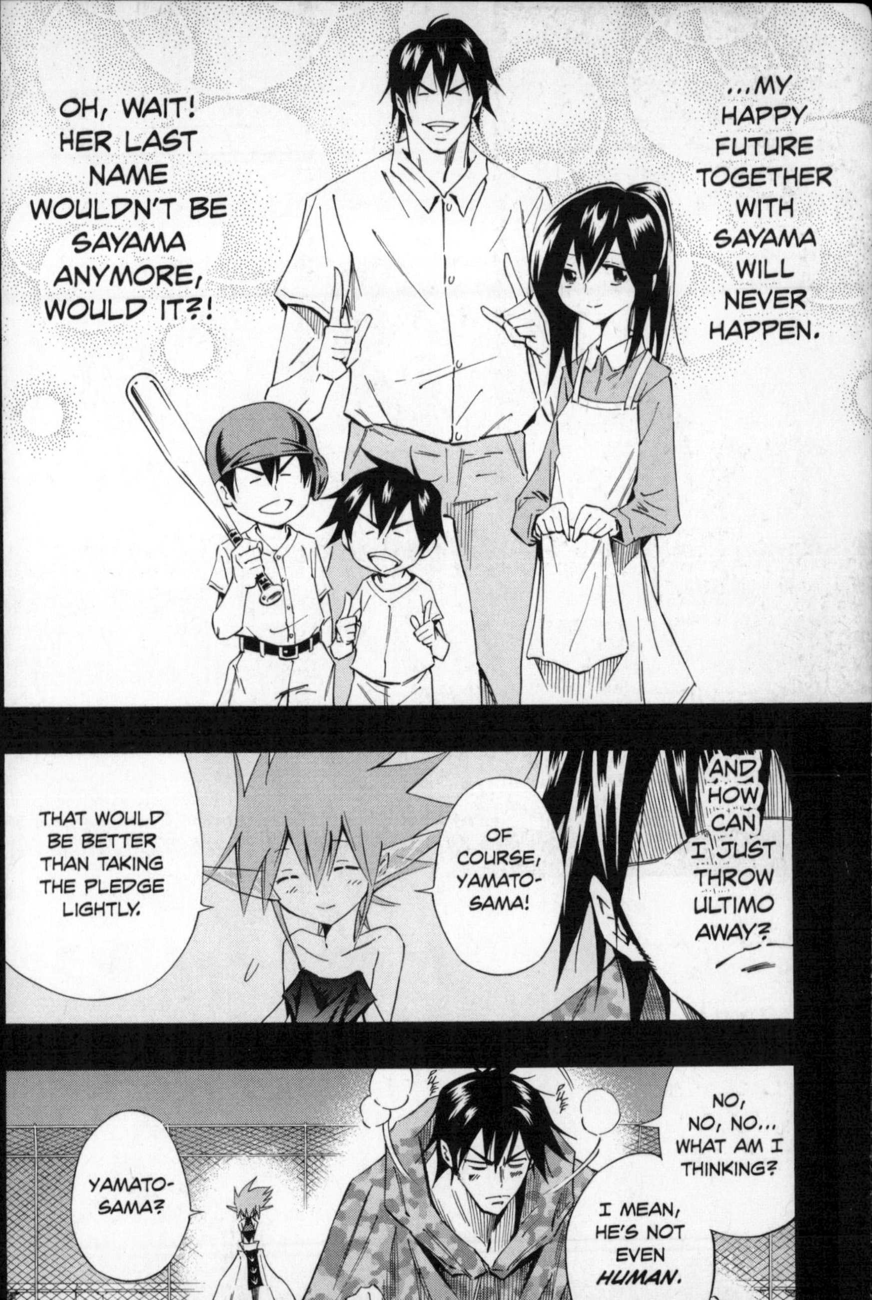
...MY HAPPY FUTURE TOGETHER WITH SAYAMA WILL NEVER HAPPEN.
OH, WAIT! HER LAST NAME WOULDN'T BE SAYAMA ANYMORE, WOULD IT?!
AND HOW CAN I JUST THROW ULTIMO AWAY?
OF COURSE, YAMATO-SAMA!
THAT WOULD BE BETTER THAN TAKING THE PLEDGE LIGHTLY.
NO, NO, NO... WHAT AM I THINKING?
I MEAN, HE'S NOT EVEN *HUMAN.*
YAMATO-SAMA?

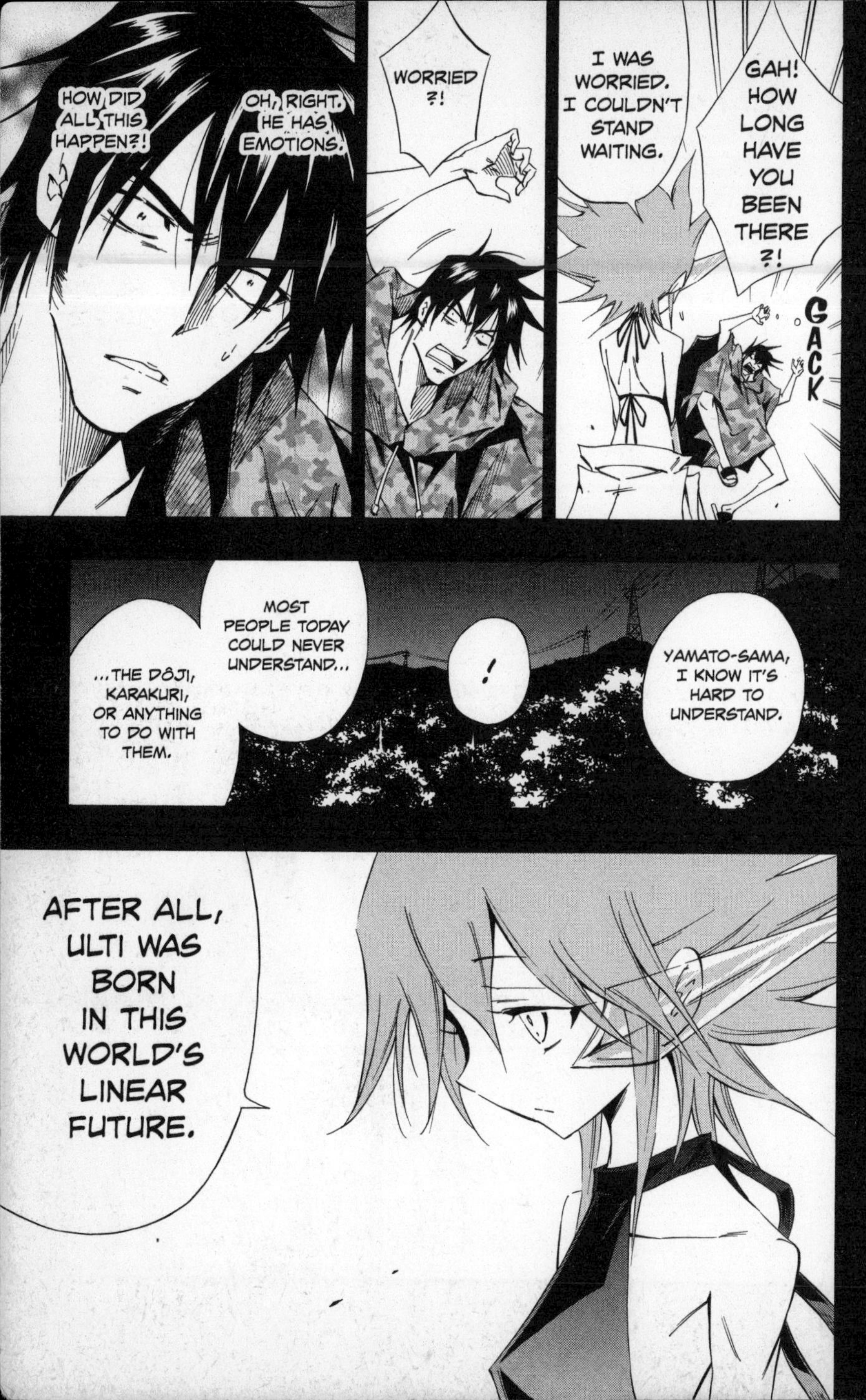
GAH! HOW LONG HAVE YOU BEEN THERE?!
I WAS WORRIED. I COULDN'T STAND WAITING.
GACK
WORRIED?!
OH, RIGHT. HE HAS EMOTIONS.
HOW DID ALL THIS HAPPEN?!
YAMATO-SAMA, I KNOW IT'S HARD TO UNDERSTAND.
!
MOST PEOPLE TODAY COULD NEVER UNDERSTAND...
...THE DÔJI, KARAKURI, OR ANYTHING TO DO WITH THEM.
AFTER ALL, ULTI WAS BORN IN THIS WORLD'S LINEAR FUTURE.

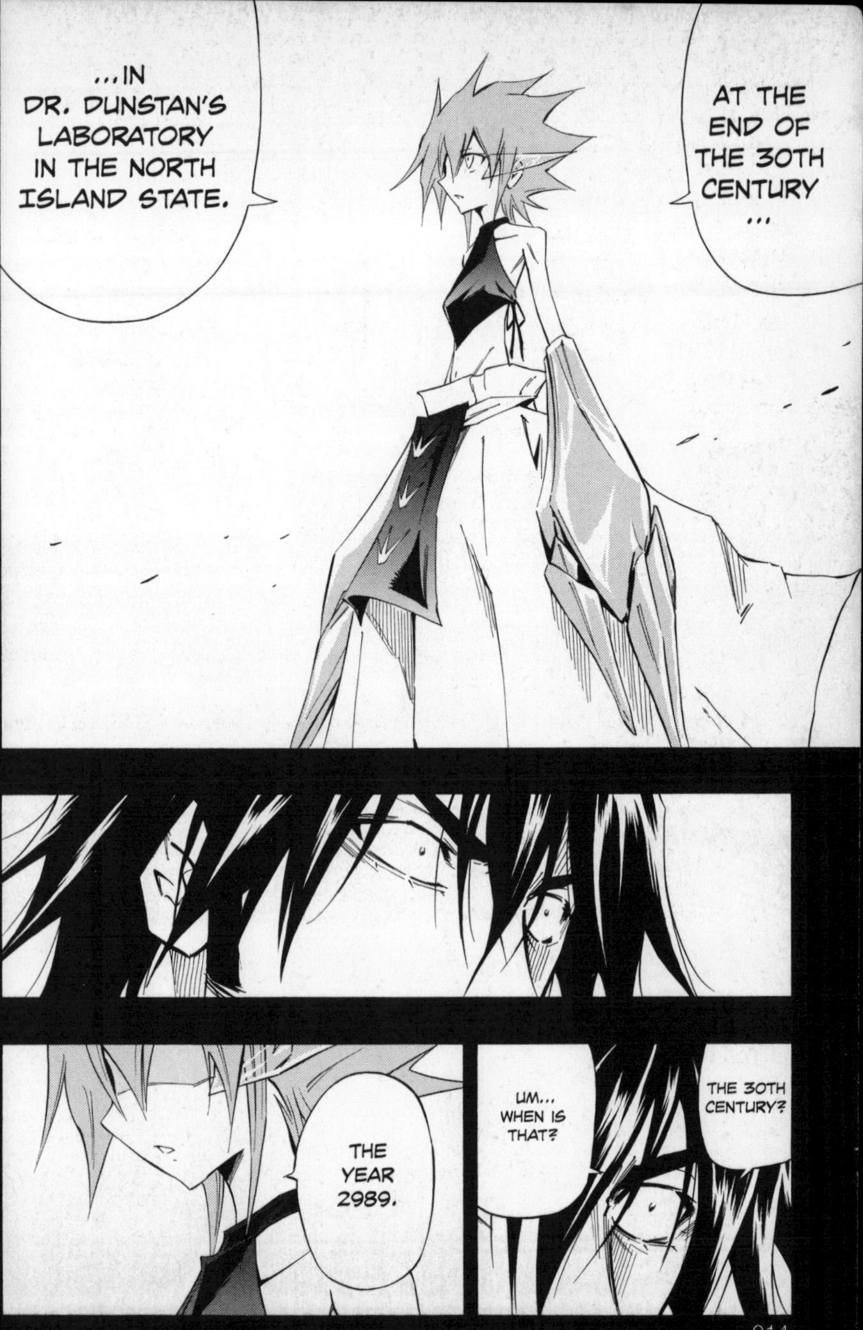
AT THE END OF THE 30TH CENTURY...
...IN DR. DUNSTAN'S LABORATORY IN THE NORTH ISLAND STATE.
THE 30TH CENTURY?
UM... WHEN IS THAT?
THE YEAR 2989.

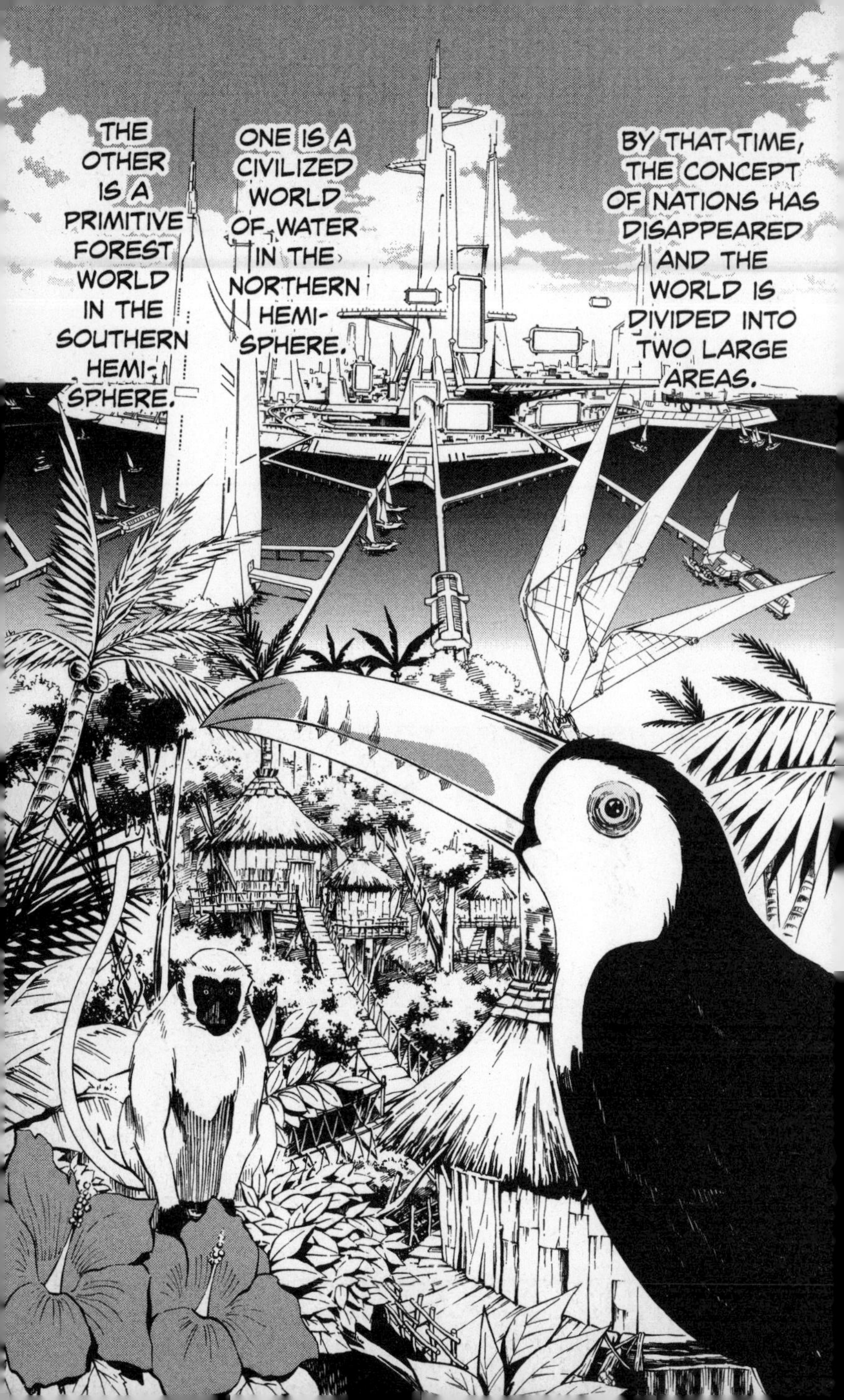
BY THAT TIME, THE CONCEPT OF NATIONS HAS DISAPPEARED AND THE WORLD IS DIVIDED INTO TWO LARGE AREAS.
ONE IS A CIVILIZED WORLD OF WATER IN THE NORTHERN HEMI-SPHERE.
THE OTHER IS A PRIMITIVE FOREST WORLD IN THE SOUTHERN HEMI-SPHERE.

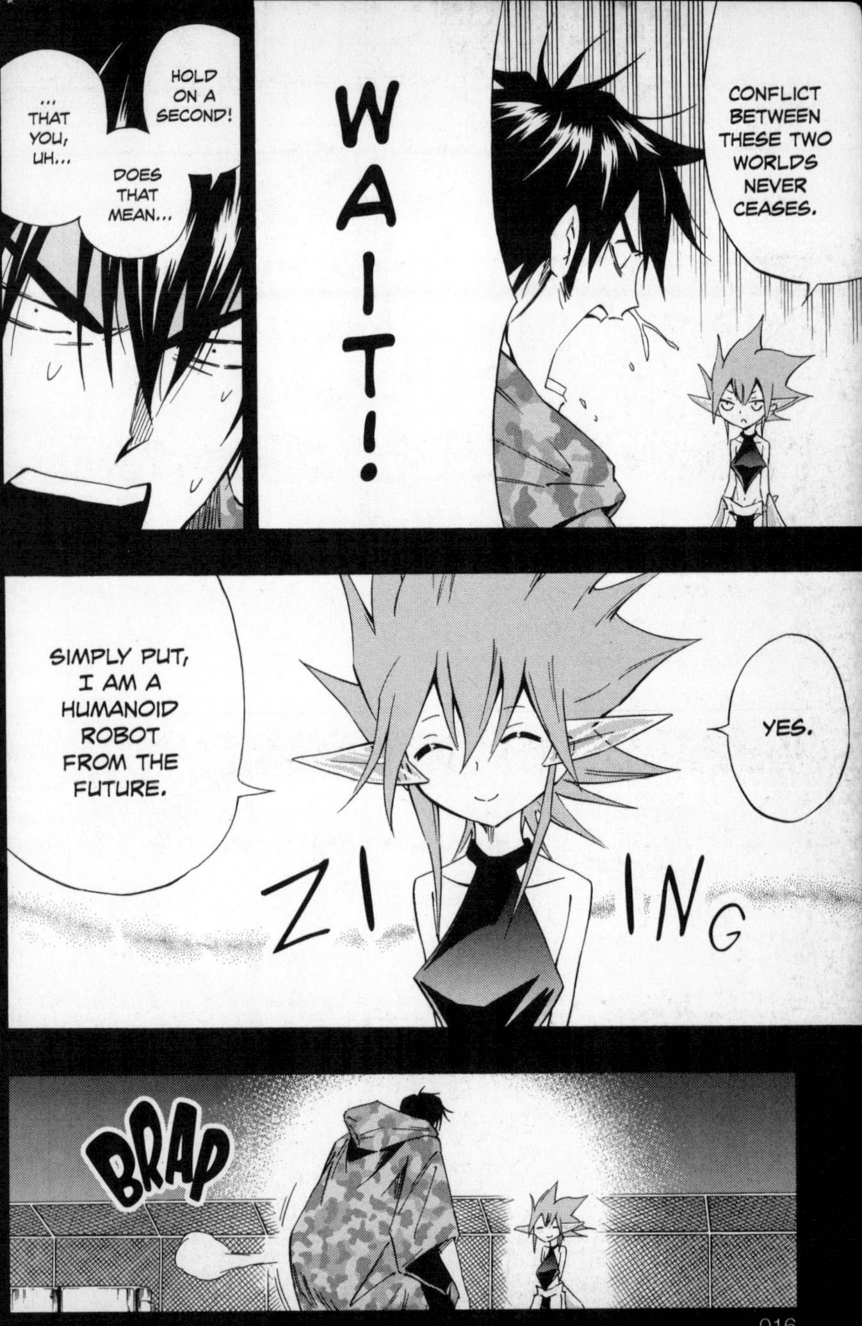
CONFLICT BETWEEN THESE TWO WORLDS NEVER CEASES.
WAIT!
HOLD ON A SECOND!
DOES THAT MEAN...
...THAT YOU, UH...
YES.
SIMPLY PUT, I AM A HUMANOID ROBOT FROM THE FUTURE.
ZIING
BRAP

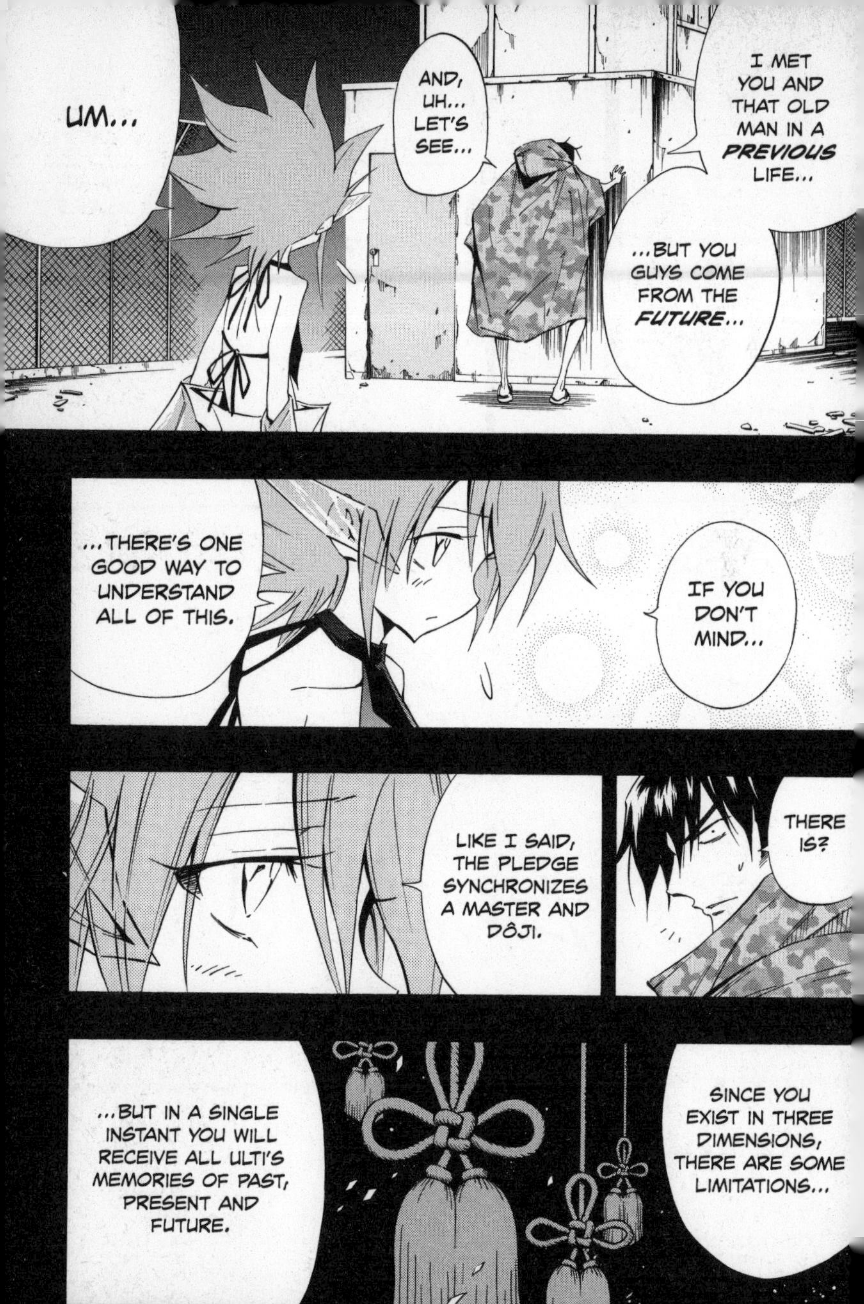
I MET YOU AND THAT OLD MAN IN A PREVIOUS LIFE...
...BUT YOU GUYS COME FROM THE FUTURE...
AND, UH... LET'S SEE...
UM...
IF YOU DON'T MIND...
...THERE'S ONE GOOD WAY TO UNDERSTAND ALL OF THIS.
THERE IS?
LIKE I SAID, THE PLEDGE SYNCHRONIZES A MASTER AND DÔJI.
SINCE YOU EXIST IN THREE DIMENSIONS, THERE ARE SOME LIMITATIONS...
...BUT IN A SINGLE INSTANT YOU WILL RECEIVE ALL ULTI'S MEMORIES OF PAST, PRESENT AND FUTURE.

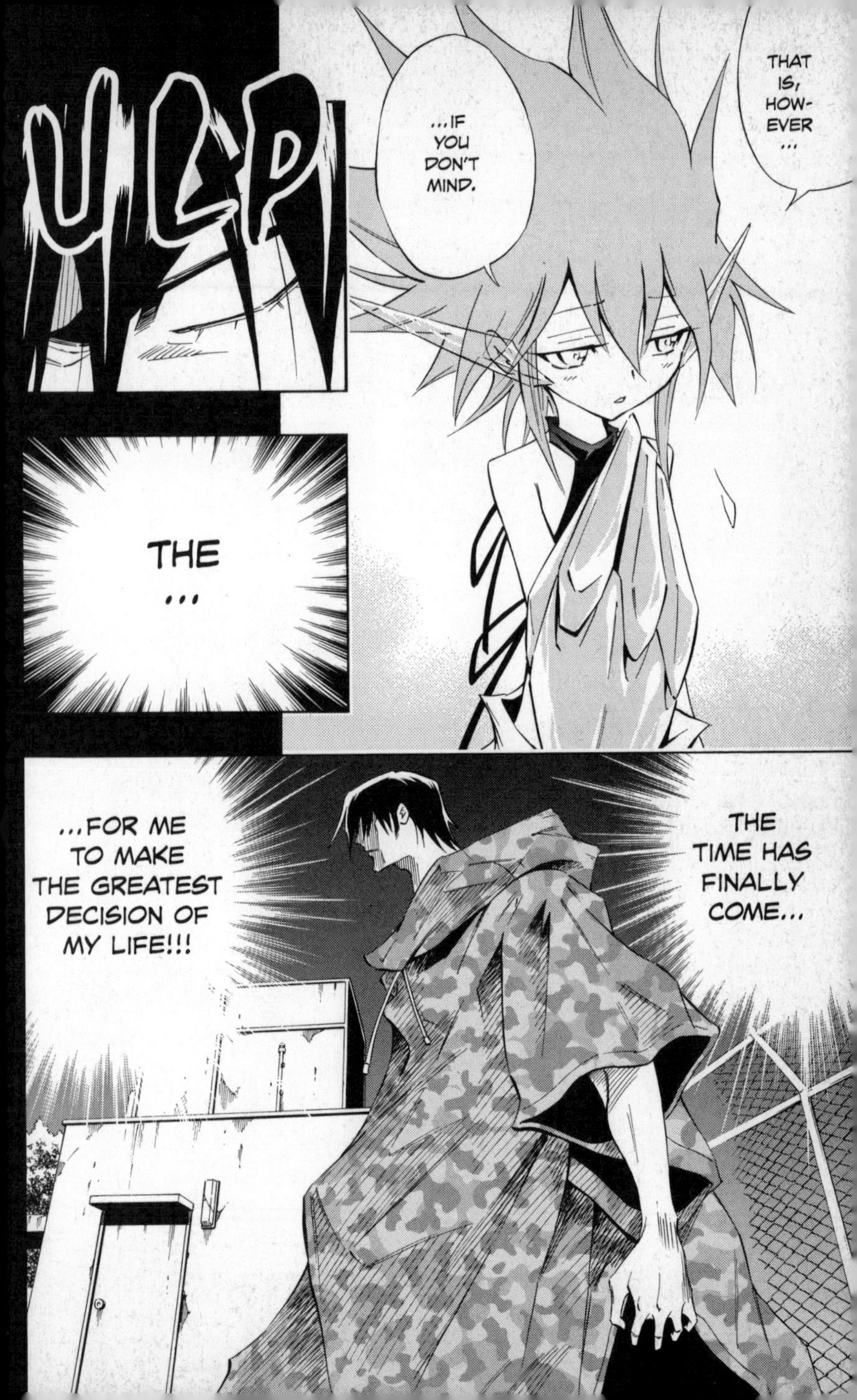
THAT IS, HOW-EVER ...
...IF YOU DON'T MIND.
UGP
THE ...
THE TIME HAS FINALLY COME...
...FOR ME TO MAKE THE GREATEST DECISION OF MY LIFE!!!

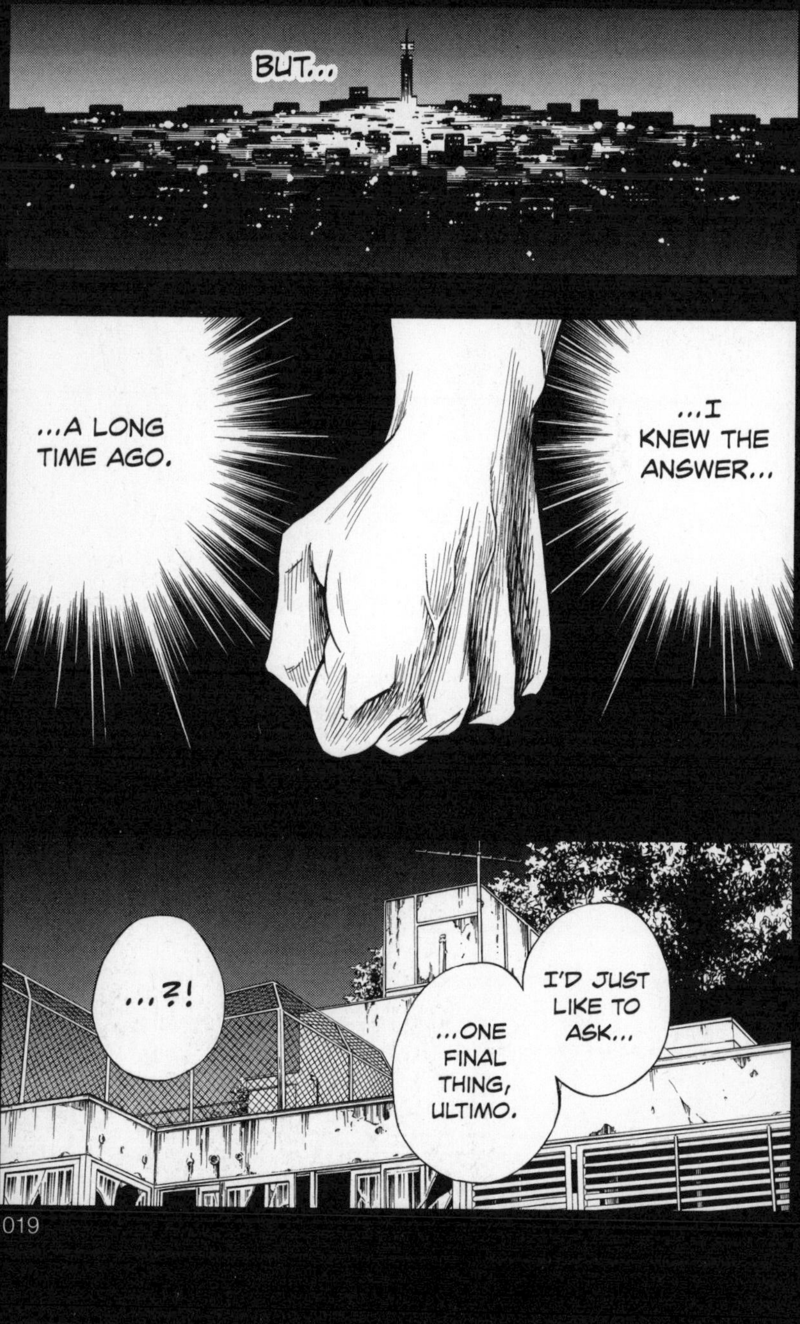
BUT...
...I KNEW THE ANSWER...
...A LONG TIME AGO.
I'D JUST LIKE TO ASK...
...ONE FINAL THING, ULTIMO.
...?!

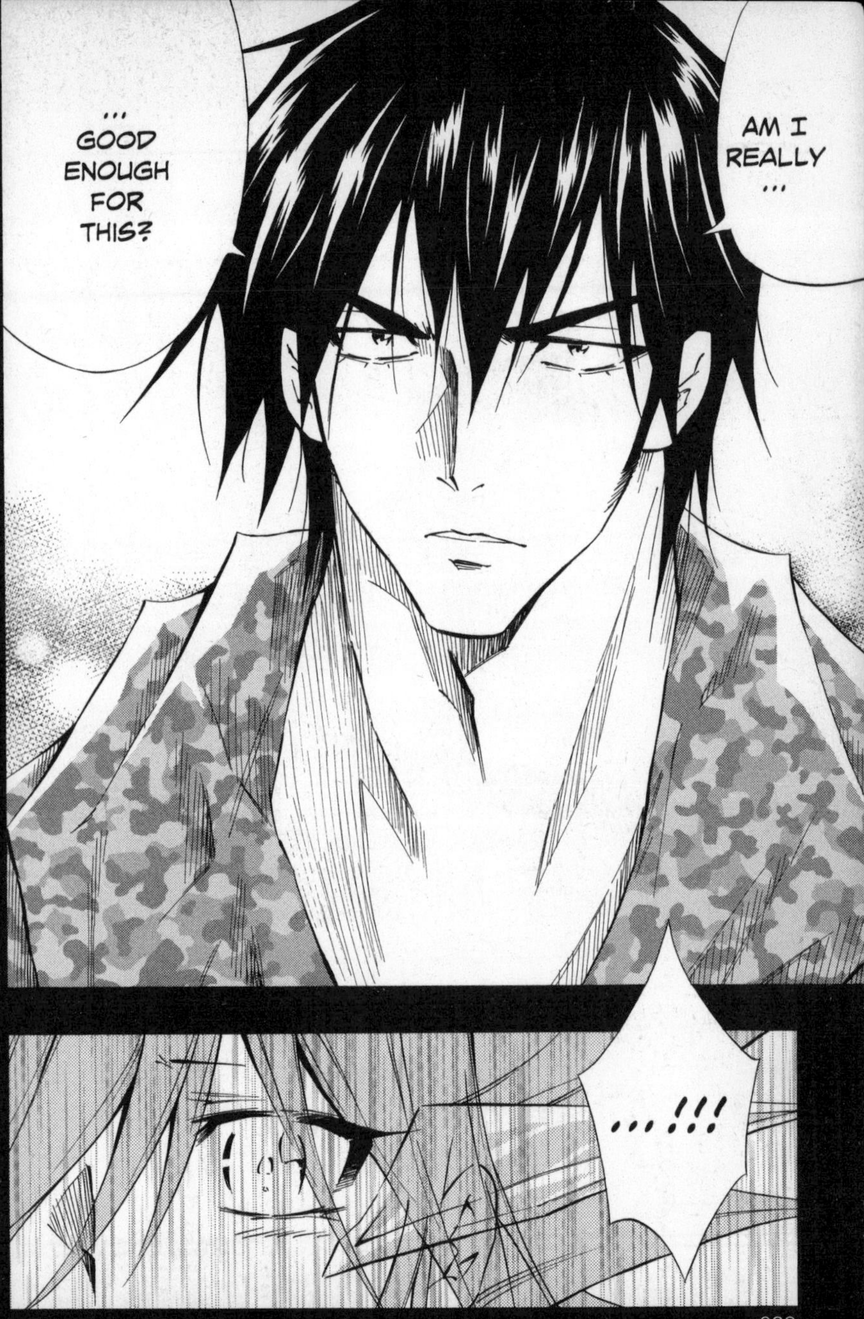
AM I REALLY ...
... GOOD ENOUGH FOR THIS?
...!!!

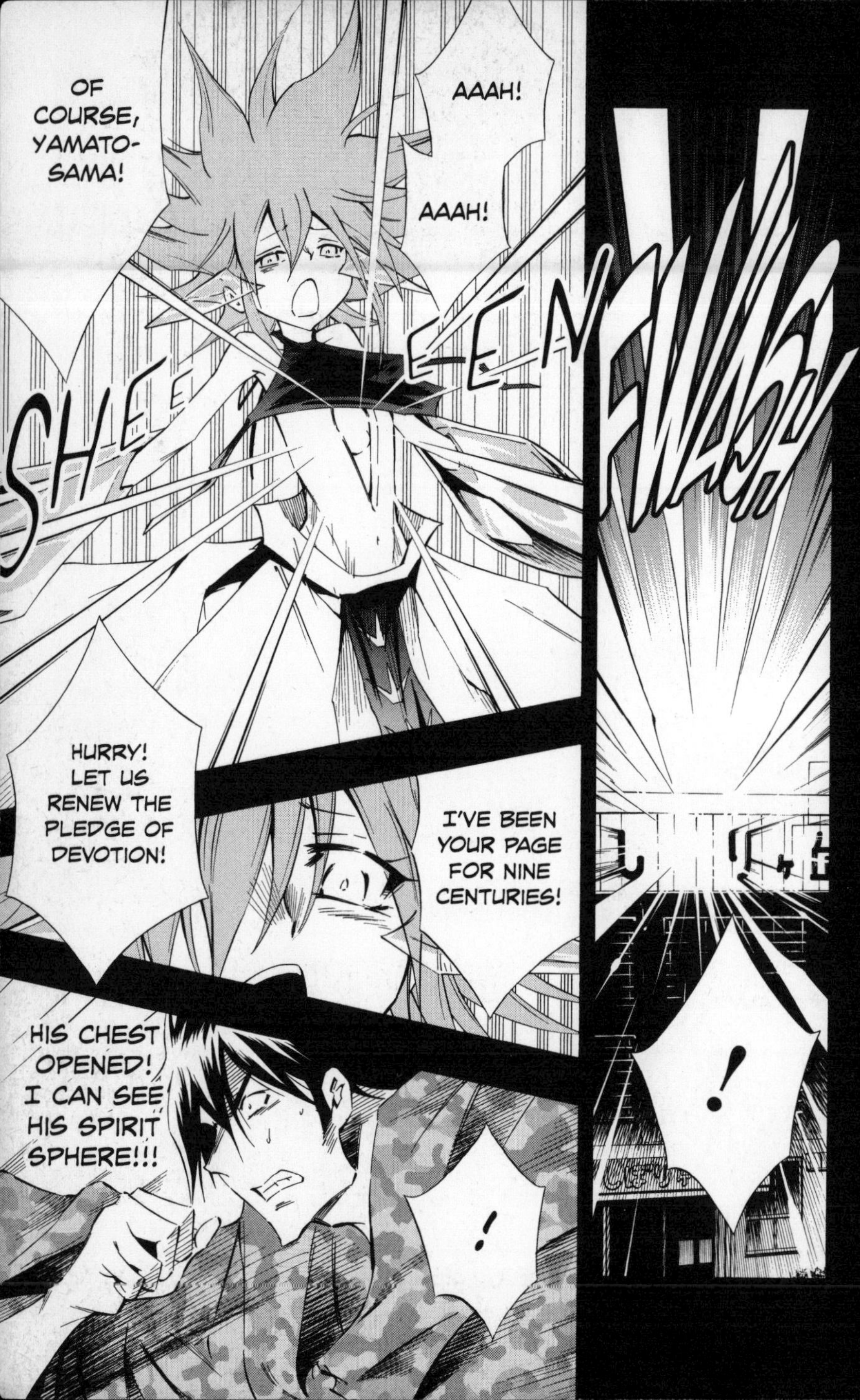
!
AAAH!
AAAH!
OF COURSE, YAMATO-SAMA!
SHEE-E-E-EN
I'VE BEEN YOUR PAGE FOR NINE CENTURIES!
HURRY! LET US RENEW THE PLEDGE OF DEVOTION!
!
HIS CHEST OPENED! I CAN SEE HIS SPIRIT SPHERE!!!

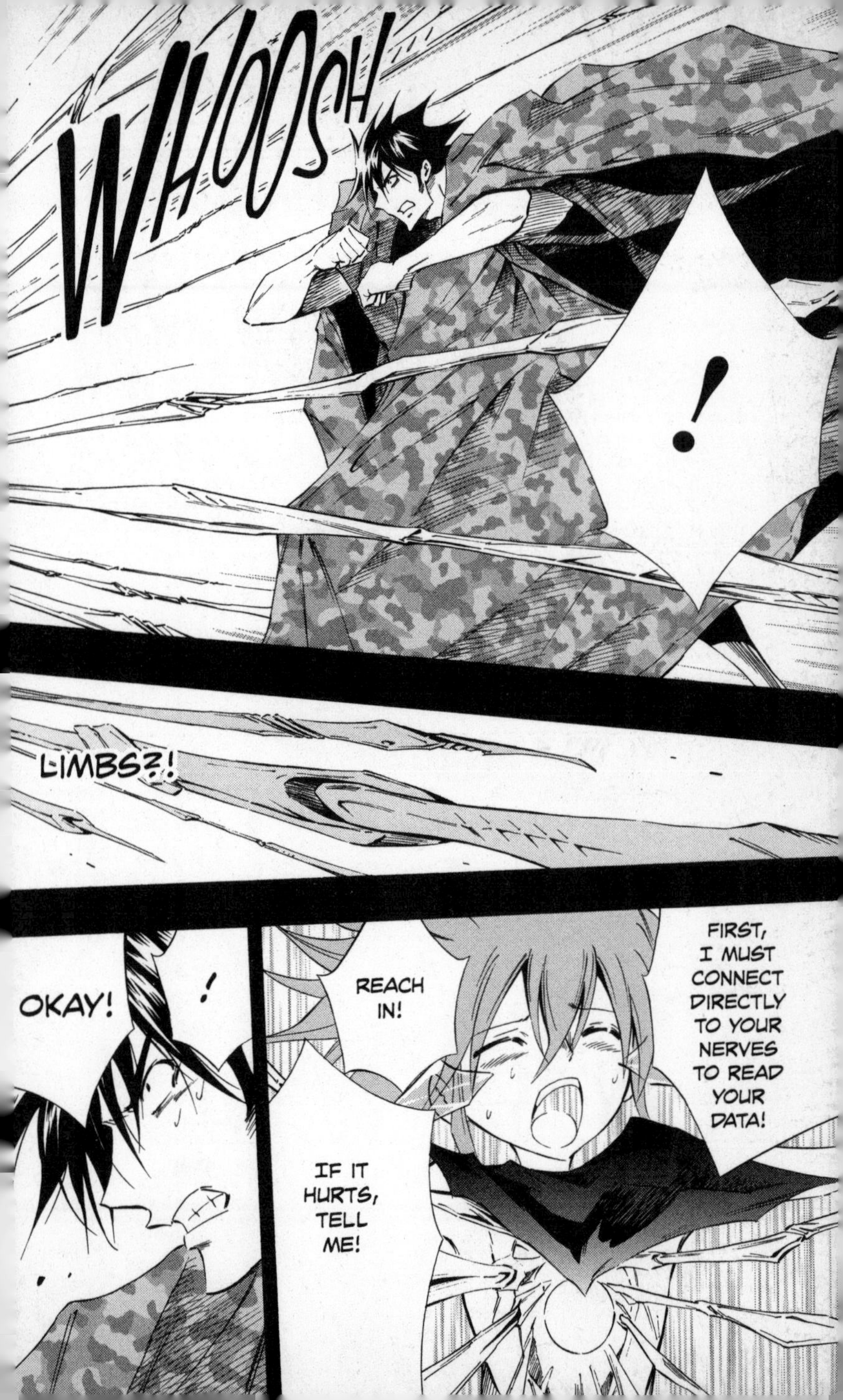
WHOOSH
!
LIMBS?!
FIRST, I MUST CONNECT DIRECTLY TO YOUR NERVES TO READ YOUR DATA!
REACH IN!
IF IT HURTS, TELL ME!
!
OKAY!

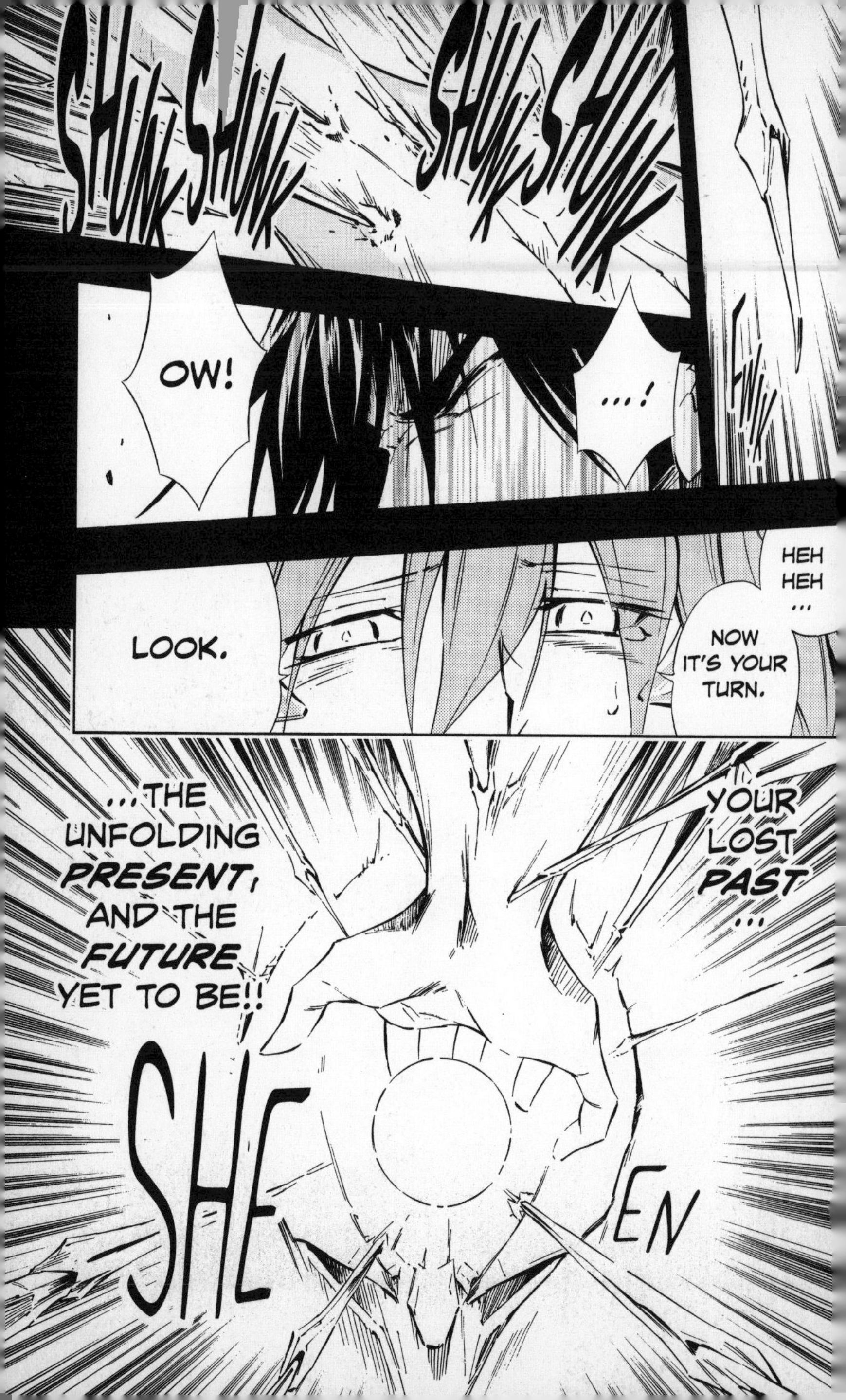
SHUNK SHUNK
SHUNK SHUNK
...!
OW!
HEH HEH ...
NOW IT'S YOUR TURN.
LOOK.
YOUR LOST PAST ...
... THE UNFOLDING PRESENT, AND THE FUTURE YET TO BE!!
SHEEN

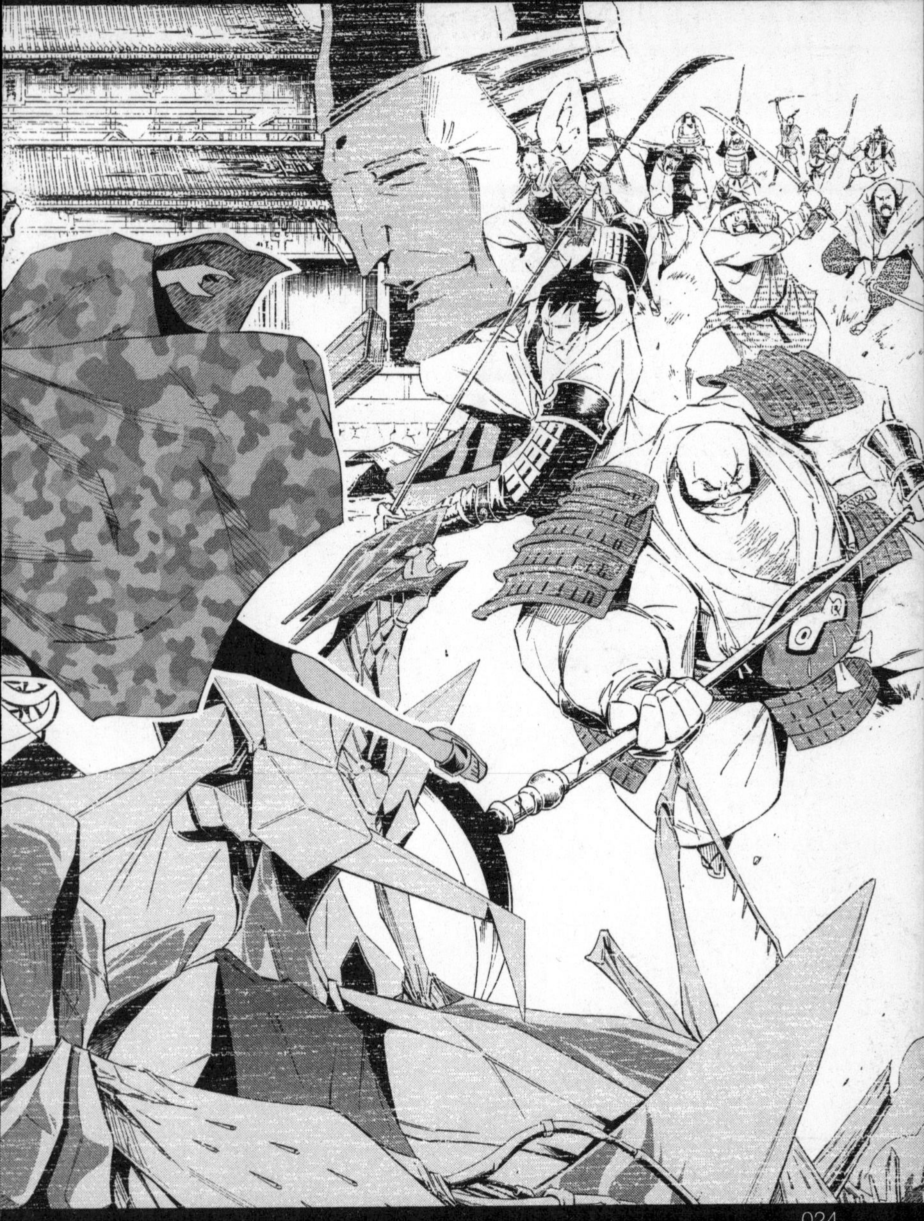

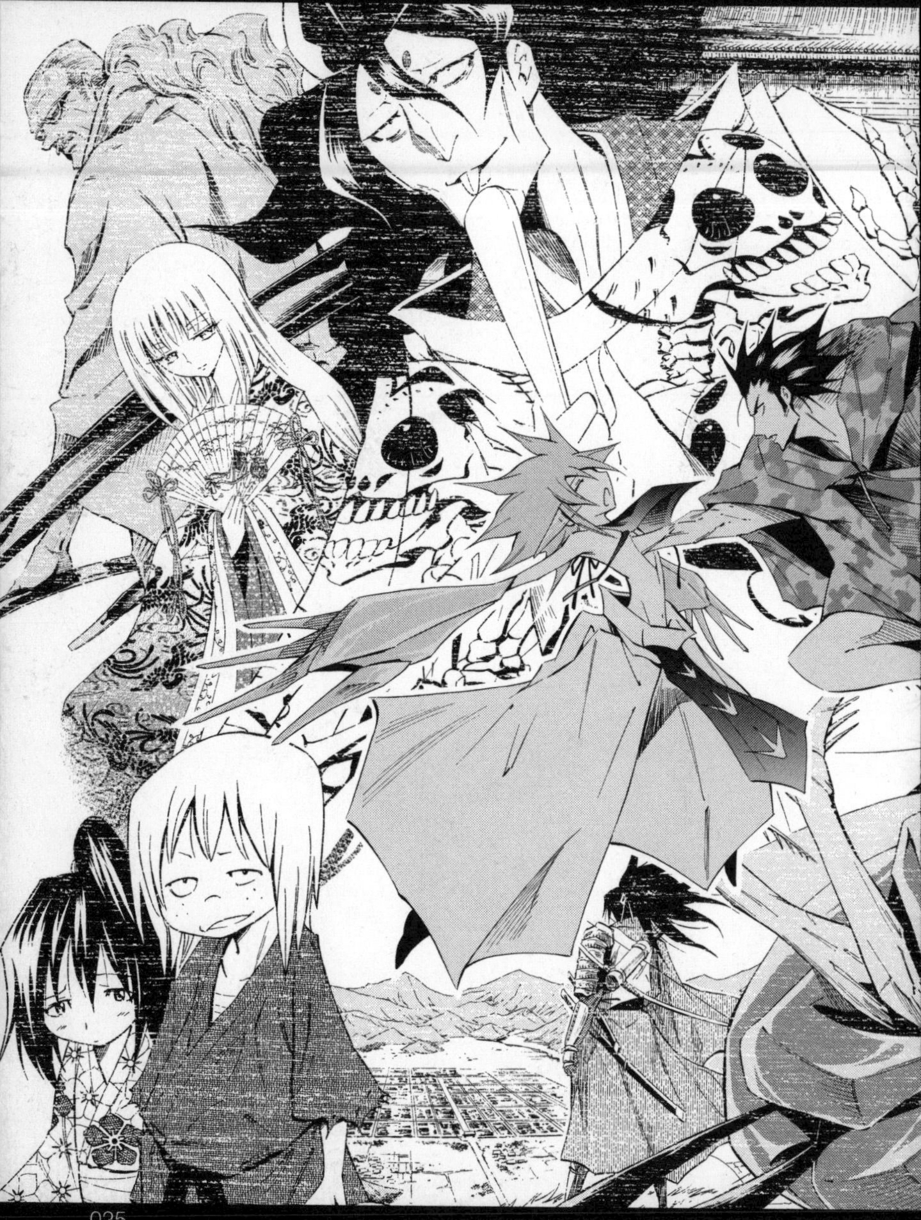

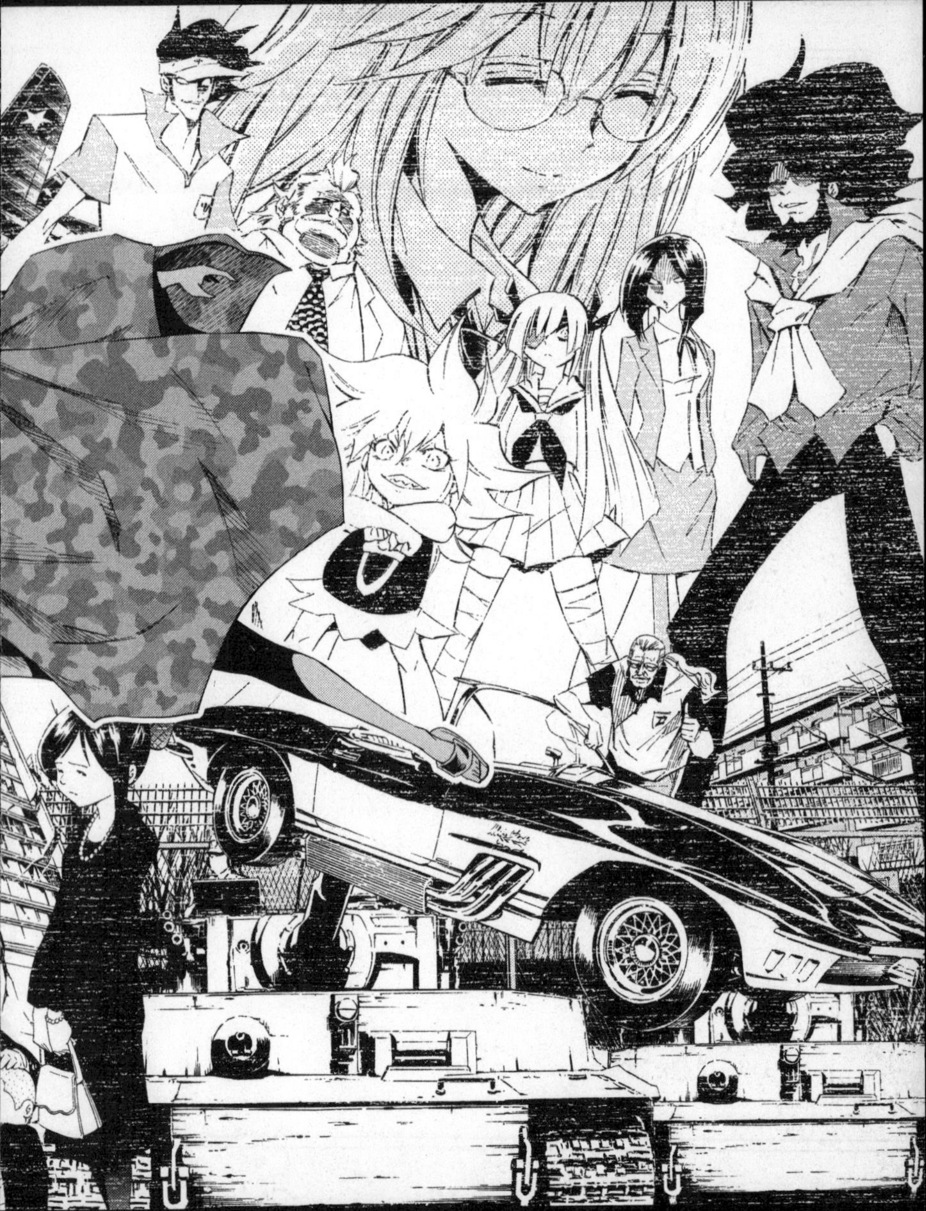

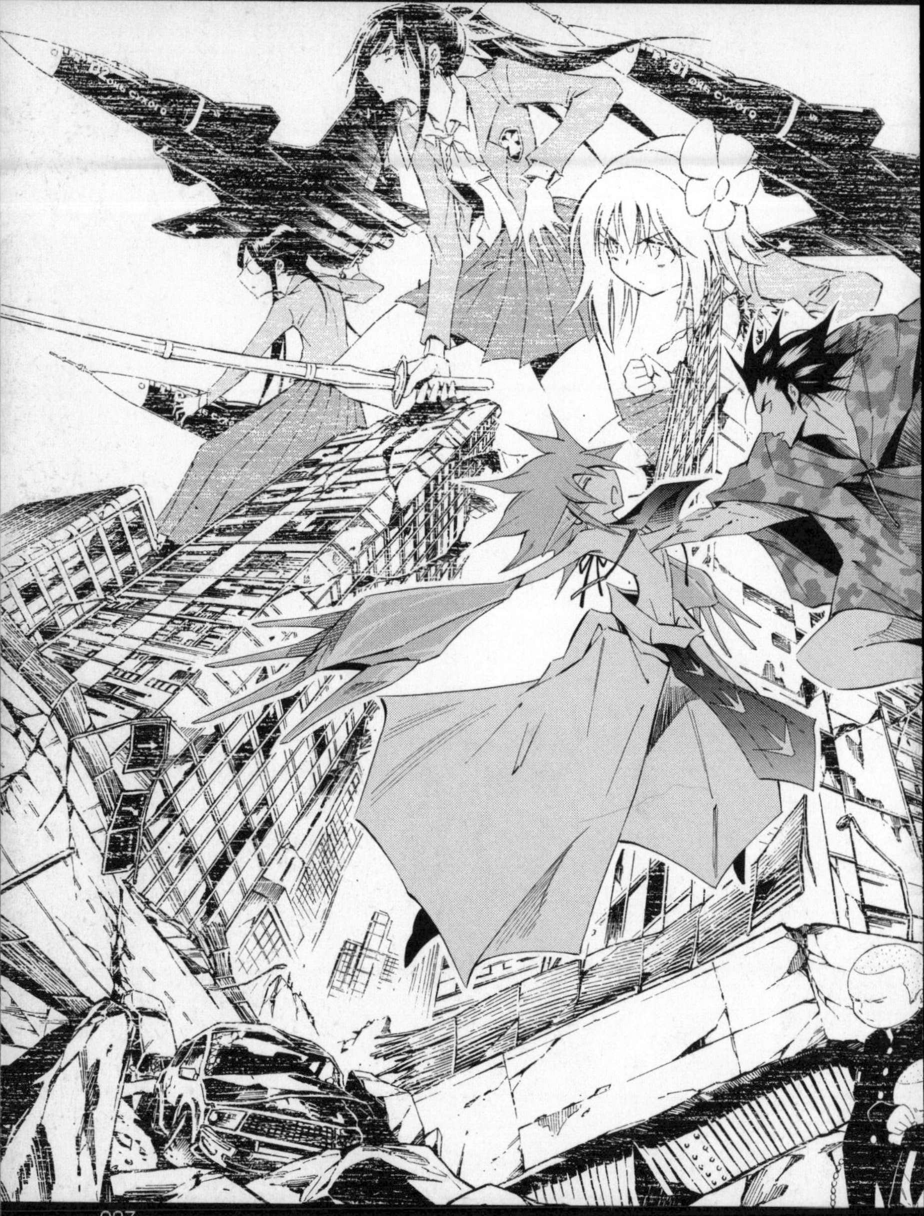

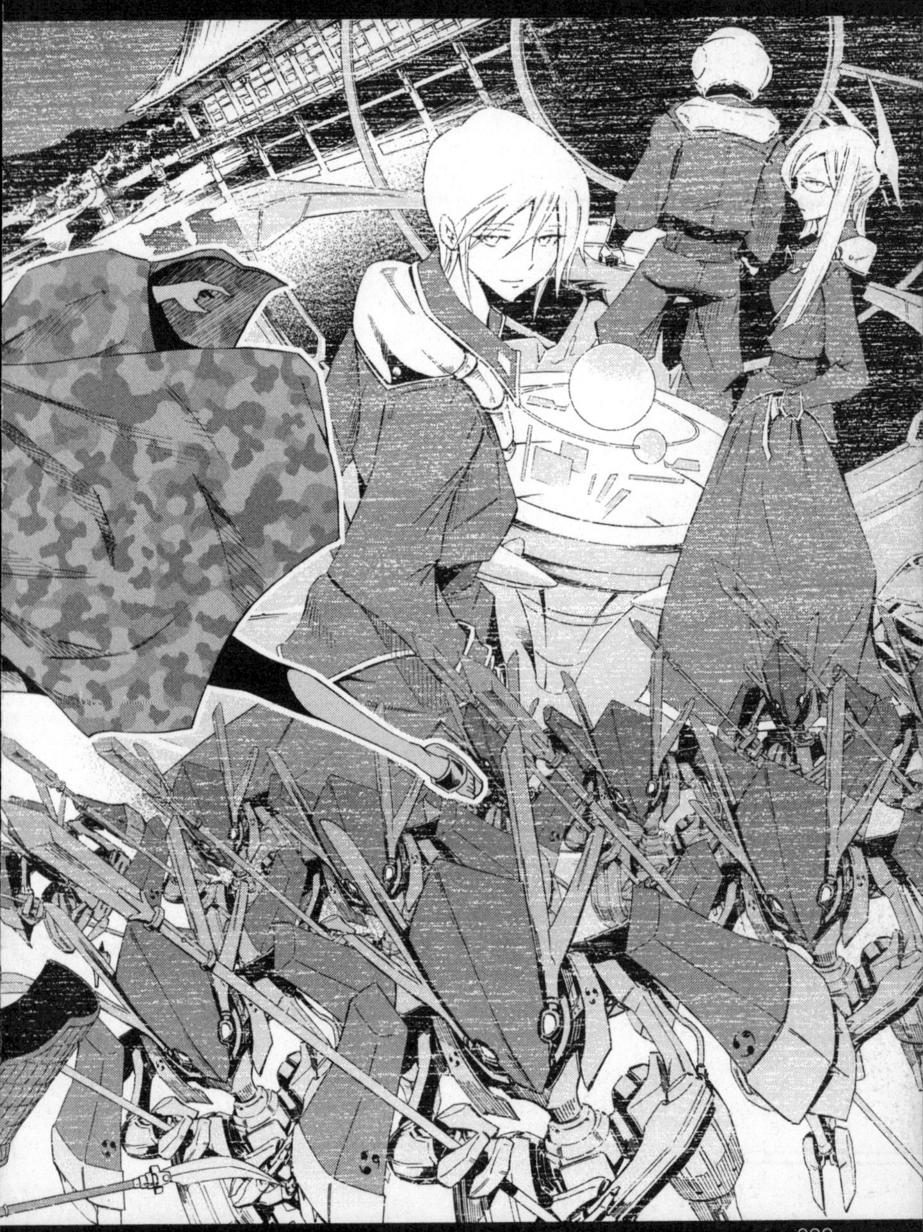

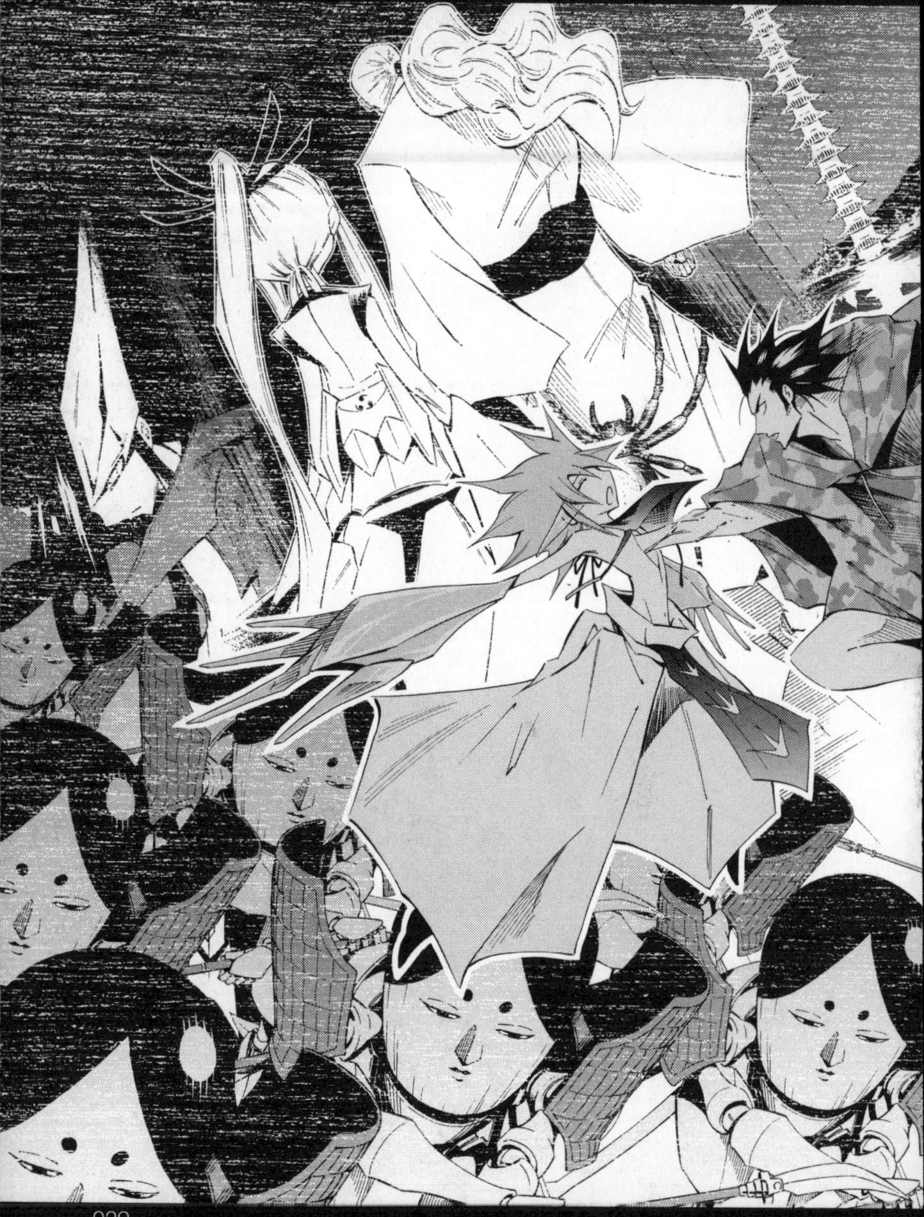

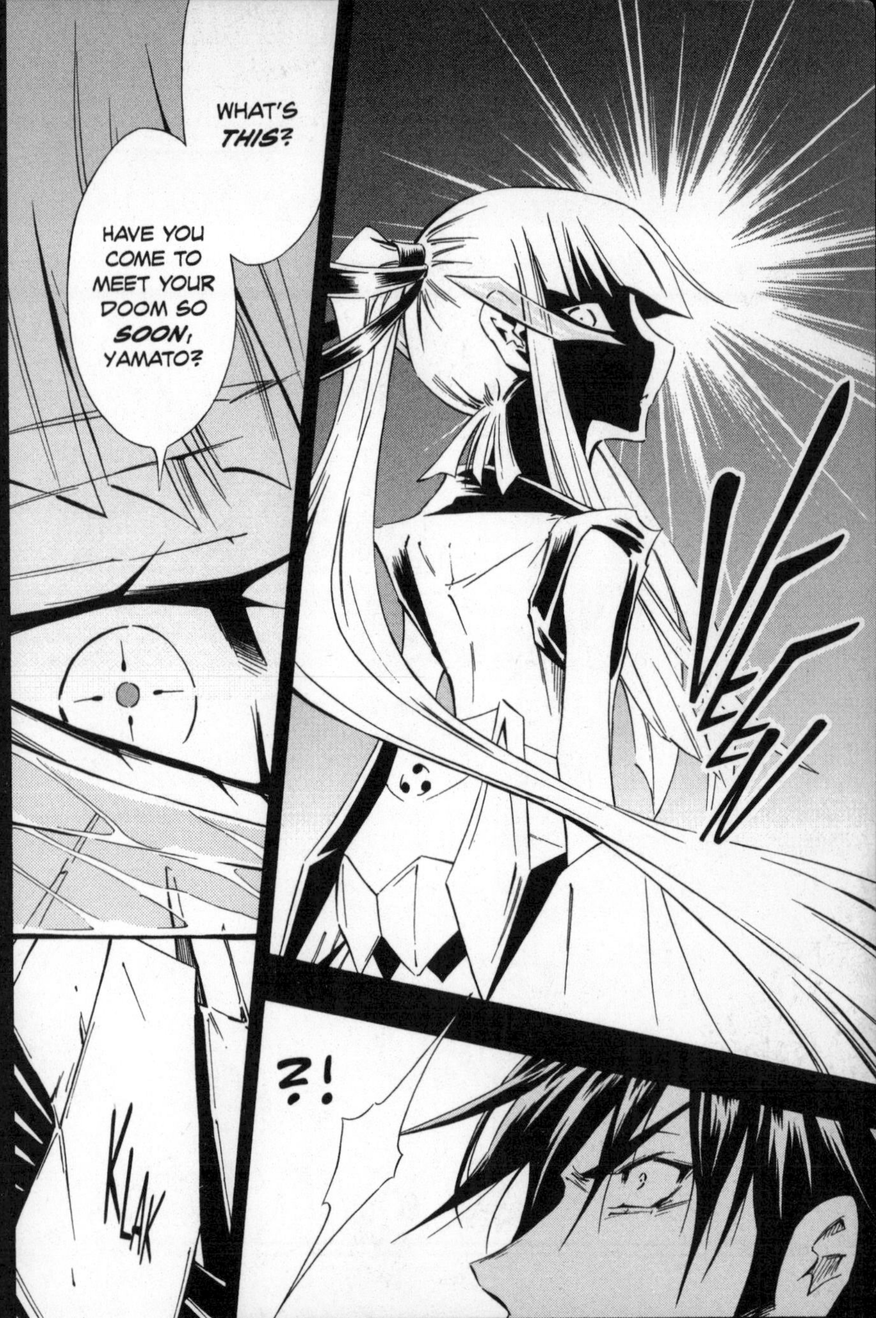
WHAT'S THIS?
HAVE YOU COME TO MEET YOUR DOOM SO SOON, YAMATO?
?!
KLAK

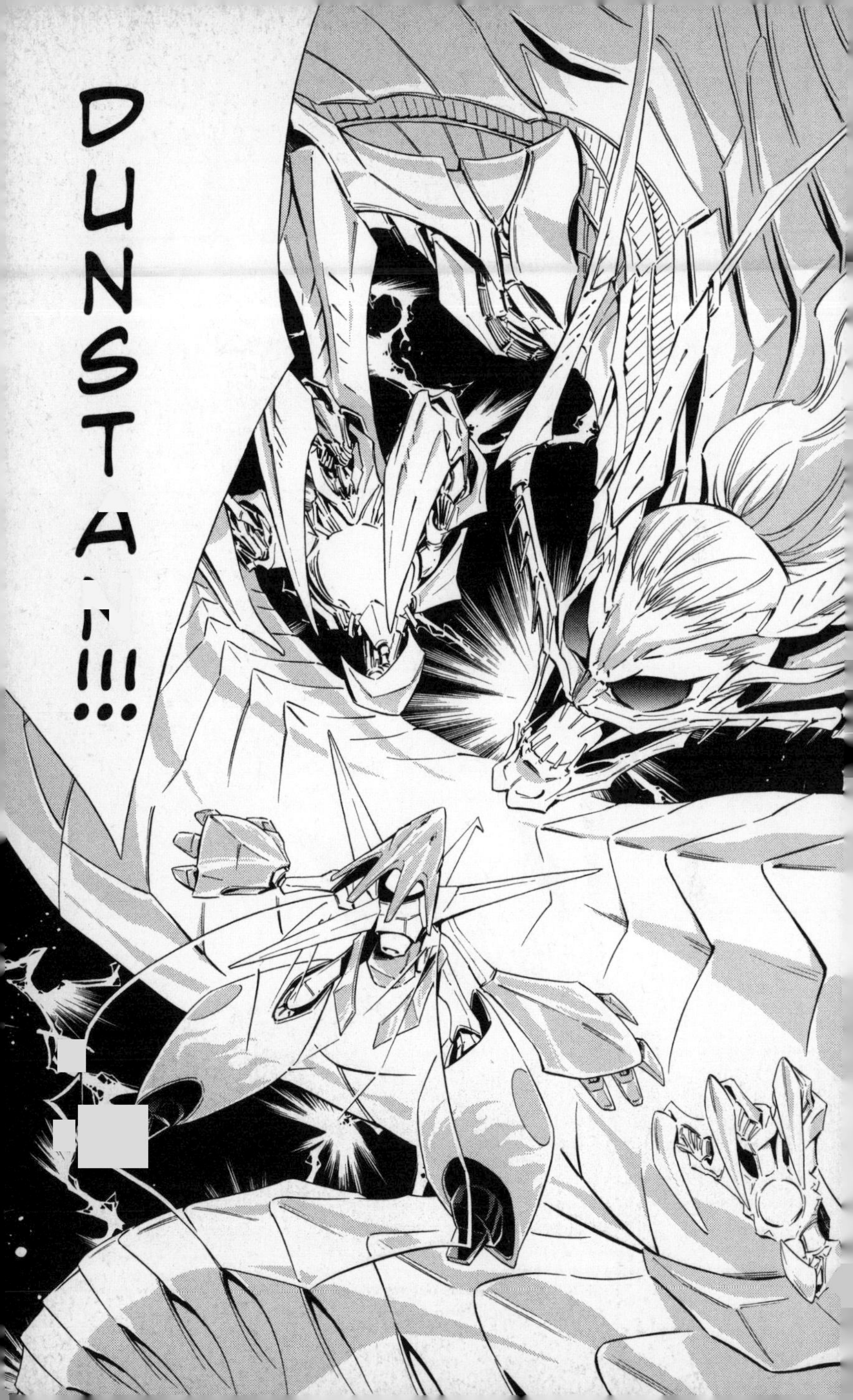
DUNSTAN!!!

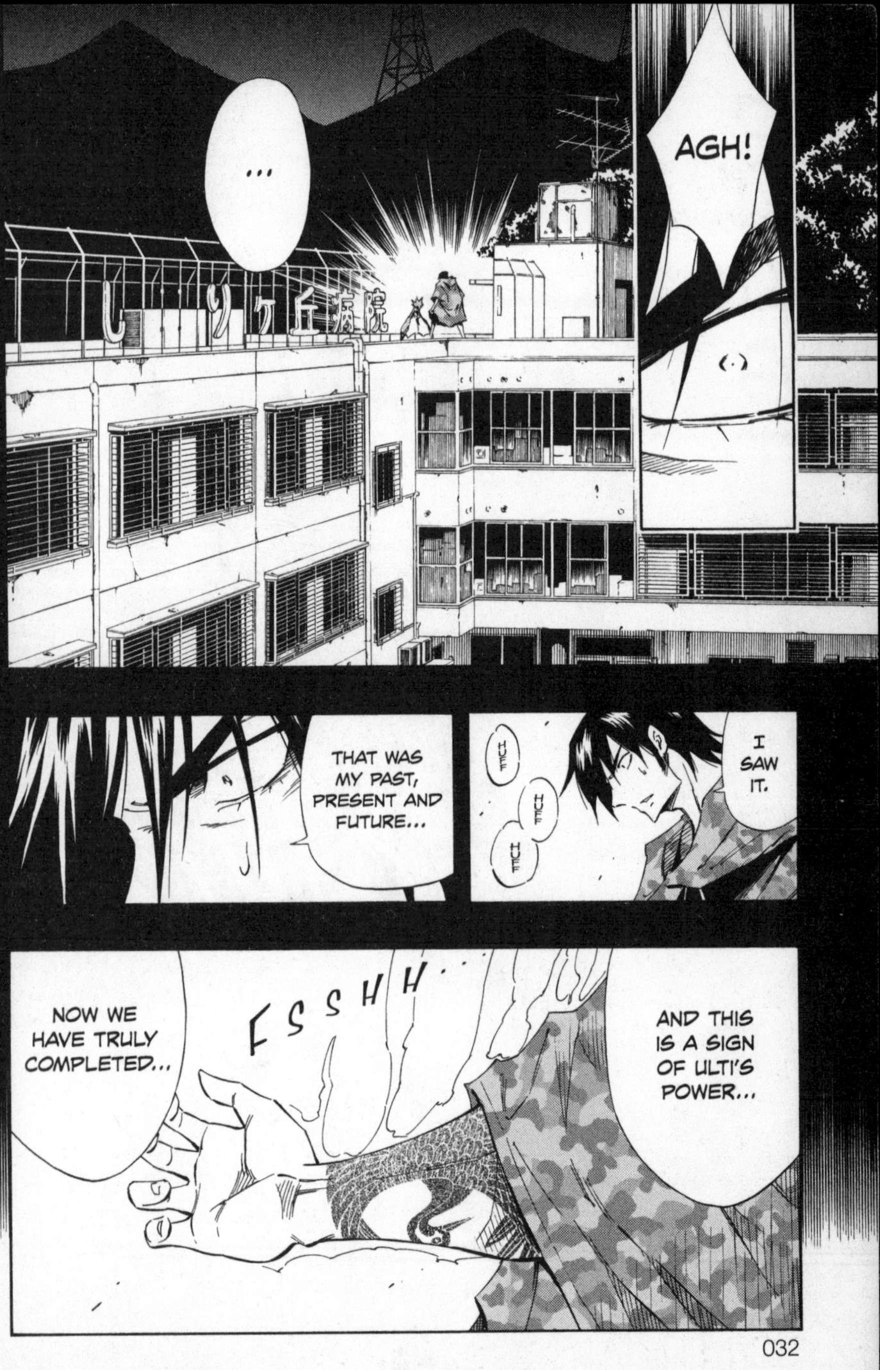
AGH!
...
HUFF
HUFF
HUFF
I SAW IT.
THAT WAS MY PAST, PRESENT AND FUTURE...
AND THIS IS A SIGN OF ULTI'S POWER...
FSSHH..
NOW WE HAVE TRULY COMPLETED...

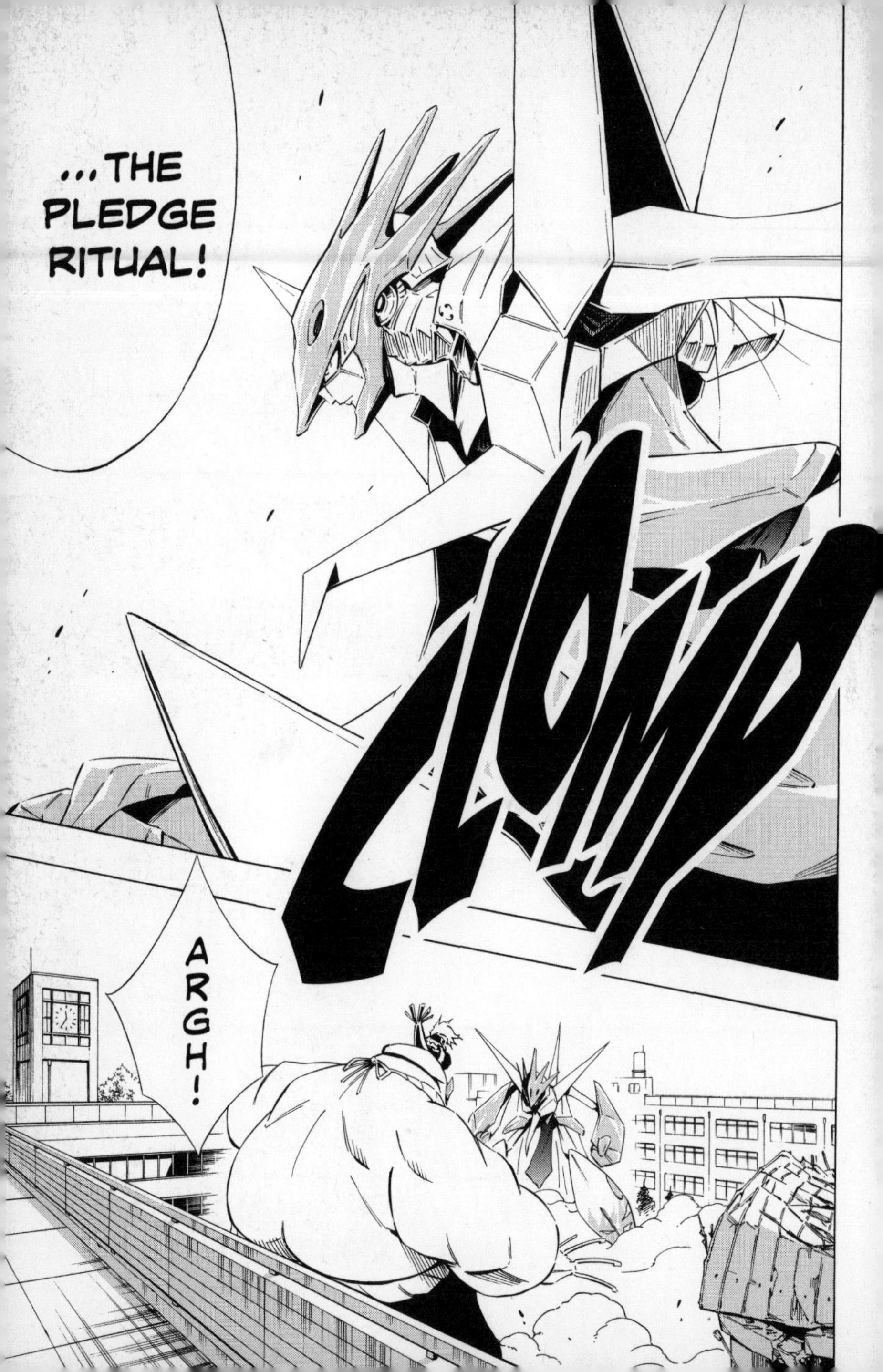
...THE PLEDGE RITUAL!
CLOMP
ARGH!

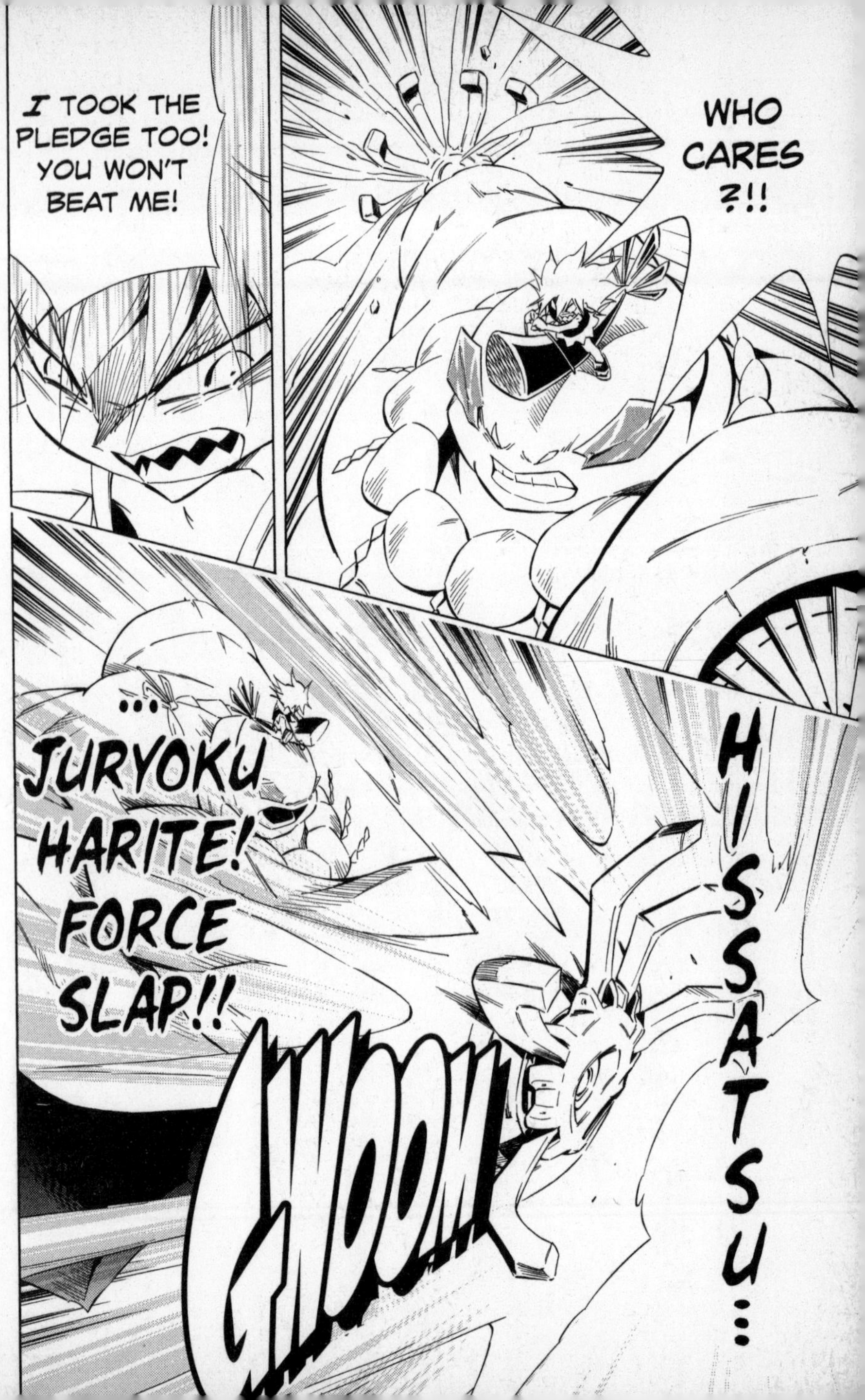
WHO CARES ?!!
I TOOK THE PLEDGE TOO! YOU WON'T BEAT ME!
HISSATSU...
...JURYOKU HARITE! FORCE SLAP!!
WHOOM

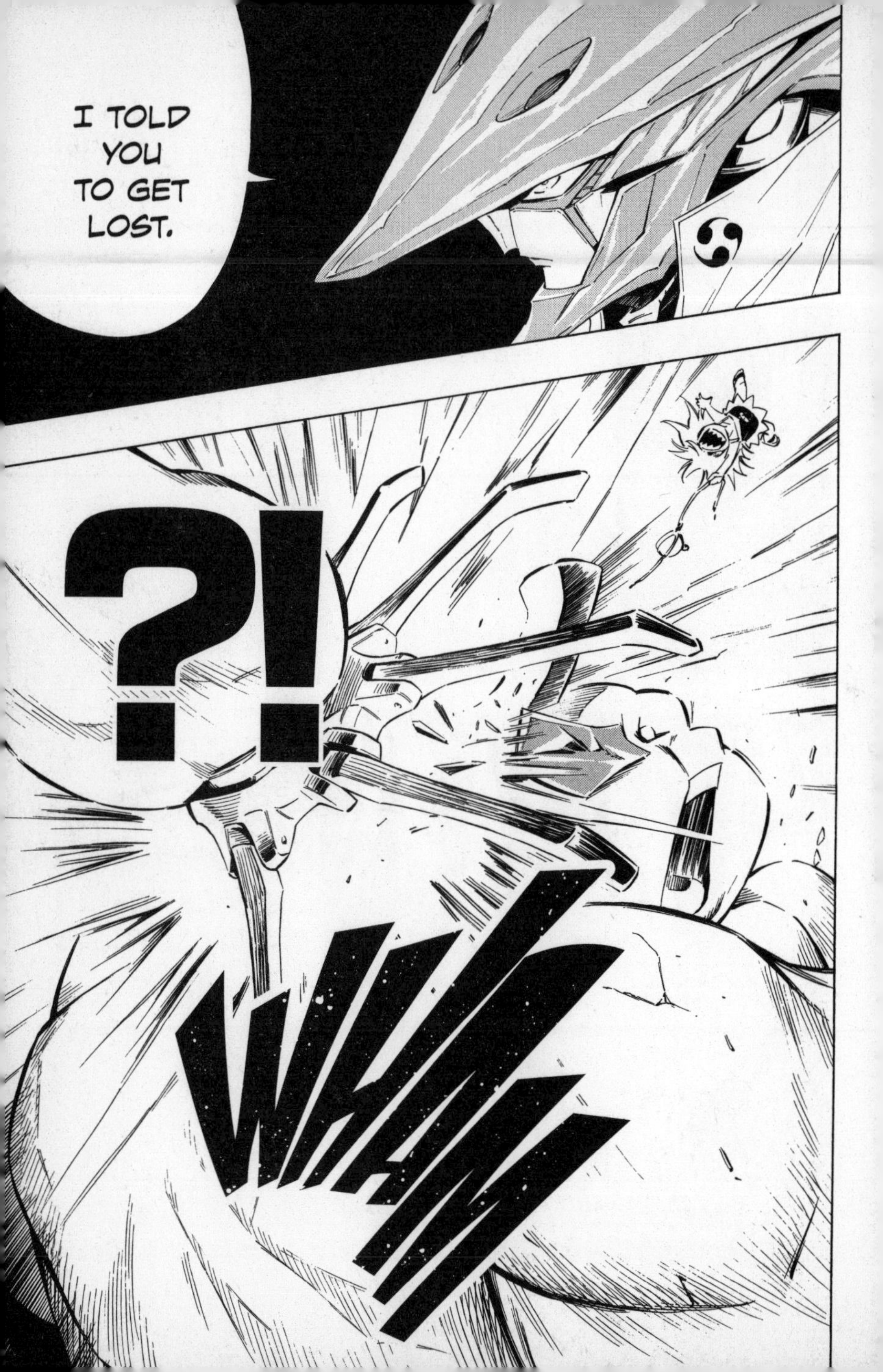
I TOLD YOU TO GET LOST.
?!
WHAM

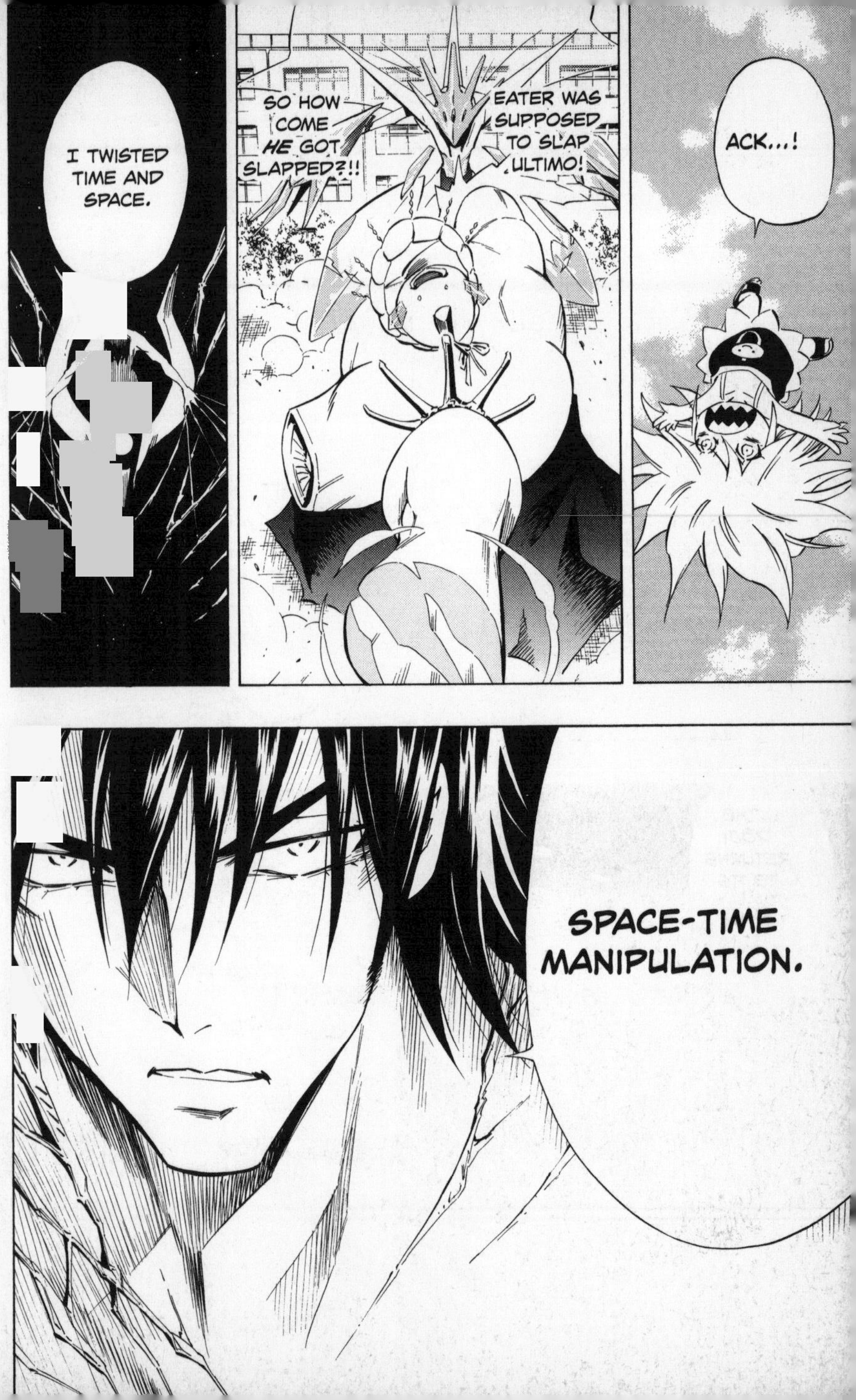
ACK...!
EATER WAS SUPPOSED TO SLAP ULTIMO!
SO HOW COME HE GOT SLAPPED?!!
I TWISTED TIME AND SPACE.
SPACE-TIME MANIPULATION.

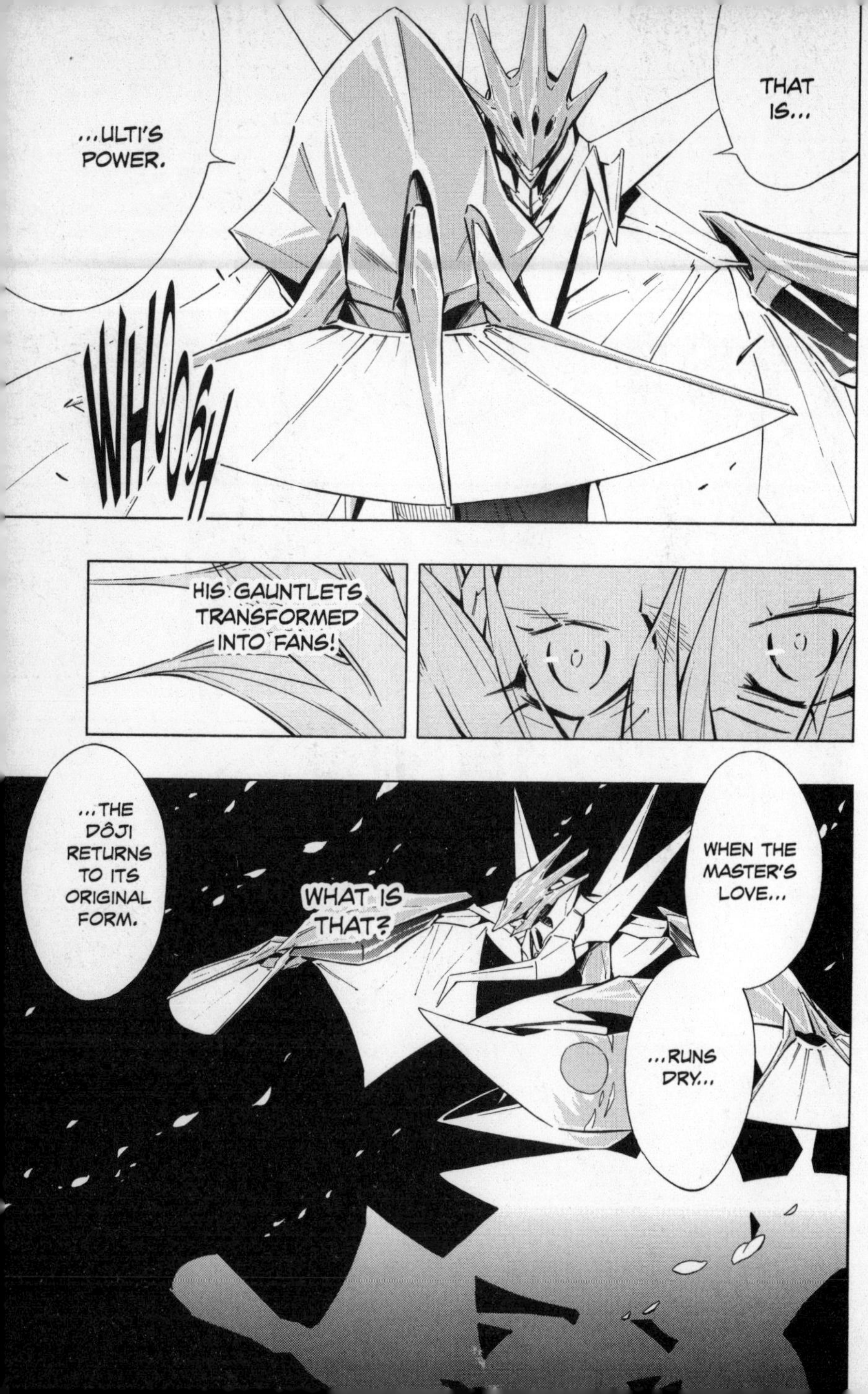
THAT IS...
...ULTI'S POWER.
WHOOSH
HIS GAUNTLETS TRANSFORMED INTO FANS!
WHEN THE MASTER'S LOVE...
...RUNS DRY...
...THE DÔJI RETURNS TO ITS ORIGINAL FORM.
WHAT IS THAT?

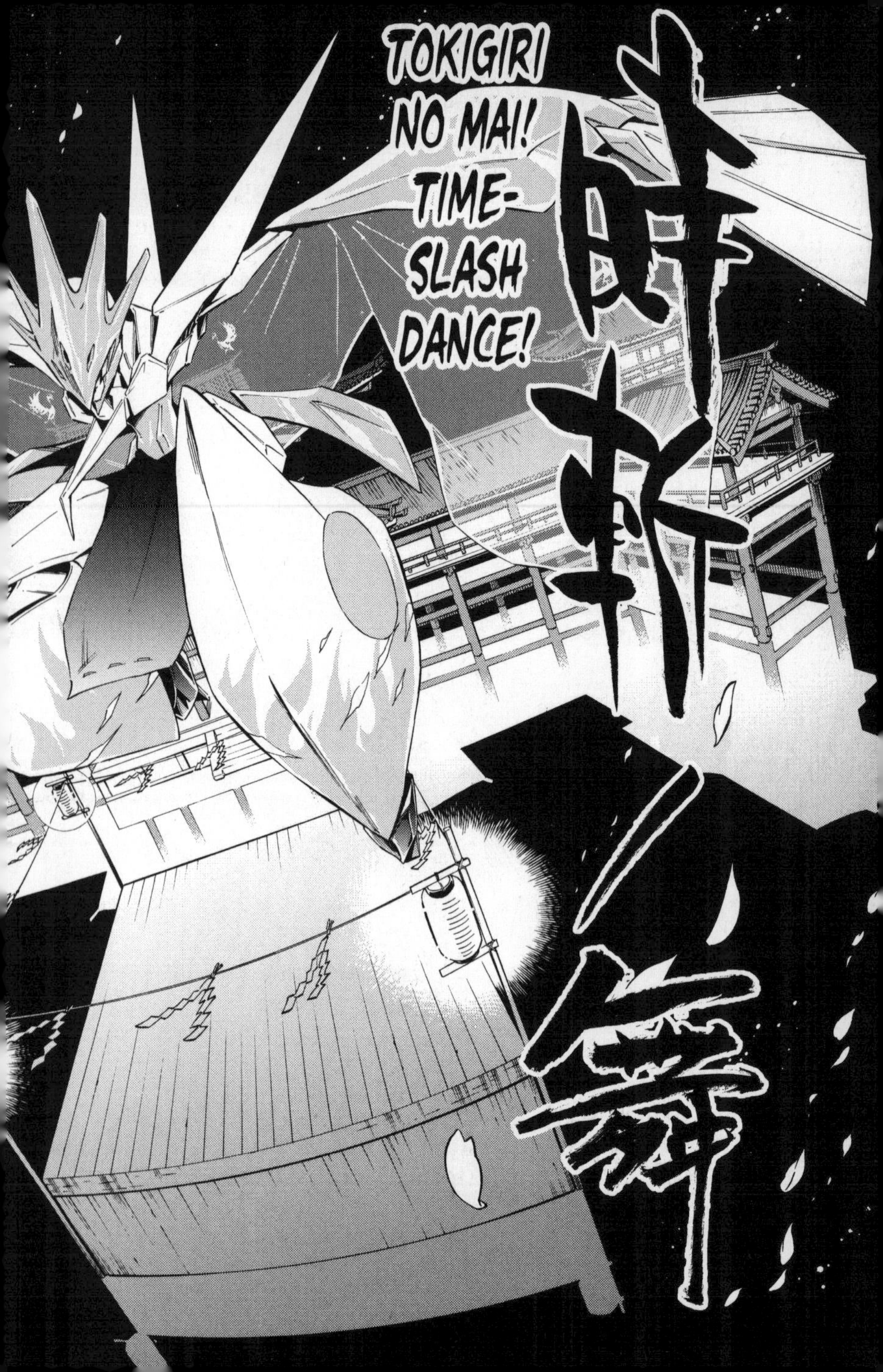
TOKIGIRI NO MAI! TIME-SLASH DANCE!
時斬ノ舞

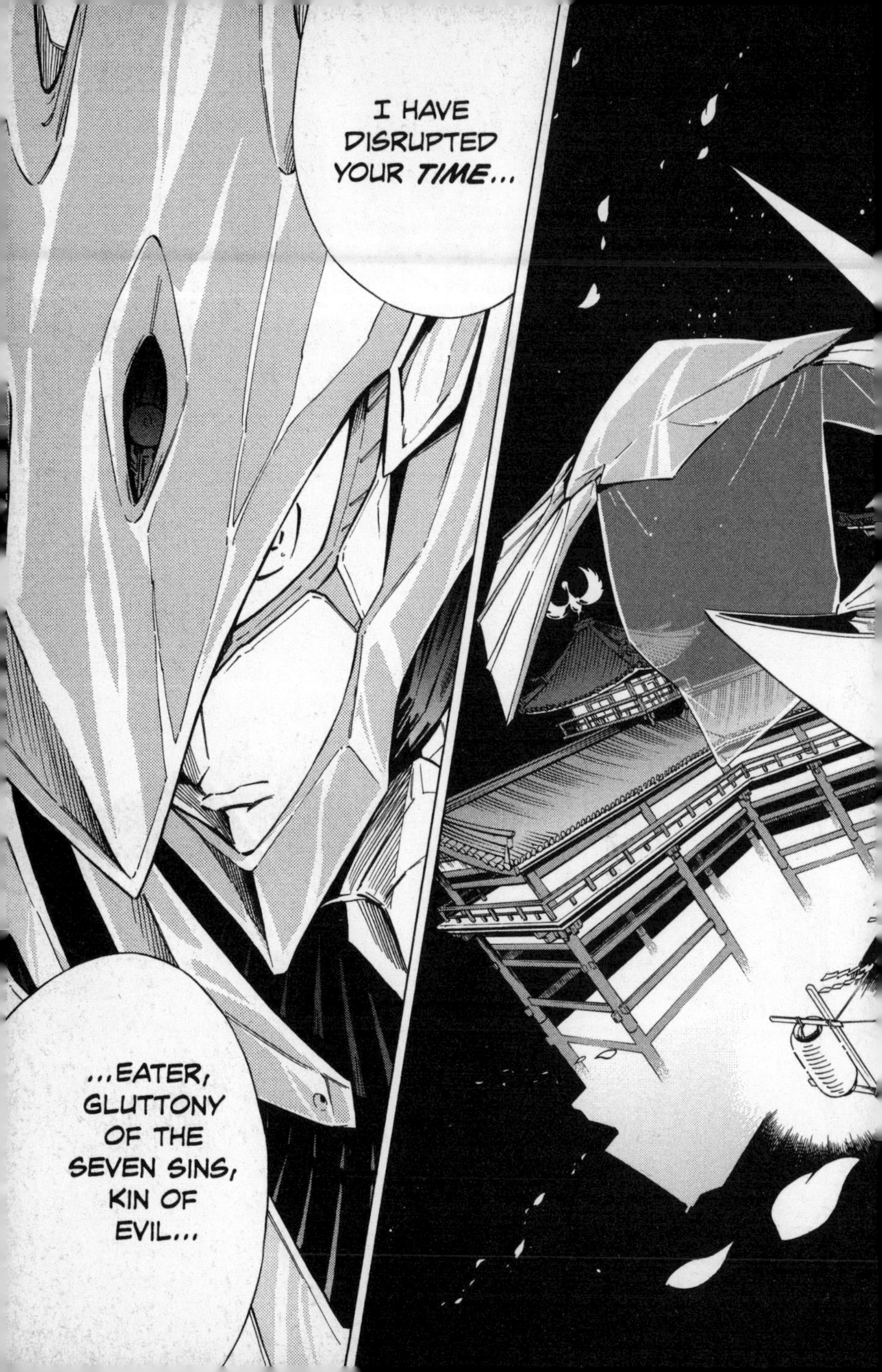
I HAVE DISRUPTED YOUR TIME...
...EATER, GLUTTONY OF THE SEVEN SINS, KIN OF EVIL...

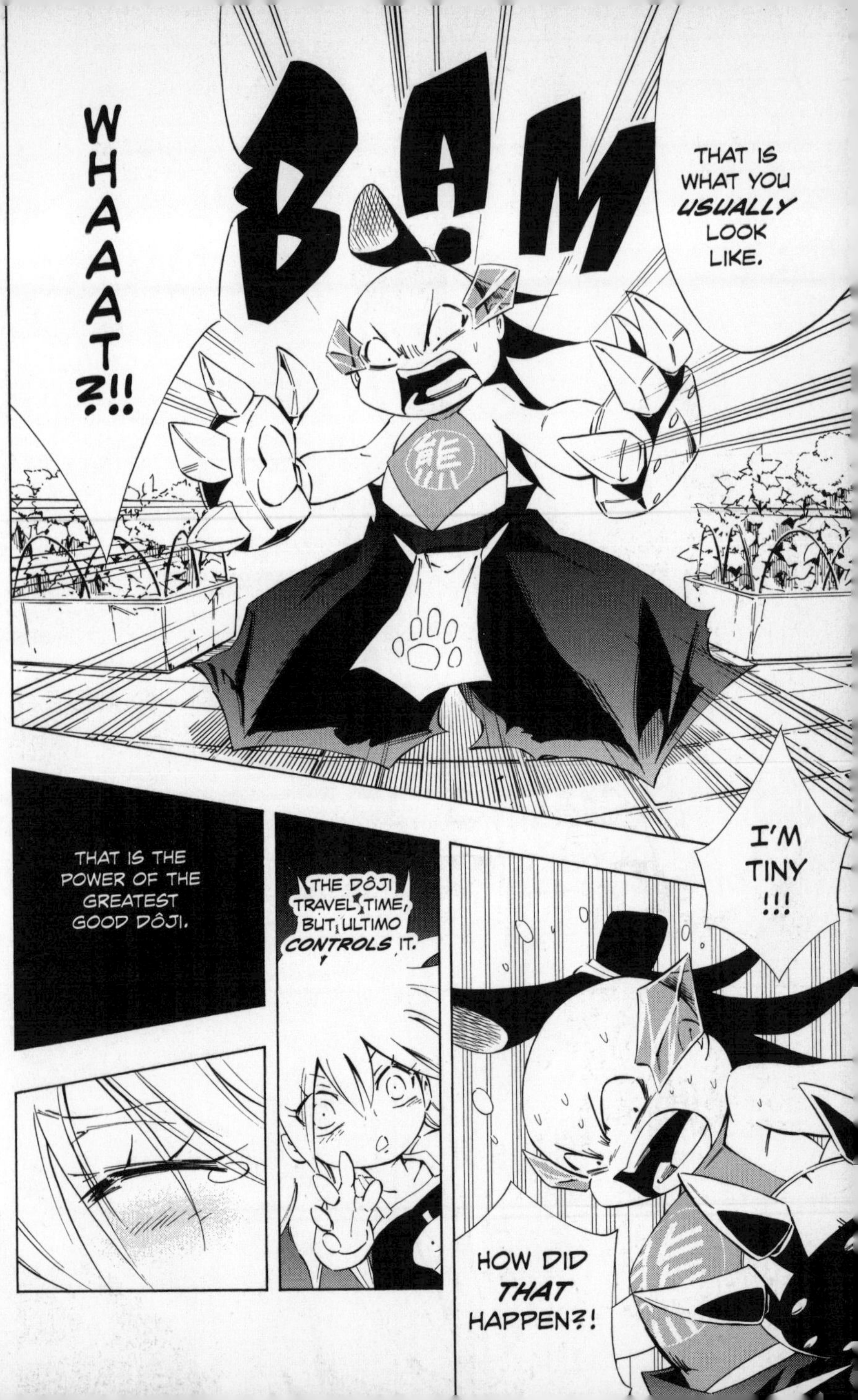
THAT IS WHAT YOU *USUALLY* LOOK LIKE.
BAM
WHAAAAT?!!
I'M TINY!!!
HOW DID *THAT* HAPPEN?!
THE DÔJI TRAVEL TIME, BUT ULTIMO *CONTROLS* IT.
THAT IS THE POWER OF THE GREATEST GOOD DÔJI.

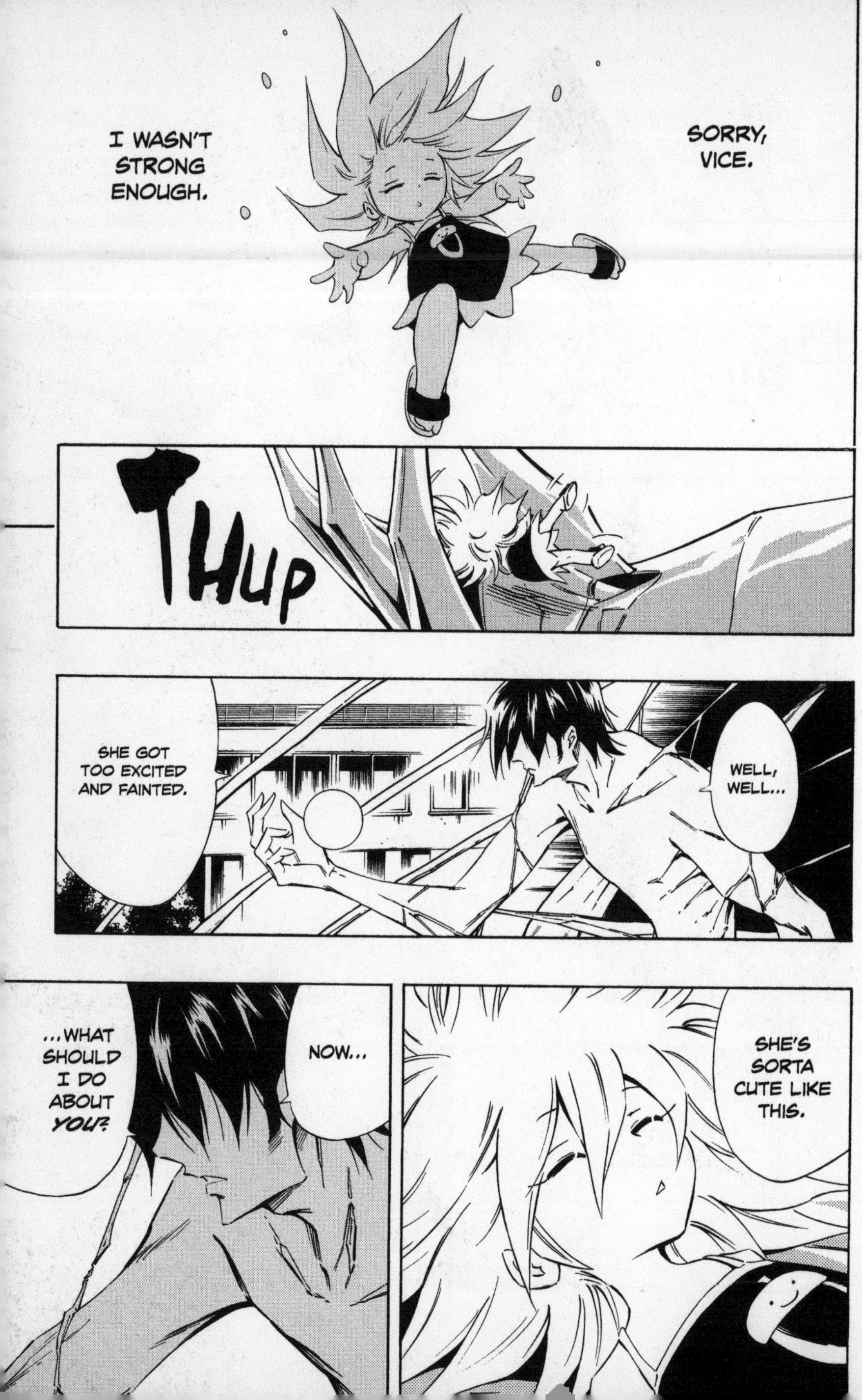
SORRY, VICE.
I WASN'T STRONG ENOUGH.
THUP
WELL, WELL...
SHE GOT TOO EXCITED AND FAINTED.
SHE'S SORTA CUTE LIKE THIS.
NOW...
...WHAT SHOULD I DO ABOUT *YOU*?

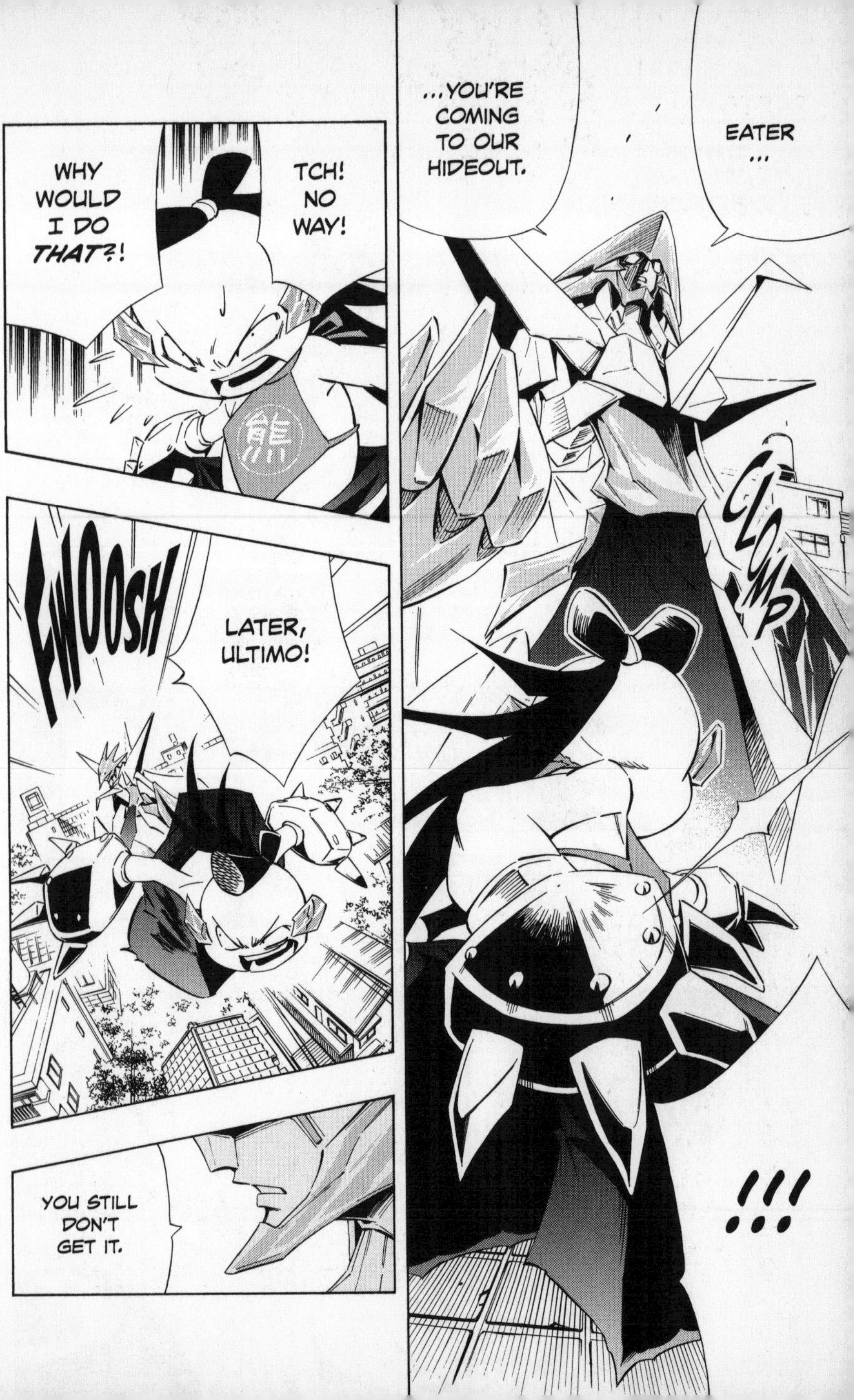
EATER ...
...YOU'RE COMING TO OUR HIDEOUT.
CLOMP
!!!
TCH! NO WAY!
WHY WOULD I DO THAT?!
FWOOSH
LATER, ULTIMO!
YOU STILL DON'T GET IT.

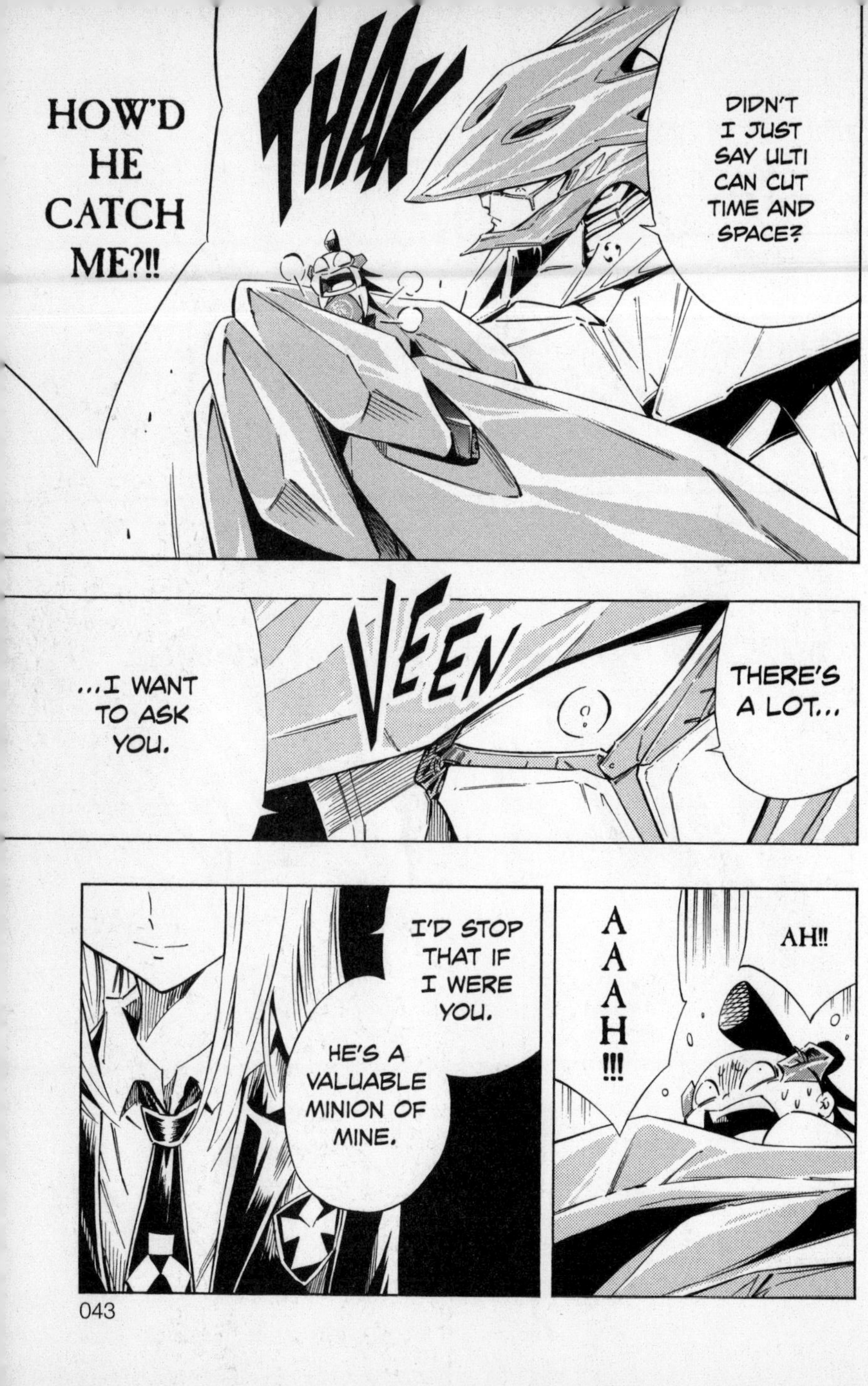
DIDN'T I JUST SAY ULTI CAN CUT TIME AND SPACE?
THAK
HOW'D HE CATCH ME?!!
THERE'S A LOT...
VEEN
...I WANT TO ASK YOU.
AH!!
AAAH!!!
I'D STOP THAT IF I WERE YOU.
HE'S A VALUABLE MINION OF MINE.

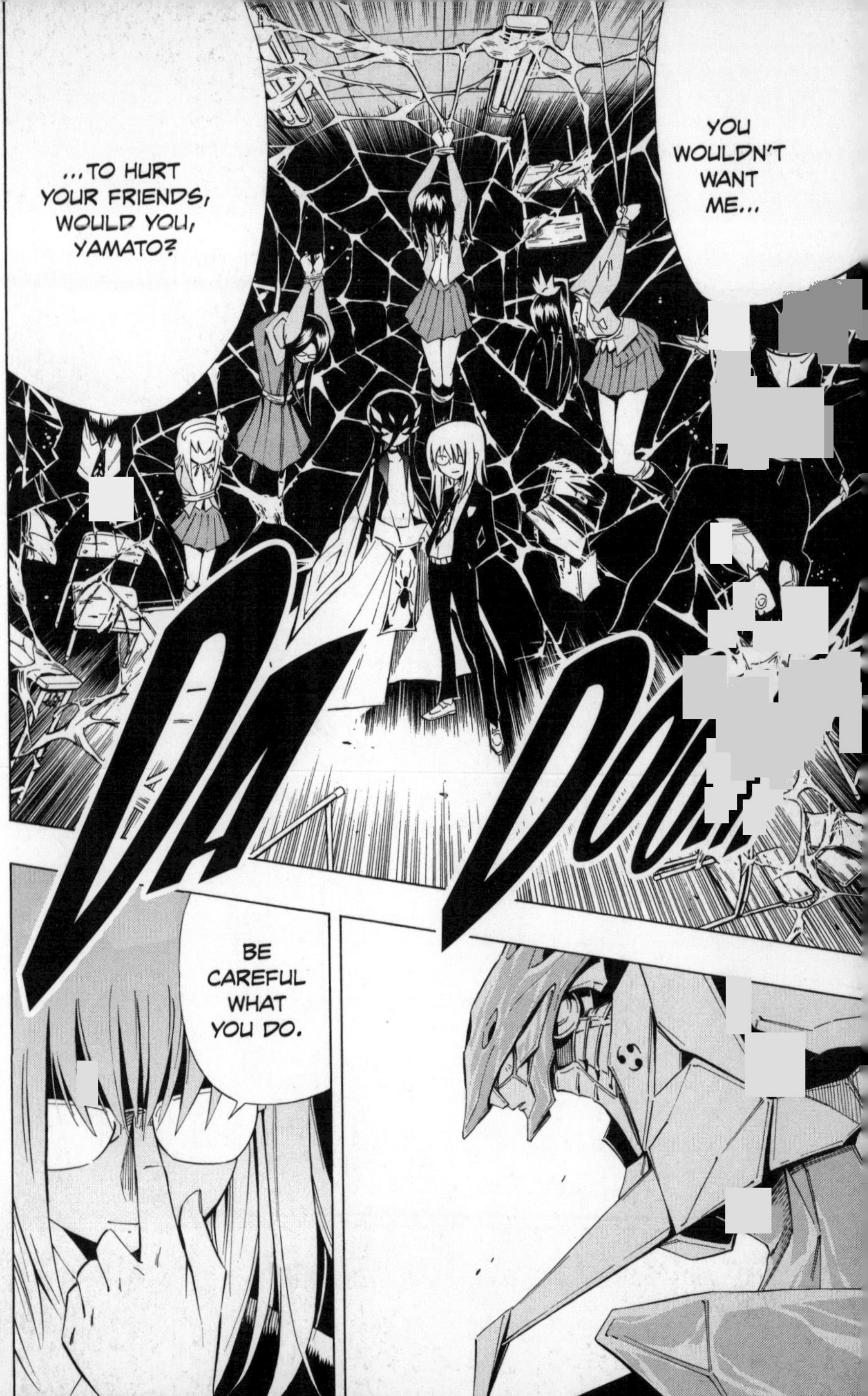
YOU WOULDN'T WANT ME...
...TO HURT YOUR FRIENDS, WOULD YOU, YAMATO?
BE CAREFUL WHAT YOU DO.

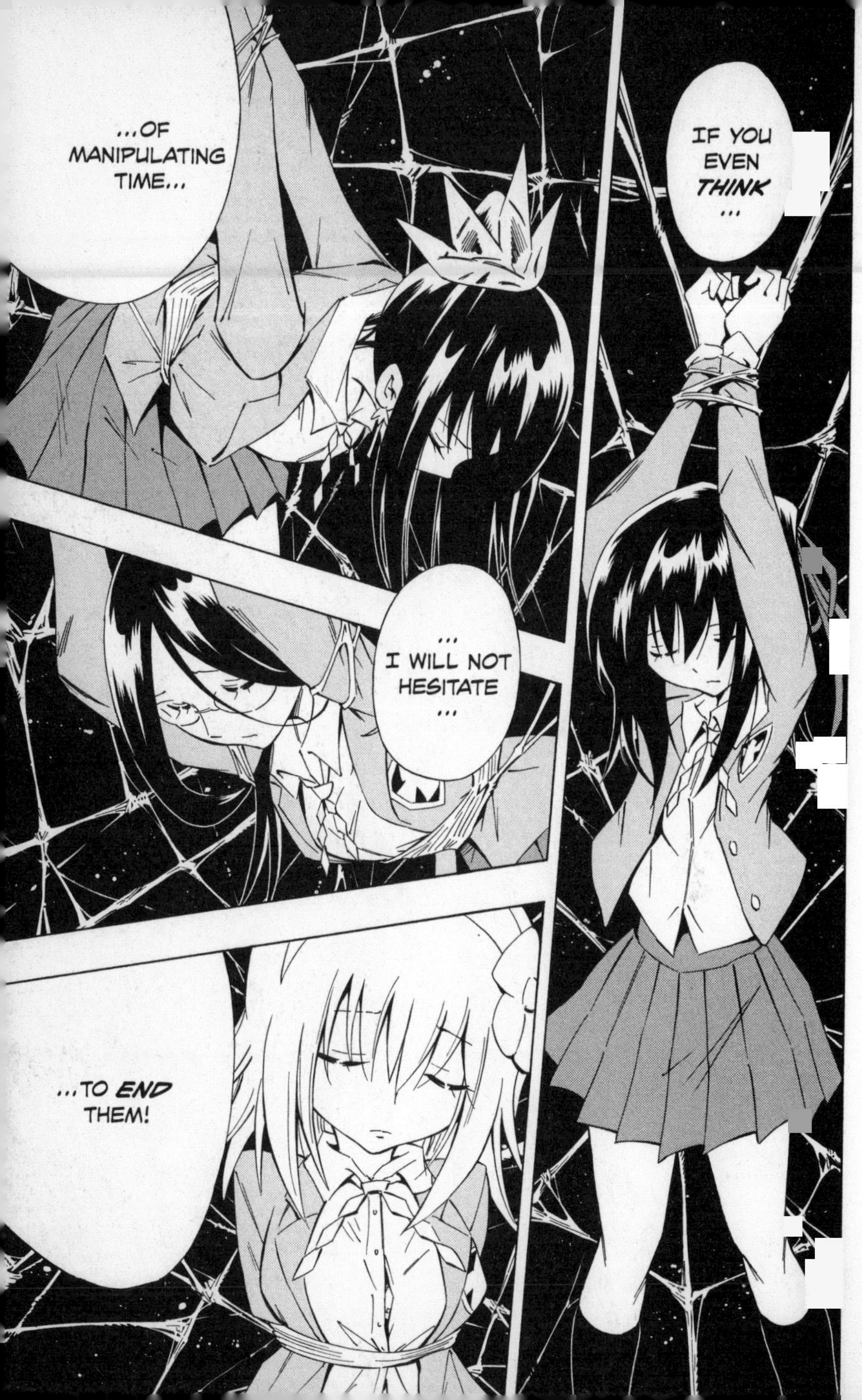
IF YOU EVEN *THINK* ...
...OF MANIPULATING TIME...
... I WILL NOT HESITATE ...
...TO *END* THEM!

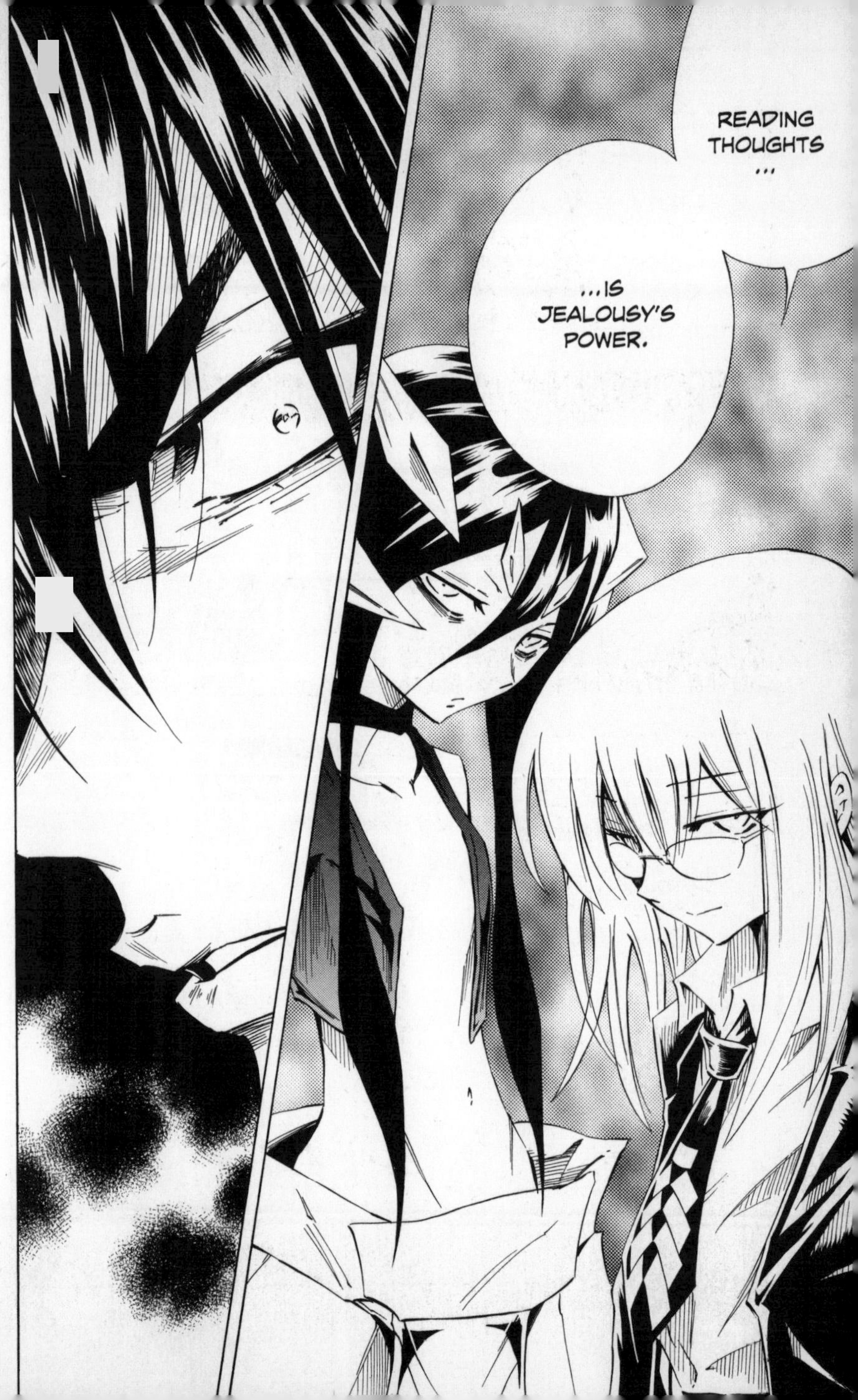
READING THOUGHTS...
...IS JEALOUSY'S POWER.

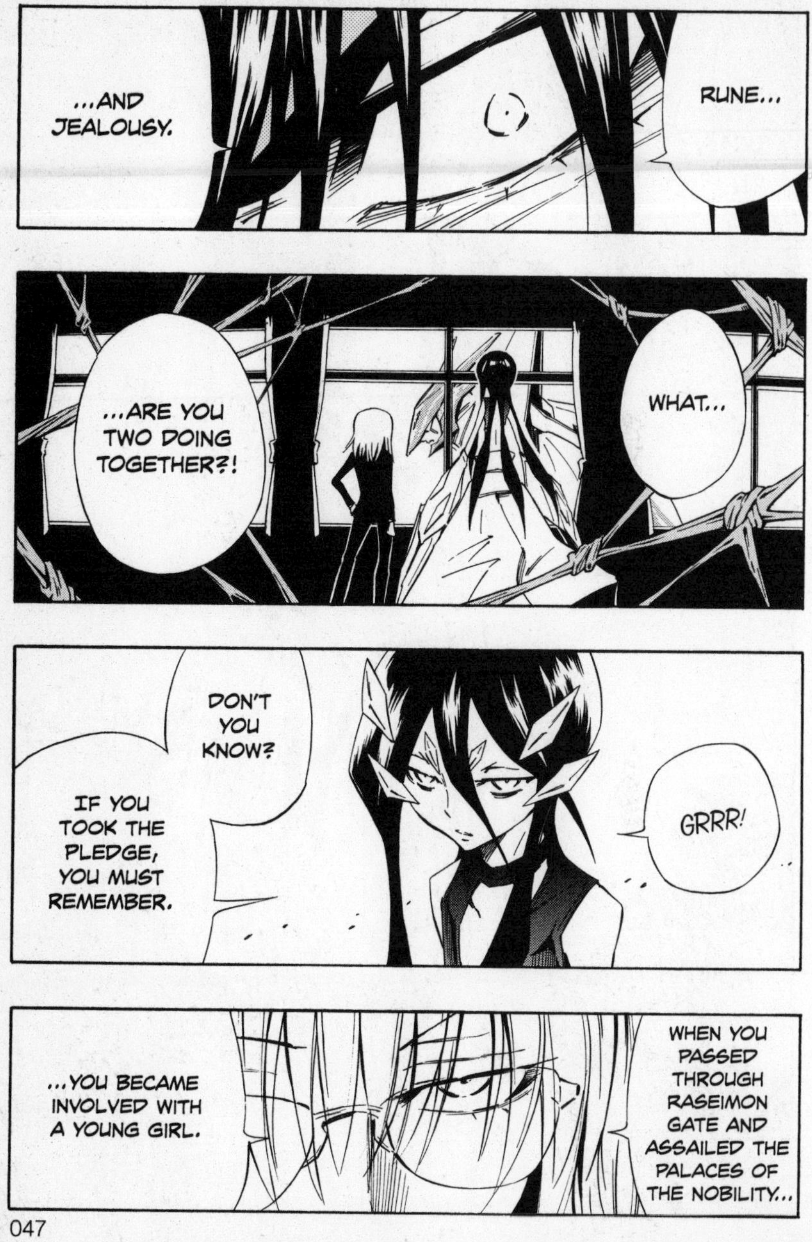
RUNE...
...AND JEALOUSY.
WHAT...
...ARE YOU TWO DOING TOGETHER?!
GRRR!
DON'T YOU KNOW?
IF YOU TOOK THE PLEDGE, YOU MUST REMEMBER.
WHEN YOU PASSED THROUGH RASEIMON GATE AND ASSAILED THE PALACES OF THE NOBILITY...
...YOU BECAME INVOLVED WITH A YOUNG GIRL.

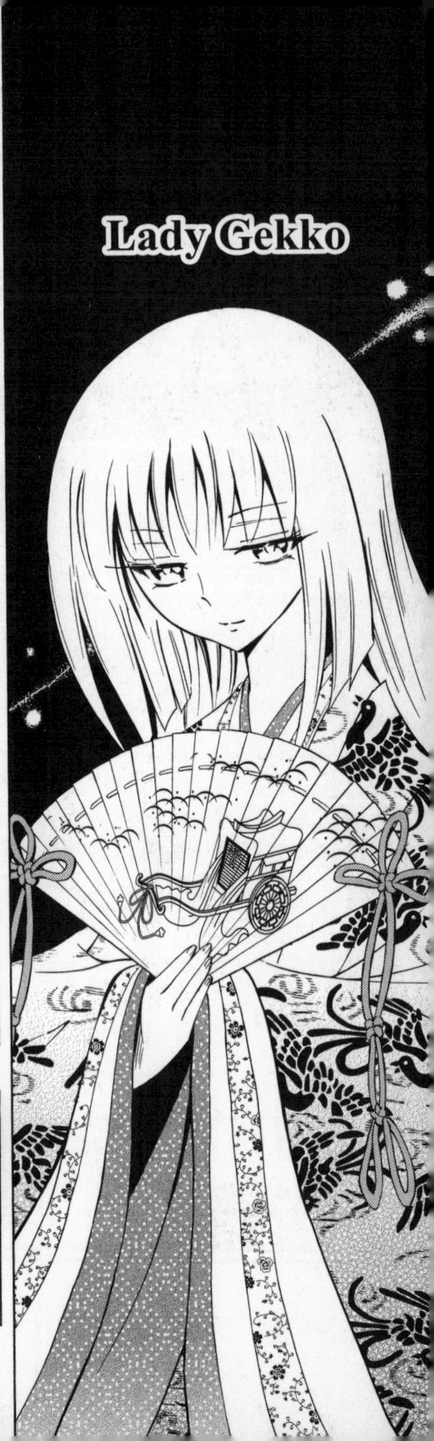
Lady Gekko

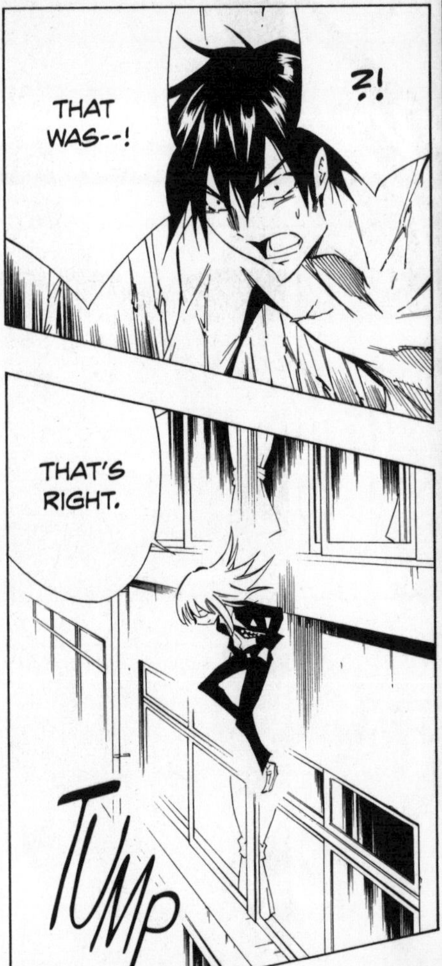
?!
THAT WAS--!
THAT'S RIGHT.
TUMP

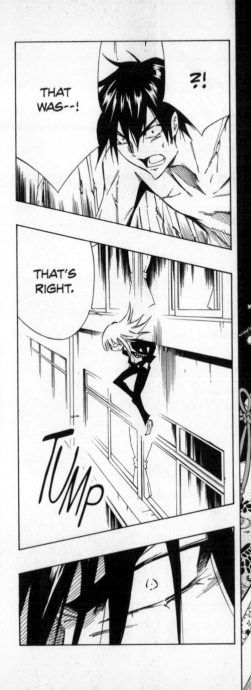

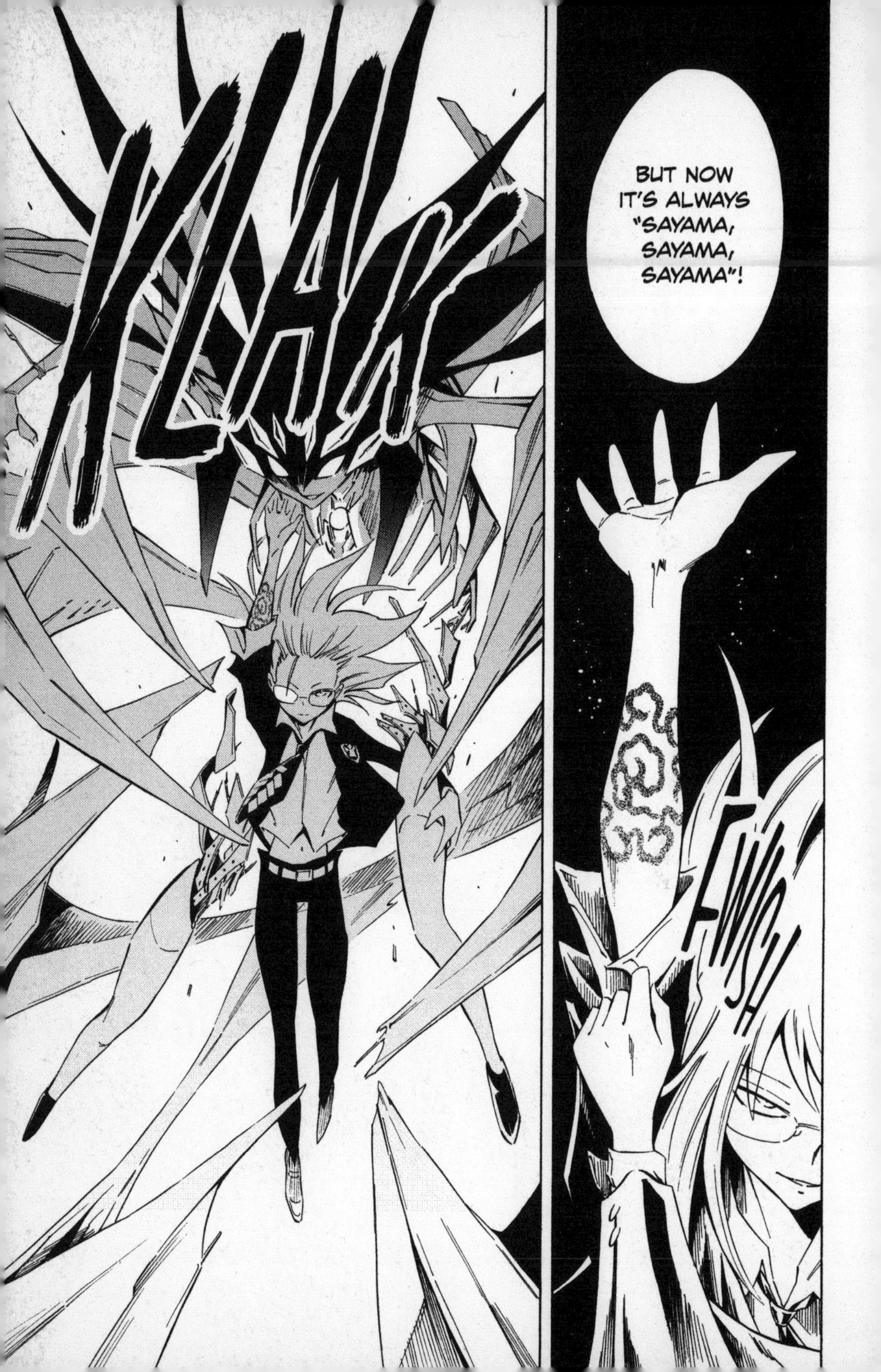
BUT NOW IT'S ALWAYS "SAYAMA, SAYAMA, SAYAMA"!
FWOOSH

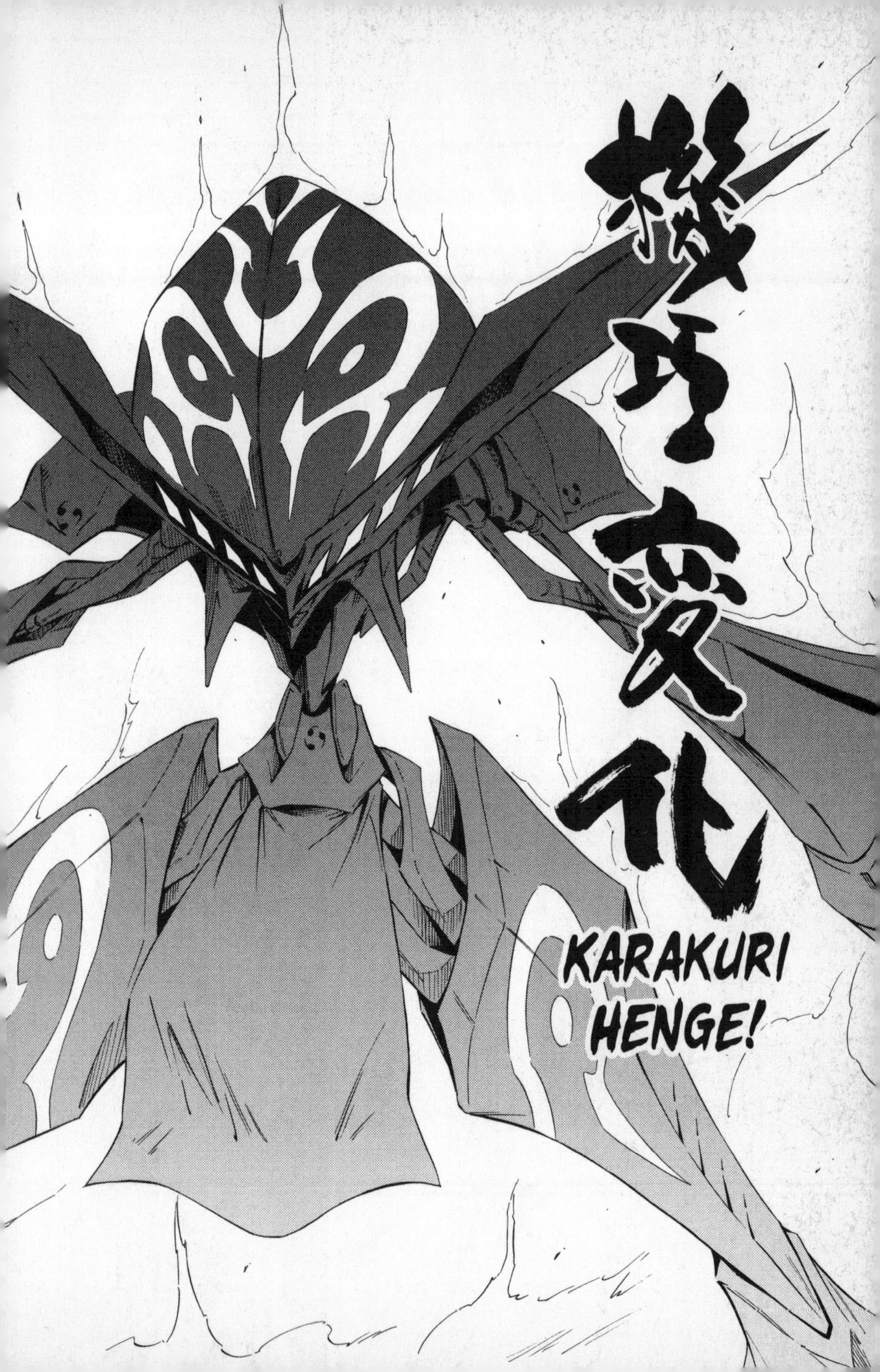
機巧変化
KARAKURI HENGE!

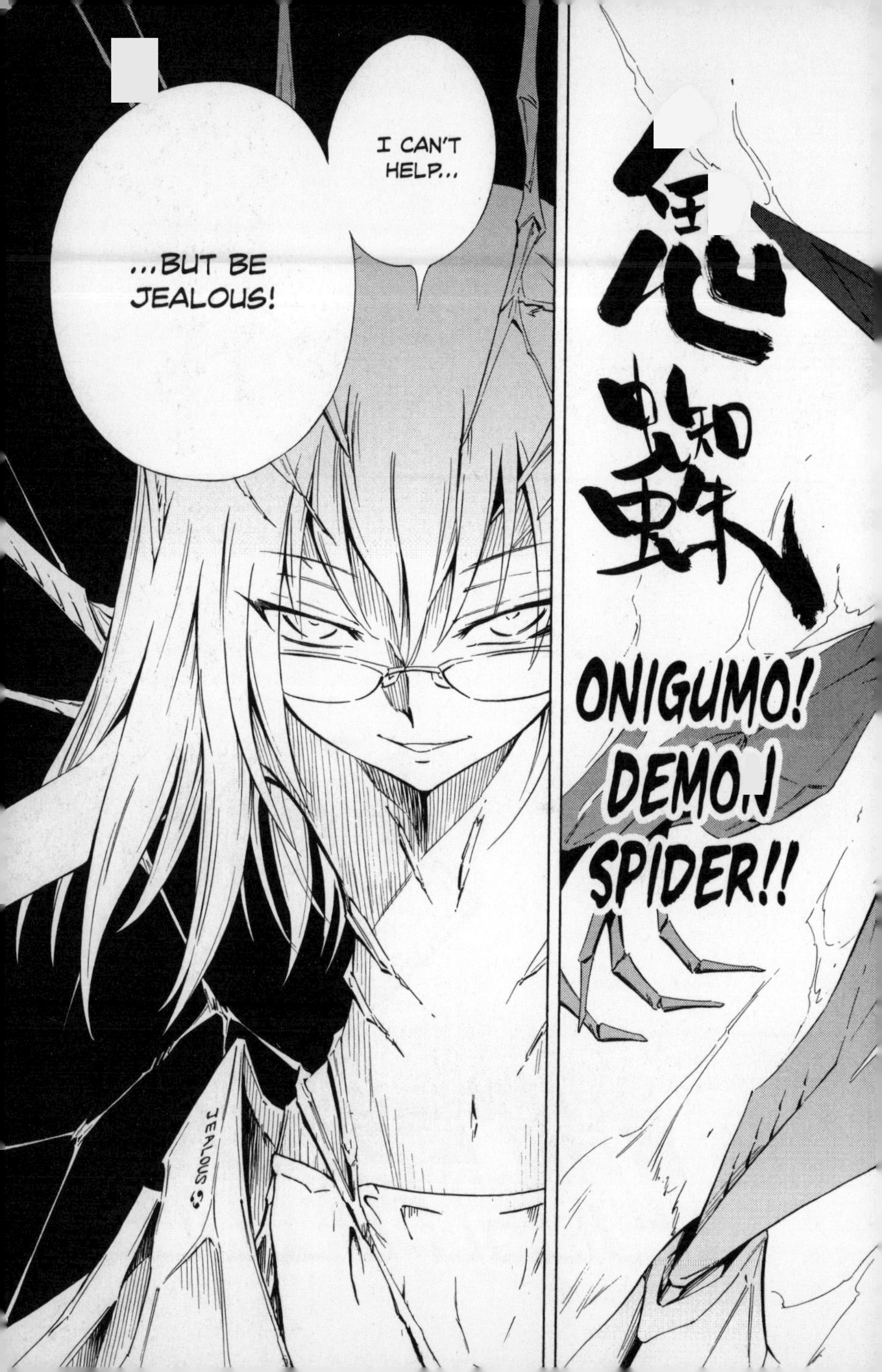
ONIGUMO! DEMON SPIDER!!
I CAN'T HELP...
...BUT BE JEALOUS!
JEALOUS

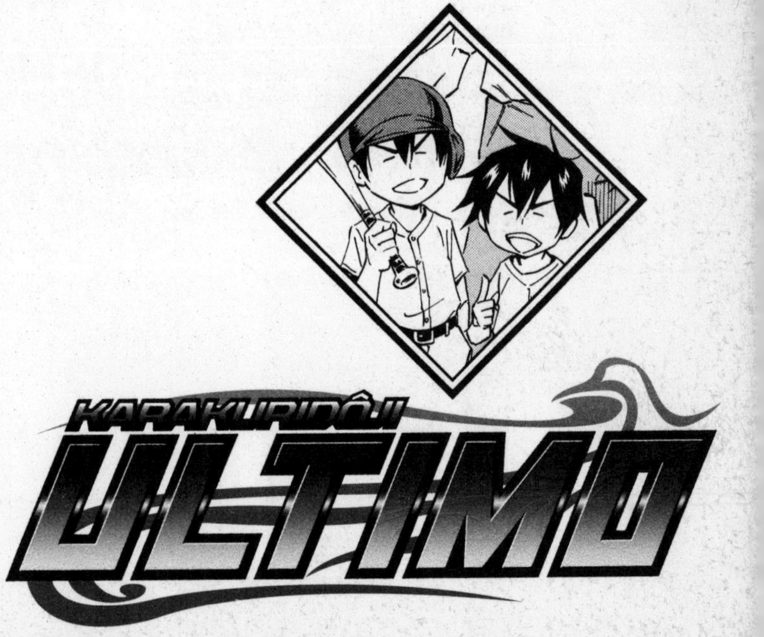

KARAKURIDÔJI
ULTIMO

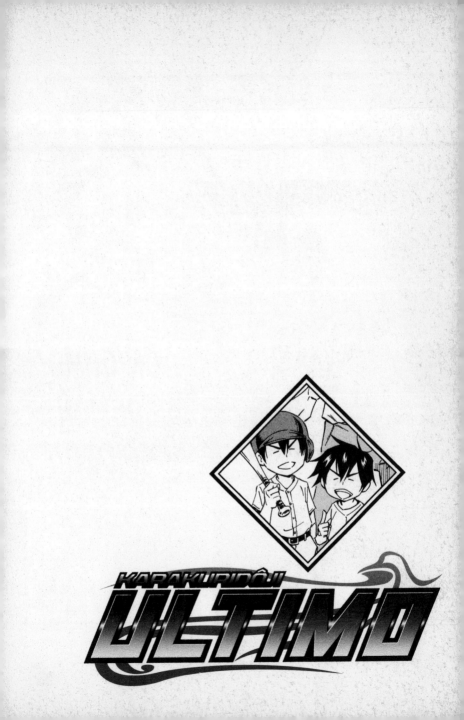

ACT 10 PERILOUS PACT

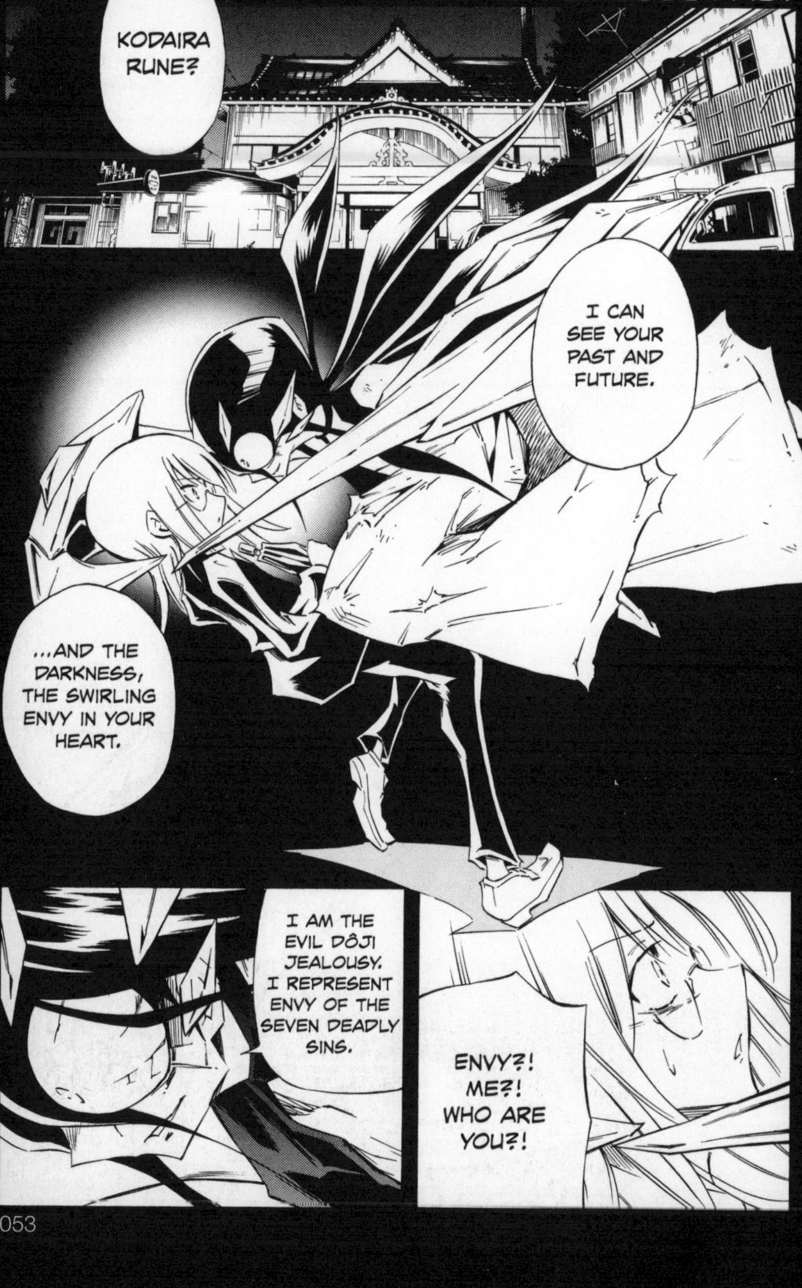
KODAIRA RUNE?
I CAN SEE YOUR PAST AND FUTURE.
...AND THE DARKNESS, THE SWIRLING ENVY IN YOUR HEART.
ENVY?! ME?! WHO ARE YOU?!
I AM THE EVIL DÔJI JEALOUSY. I REPRESENT ENVY OF THE SEVEN DEADLY SINS.

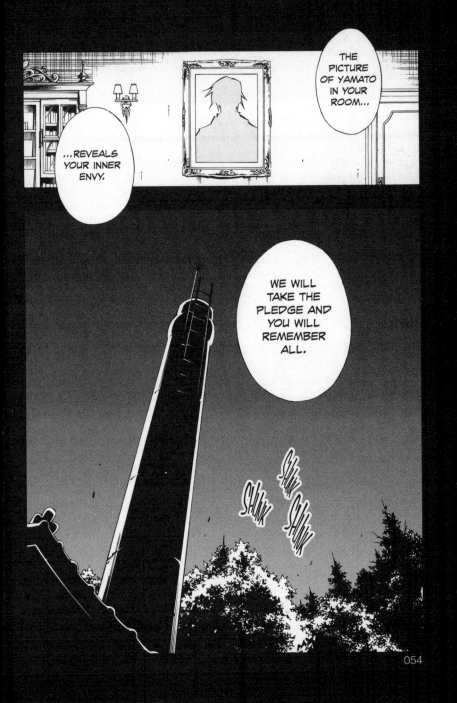

THE PICTURE OF YAMATO IN YOUR ROOM...

...REVEALS YOUR INNER ENVY.

WE WILL TAKE THE PLEDGE AND YOU WILL REMEMBER ALL.

SHLINK
SHLINK
SHLINK

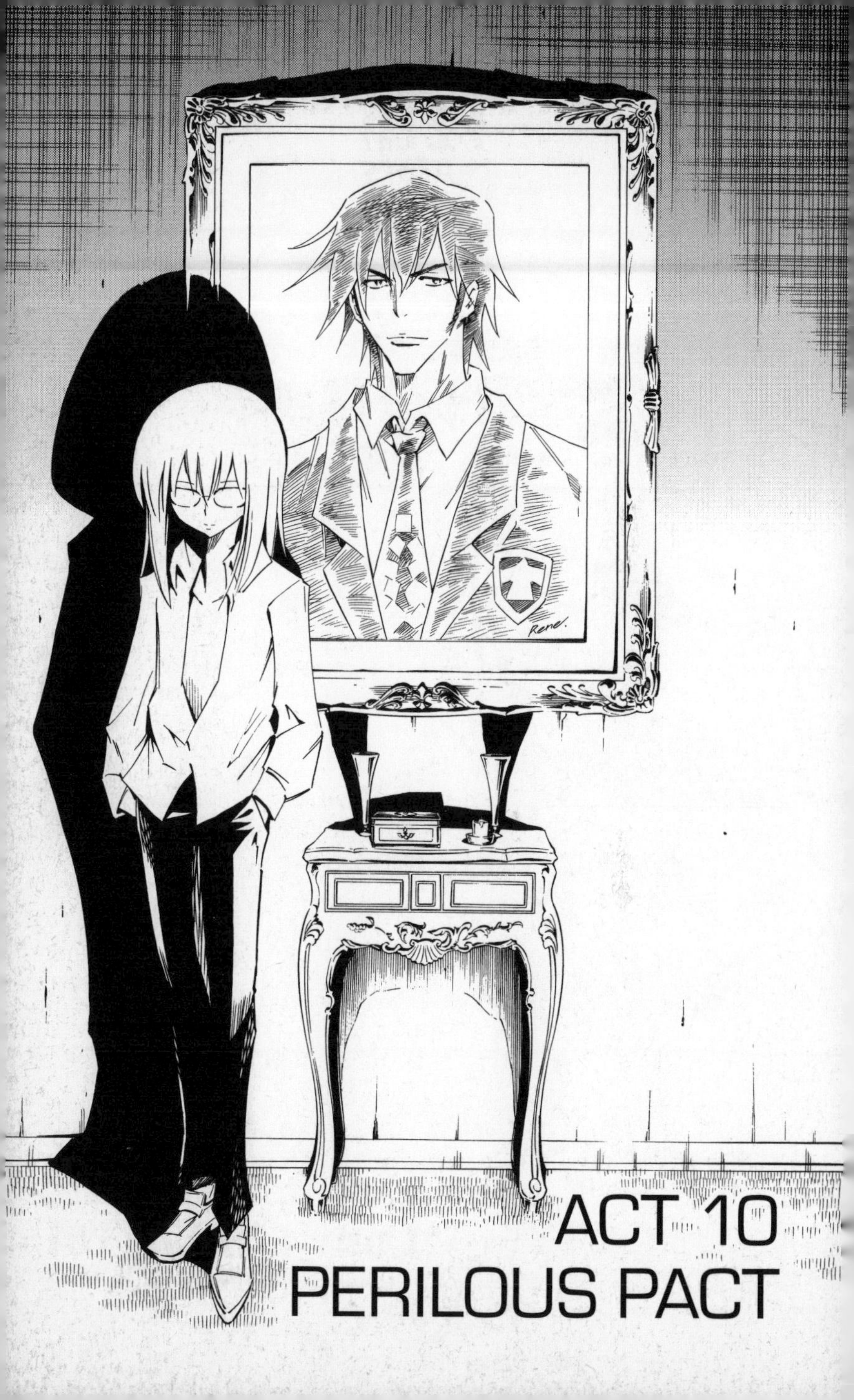
Rene.

ACT 10
PERILOUS PACT

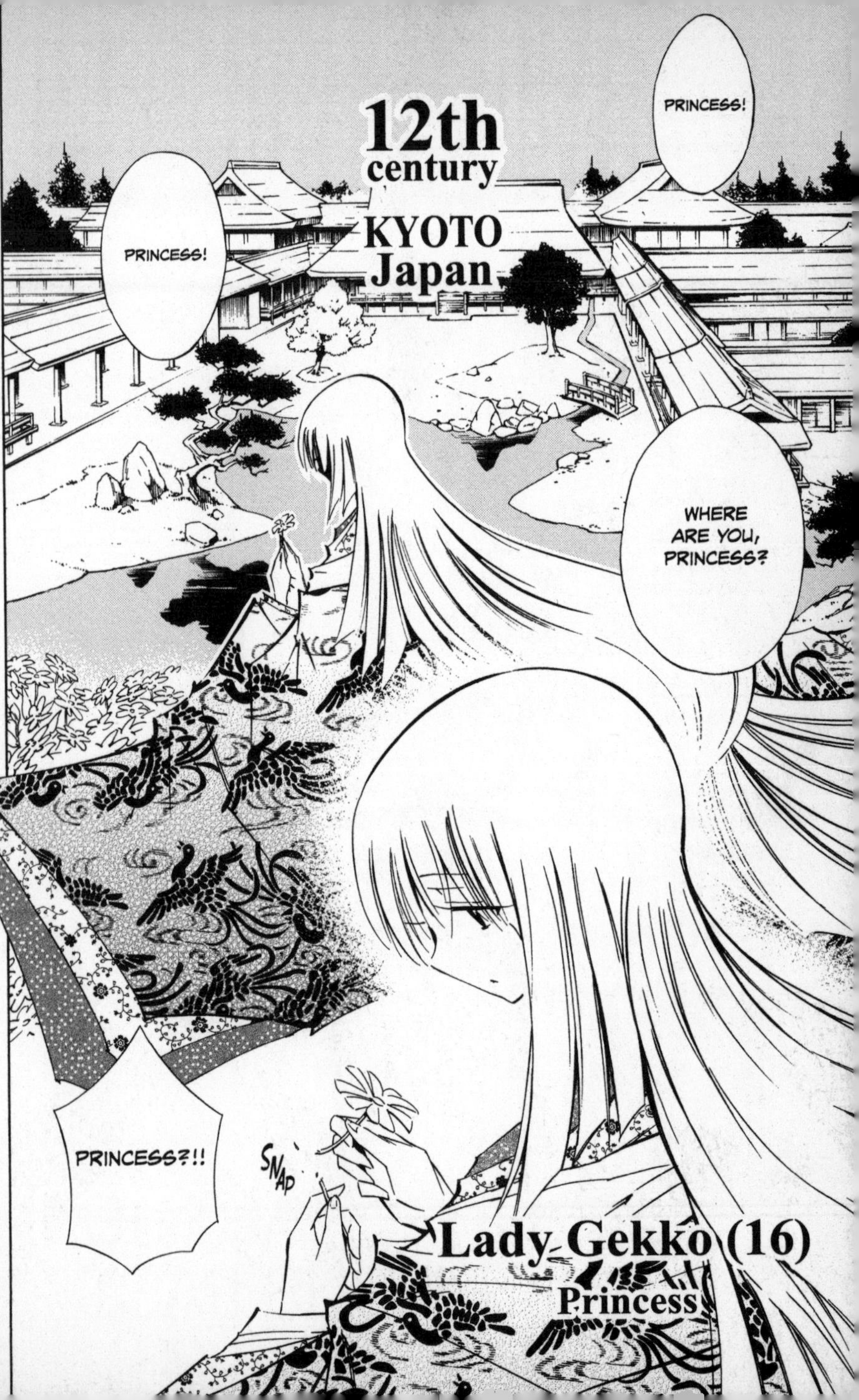
PRINCESS!
12th century
KYOTO Japan
PRINCESS!
WHERE ARE YOU, PRINCESS?
PRINCESS?!!
SNAP
Lady Gekko (16)
Princess

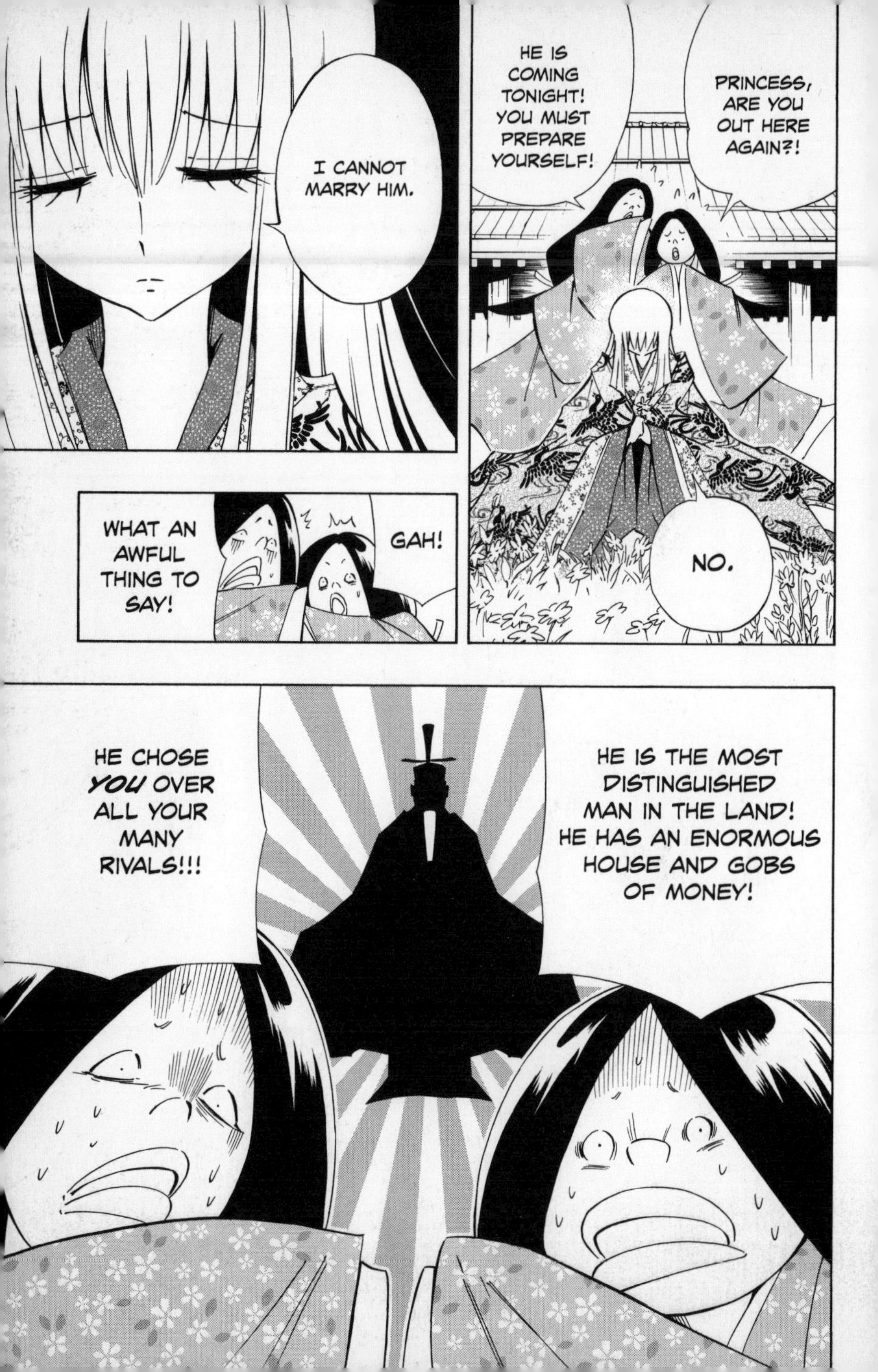
PRINCESS, ARE YOU OUT HERE AGAIN?!
HE IS COMING TONIGHT! YOU MUST PREPARE YOURSELF!
NO.
I CANNOT MARRY HIM.
GAH!
WHAT AN AWFUL THING TO SAY!
HE IS THE MOST DISTINGUISHED MAN IN THE LAND! HE HAS AN ENORMOUS HOUSE AND GOBS OF MONEY!
HE CHOSE *YOU* OVER ALL YOUR MANY RIVALS!!!

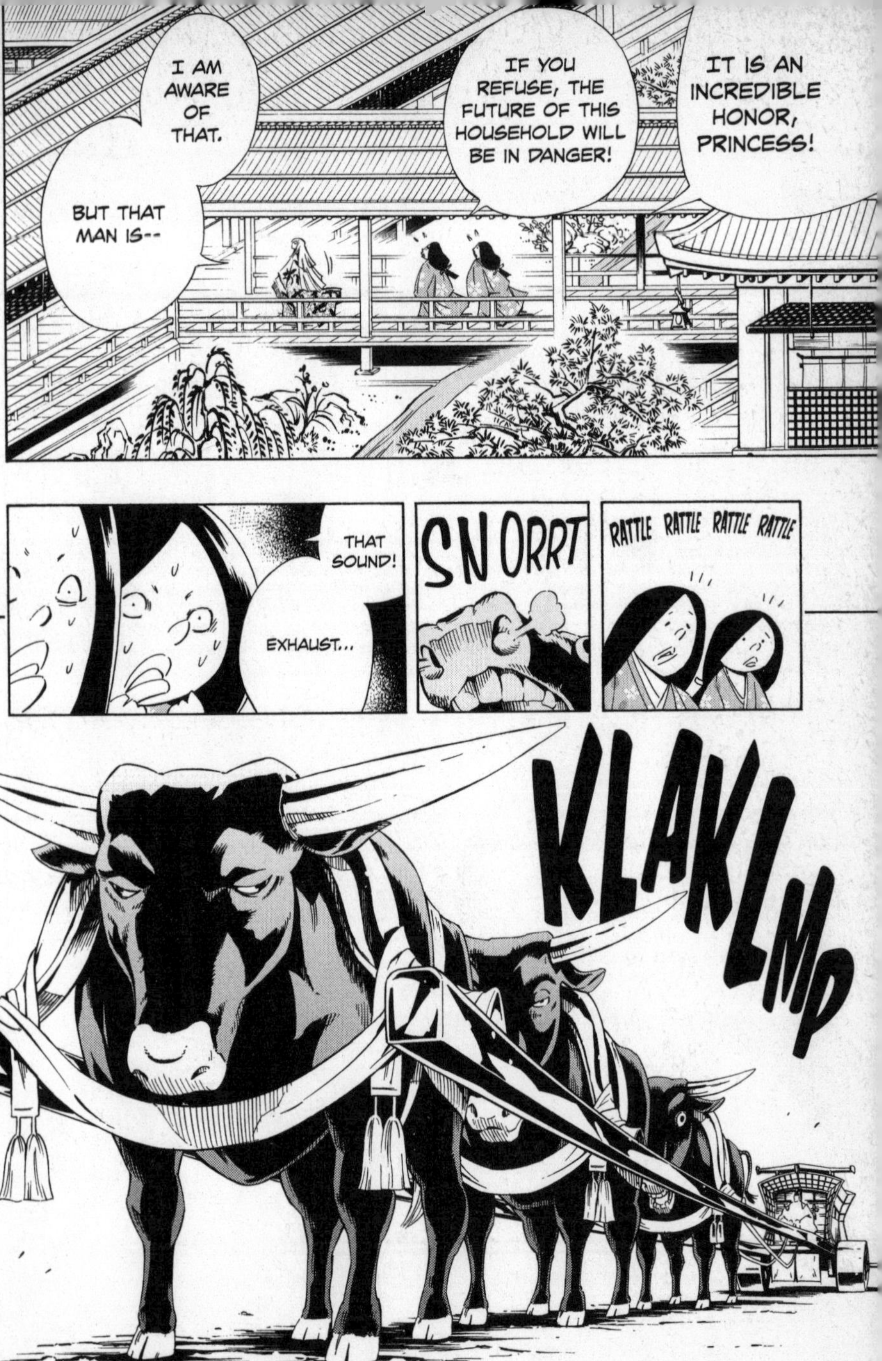
IT IS AN INCREDIBLE HONOR, PRINCESS!
IF YOU REFUSE, THE FUTURE OF THIS HOUSEHOLD WILL BE IN DANGER!
I AM AWARE OF THAT.
BUT THAT MAN IS--
RATTLE RATTLE RATTLE RATTLE
SNORRT
THAT SOUND!
EXHAUST...
KLAKLMP

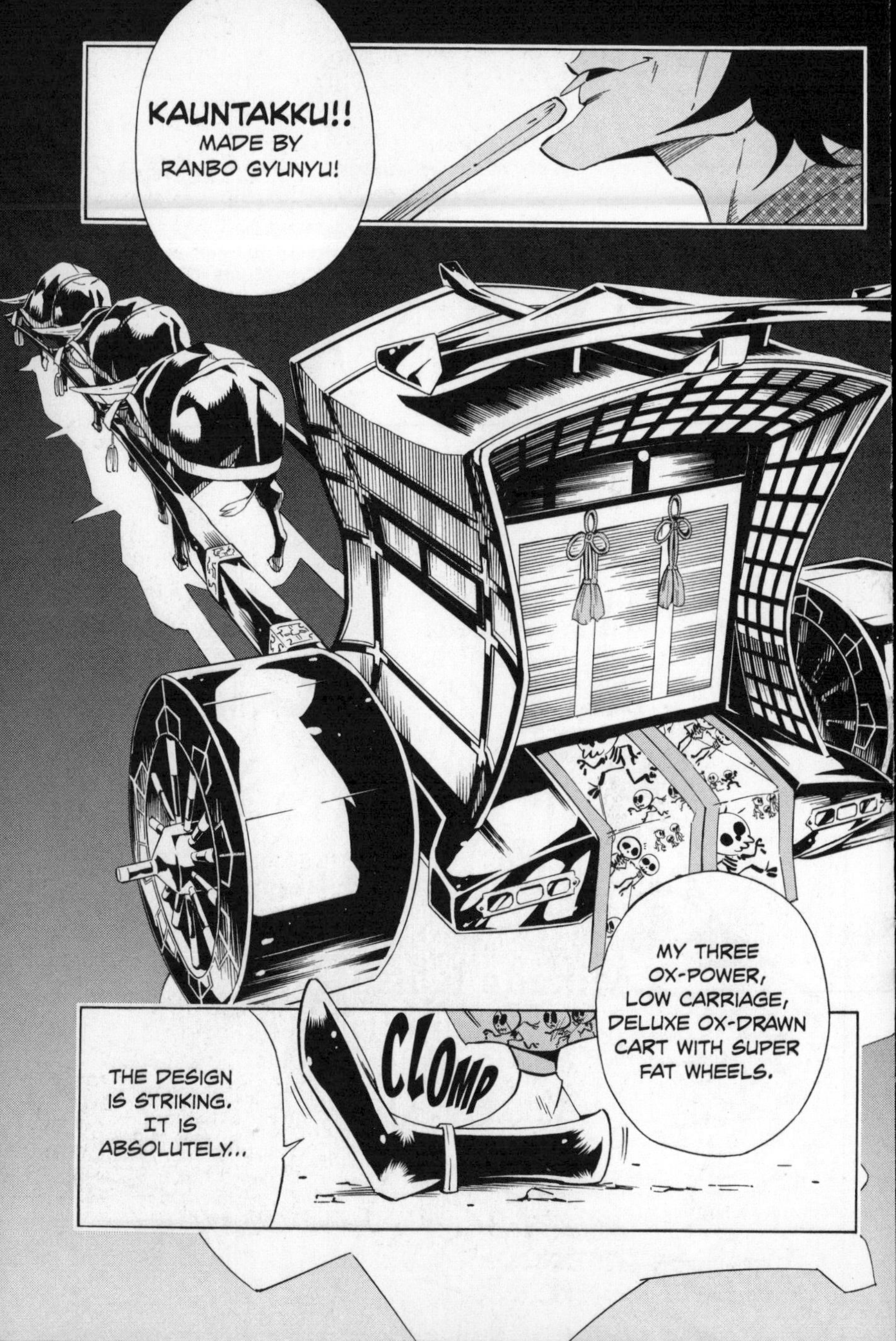
KAUNTAKKU!! MADE BY RANBO GYUNYU!
MY THREE OX-POWER, LOW CARRIAGE, DELUXE OX-DRAWN CART WITH SUPER FAT WHEELS.
CLOMP
THE DESIGN IS STRIKING. IT IS ABSOLUTELY...

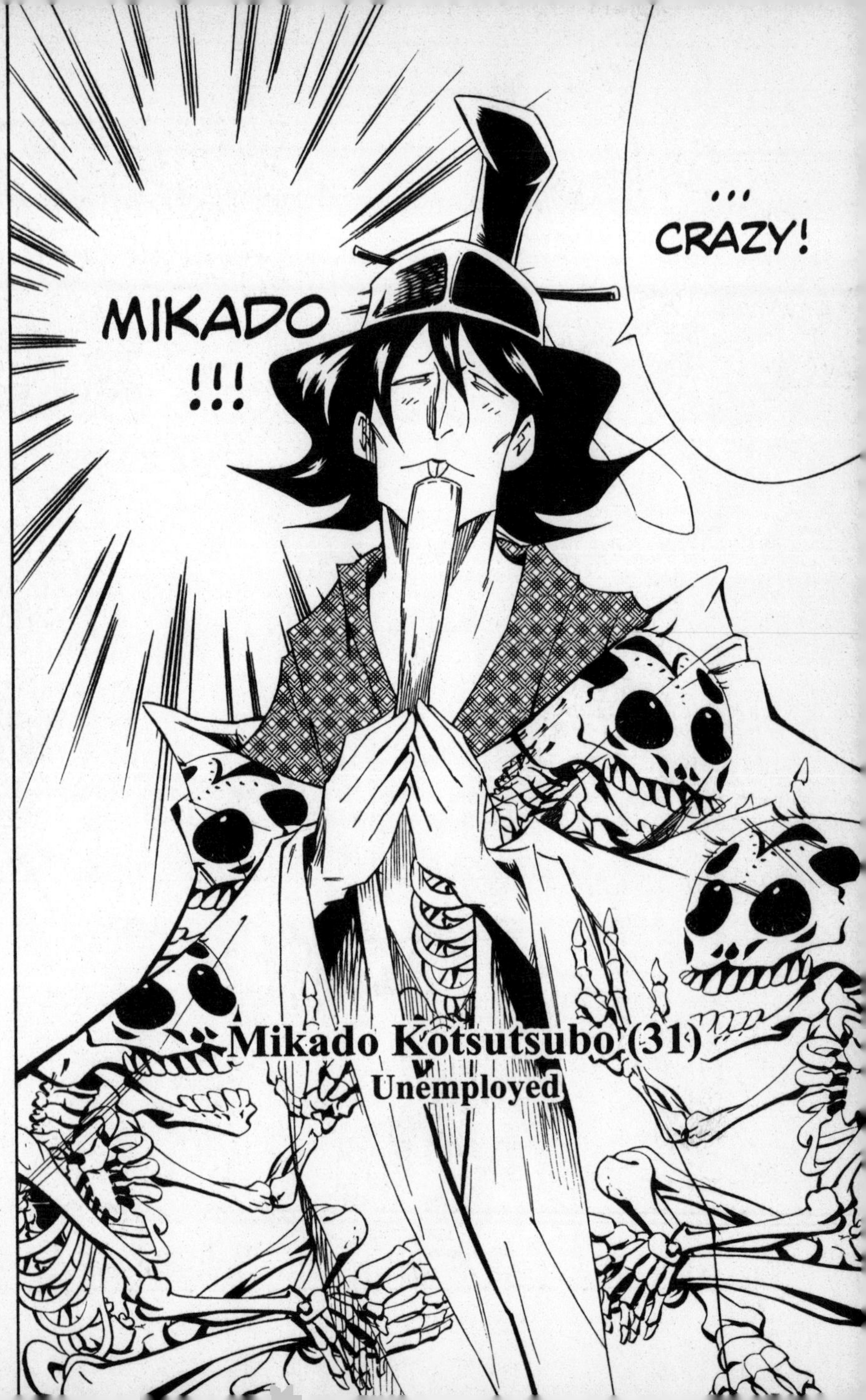
...CRAZY!
MIKADO!!!
Mikado Kotsutsubo (31)
Unemployed

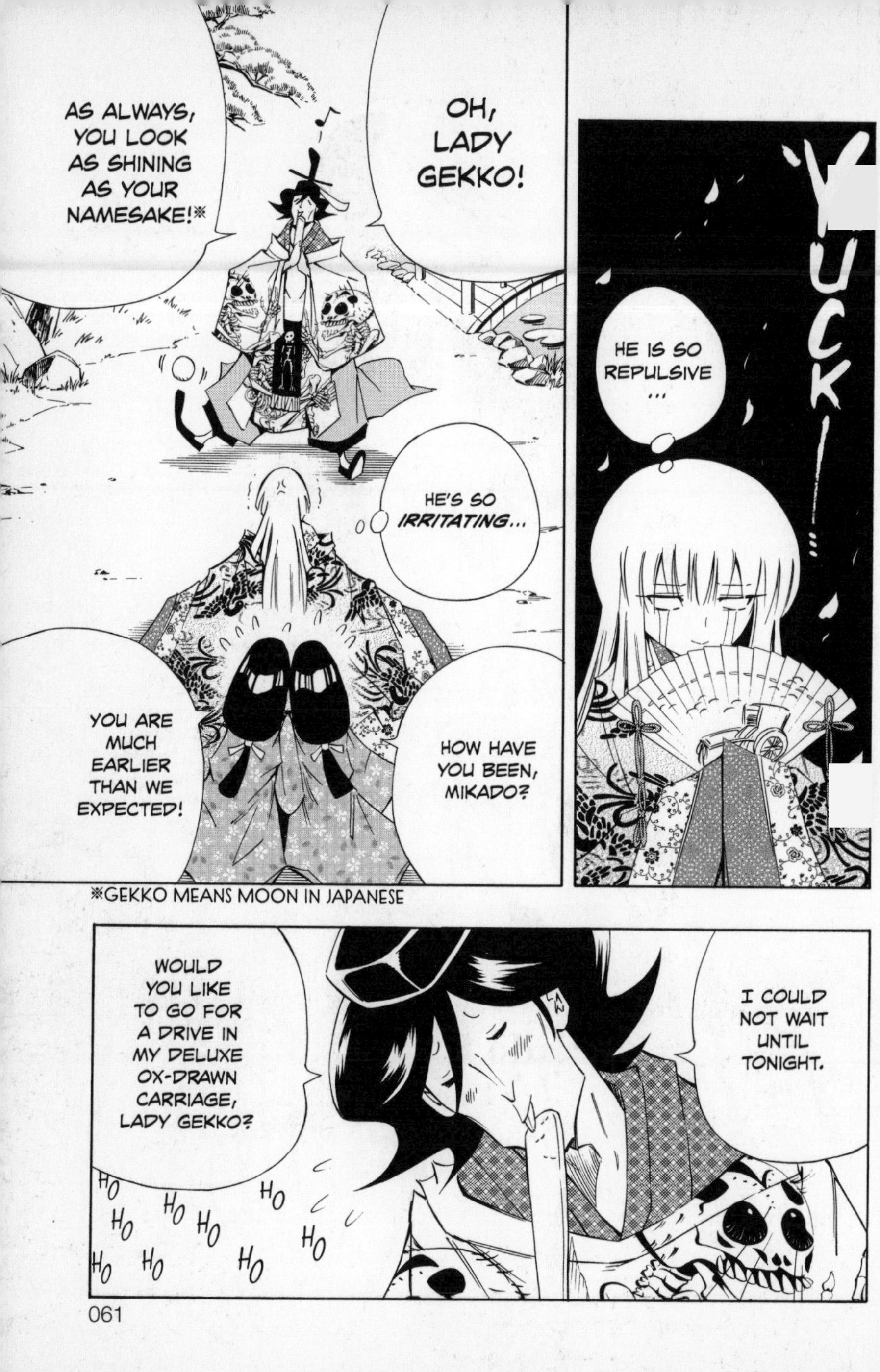
YUCK!...
HE IS SO REPULSIVE ...
OH, LADY GEKKO!
AS ALWAYS, YOU LOOK AS SHINING AS YOUR NAMESAKE!※
HE'S SO *IRRITATING...*
HOW HAVE YOU BEEN, MIKADO?
YOU ARE MUCH EARLIER THAN WE EXPECTED!
I COULD NOT WAIT UNTIL TONIGHT.
WOULD YOU LIKE TO GO FOR A DRIVE IN MY DELUXE OX-DRAWN CARRIAGE, LADY GEKKO?
HO HO HO HO HO HO HO HO HO

※GEKKO MEANS MOON IN JAPANESE

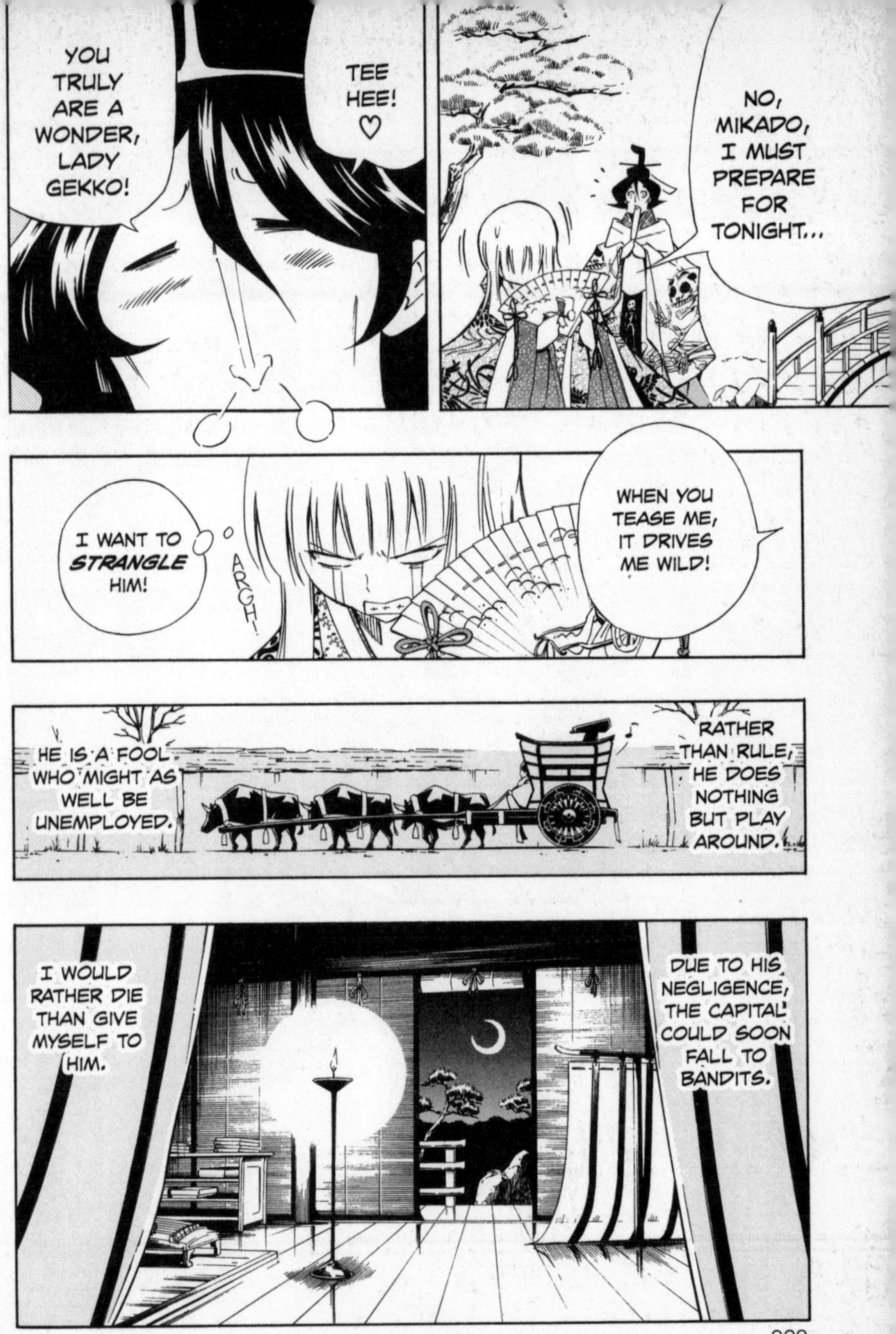
NO, MIKADO, I MUST PREPARE FOR TONIGHT...
TEE HEE! ♡
YOU TRULY ARE A WONDER, LADY GEKKO!
WHEN YOU TEASE ME, IT DRIVES ME WILD!
ARGH!
I WANT TO *STRANGLE* HIM!
RATHER THAN RULE, HE DOES NOTHING BUT PLAY AROUND.
HE IS A FOOL WHO MIGHT AS WELL BE UNEMPLOYED.
DUE TO HIS NEGLIGENCE, THE CAPITAL COULD SOON FALL TO BANDITS.
I WOULD RATHER DIE THAN GIVE MYSELF TO HIM.

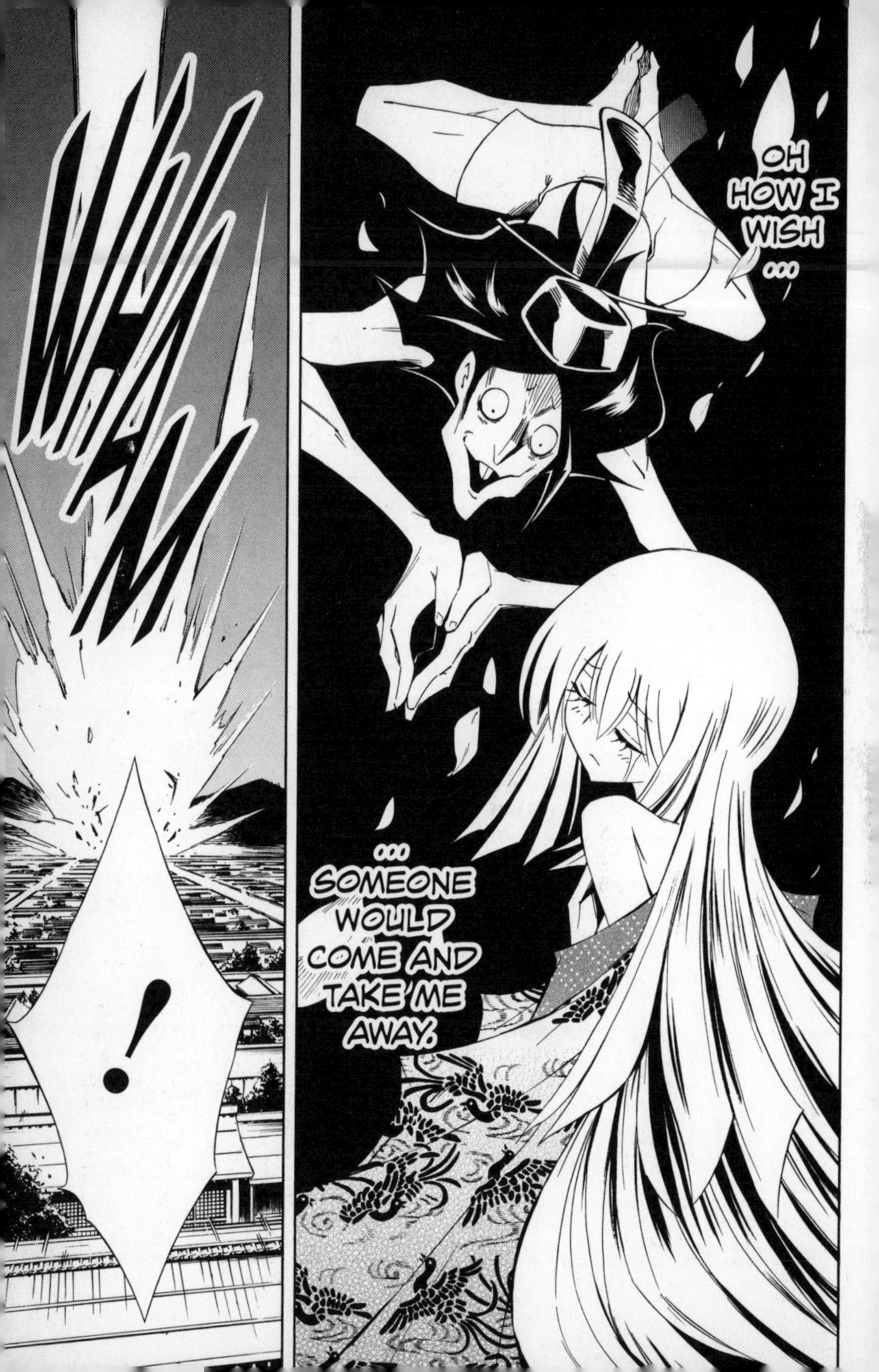
OH HOW I WISH ...
... SOMEONE WOULD COME AND TAKE ME AWAY.
WHAM
!

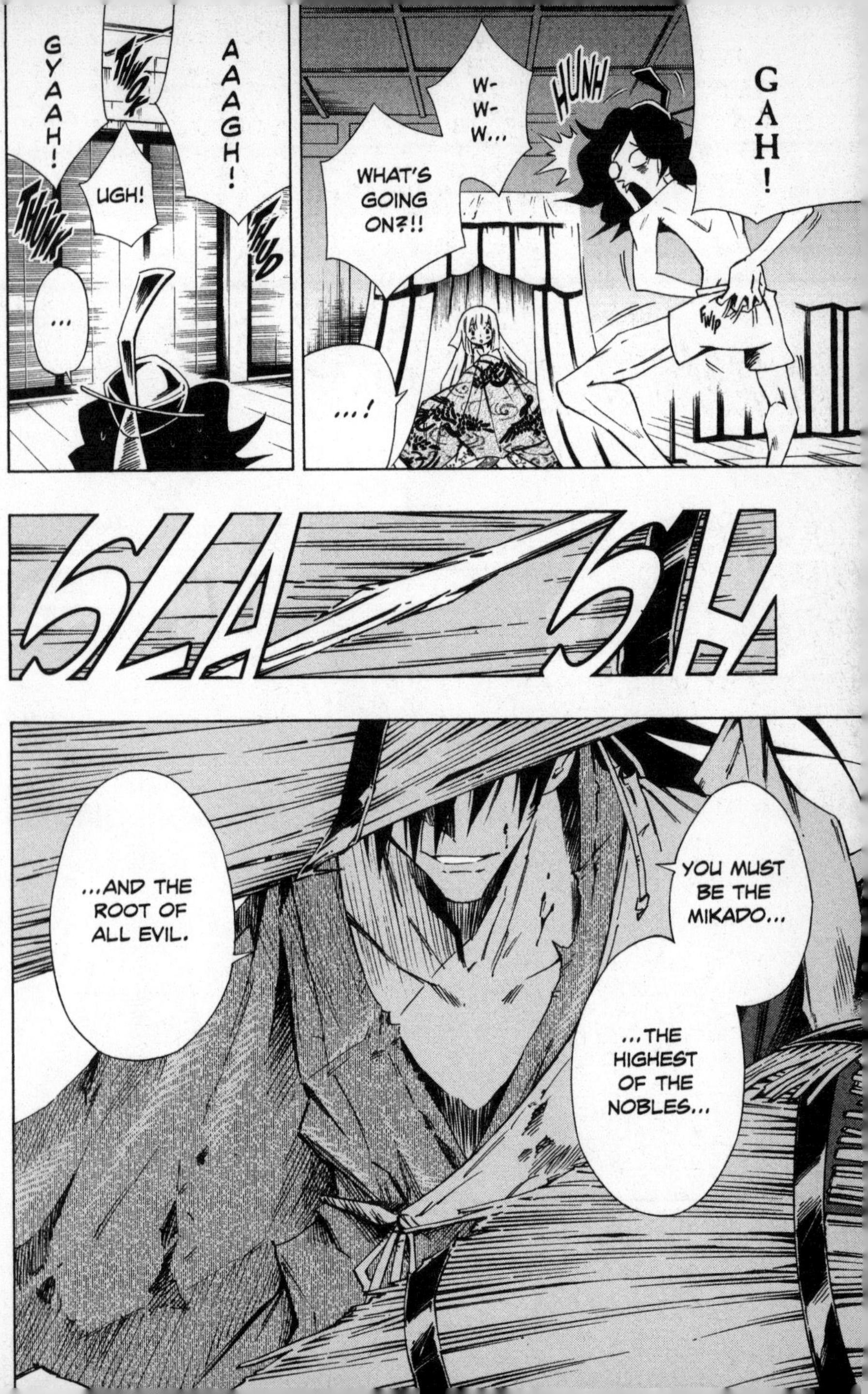
GAH!
HUNH
W-W-W...
WHAT'S GOING ON?!!
FWIP
...!
AAAGH!
GYAAH!
UGH!
THUNK
THUD
...
YOU MUST BE THE MIKADO...
...THE HIGHEST OF THE NOBLES...
...AND THE ROOT OF ALL EVIL.

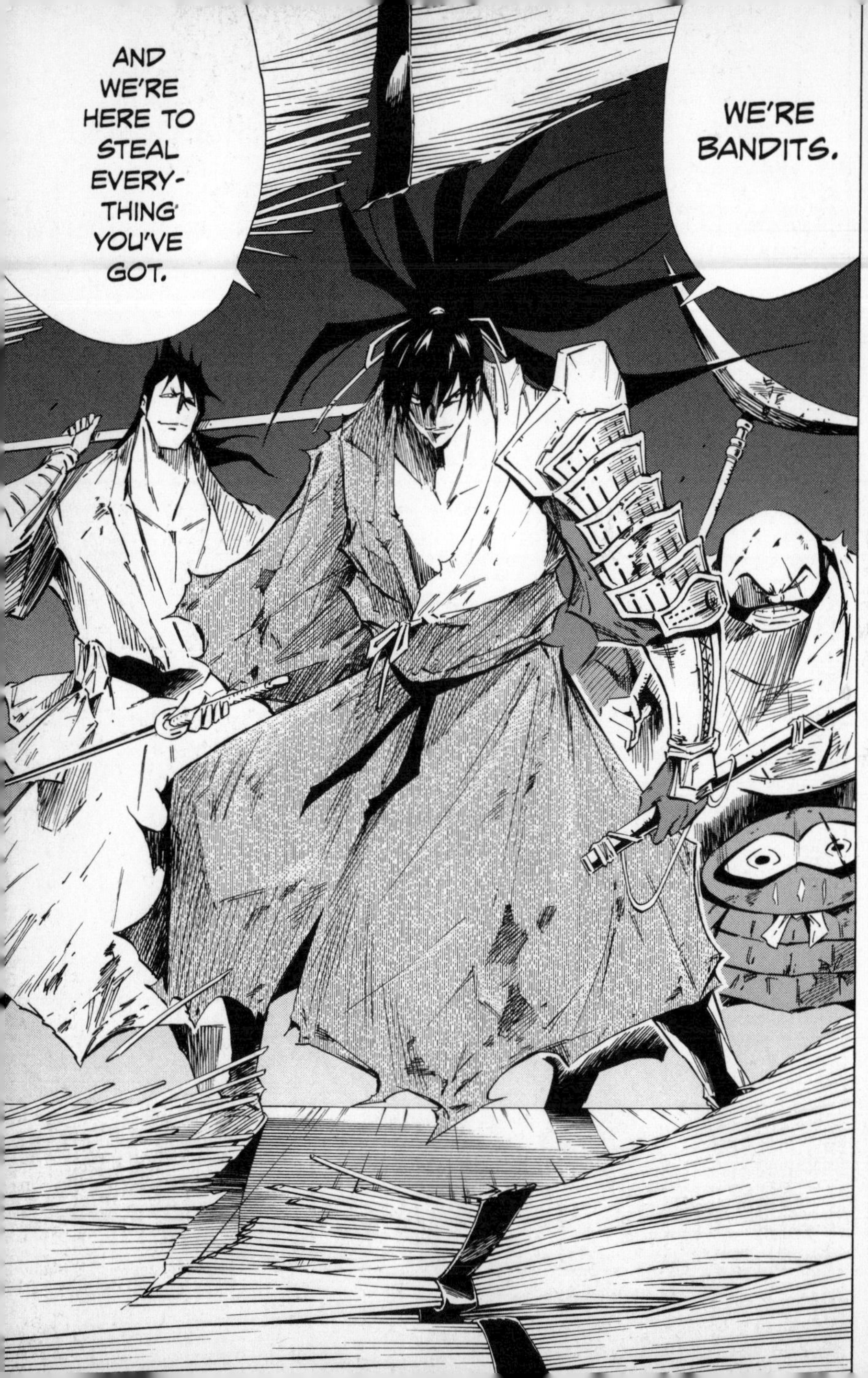
WE'RE BANDITS.
AND WE'RE HERE TO STEAL EVERYTHING YOU'VE GOT.

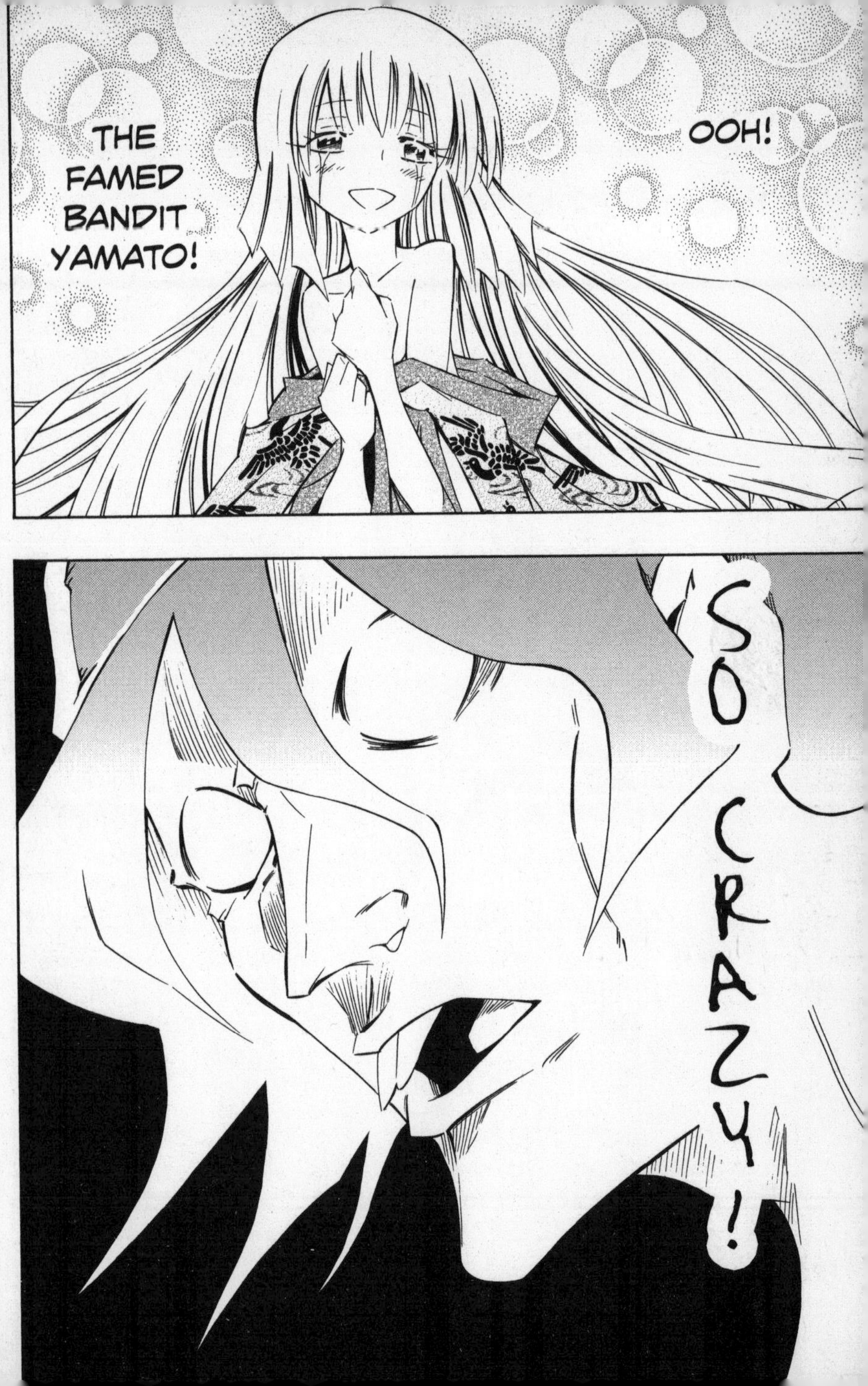
OOH!
THE FAMED BANDIT YAMATO!
SO CRAZY!

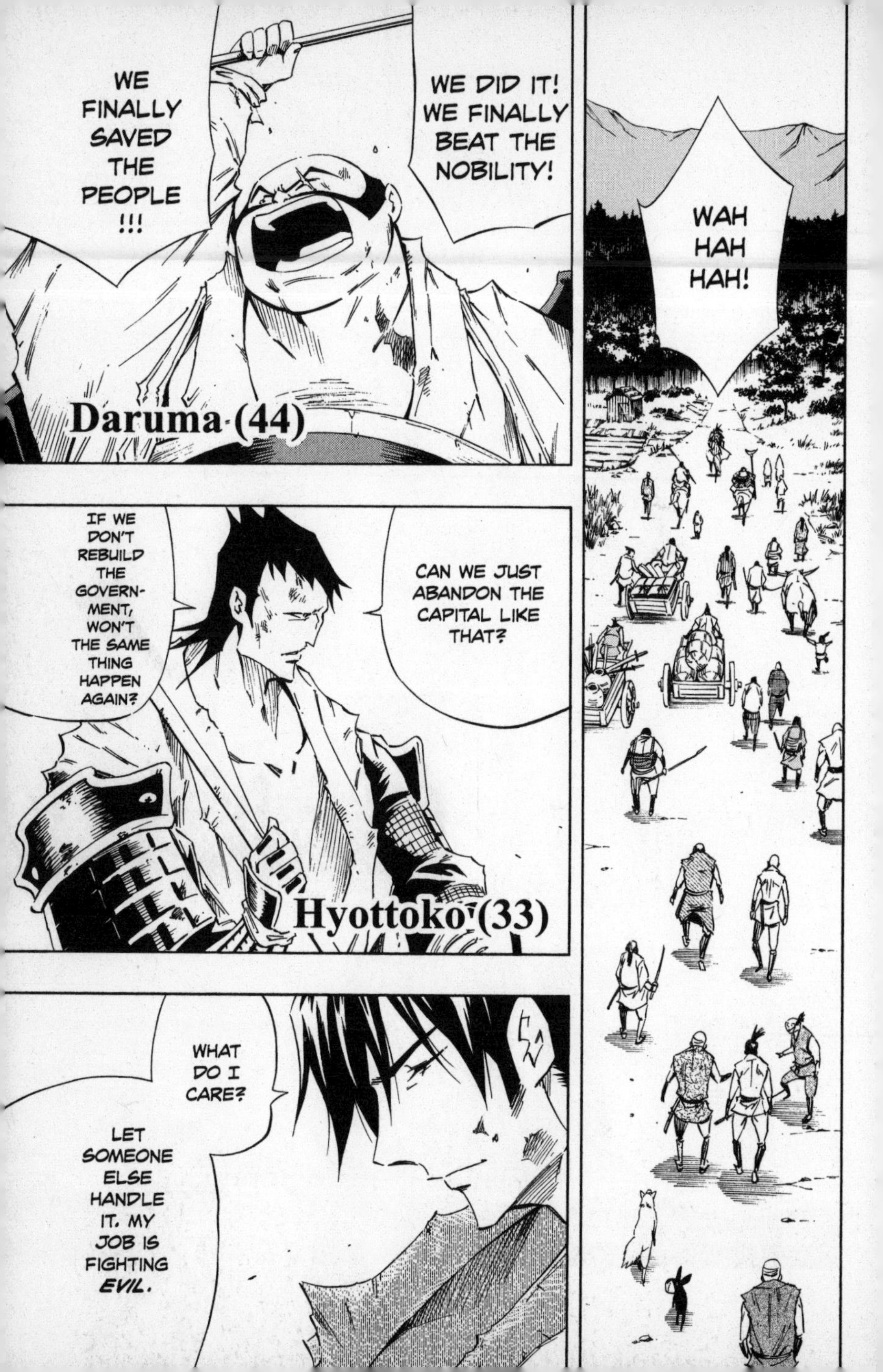
WAH HAH HAH!
WE DID IT! WE FINALLY BEAT THE NOBILITY!
WE FINALLY SAVED THE PEOPLE!!!
Daruma (44)
CAN WE JUST ABANDON THE CAPITAL LIKE THAT?
IF WE DON'T REBUILD THE GOVERN-MENT, WON'T THE SAME THING HAPPEN AGAIN?
Hyottoko (33)
WHAT DO I CARE?
LET SOMEONE ELSE HANDLE IT. MY JOB IS FIGHTING *EVIL*.

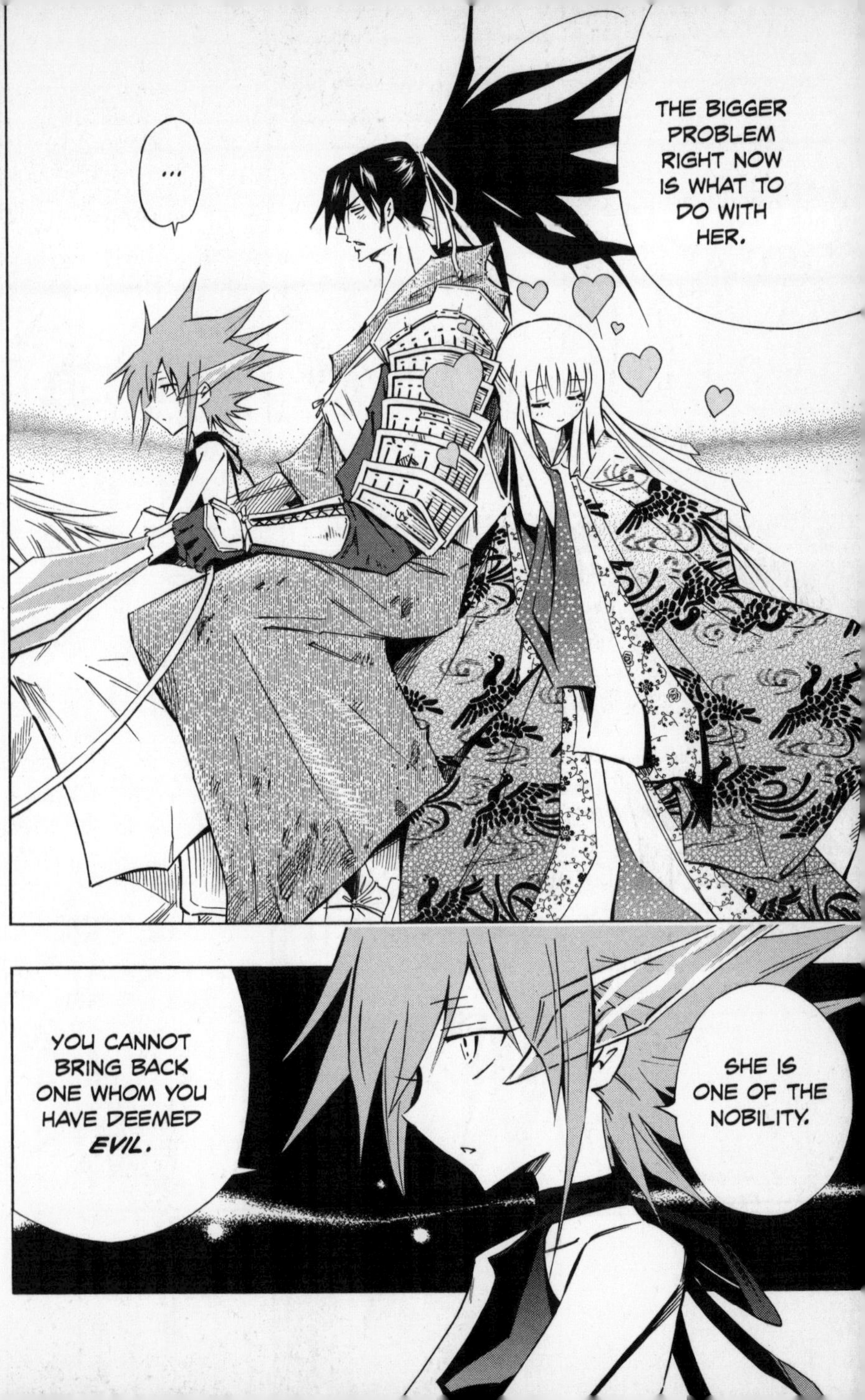
THE BIGGER PROBLEM RIGHT NOW IS WHAT TO DO WITH HER.
...
SHE IS ONE OF THE NOBILITY.
YOU CANNOT BRING BACK ONE WHOM YOU HAVE DEEMED *EVIL*.

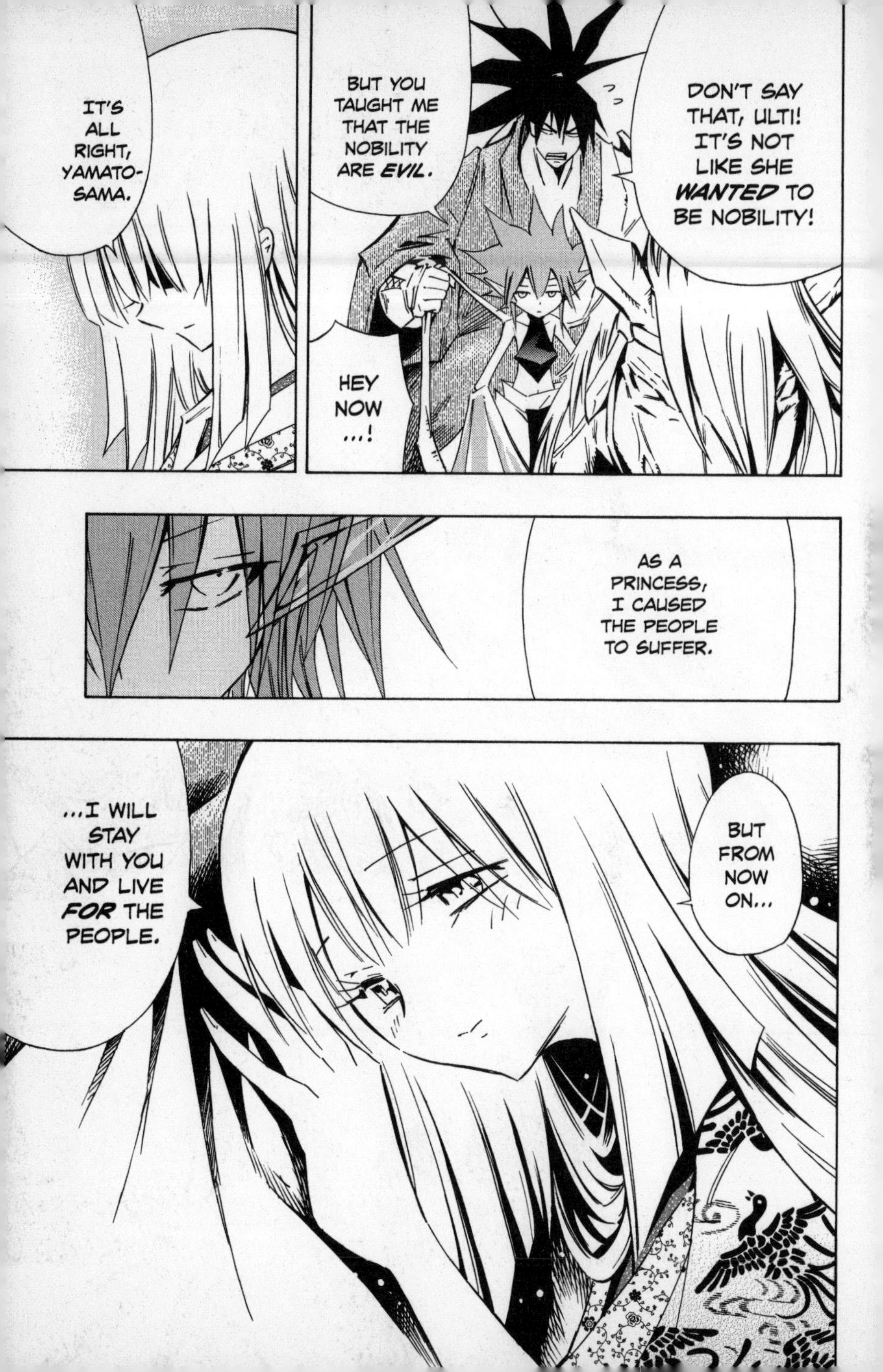
DON'T SAY THAT, ULTI! IT'S NOT LIKE SHE *WANTED* TO BE NOBILITY!
BUT YOU TAUGHT ME THAT THE NOBILITY ARE *EVIL*.
HEY NOW ...!
IT'S ALL RIGHT, YAMATO-SAMA.
AS A PRINCESS, I CAUSED THE PEOPLE TO SUFFER.
BUT FROM NOW ON...
...I WILL STAY WITH YOU AND LIVE *FOR* THE PEOPLE.

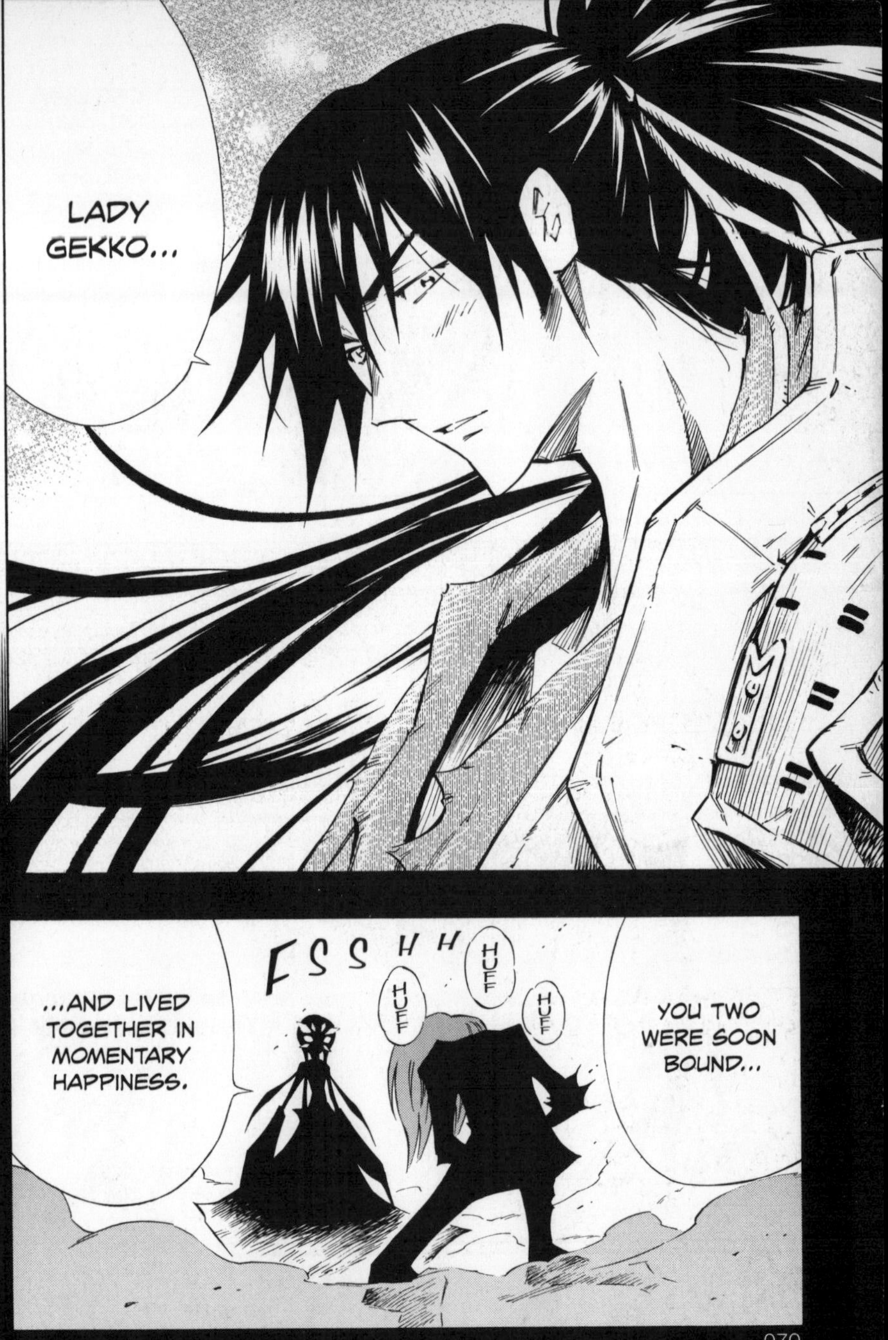
LADY GEKKO...
YOU TWO WERE SOON BOUND...
HUFF
HUFF
HUFF
FSSHH
...AND LIVED TOGETHER IN MOMENTARY HAPPINESS.

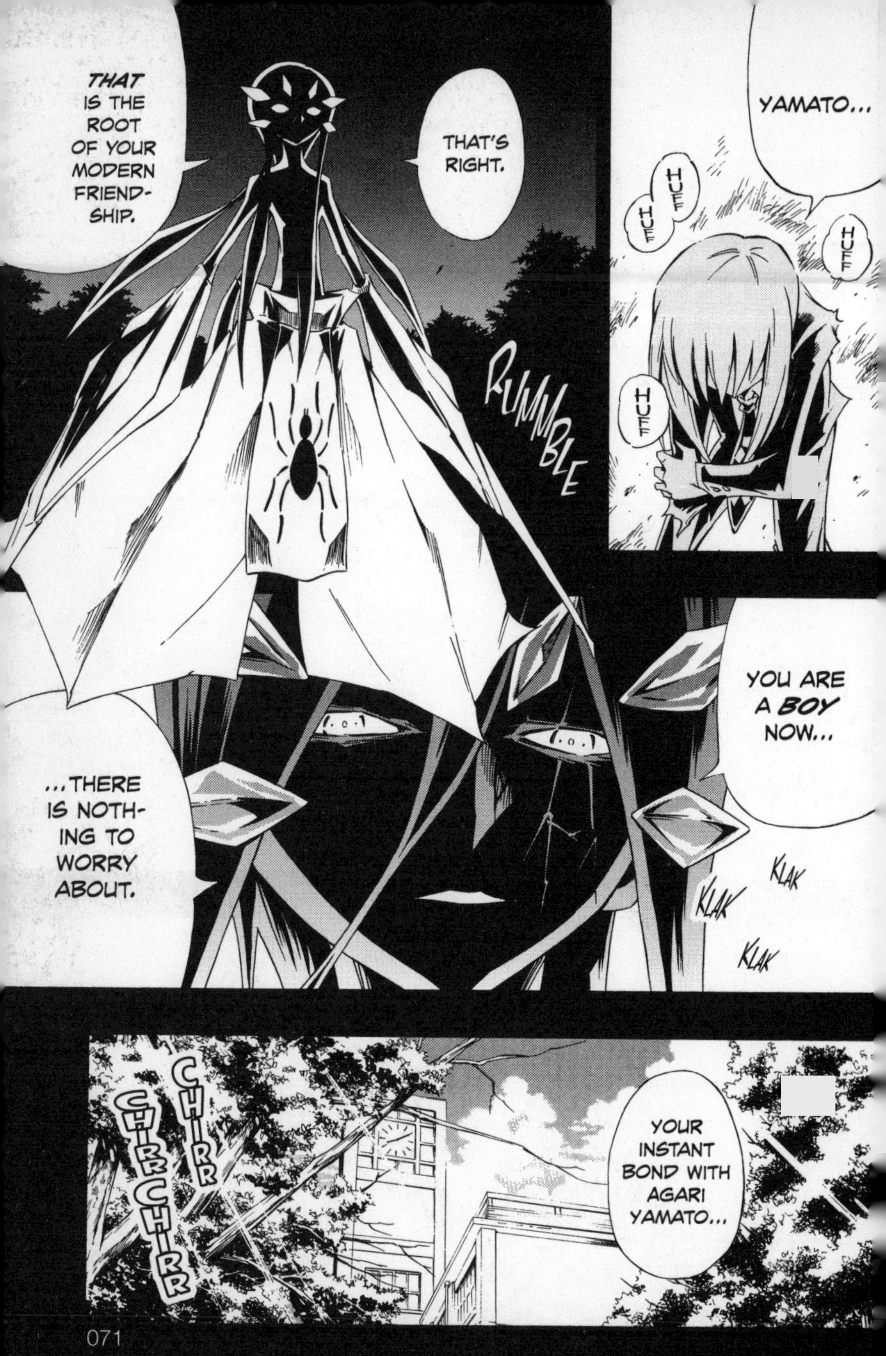
YAMATO...
HUFF HUFF
HUFF
HUFF
HUFF
THAT'S RIGHT.
THAT IS THE ROOT OF YOUR MODERN FRIEND-SHIP.
RUMMBLE
YOU ARE A *BOY* NOW...
KLAK
KLAK
KLAK
...THERE IS NOTH-ING TO WORRY ABOUT.
YOUR INSTANT BOND WITH AGARI YAMATO...
CHIRR
CHIRR CHIRR

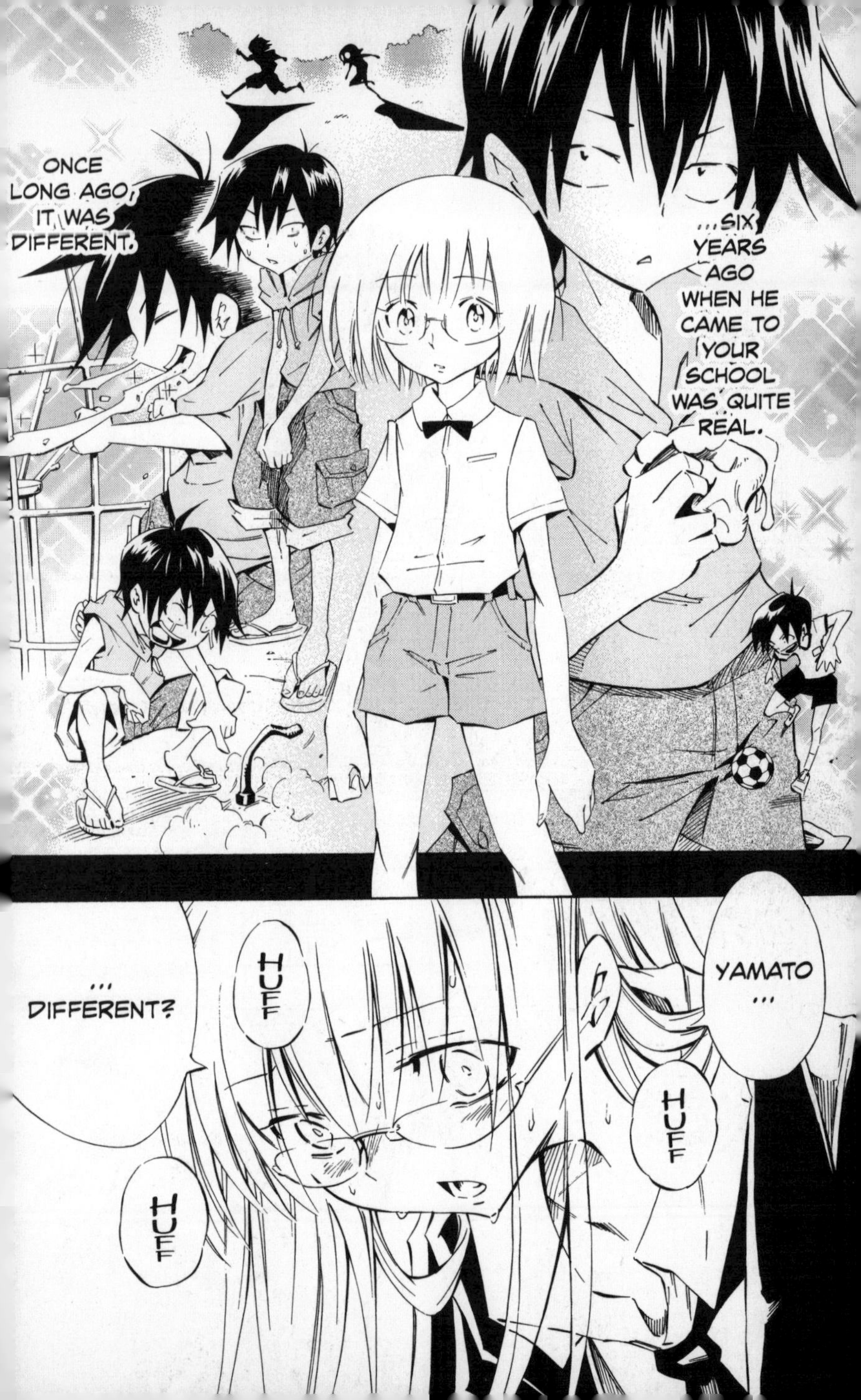
...SIX YEARS AGO WHEN HE CAME TO YOUR SCHOOL WAS QUITE REAL.
ONCE LONG AGO, IT WAS DIFFERENT.
YAMATO ...
HUFF
... DIFFERENT?
HUFF
HUFF

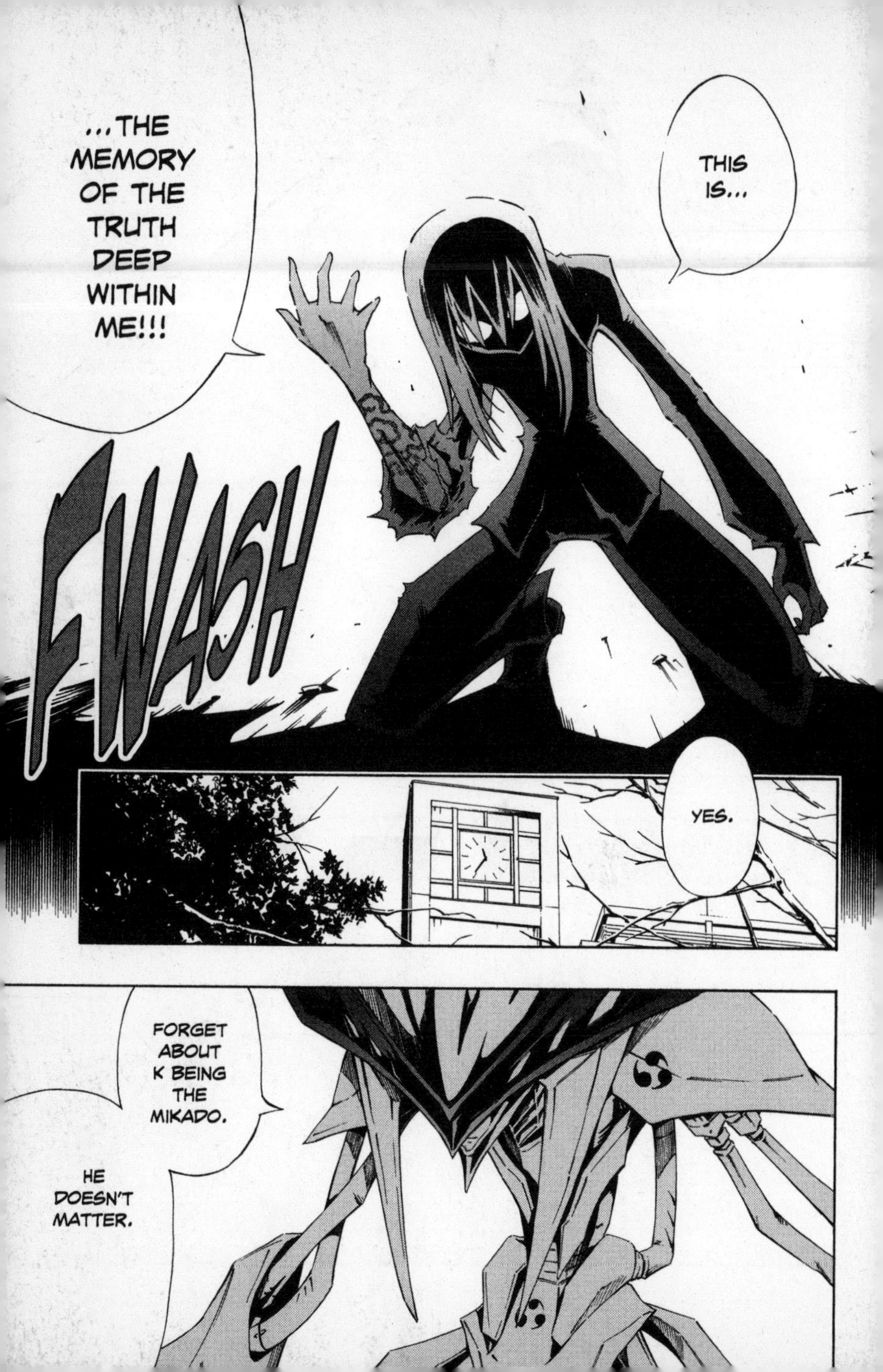
THIS IS...
...THE MEMORY OF THE TRUTH DEEP WITHIN ME!!!
FWASH
YES.
FORGET ABOUT K BEING THE MIKADO.
HE DOESN'T MATTER.

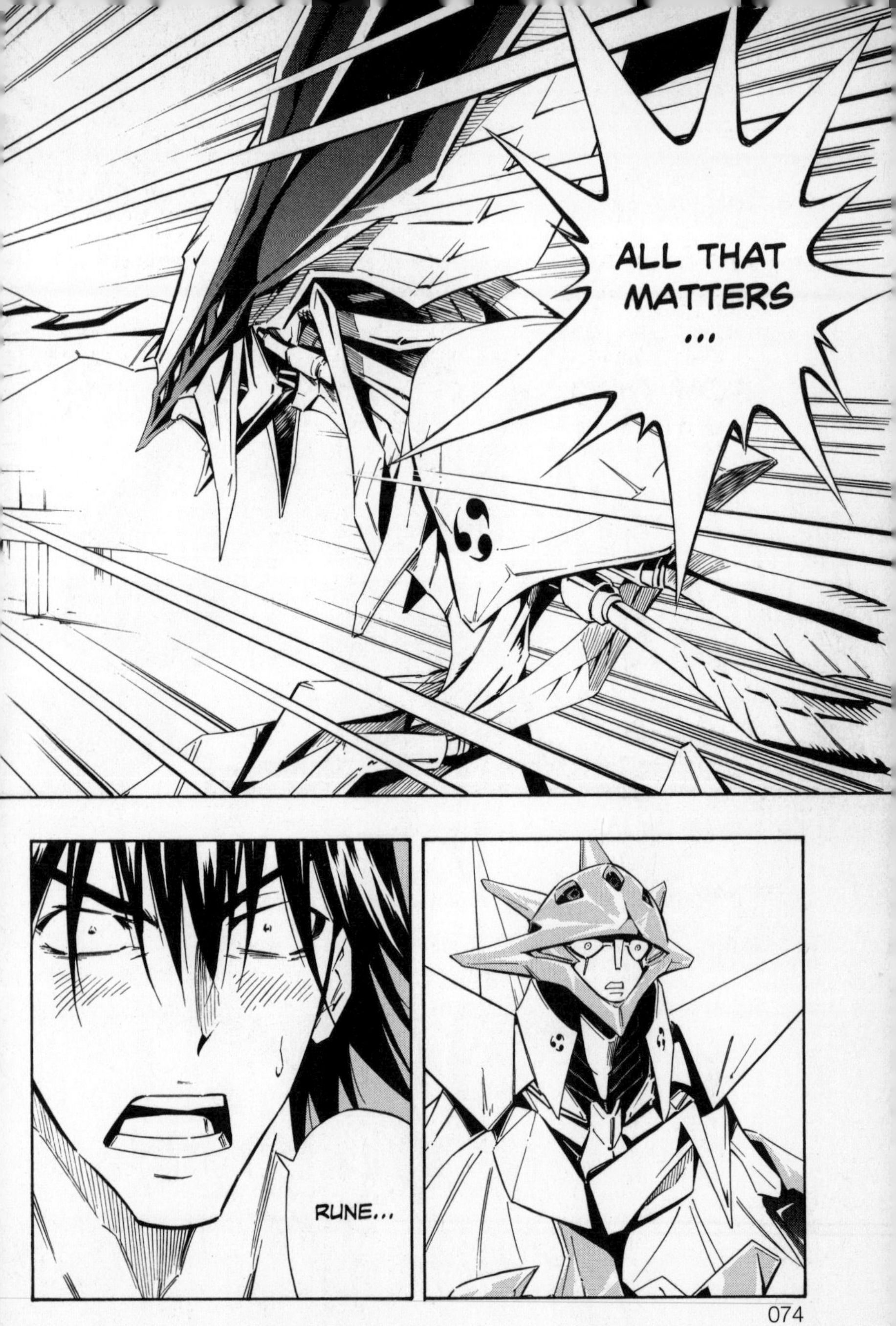
ALL THAT MATTERS ...
RUNE...

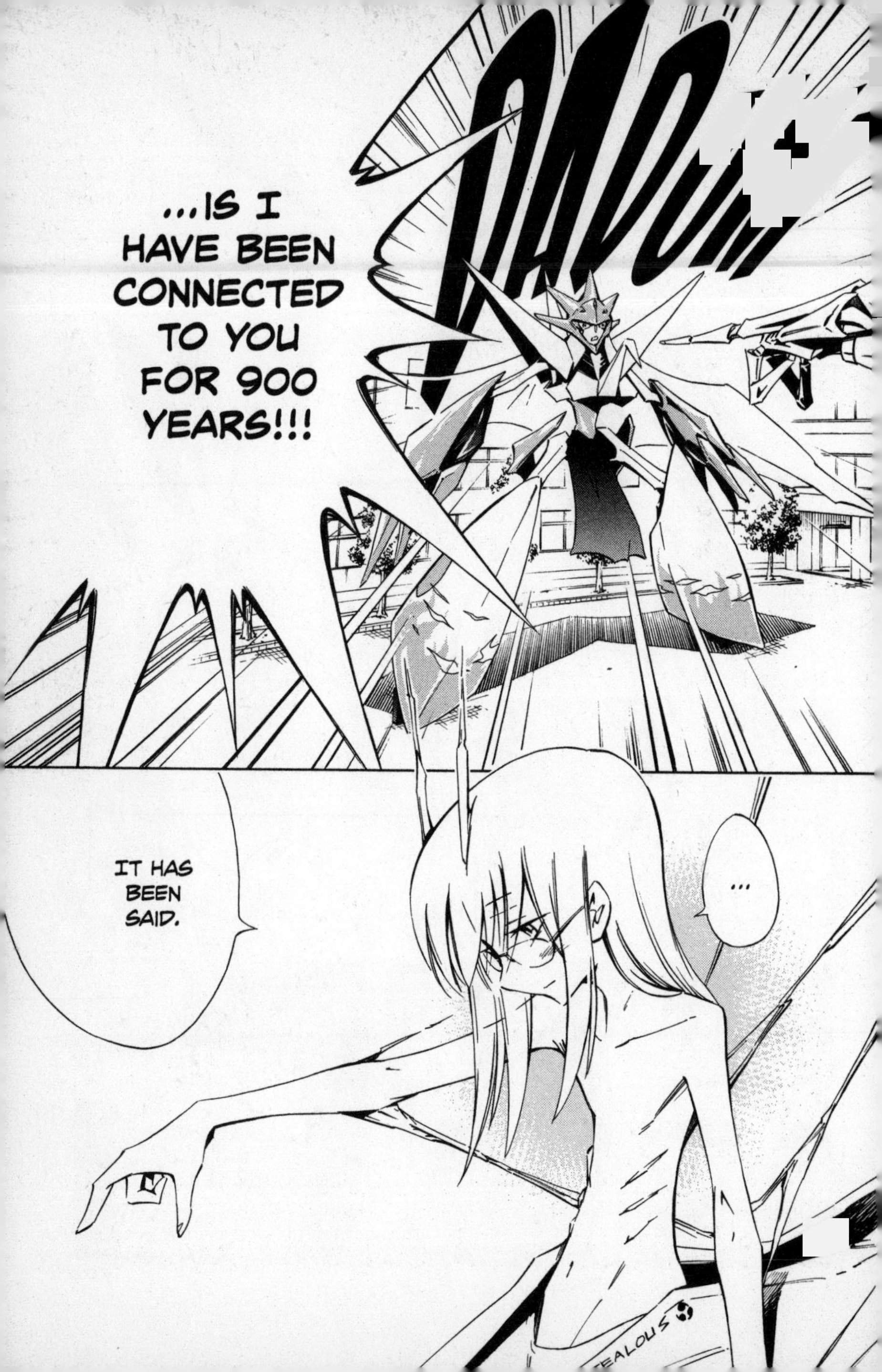
...IS I HAVE BEEN CONNECTED TO YOU FOR 900 YEARS!!!
...
IT HAS BEEN SAID.

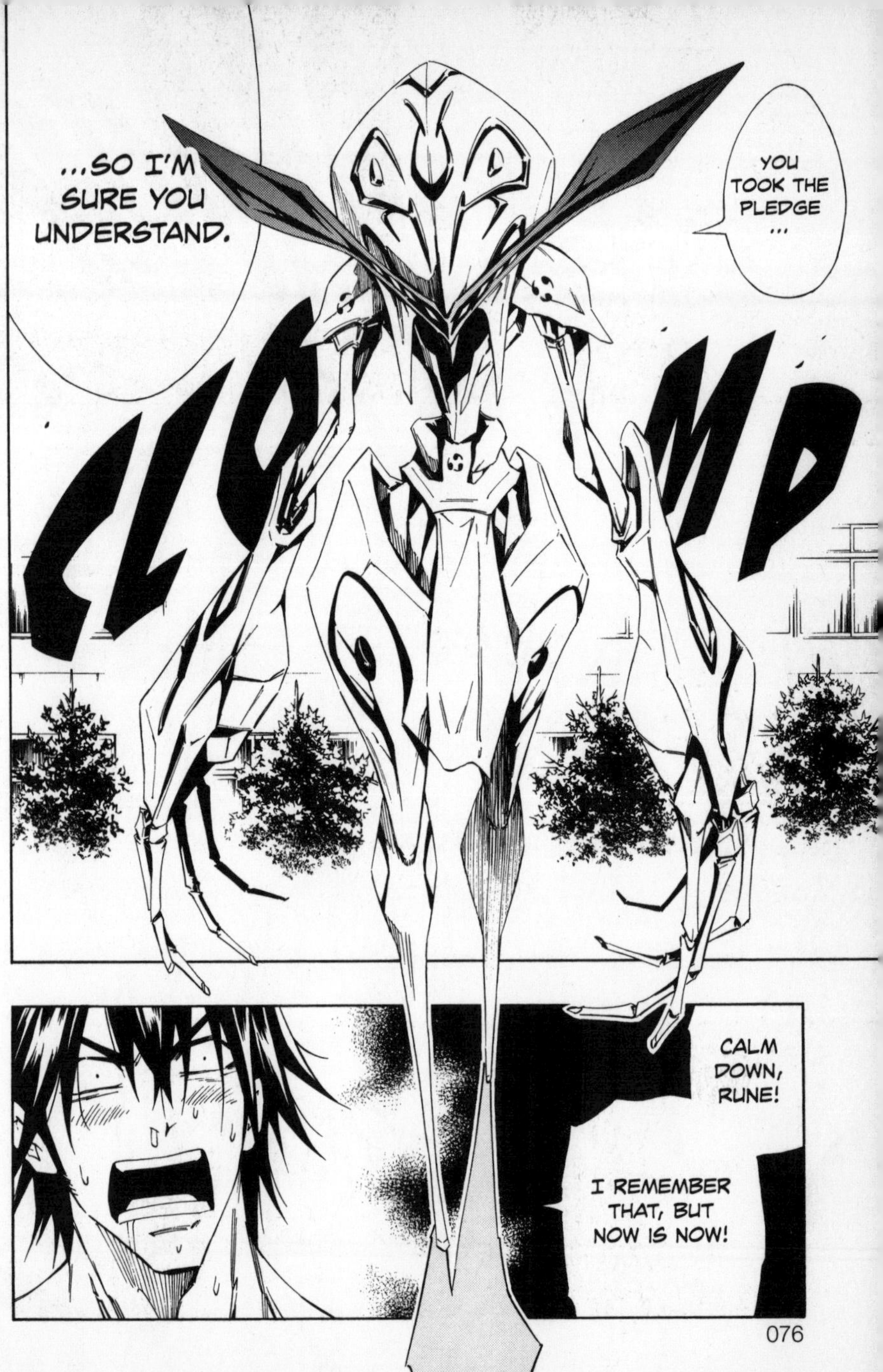
YOU TOOK THE PLEDGE ...
...SO I'M SURE YOU UNDERSTAND.
CLOMP
CALM DOWN, RUNE!
I REMEMBER THAT, BUT NOW IS NOW!

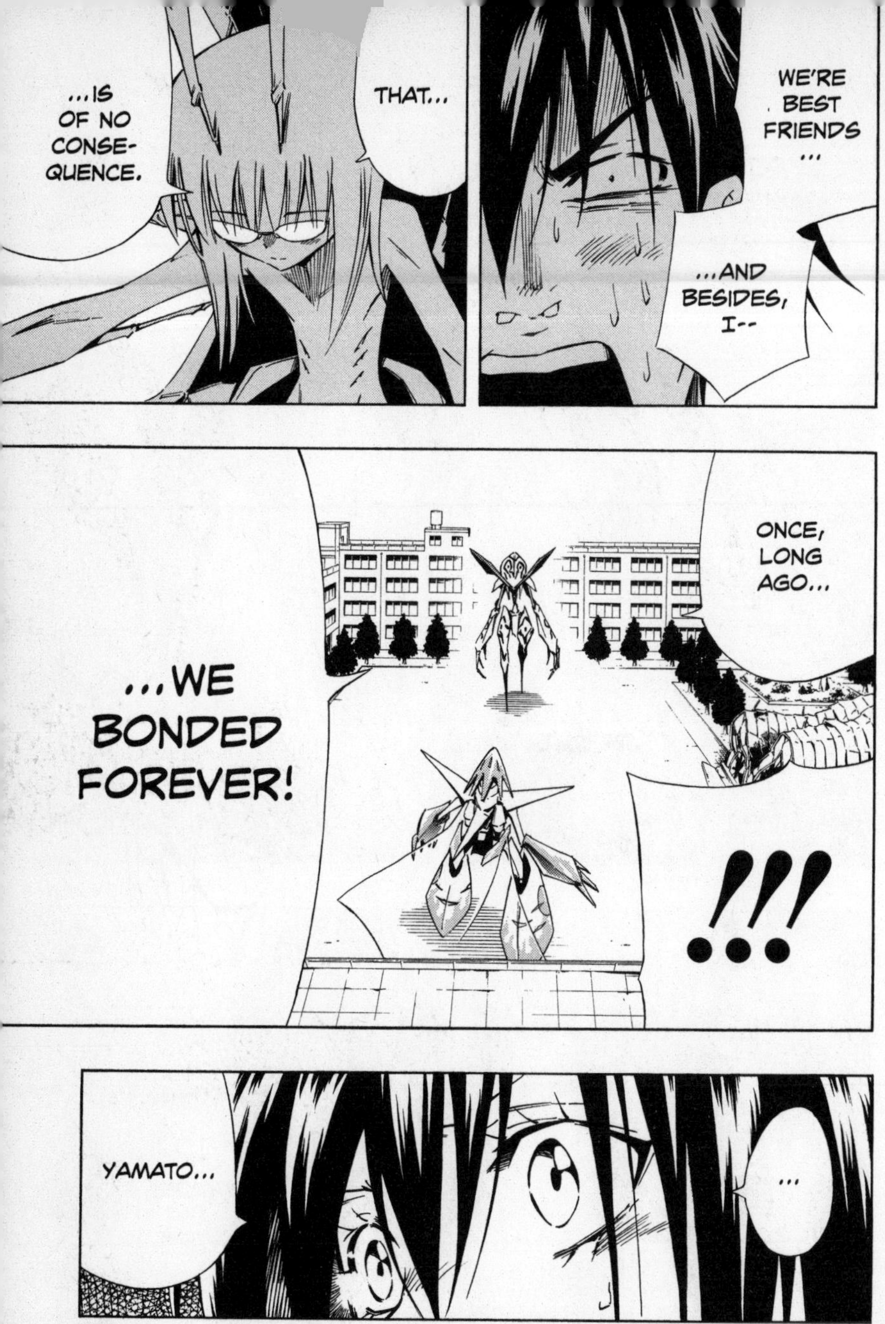
WE'RE BEST FRIENDS...
...AND BESIDES, I--
THAT...
...IS OF NO CONSEQUENCE.
ONCE, LONG AGO...
...WE BONDED FOREVER!
!!!
...
YAMATO...

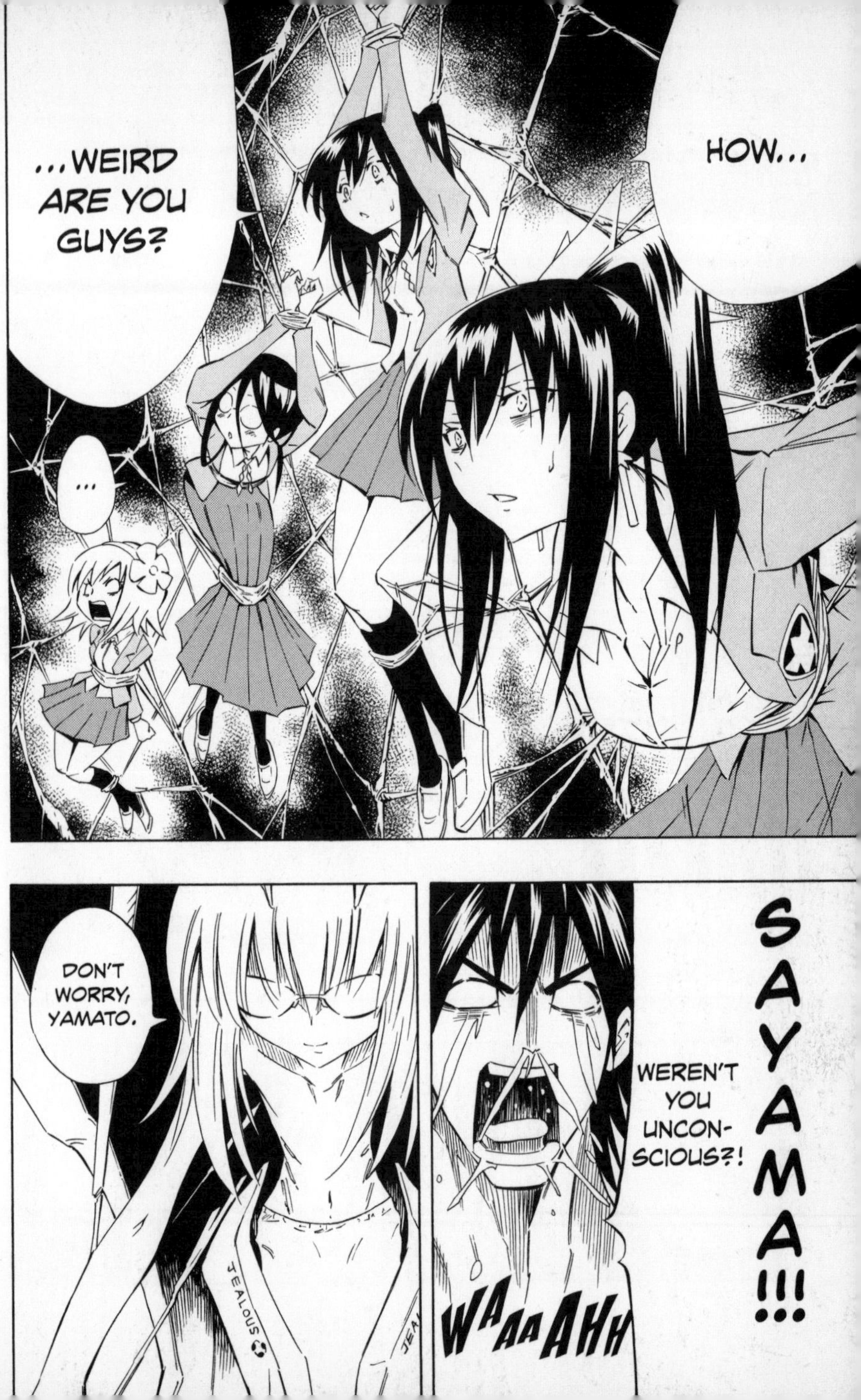
HOW...
...WEIRD ARE YOU GUYS?
...
SAYAMA!!!
WEREN'T YOU UNCON-SCIOUS?!
WAAAAHH
DON'T WORRY, YAMATO.
JEALOUS

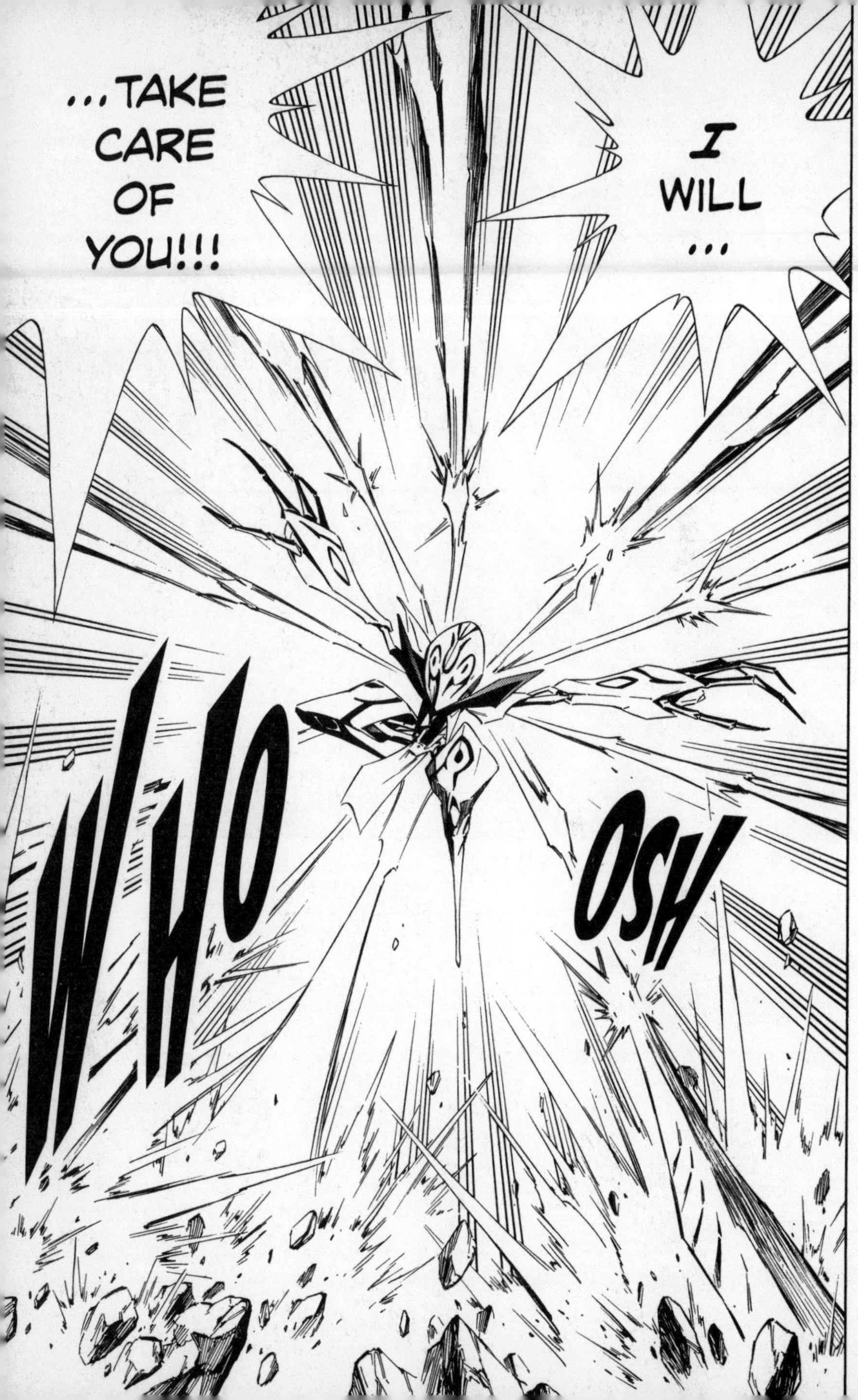
I WILL ...
...TAKE CARE OF YOU!!!
WHOOSH

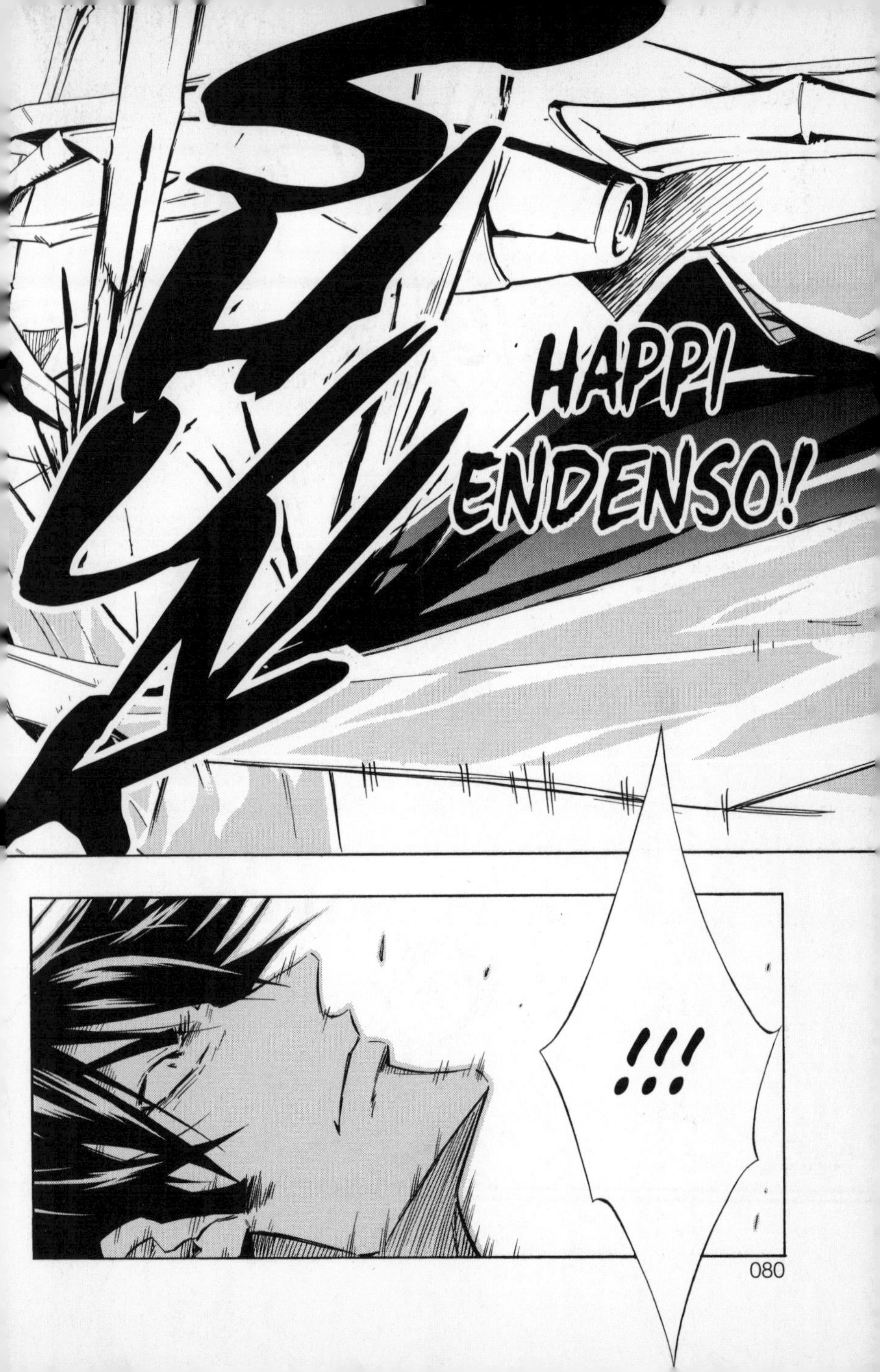
HAPPI ENDENSO!
!!!

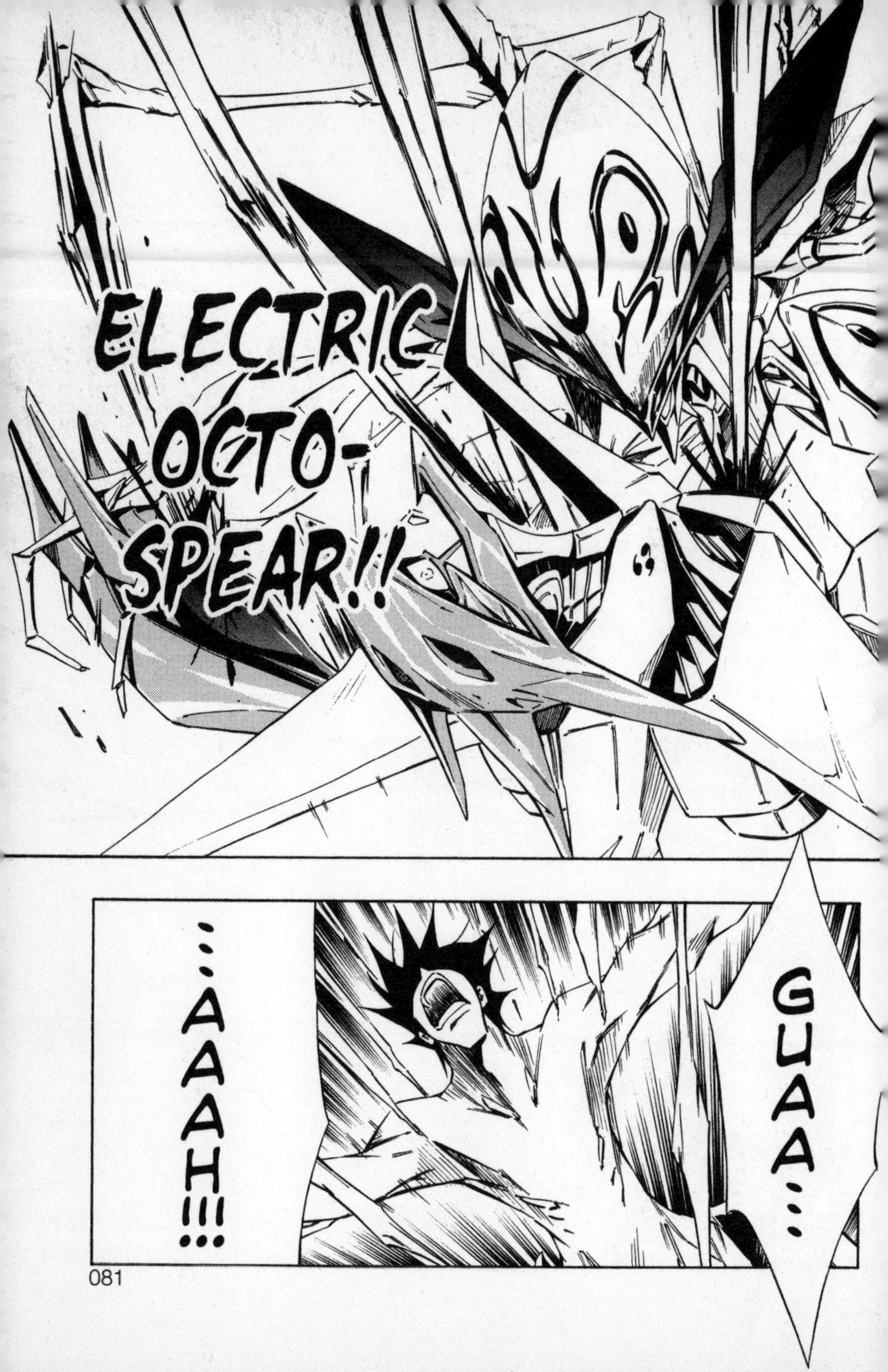
ELECTRIC OCTO-SPEAR!!
GUAA...
...AAAH!!!

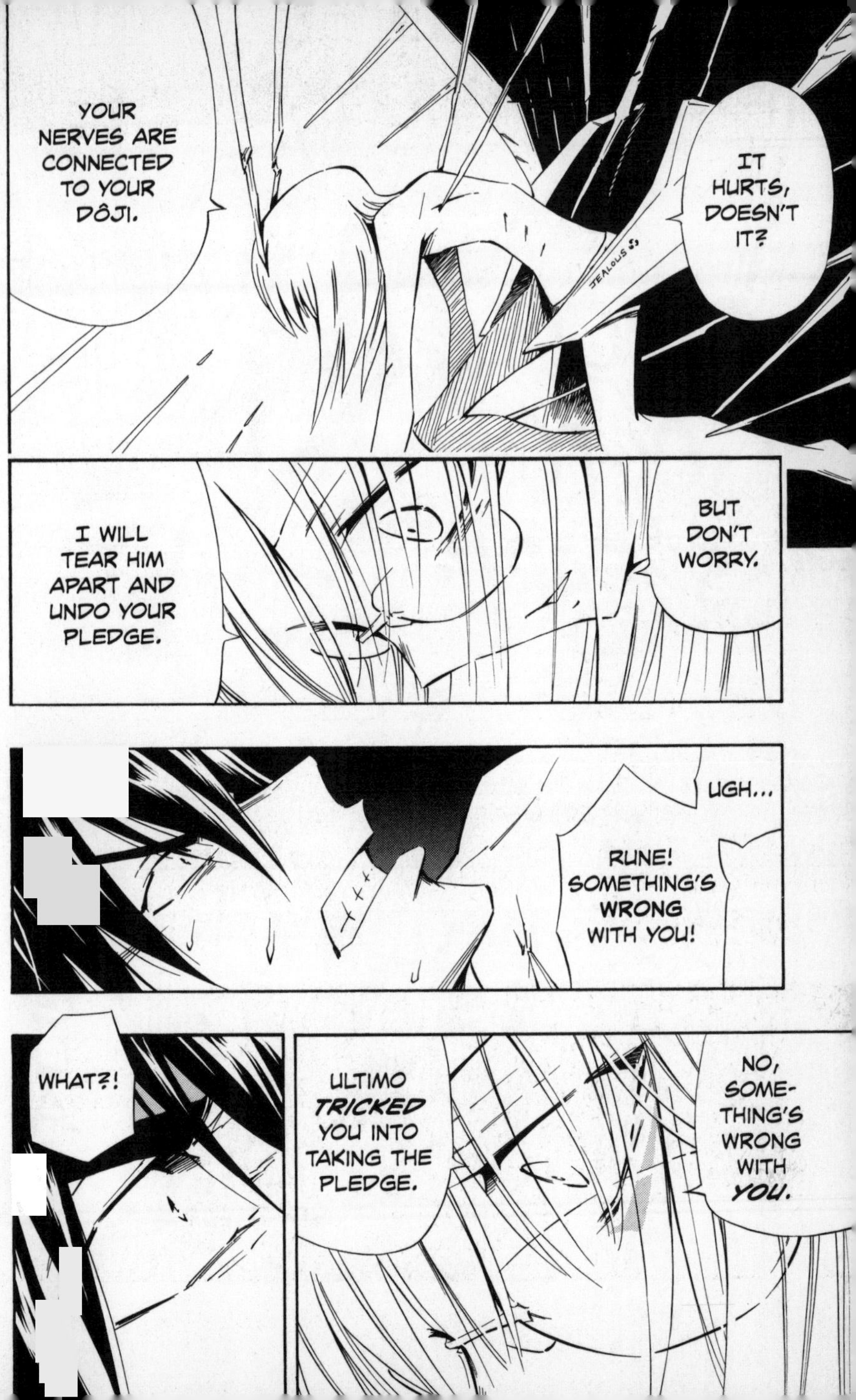
IT HURTS, DOESN'T IT?
JEALOUS
YOUR NERVES ARE CONNECTED TO YOUR DÔJI.
BUT DON'T WORRY.
I WILL TEAR HIM APART AND UNDO YOUR PLEDGE.
UGH...
RUNE! SOMETHING'S WRONG WITH YOU!
NO, SOME-THING'S WRONG WITH *YOU*.
ULTIMO *TRICKED* YOU INTO TAKING THE PLEDGE.
WHAT?!

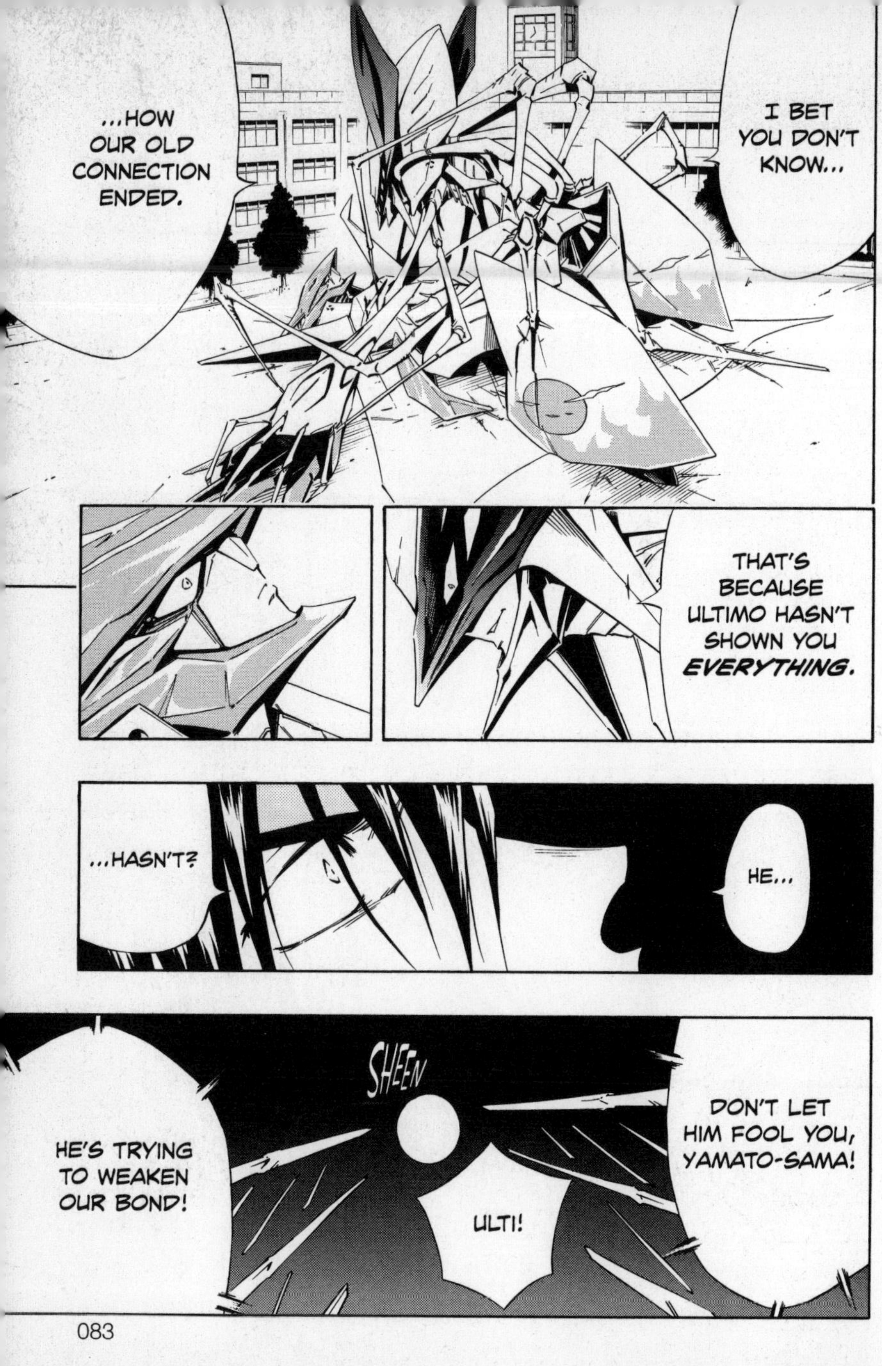
I BET YOU DON'T KNOW...
...HOW OUR OLD CONNECTION ENDED.
THAT'S BECAUSE ULTIMO HASN'T SHOWN YOU *EVERYTHING*.
HE...
...HASN'T?
DON'T LET HIM FOOL YOU, YAMATO-SAMA!
SHEEN
ULTI!
HE'S TRYING TO WEAKEN OUR BOND!

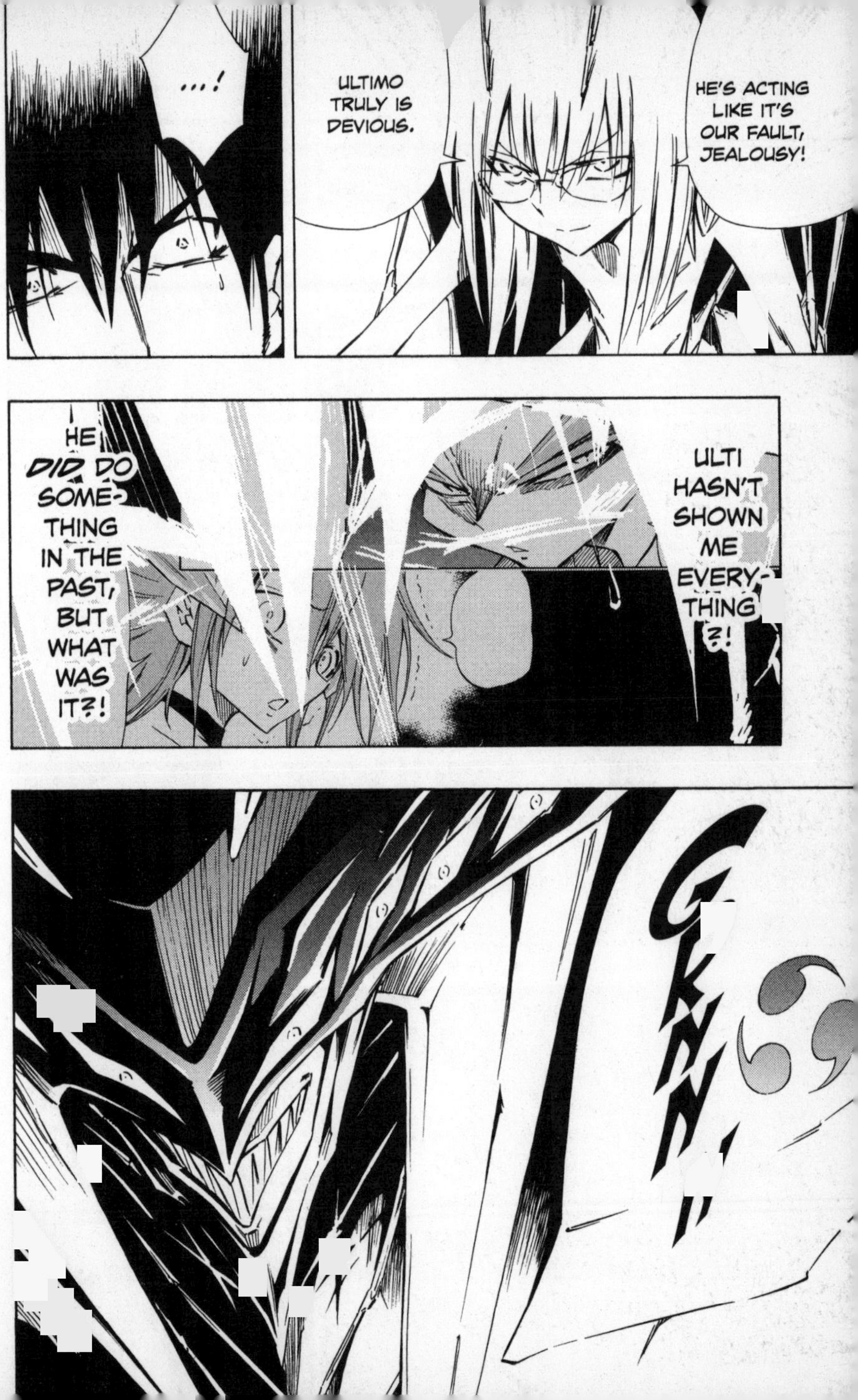
HE'S ACTING LIKE IT'S OUR FAULT, JEALOUSY!
ULTIMO TRULY IS DEVIOUS.
...!
ULTI HASN'T SHOWN ME EVERYTHING?!
HE DID DO SOMETHING IN THE PAST, BUT WHAT WAS IT?!

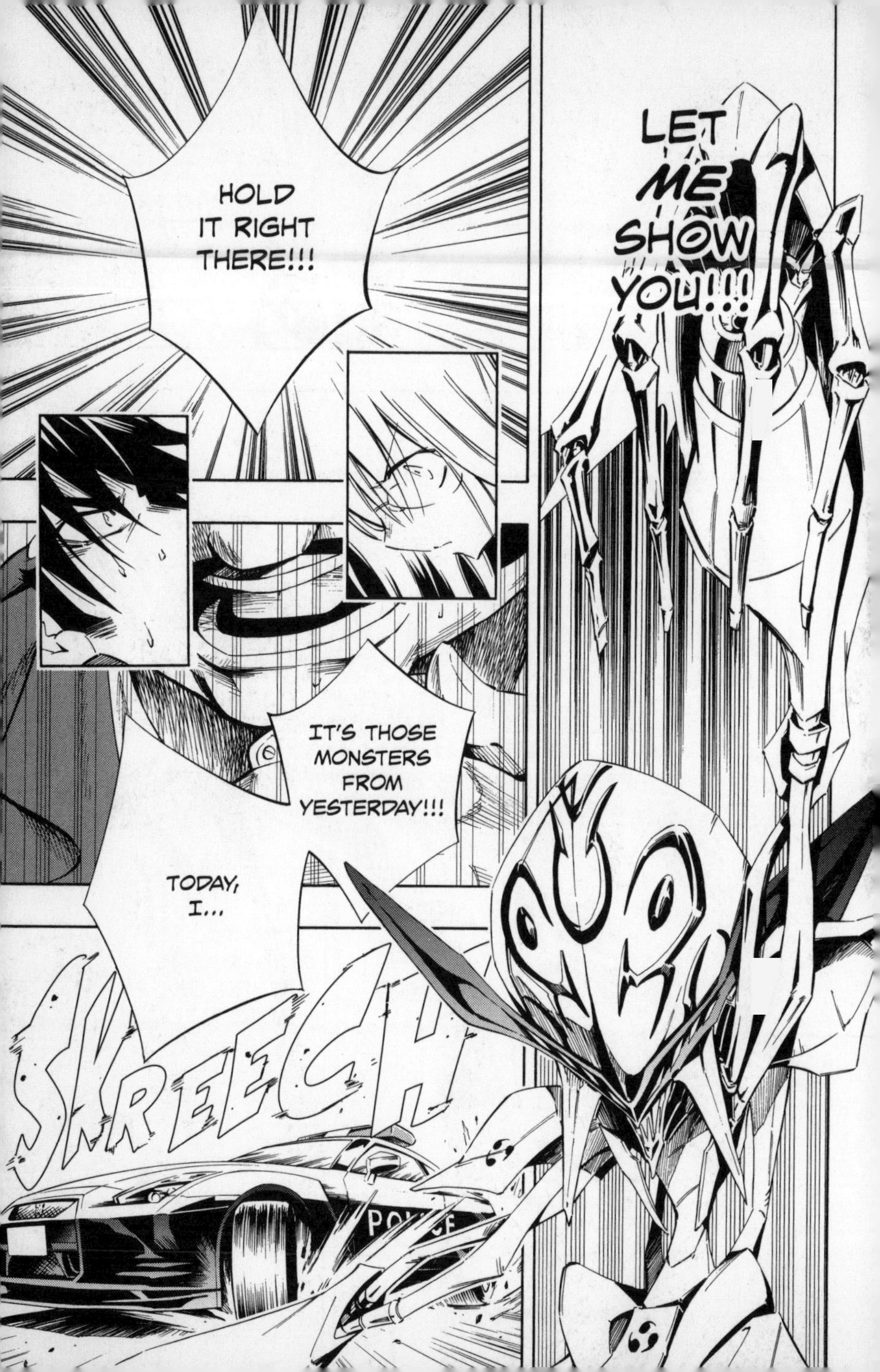
LET ME SHOW YOU!!!
HOLD IT RIGHT THERE!!!
IT'S THOSE MONSTERS FROM YESTERDAY!!!
TODAY, I...
SHREECH
POLICE

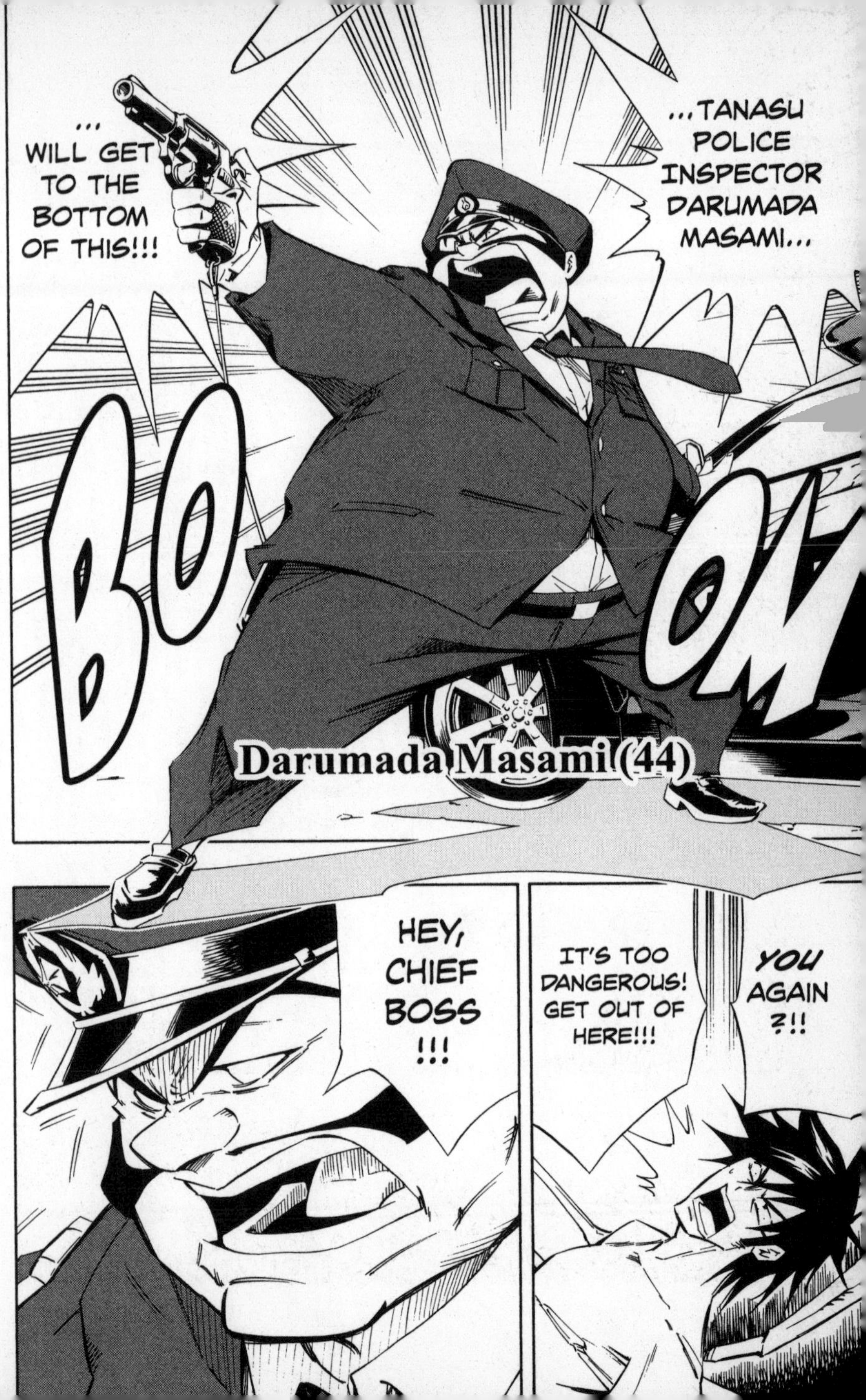
...TANASU POLICE INSPECTOR DARUMADA MASAMI...
...WILL GET TO THE BOTTOM OF THIS!!!
BOOM
Darumada Masami (44)
YOU AGAIN?!!
IT'S TOO DANGEROUS! GET OUT OF HERE!!!
HEY, CHIEF BOSS!!!

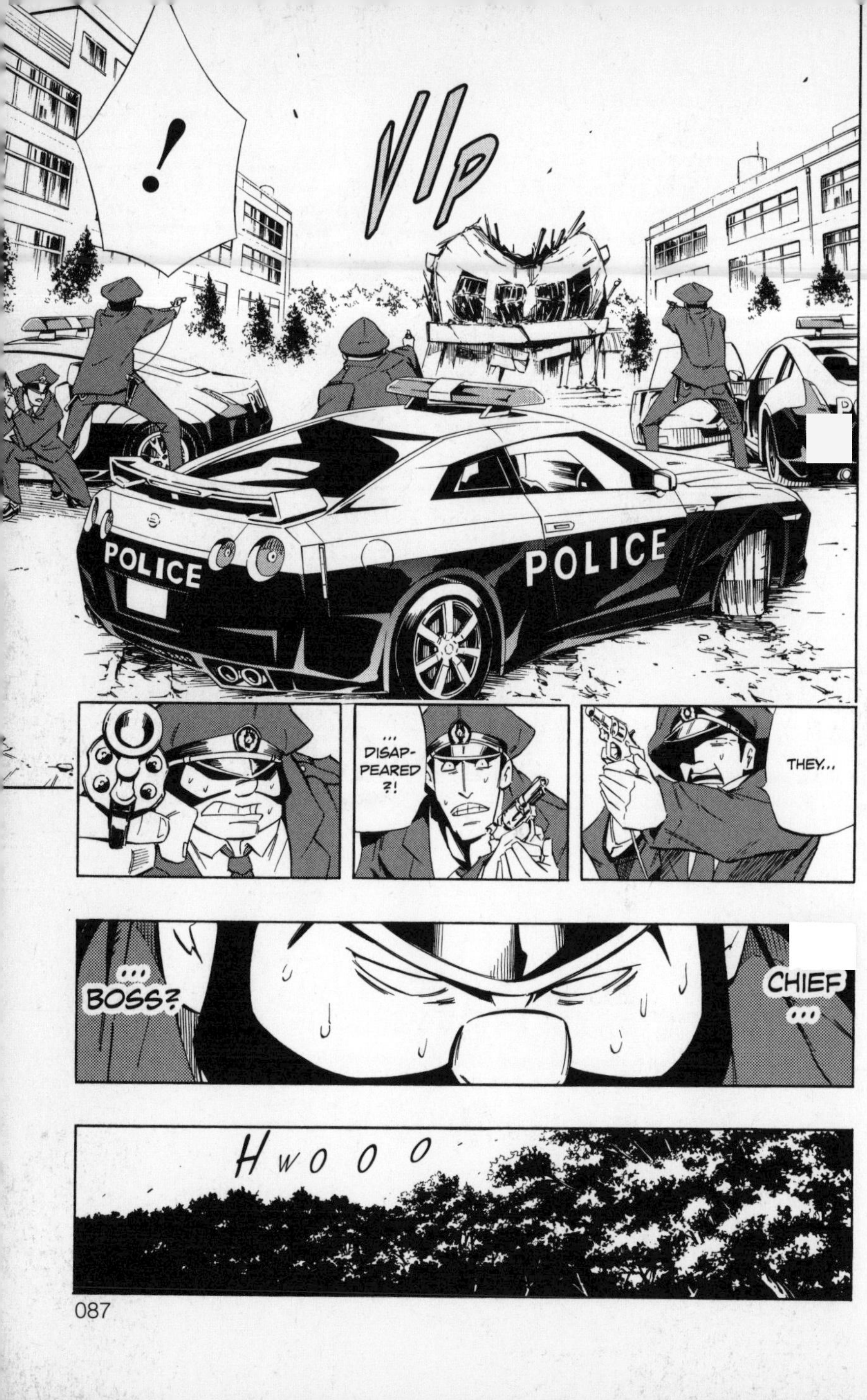
VIP
!
THEY...
... DISAP-PEARED ?!
CHIEF ...
... BOSS?
HWOOO

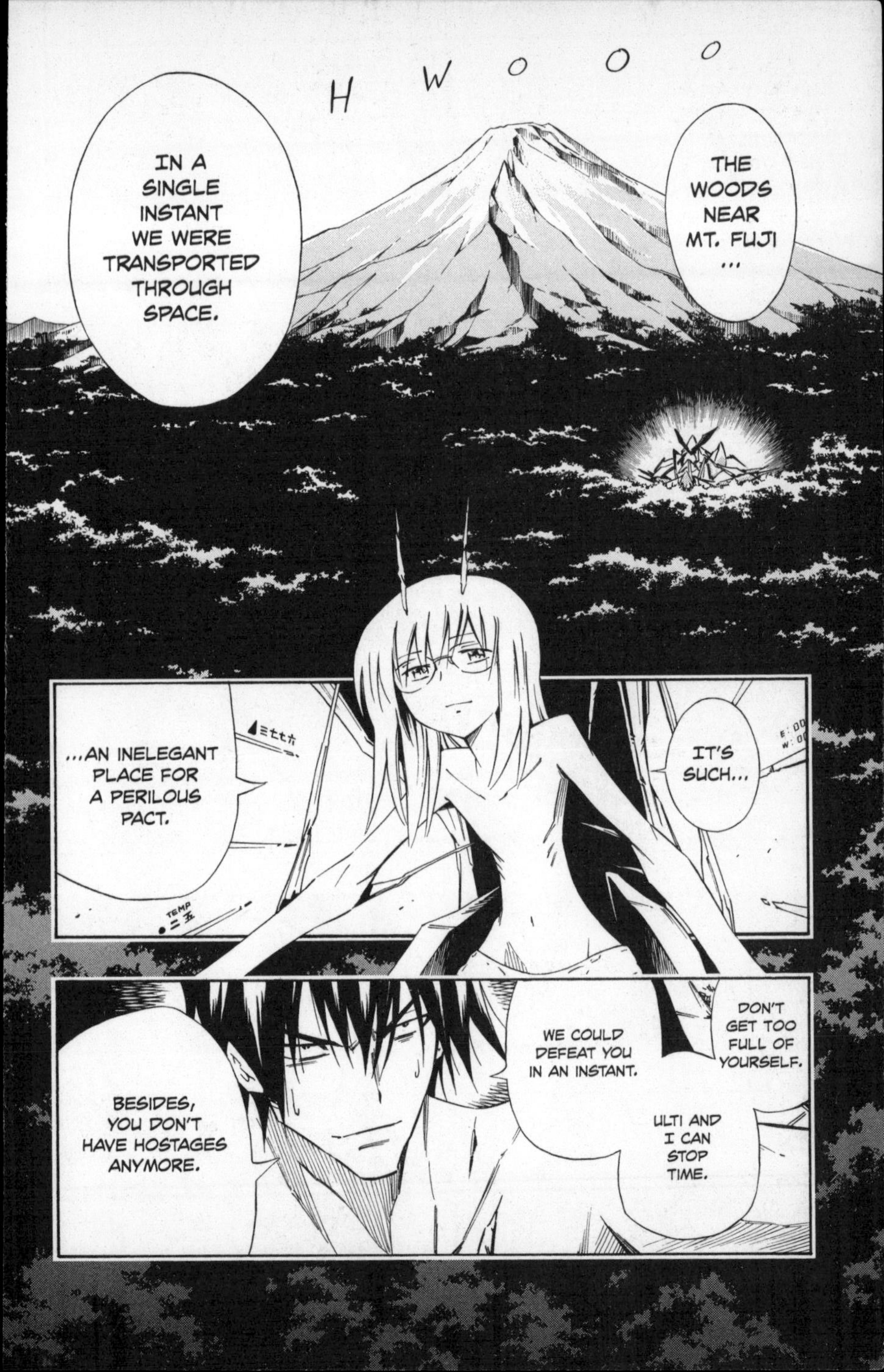
HWOOO
THE WOODS NEAR MT. FUJI ...
IN A SINGLE INSTANT WE WERE TRANSPORTED THROUGH SPACE.
IT'S SUCH...
...AN INELEGANT PLACE FOR A PERILOUS PACT.
DON'T GET TOO FULL OF YOURSELF.
ULTI AND I CAN STOP TIME.
WE COULD DEFEAT YOU IN AN INSTANT.
BESIDES, YOU DON'T HAVE HOSTAGES ANYMORE.

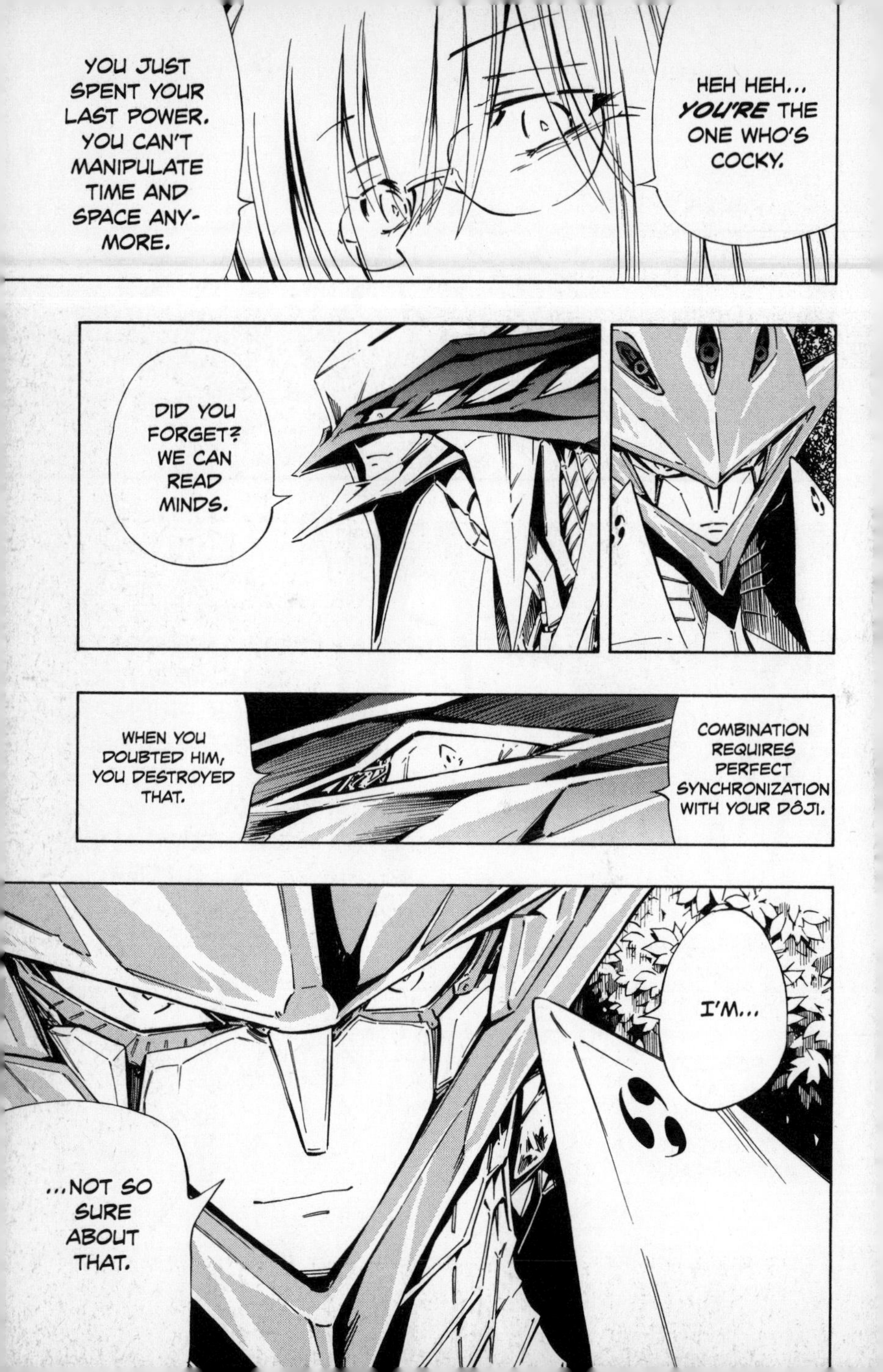
HEH HEH... *YOU'RE* THE ONE WHO'S COCKY.
YOU JUST SPENT YOUR LAST POWER. YOU CAN'T MANIPULATE TIME AND SPACE ANY-MORE.
DID YOU FORGET? WE CAN READ MINDS.
COMBINATION REQUIRES PERFECT SYNCHRONIZATION WITH YOUR DÔJI.
WHEN YOU DOUBTED HIM, YOU DESTROYED THAT.
I'M...
...NOT SO SURE ABOUT THAT.

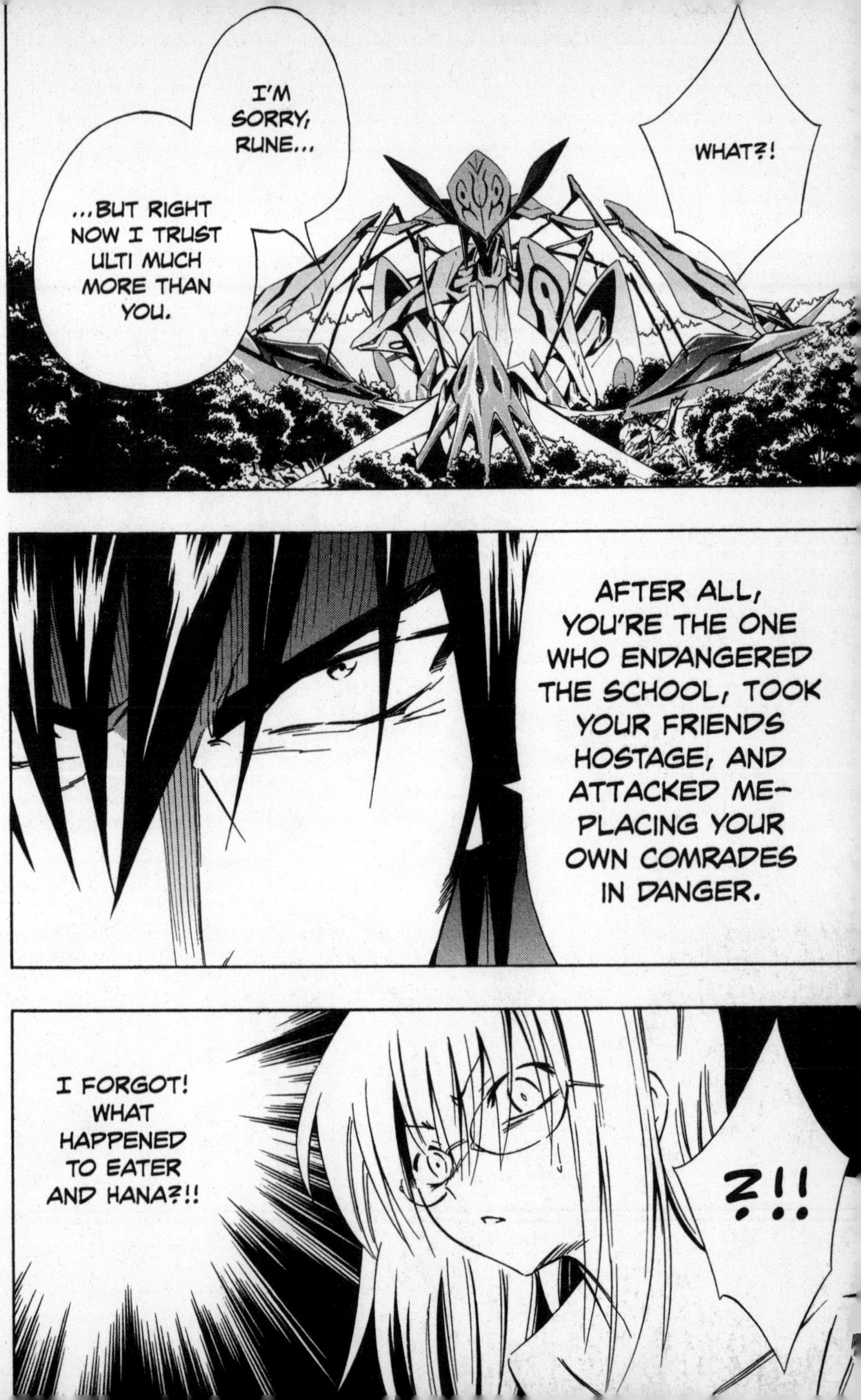
WHAT?!
I'M SORRY, RUNE...
...BUT RIGHT NOW I TRUST ULTI MUCH MORE THAN YOU.
AFTER ALL, YOU'RE THE ONE WHO ENDANGERED THE SCHOOL, TOOK YOUR FRIENDS HOSTAGE, AND ATTACKED ME– PLACING YOUR OWN COMRADES IN DANGER.
?!!
I FORGOT! WHAT HAPPENED TO EATER AND HANA?!!

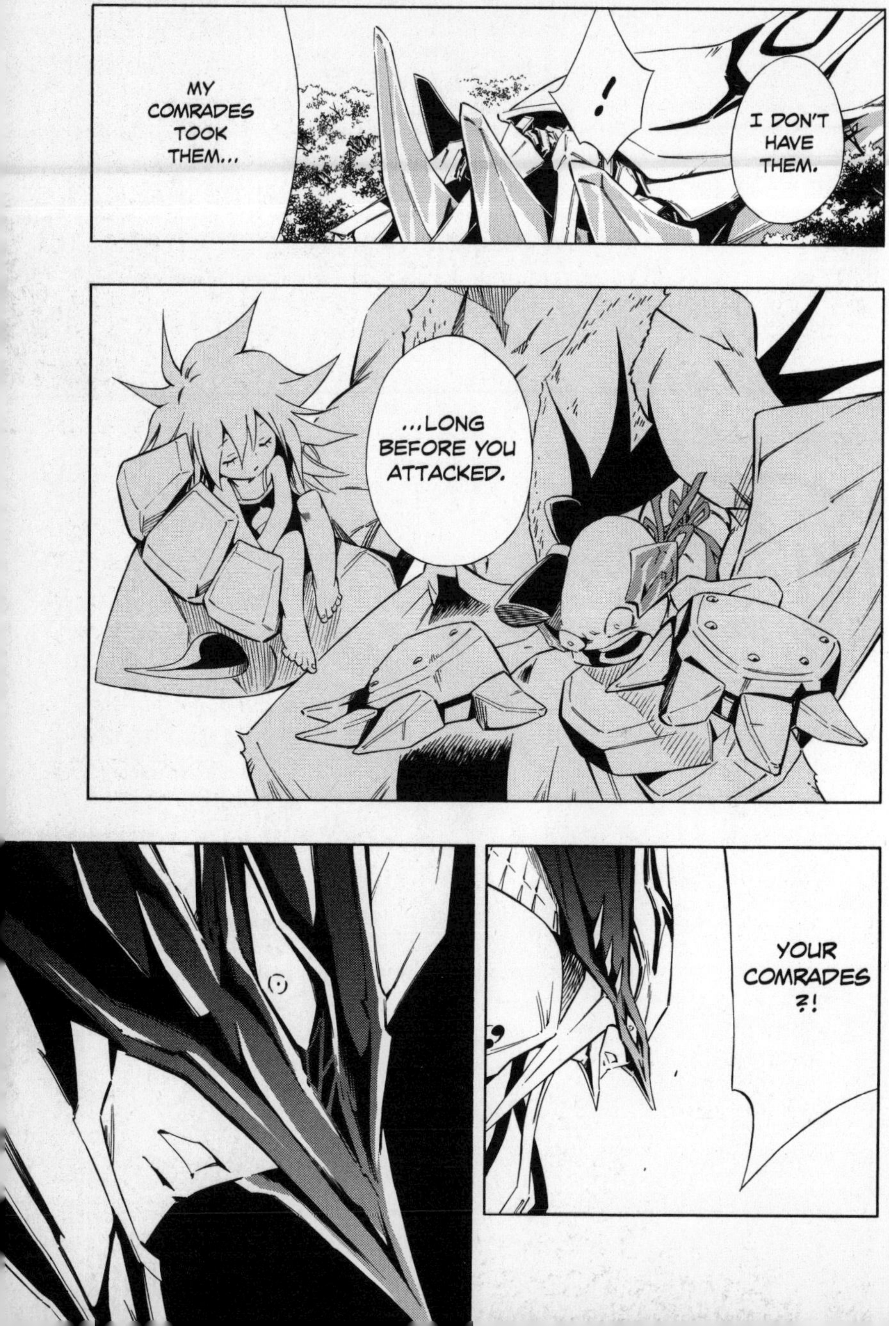
I DON'T HAVE THEM.
!
MY COMRADES TOOK THEM...
...LONG BEFORE YOU ATTACKED.
YOUR COMRADES ?!

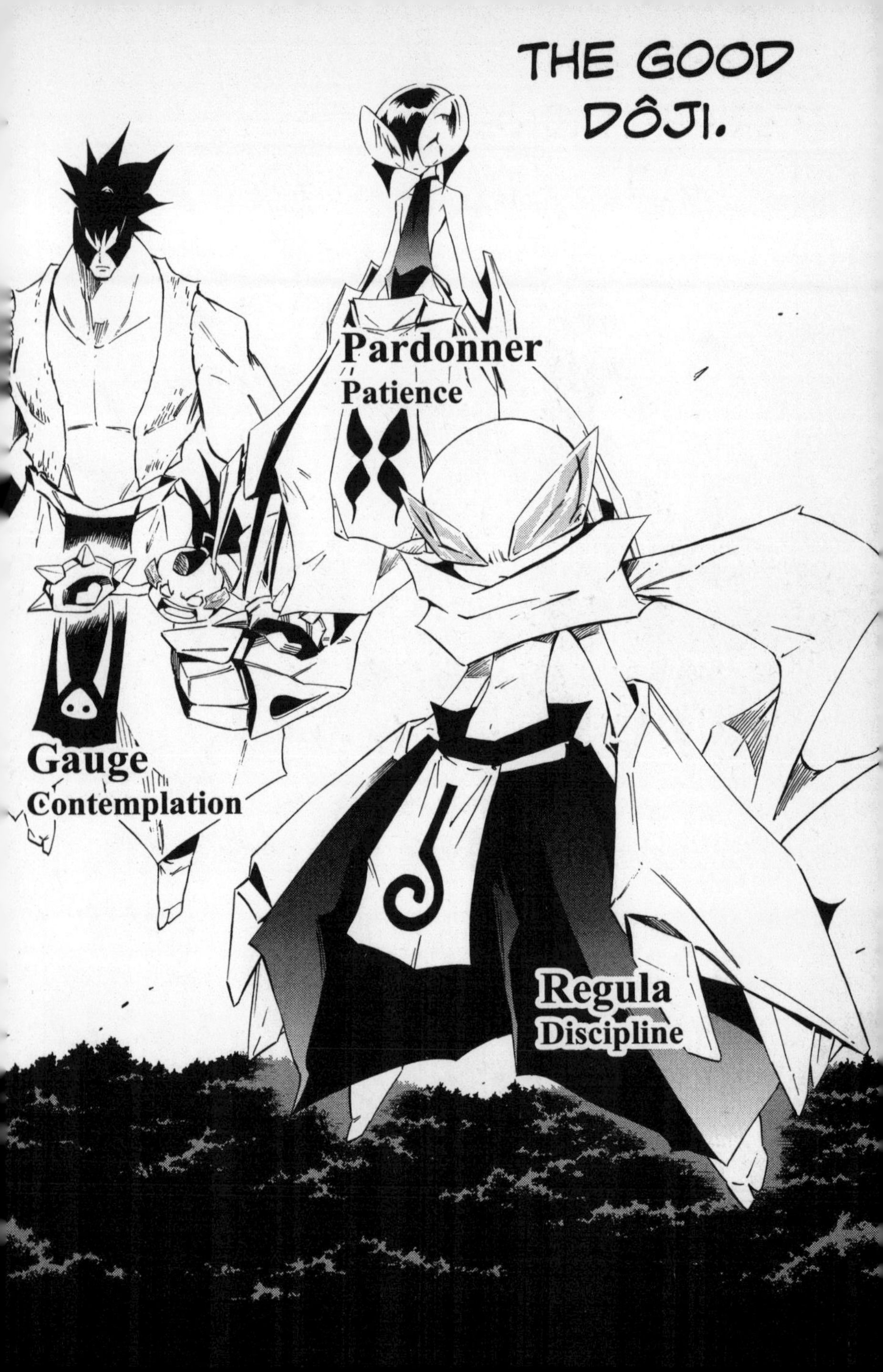
THE GOOD DÔJI.
Pardonner
Patience
Gauge
Contemplation
Regula
Discipline

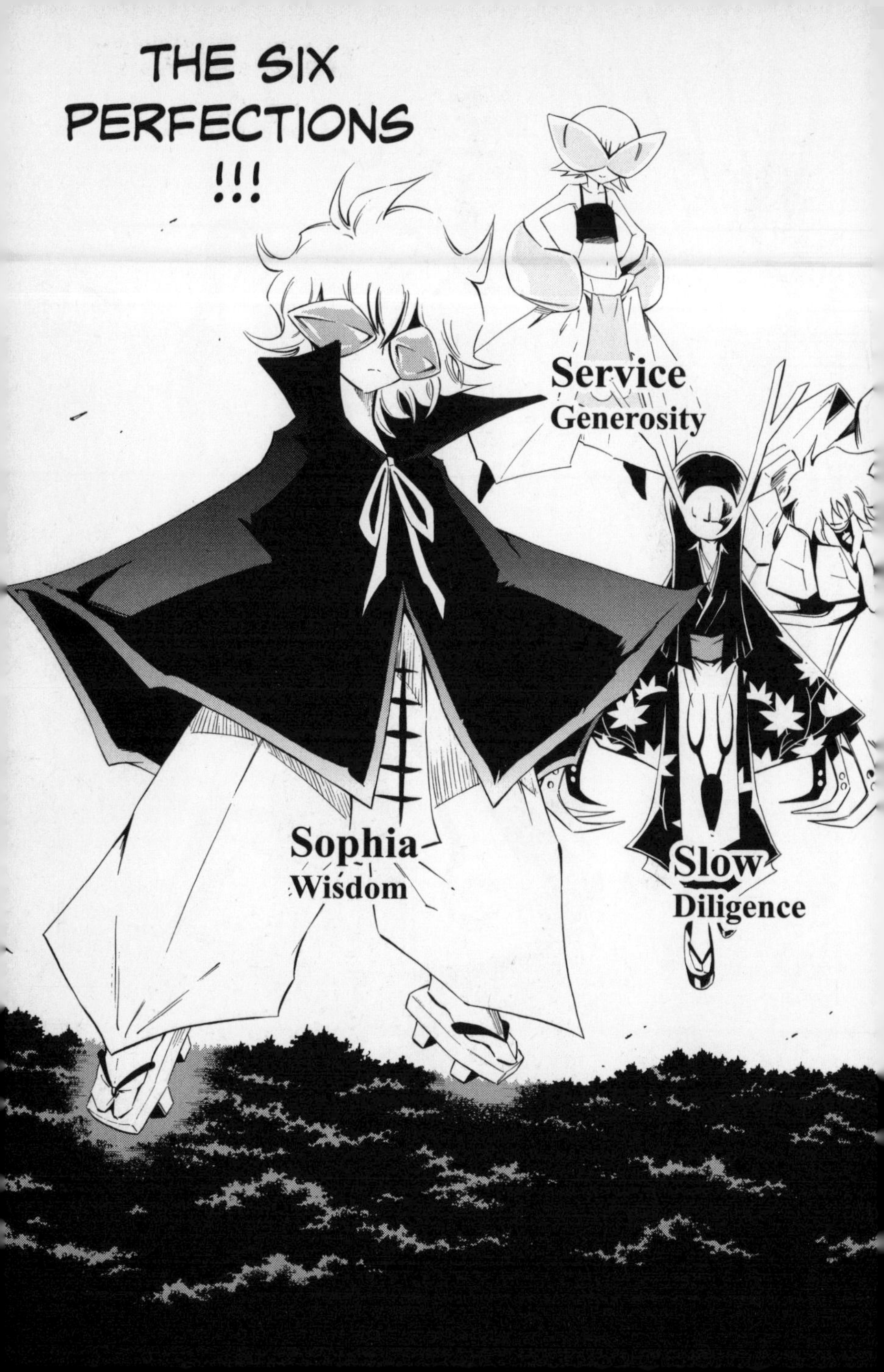
THE SIX PERFECTIONS !!!
Service
Generosity
Slow
Diligence
Sophia
Wisdom

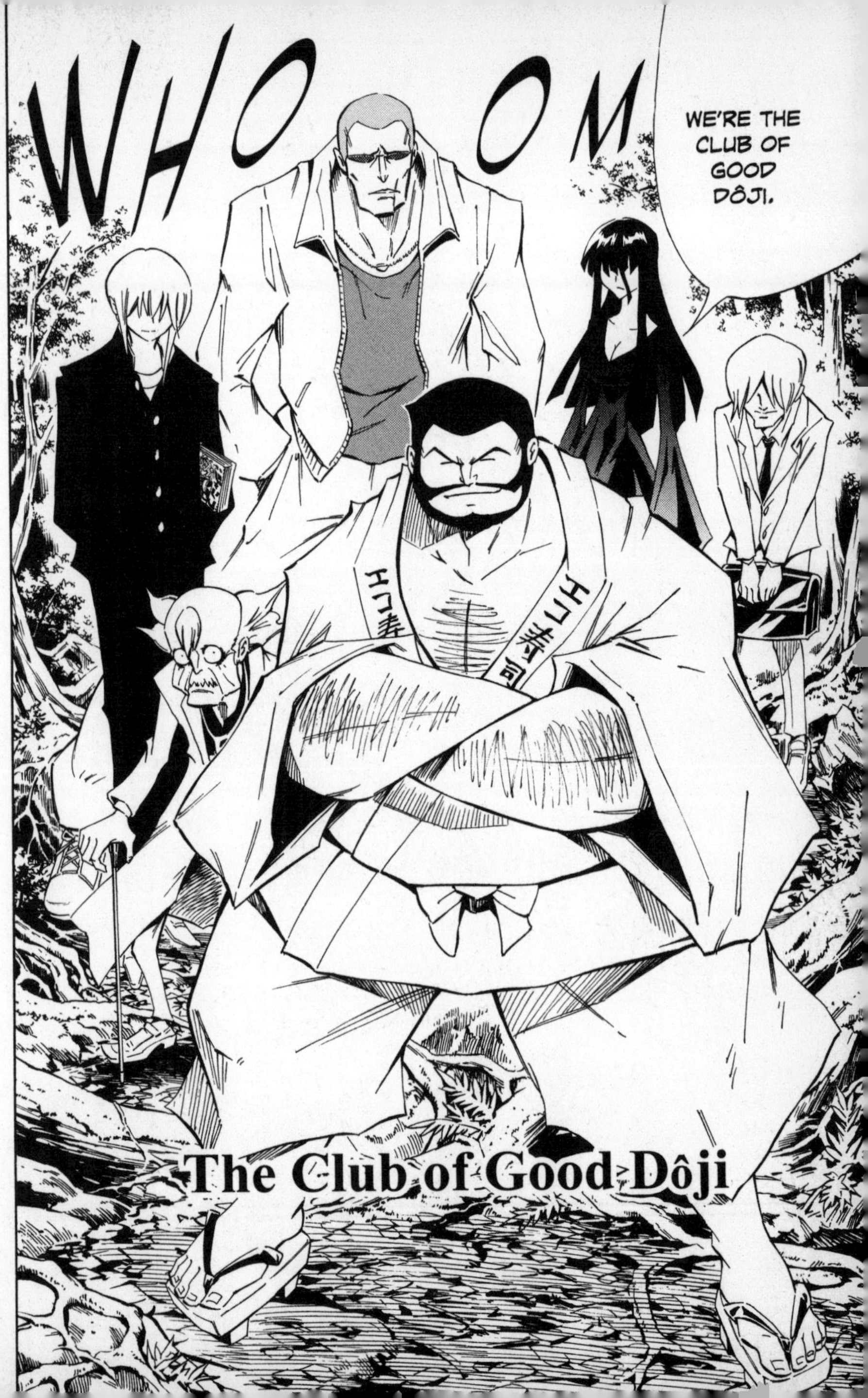
WE'RE THE CLUB OF GOOD DÔJI.
WHOOM
The Club of Good Dôji

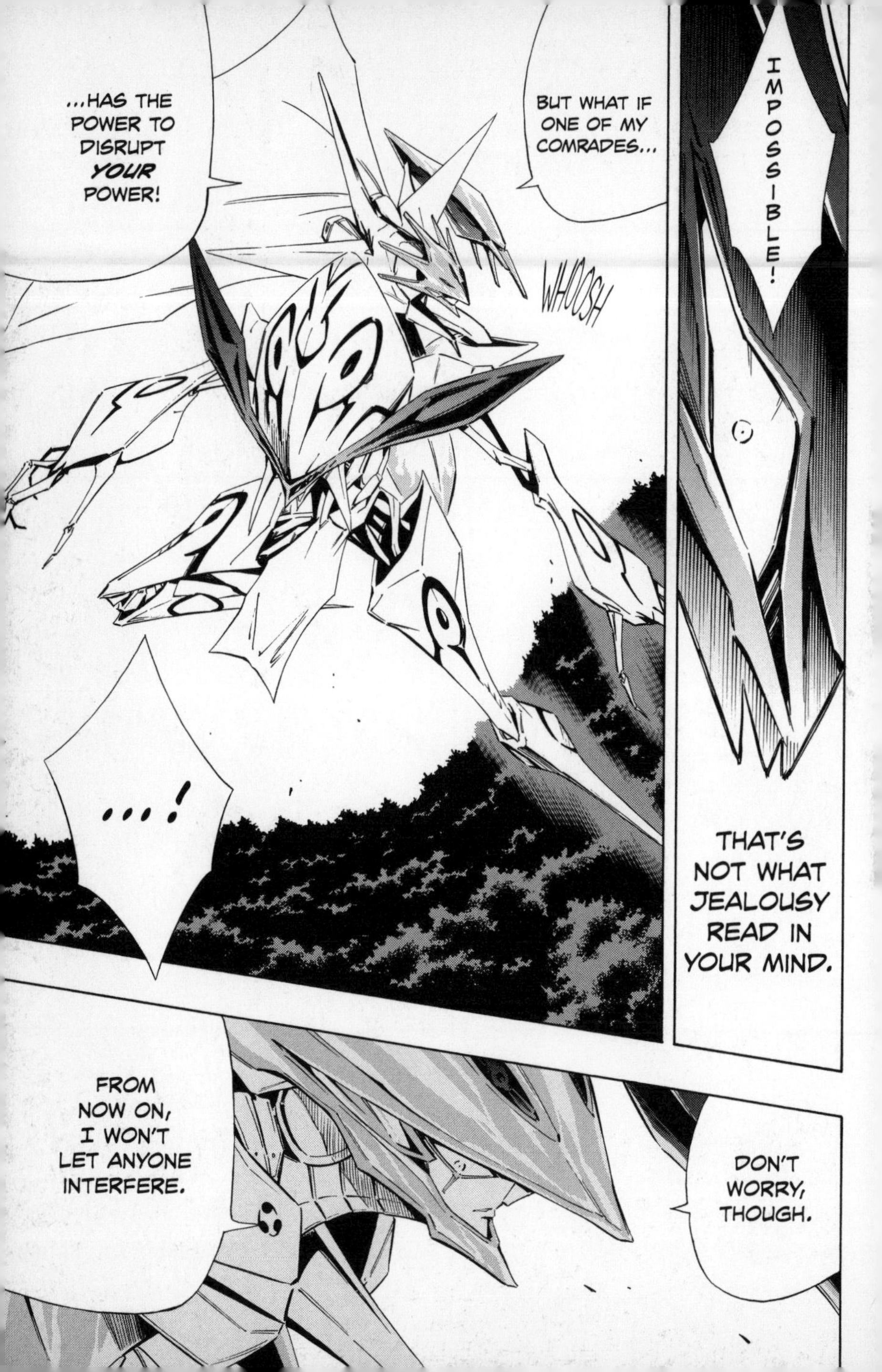
IMPOSSIBLE!
THAT'S NOT WHAT JEALOUSY READ IN YOUR MIND.
BUT WHAT IF ONE OF MY COMRADES...
...HAS THE POWER TO DISRUPT *YOUR* POWER!
WHOOSH
...!
DON'T WORRY, THOUGH.
FROM NOW ON, I WON'T LET ANYONE INTERFERE.

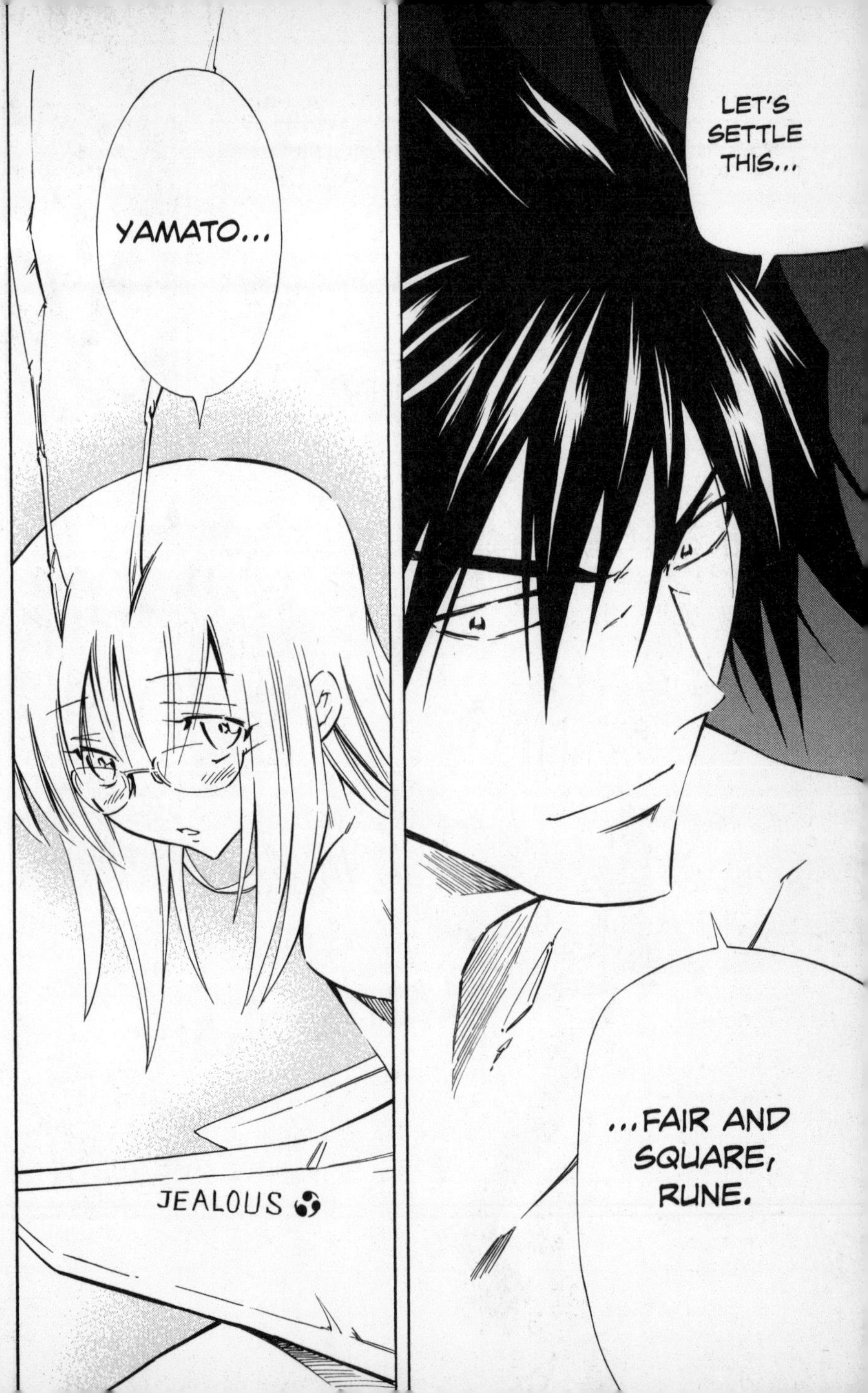
LET'S SETTLE THIS...
...FAIR AND SQUARE, RUNE.
YAMATO...
JEALOUS

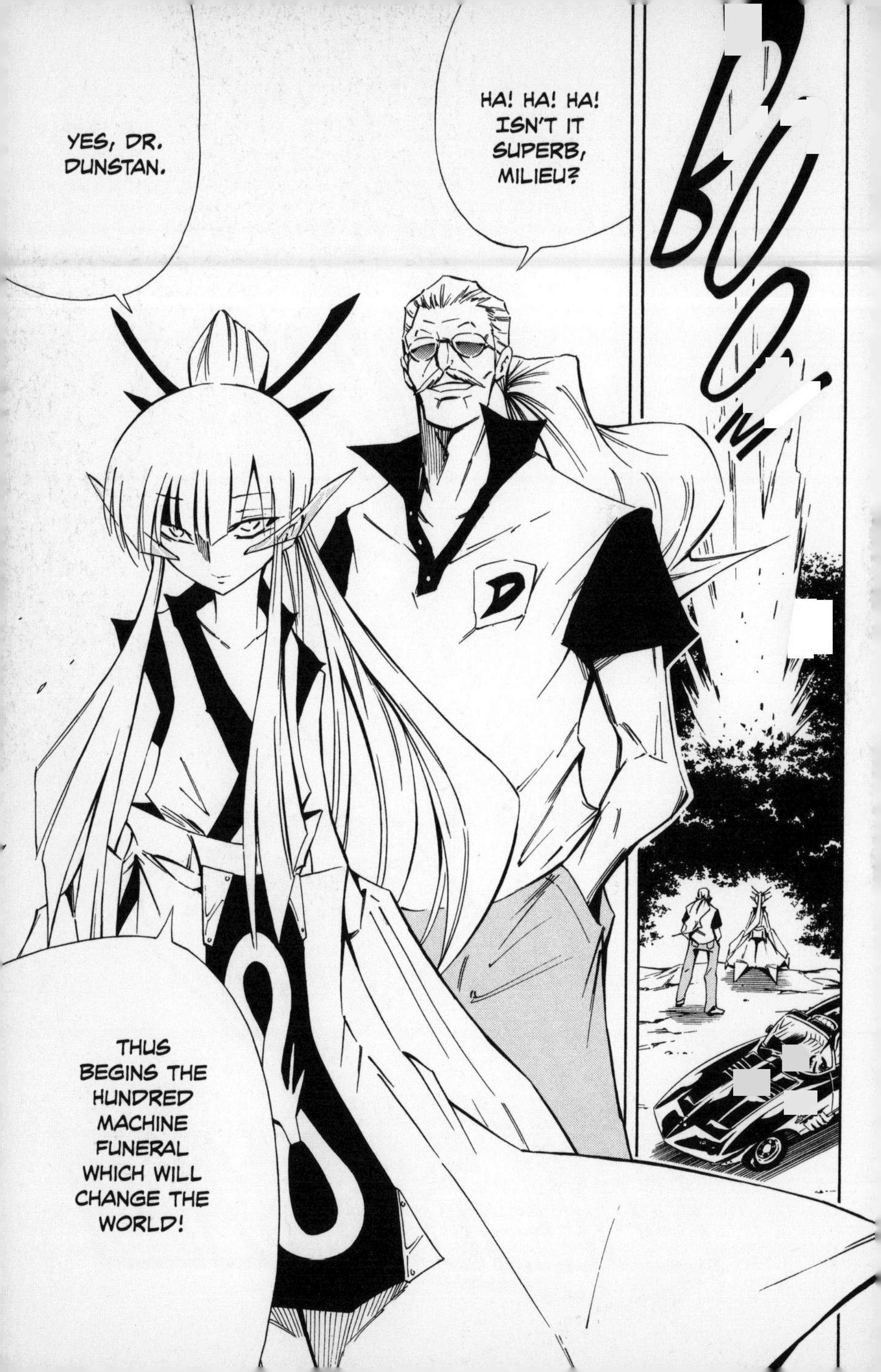
HA! HA! HA! ISN'T IT SUPERB, MILIEU?
YES, DR. DUNSTAN.
THUS BEGINS THE HUNDRED MACHINE FUNERAL WHICH WILL CHANGE THE WORLD!

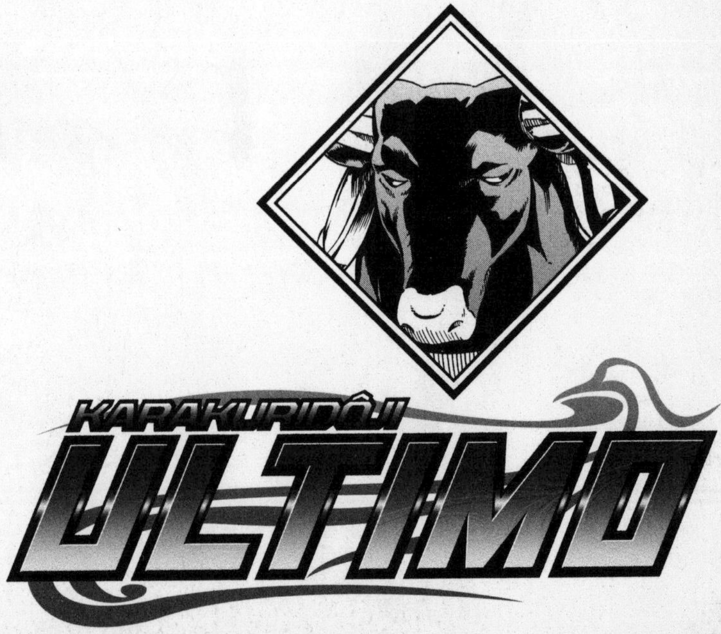

KARAKURIDÔJI
ULTIMO

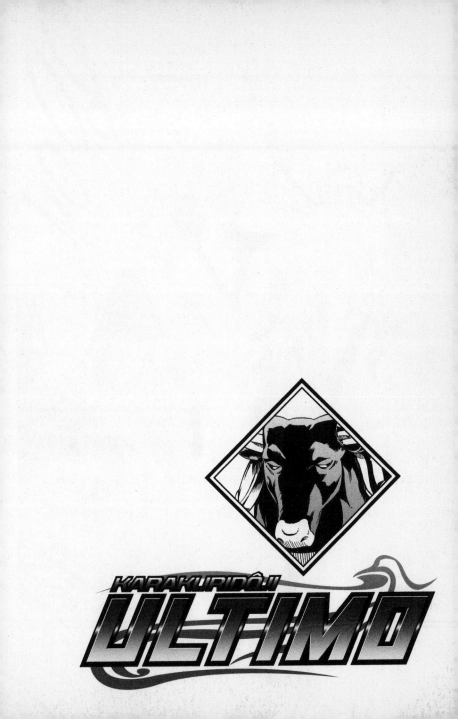

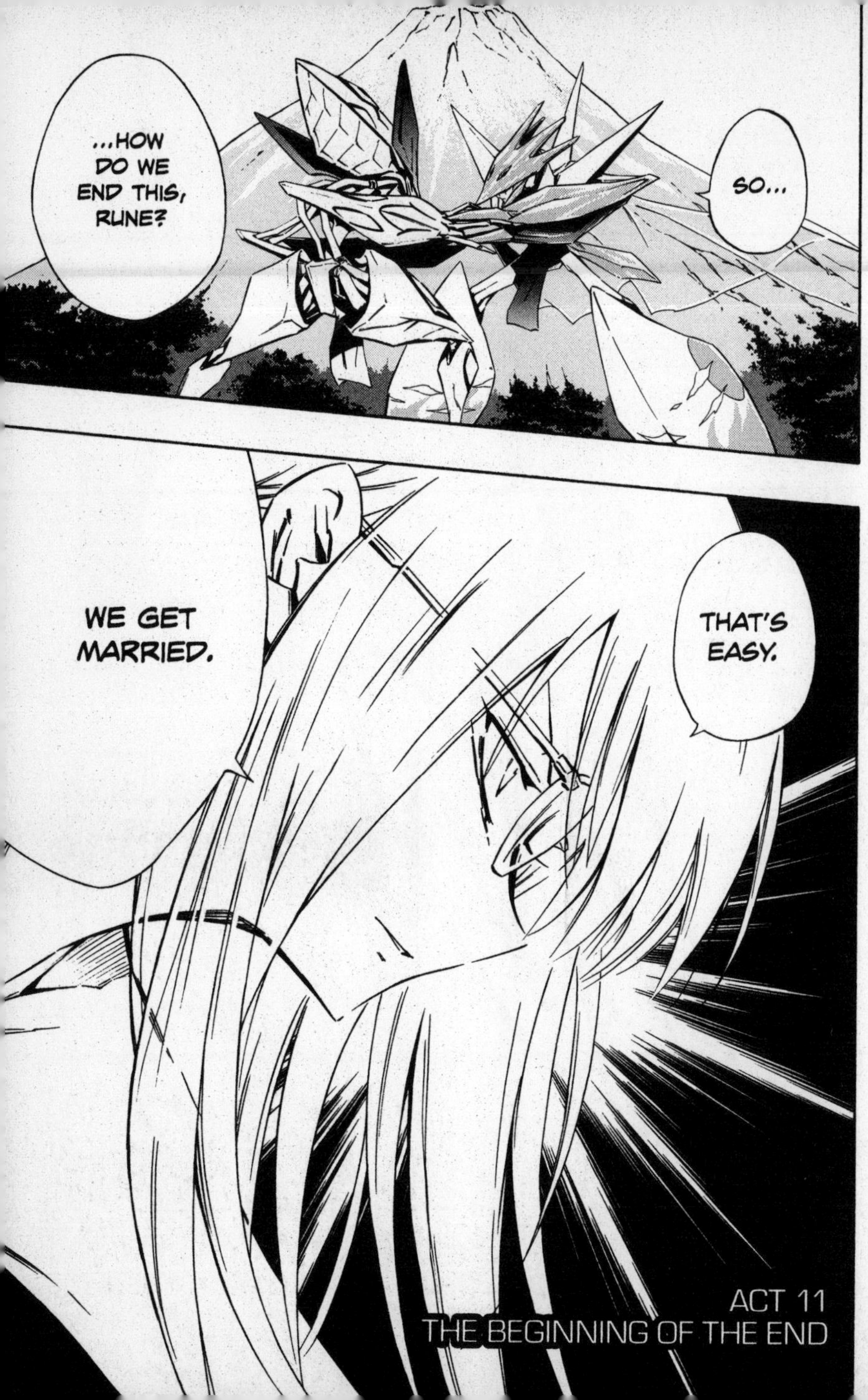
SO...
...HOW DO WE END THIS, RUNE?
THAT'S EASY.
WE GET MARRIED.
ACT 11
THE BEGINNING OF THE END

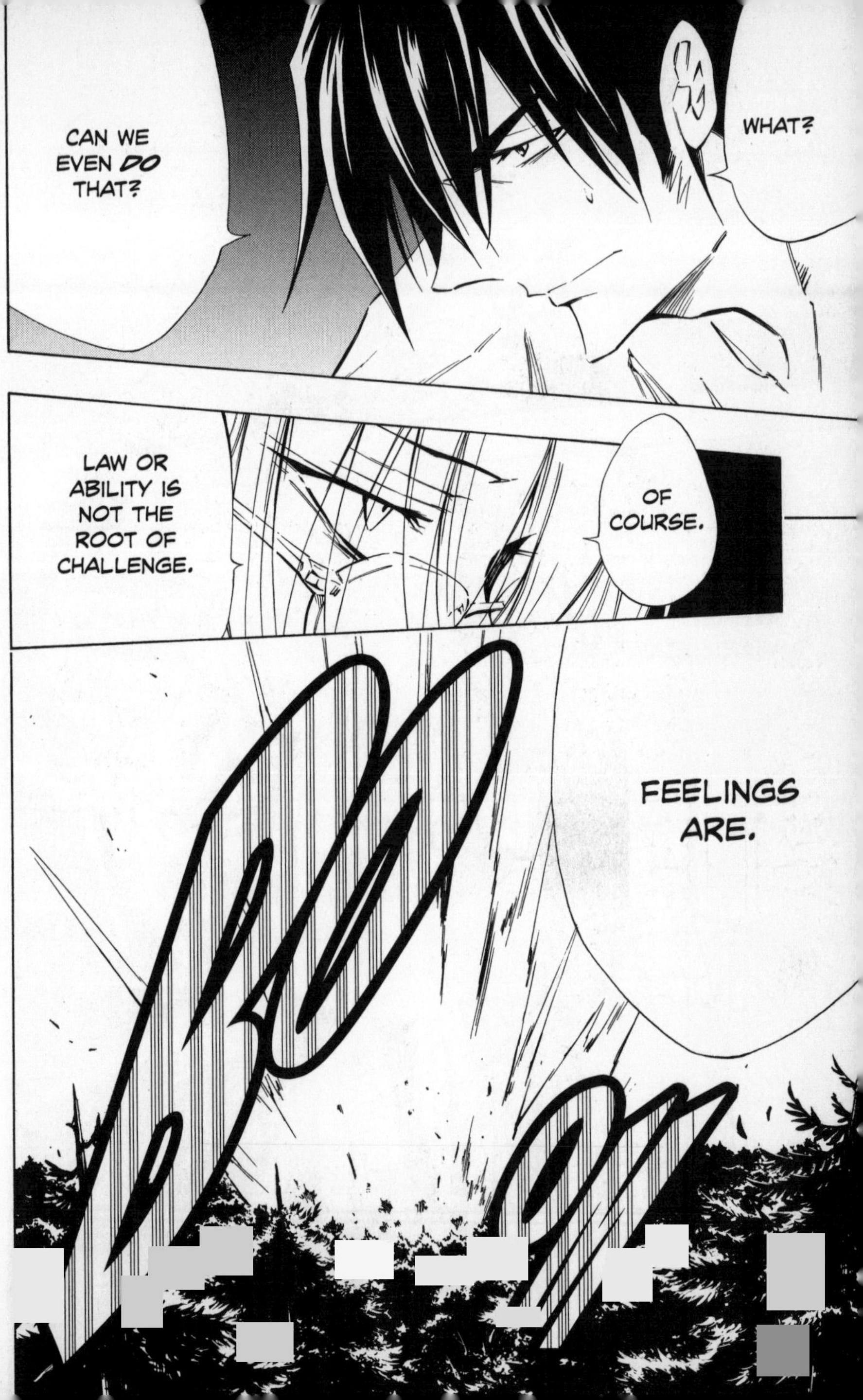
WHAT?
CAN WE EVEN *DO* THAT?
OF COURSE.
LAW OR ABILITY IS NOT THE ROOT OF CHALLENGE.
FEELINGS ARE.

ACT 11
THE BEGINNING OF THE END

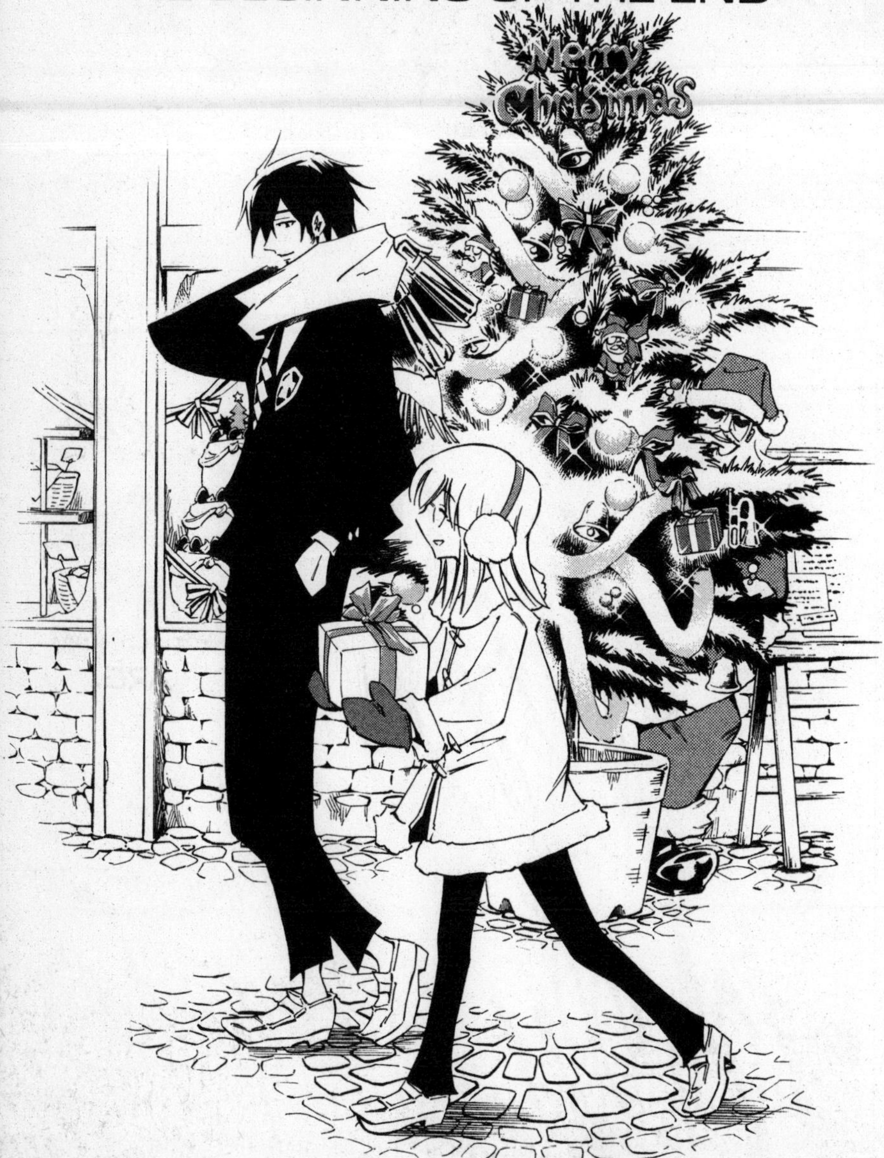
Merry Christmas

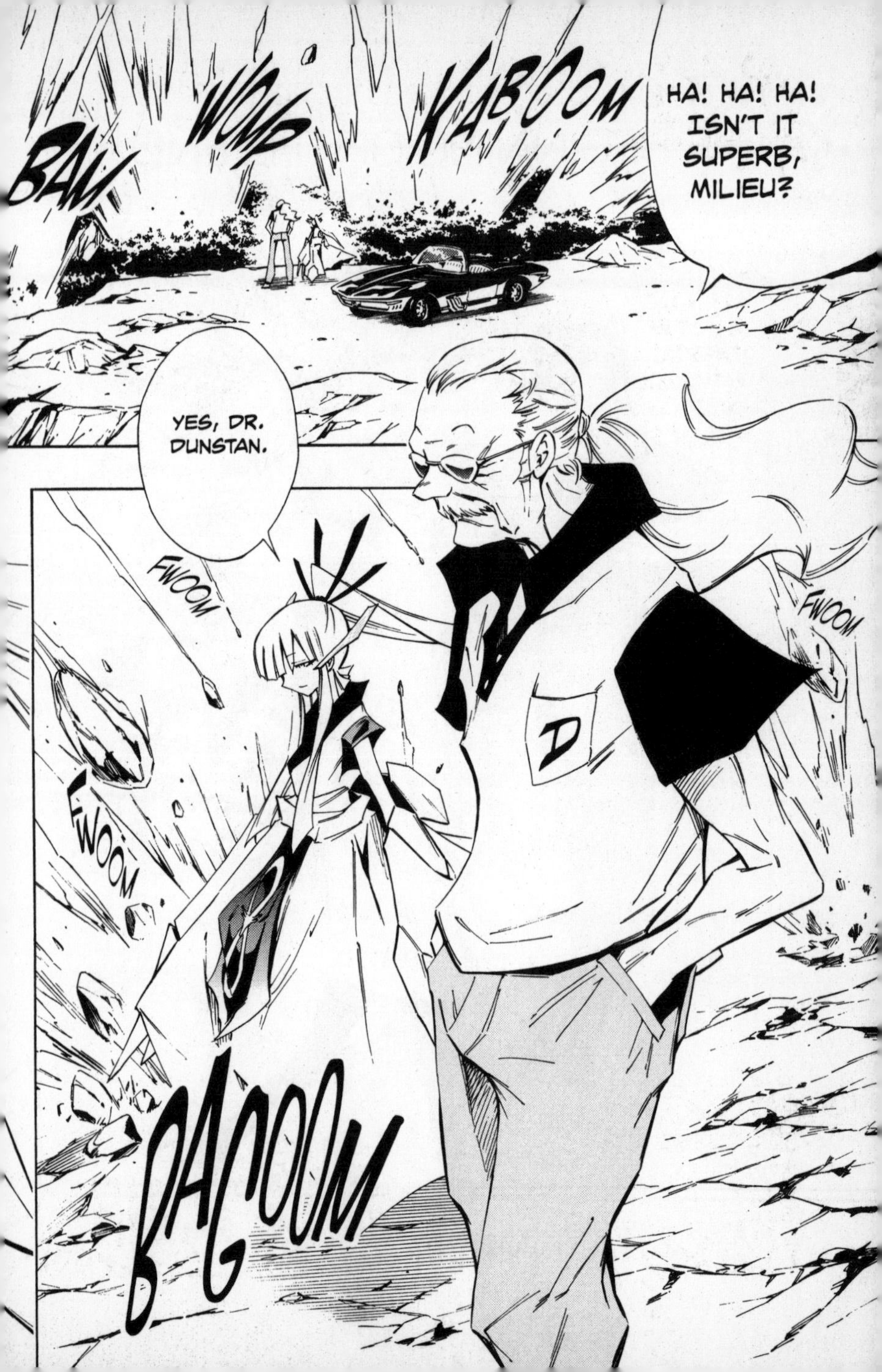
HA! HA! HA! ISN'T IT SUPERB, MILIEU?
KABOOM
WOMP
BAM
YES, DR. DUNSTAN.
FWOOM
FWOOM
FWOOM
BAGOOM

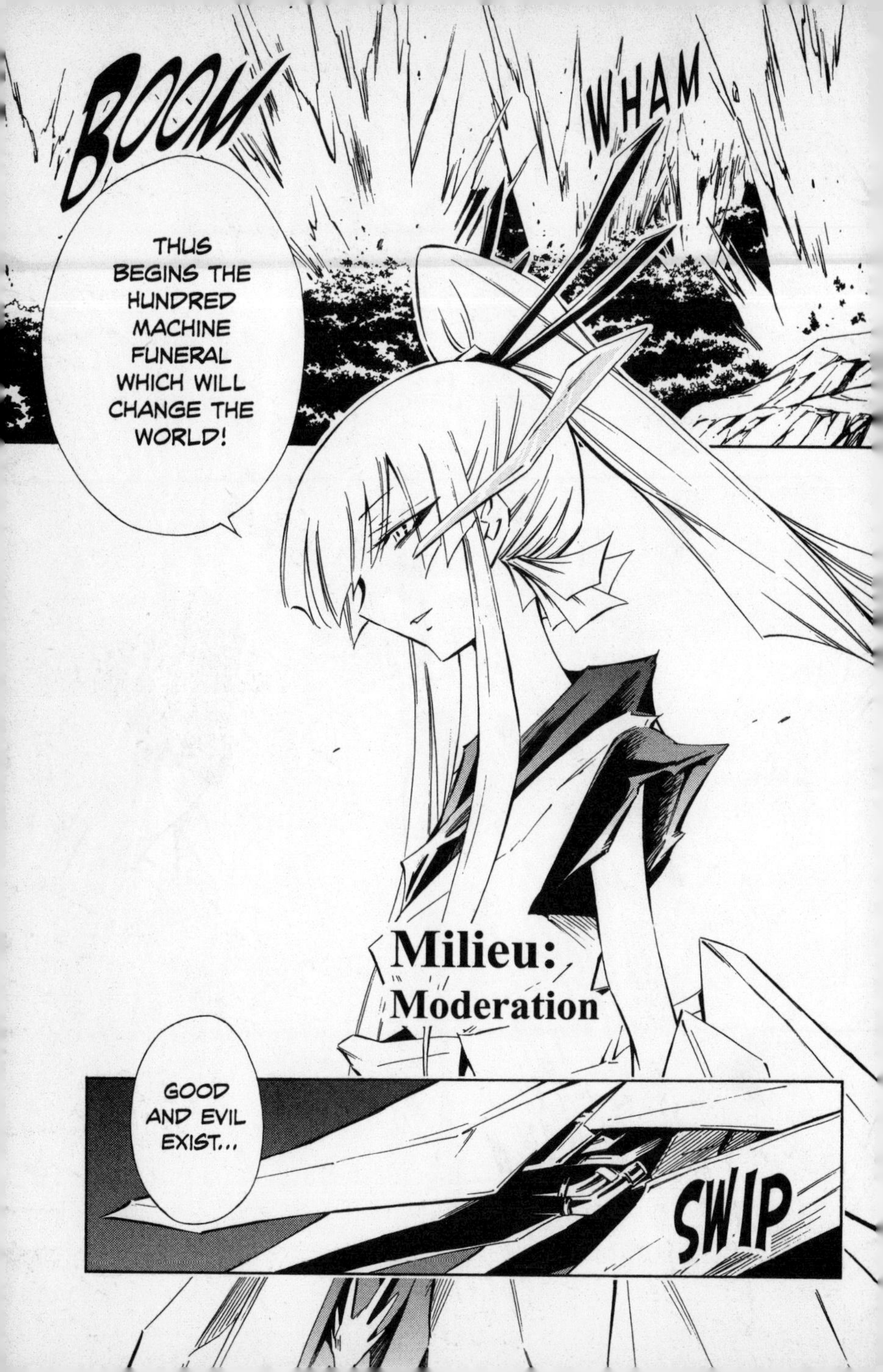
BOOM
WHAM
THUS BEGINS THE HUNDRED MACHINE FUNERAL WHICH WILL CHANGE THE WORLD!
Milieu: Moderation
GOOD AND EVIL EXIST...
SWIP

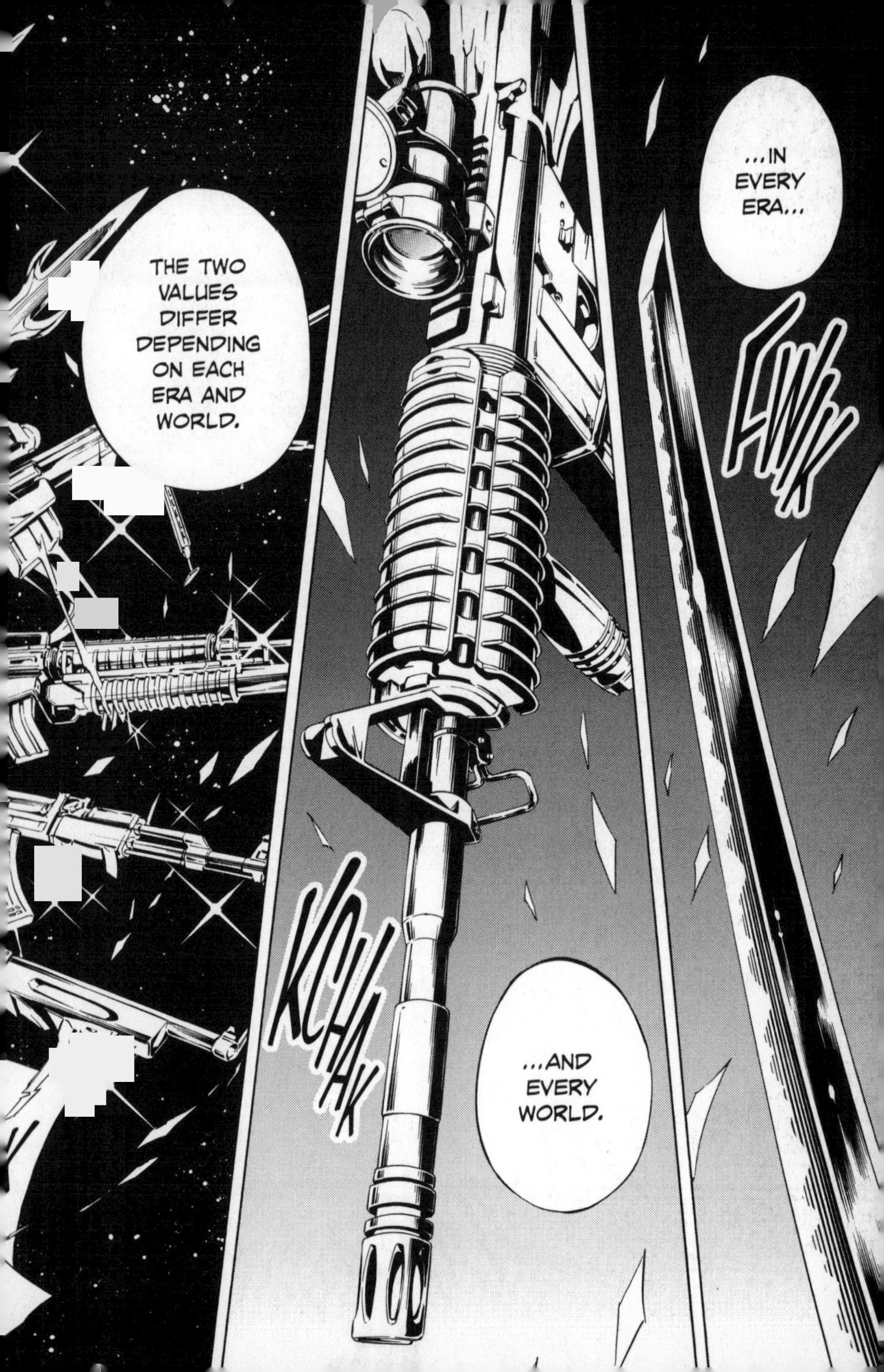
...IN EVERY ERA...
KCHAK
...AND EVERY WORLD.
THE TWO VALUES DIFFER DEPENDING ON EACH ERA AND WORLD.

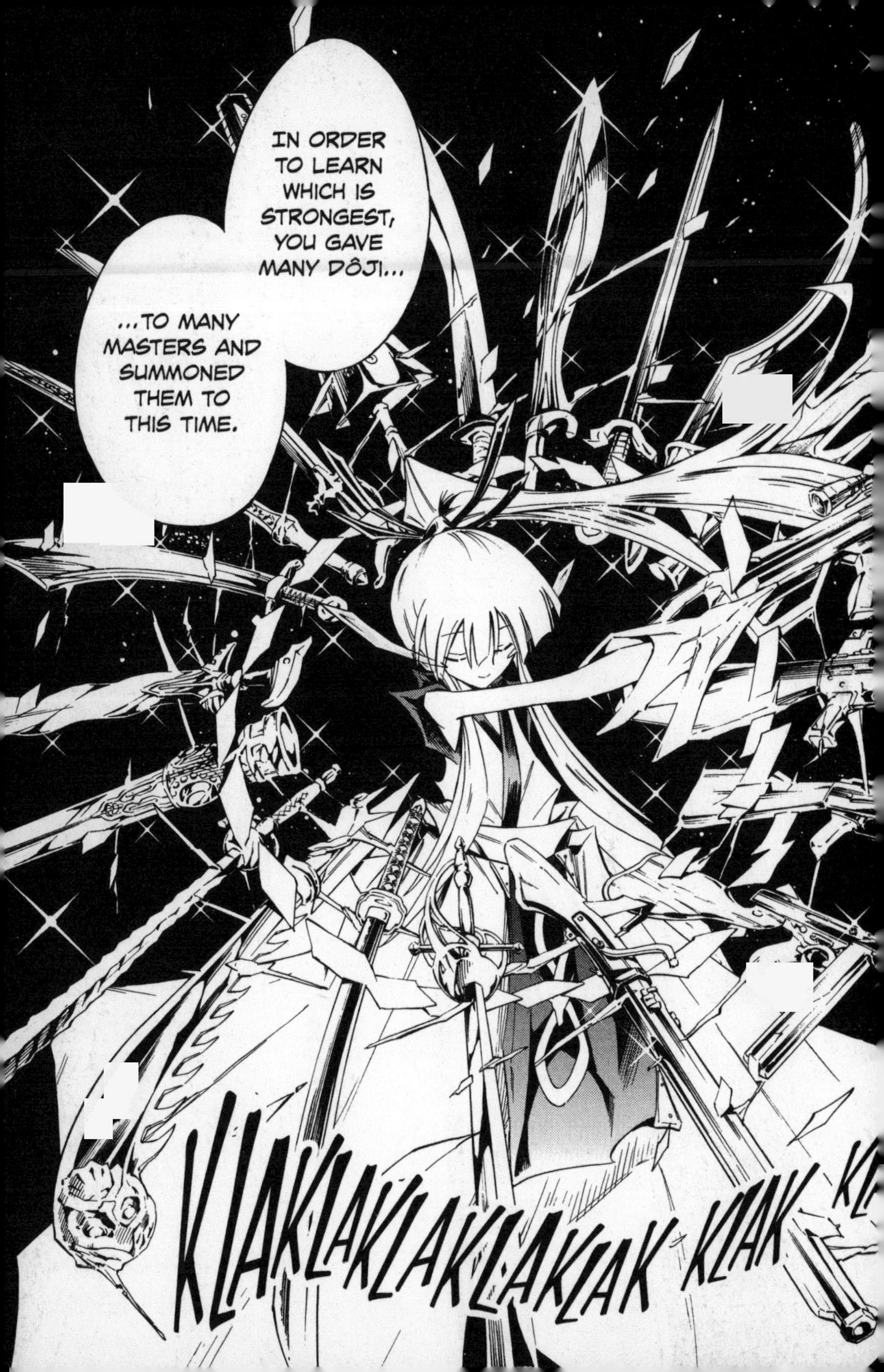

IN ORDER TO LEARN WHICH IS STRONGEST, YOU GAVE MANY DÔJI...
...TO MANY MASTERS AND SUMMONED THEM TO THIS TIME.
KLAKLAKLAKLAKLAKLAK KLAK KLAK

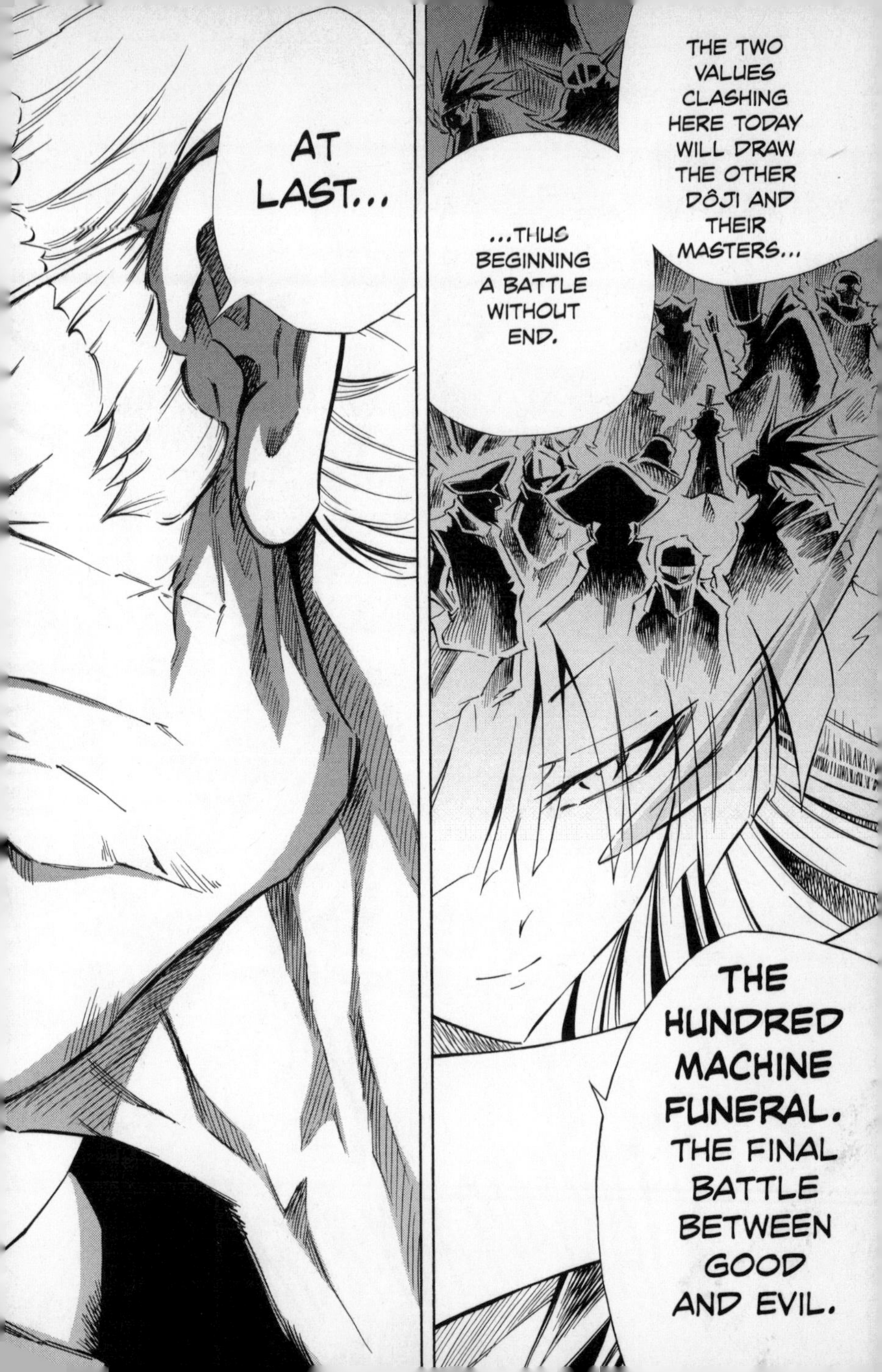
THE TWO VALUES CLASHING HERE TODAY WILL DRAW THE OTHER DÔJI AND THEIR MASTERS...
...THUS BEGINNING A BATTLE WITHOUT END.
THE HUNDRED MACHINE FUNERAL. THE FINAL BATTLE BETWEEN GOOD AND EVIL.
AT LAST...

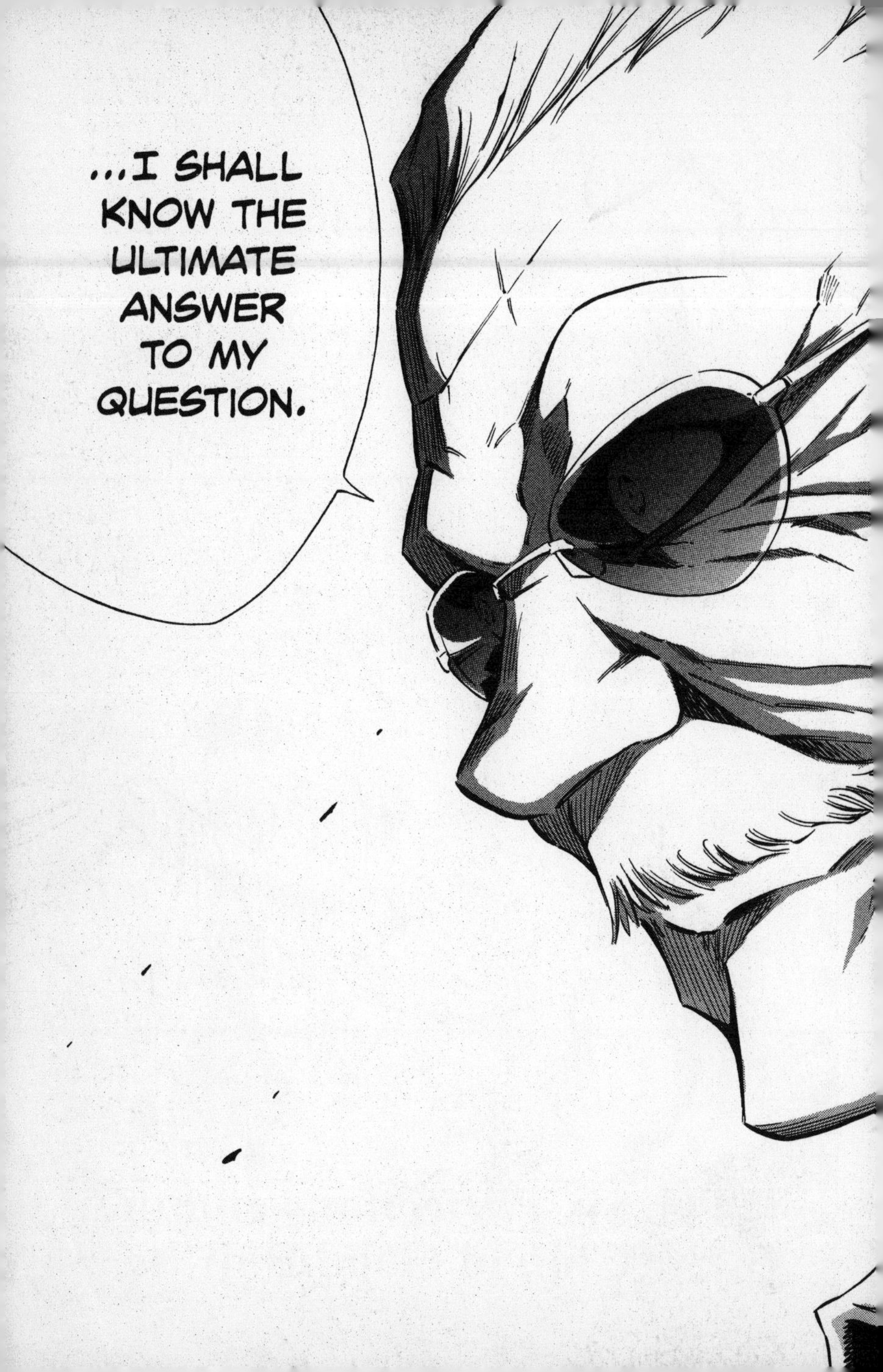
...I SHALL KNOW THE ULTIMATE ANSWER TO MY QUESTION.

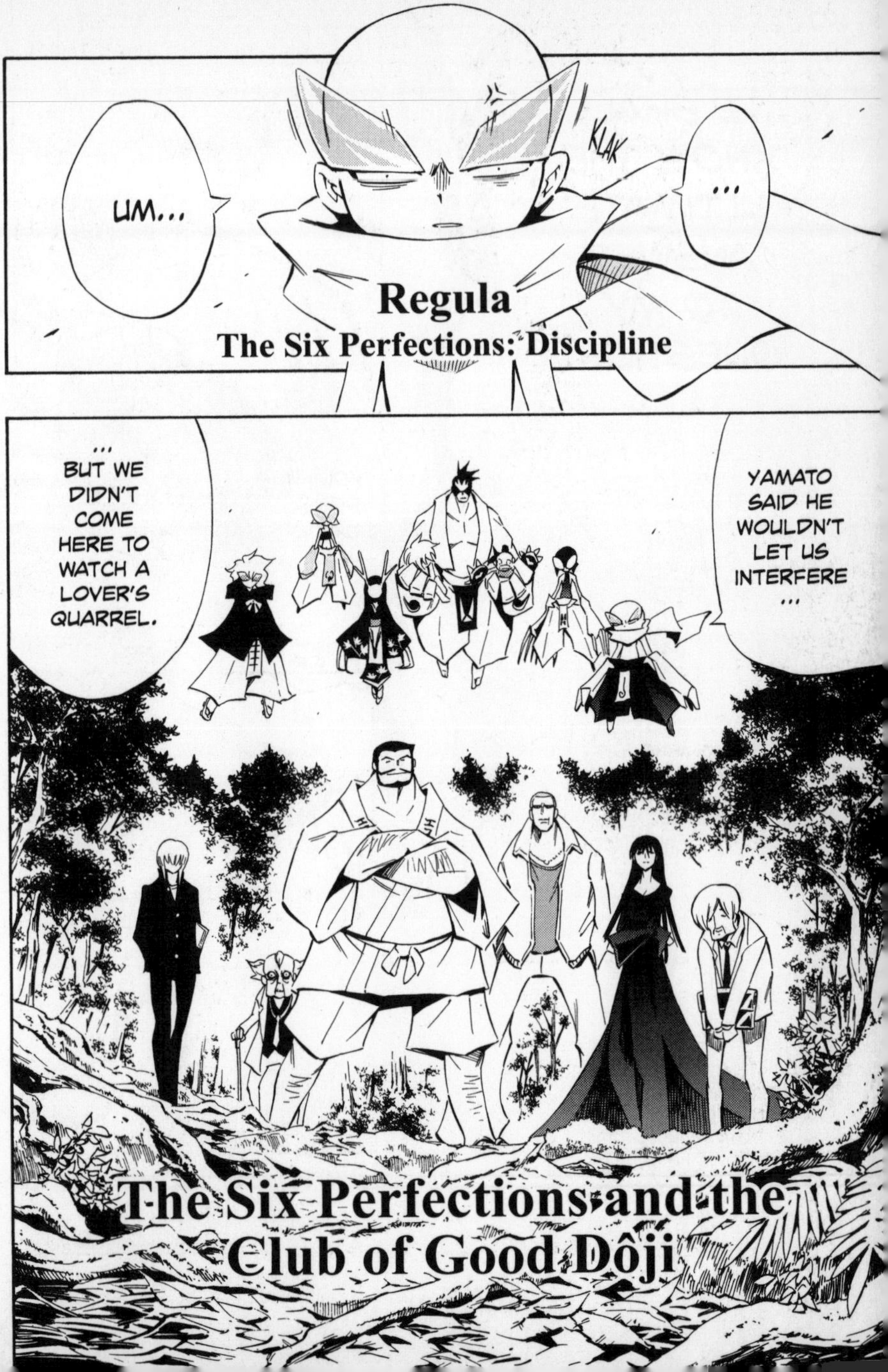
...
KLAK
UM...
Regula
The Six Perfections: Discipline
YAMATO SAID HE WOULDN'T LET US INTERFERE ...
... BUT WE DIDN'T COME HERE TO WATCH A LOVER'S QUARREL.
The Six Perfections and the Club of Good Dôji

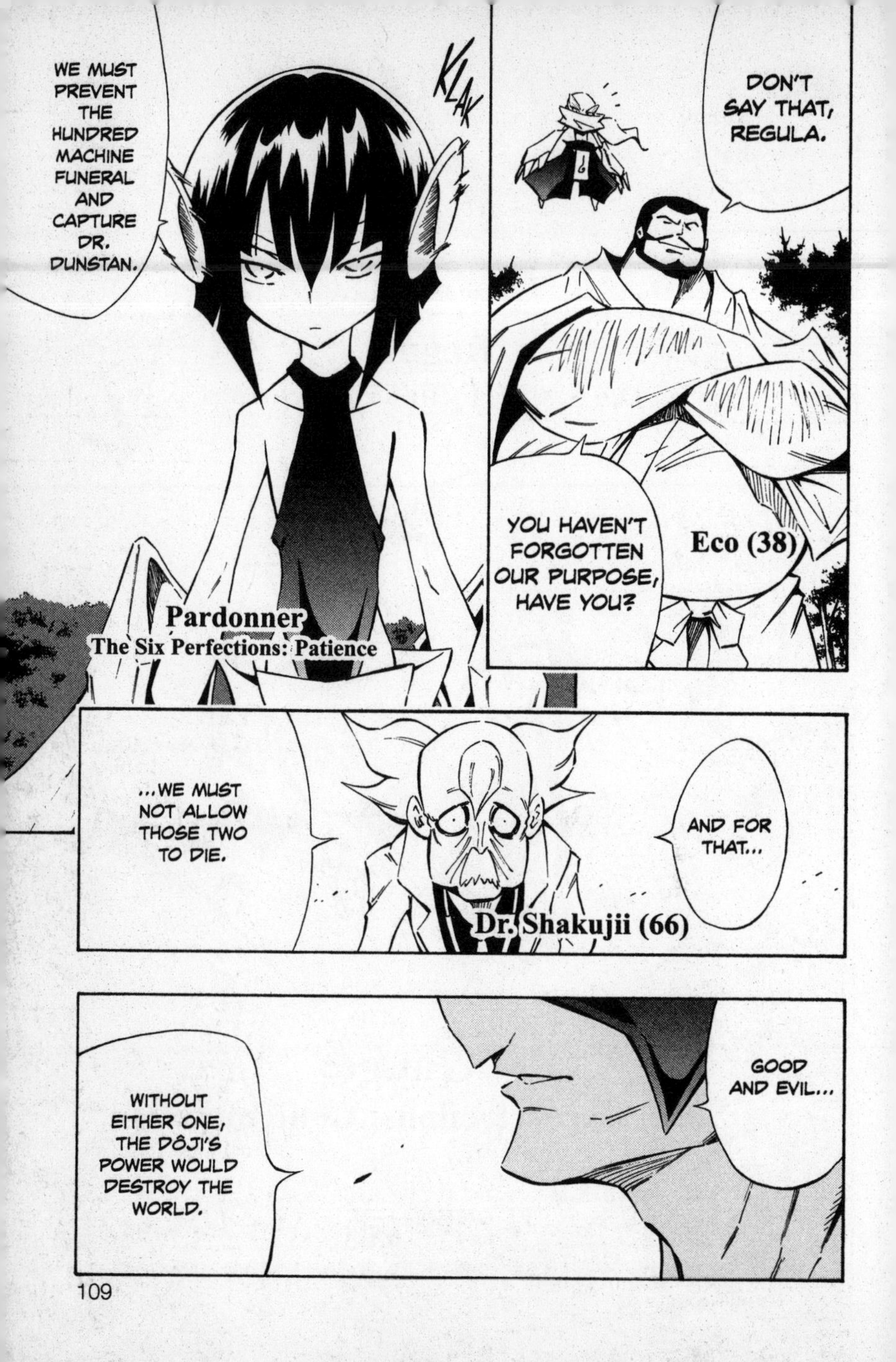
DON'T SAY THAT, REGULA.
YOU HAVEN'T FORGOTTEN OUR PURPOSE, HAVE YOU?
Eco (38)
KLAK
WE MUST PREVENT THE HUNDRED MACHINE FUNERAL AND CAPTURE DR. DUNSTAN.
Pardonner
The Six Perfections: Patience
AND FOR THAT...
...WE MUST NOT ALLOW THOSE TWO TO DIE.
Dr. Shakujii (66)
GOOD AND EVIL...
WITHOUT EITHER ONE, THE DÔJI'S POWER WOULD DESTROY THE WORLD.

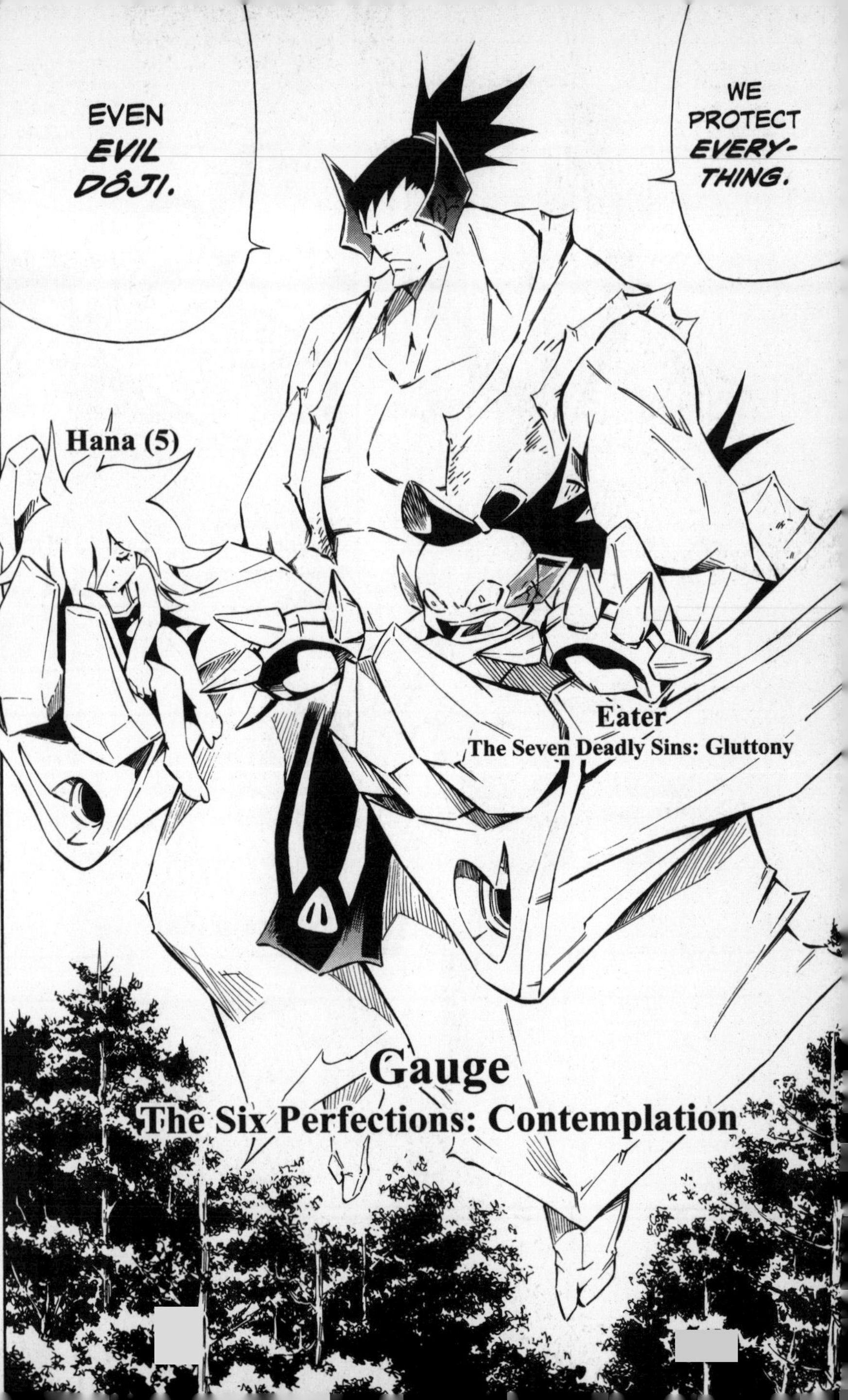
WE PROTECT EVERYTHING.
EVEN EVIL DÔJI.
Hana (5)
Eater
The Seven Deadly Sins: Gluttony
Gauge
The Six Perfections: Contemplation

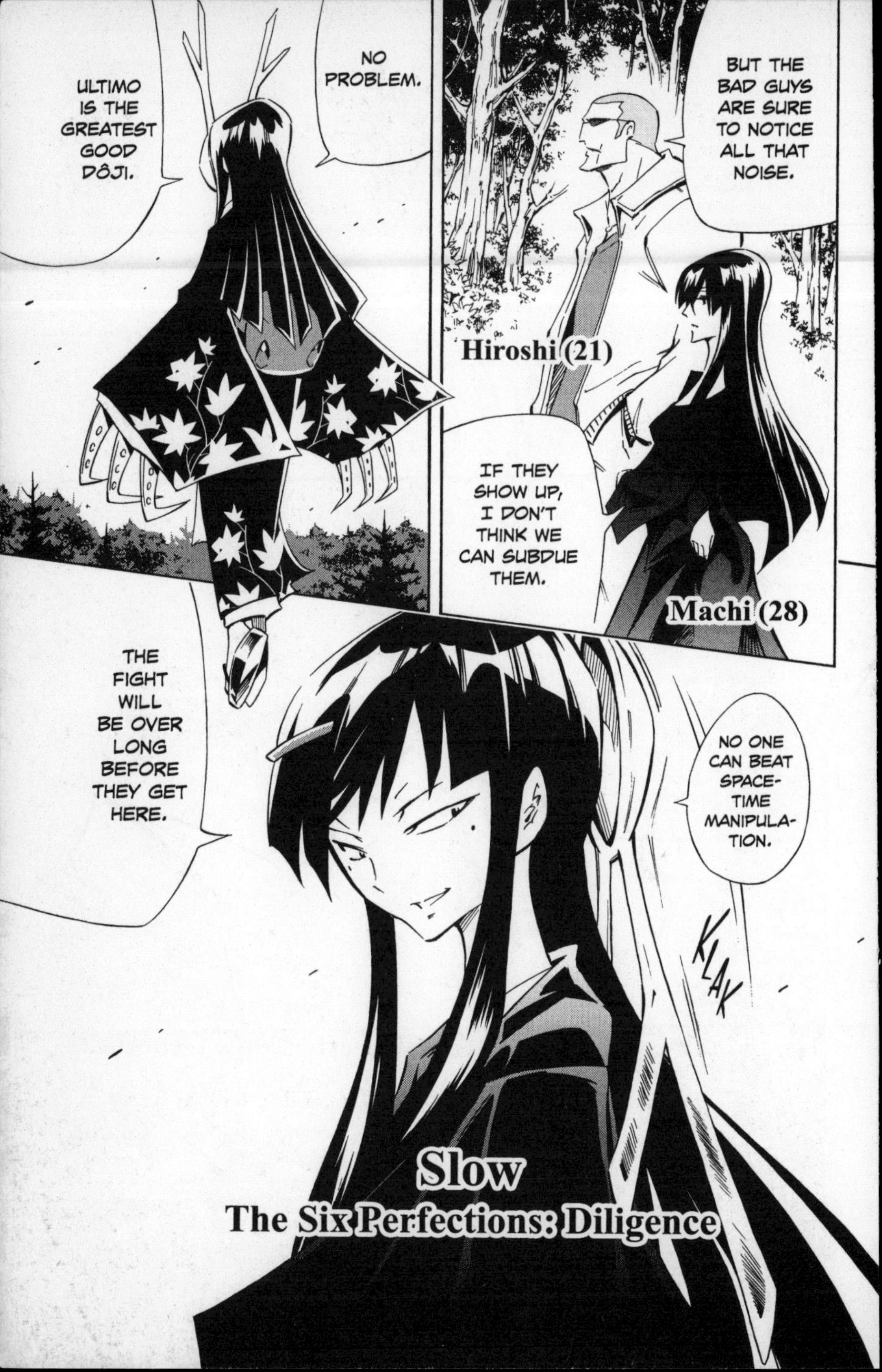
BUT THE BAD GUYS ARE SURE TO NOTICE ALL THAT NOISE.
Hiroshi (21)
IF THEY SHOW UP, I DON'T THINK WE CAN SUBDUE THEM.
Machi (28)
NO PROBLEM.
ULTIMO IS THE GREATEST GOOD DÔJI.
NO ONE CAN BEAT SPACE-TIME MANIPULATION.
THE FIGHT WILL BE OVER LONG BEFORE THEY GET HERE.
KLAK
Slow
The Six Perfections: Diligence

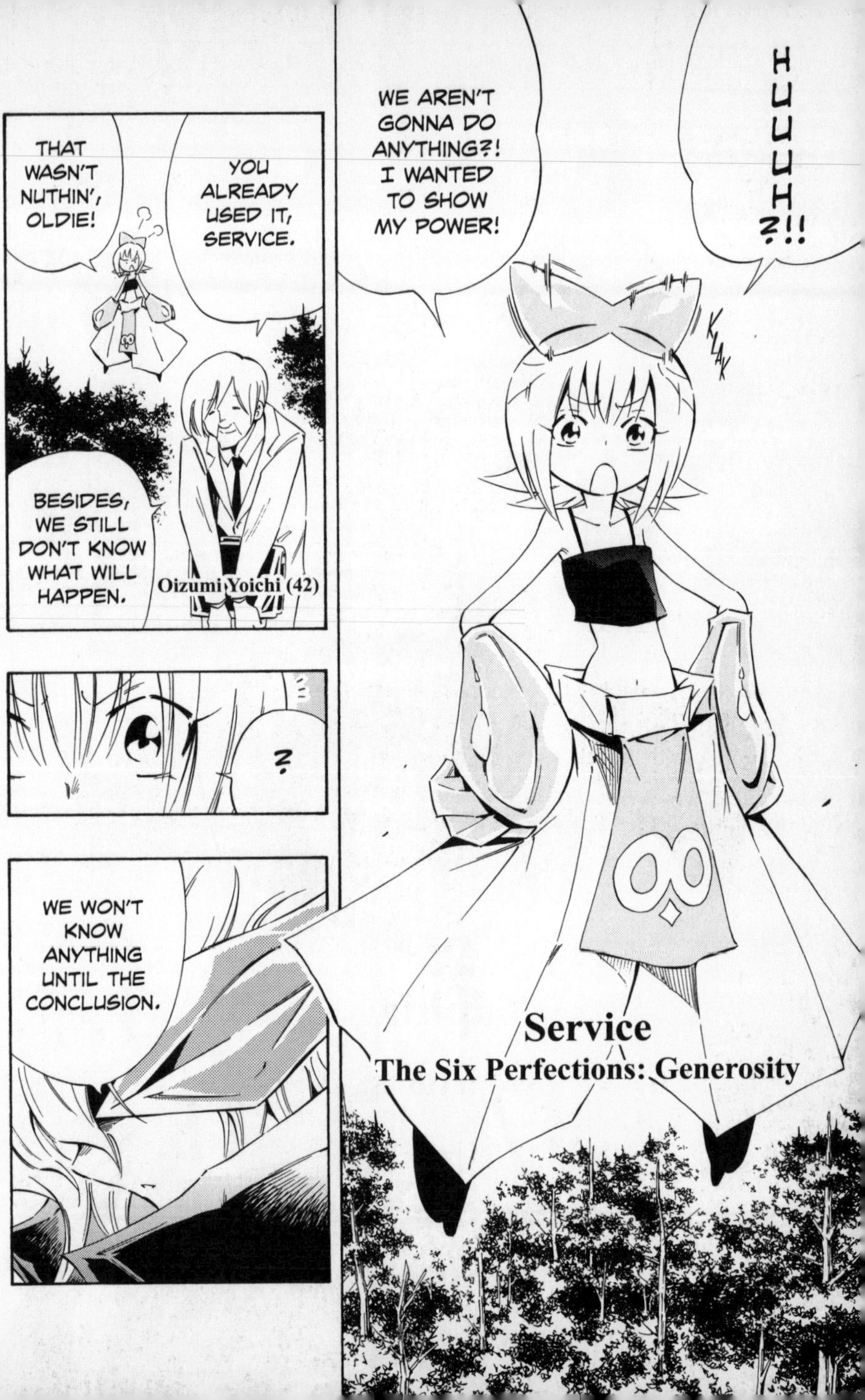
HUUUH?!!
WE AREN'T GONNA DO ANYTHING?! I WANTED TO SHOW MY POWER!
KLAK
Service
The Six Perfections: Generosity
YOU ALREADY USED IT, SERVICE.
THAT WASN'T NUTHIN', OLDIE!
BESIDES, WE STILL DON'T KNOW WHAT WILL HAPPEN.
Oizumi Yoichi (42)
?
WE WON'T KNOW ANYTHING UNTIL THE CONCLUSION.

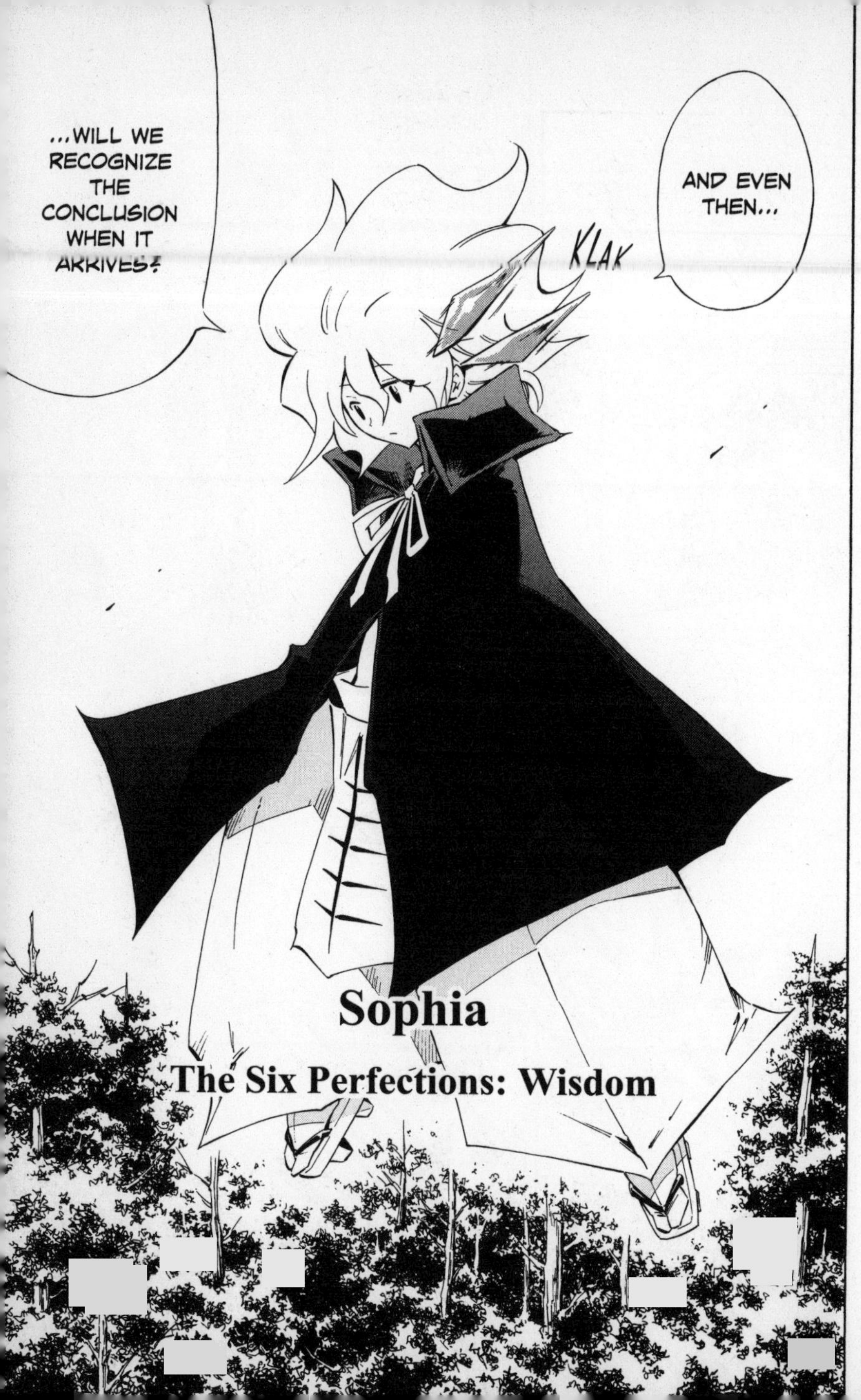
AND EVEN THEN...
KLAK
...WILL WE RECOGNIZE THE CONCLUSION WHEN IT ARRIVES?
Sophia
The Six Perfections: Wisdom

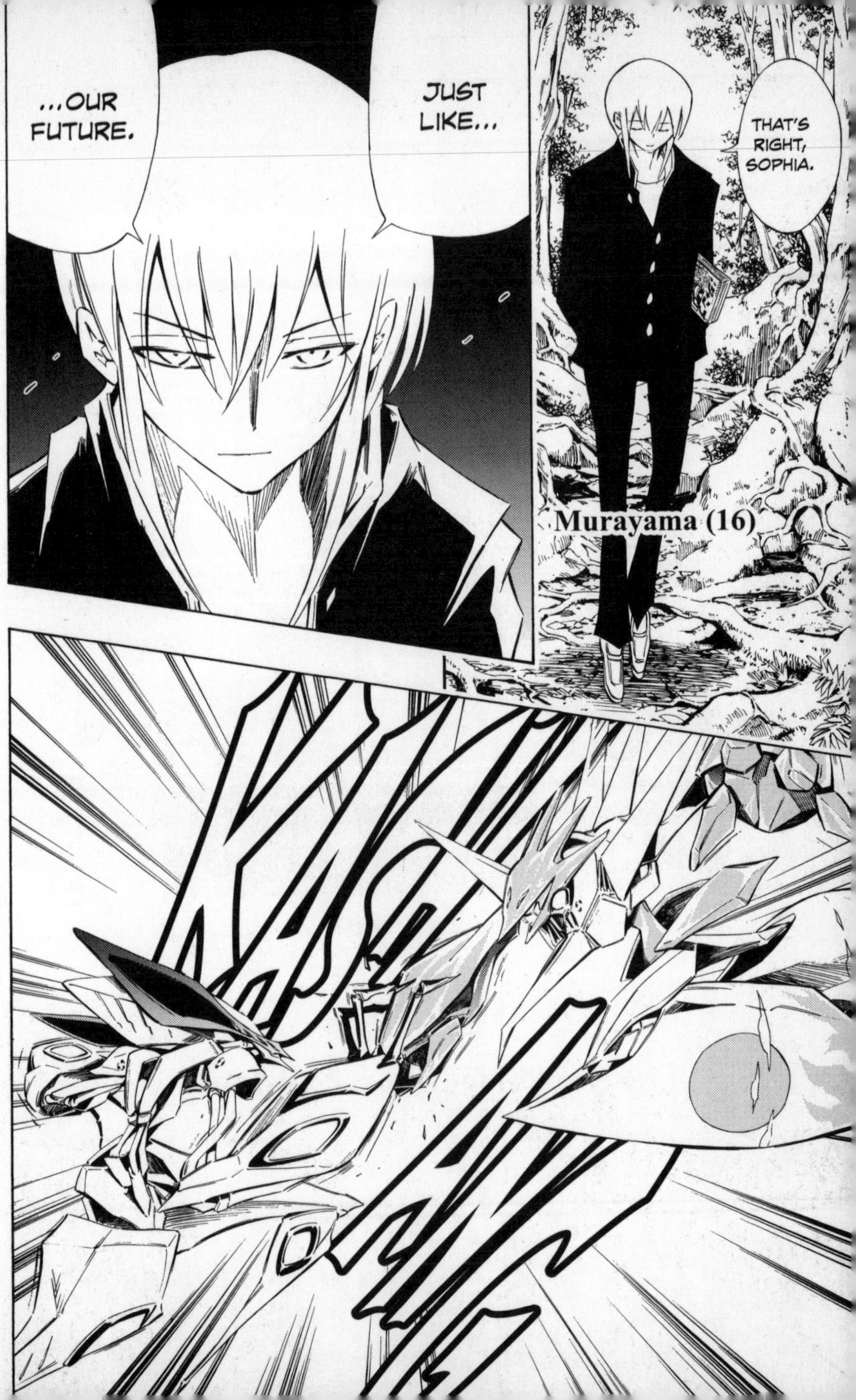
THAT'S RIGHT, SOPHIA.
Murayama (16)
JUST LIKE...
...OUR FUTURE.

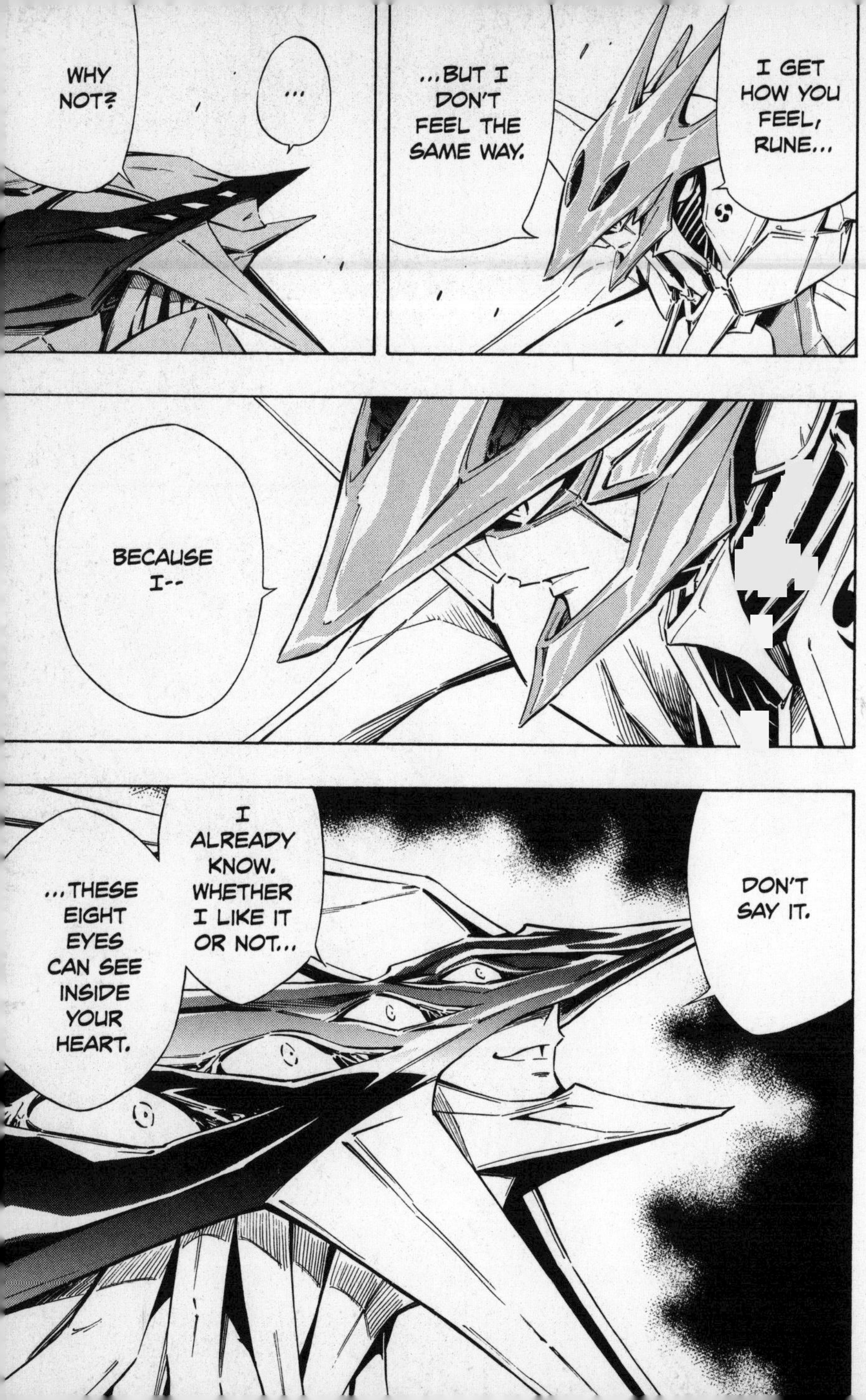
I GET HOW YOU FEEL, RUNE...
...BUT I DON'T FEEL THE SAME WAY.
...
WHY NOT?
BECAUSE I--
DON'T SAY IT.
I ALREADY KNOW. WHETHER I LIKE IT OR NOT...
...THESE EIGHT EYES CAN SEE INSIDE YOUR HEART.

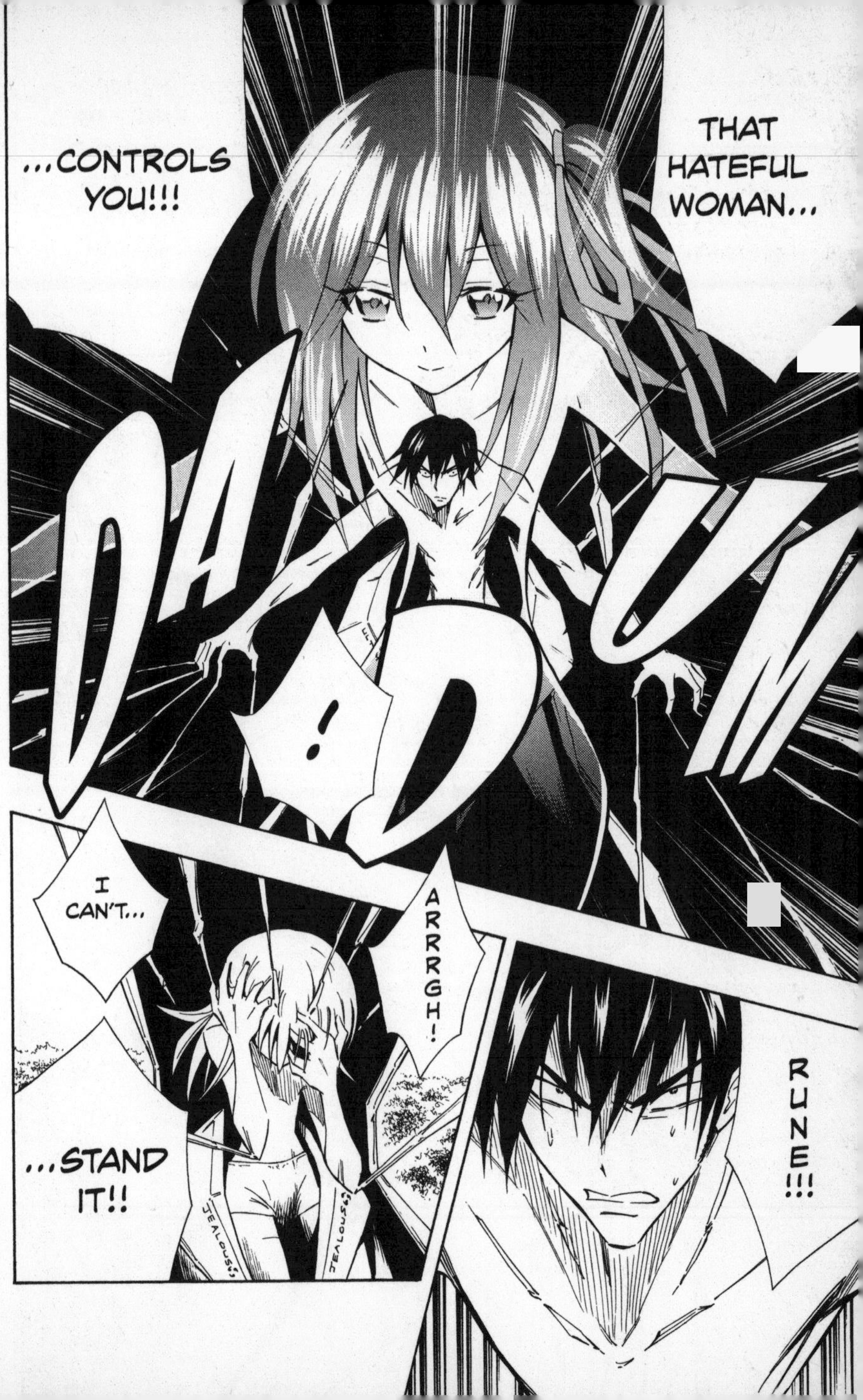
THAT HATEFUL WOMAN...
...CONTROLS YOU!!!
DA DUM
RUNE!!!
ARRRGH!
I CAN'T...
...STAND IT!!
JEALOUS
JEALOUS

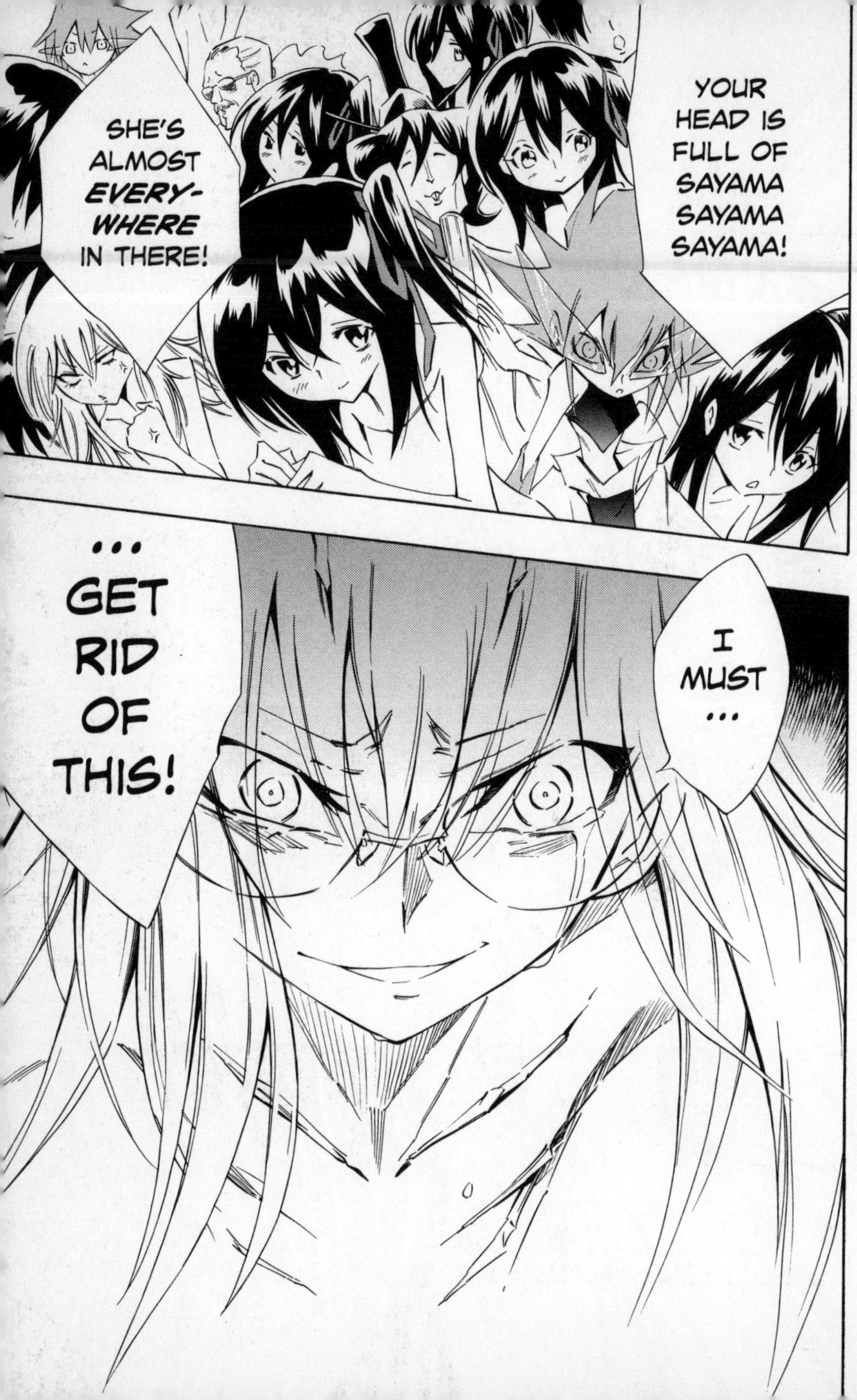
YOUR HEAD IS FULL OF SAYAMA SAYAMA SAYAMA!
SHE'S ALMOST *EVERY-WHERE* IN THERE!
I MUST...
...GET RID OF THIS!

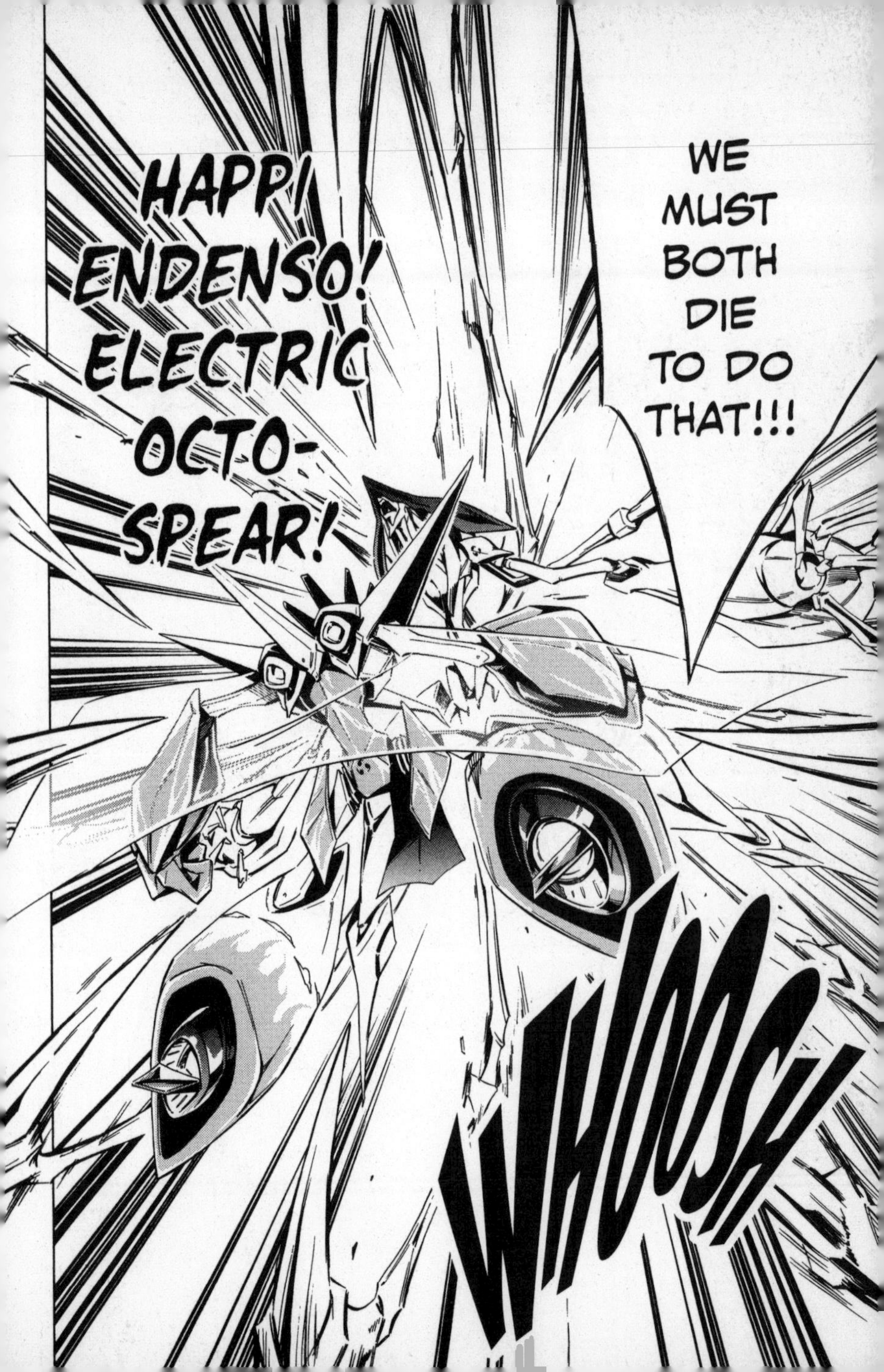
WE MUST BOTH DIE TO DO THAT!!!
HAPPI ENDENSO! ELECTRIC OCTO-SPEAR!
WHOOSH

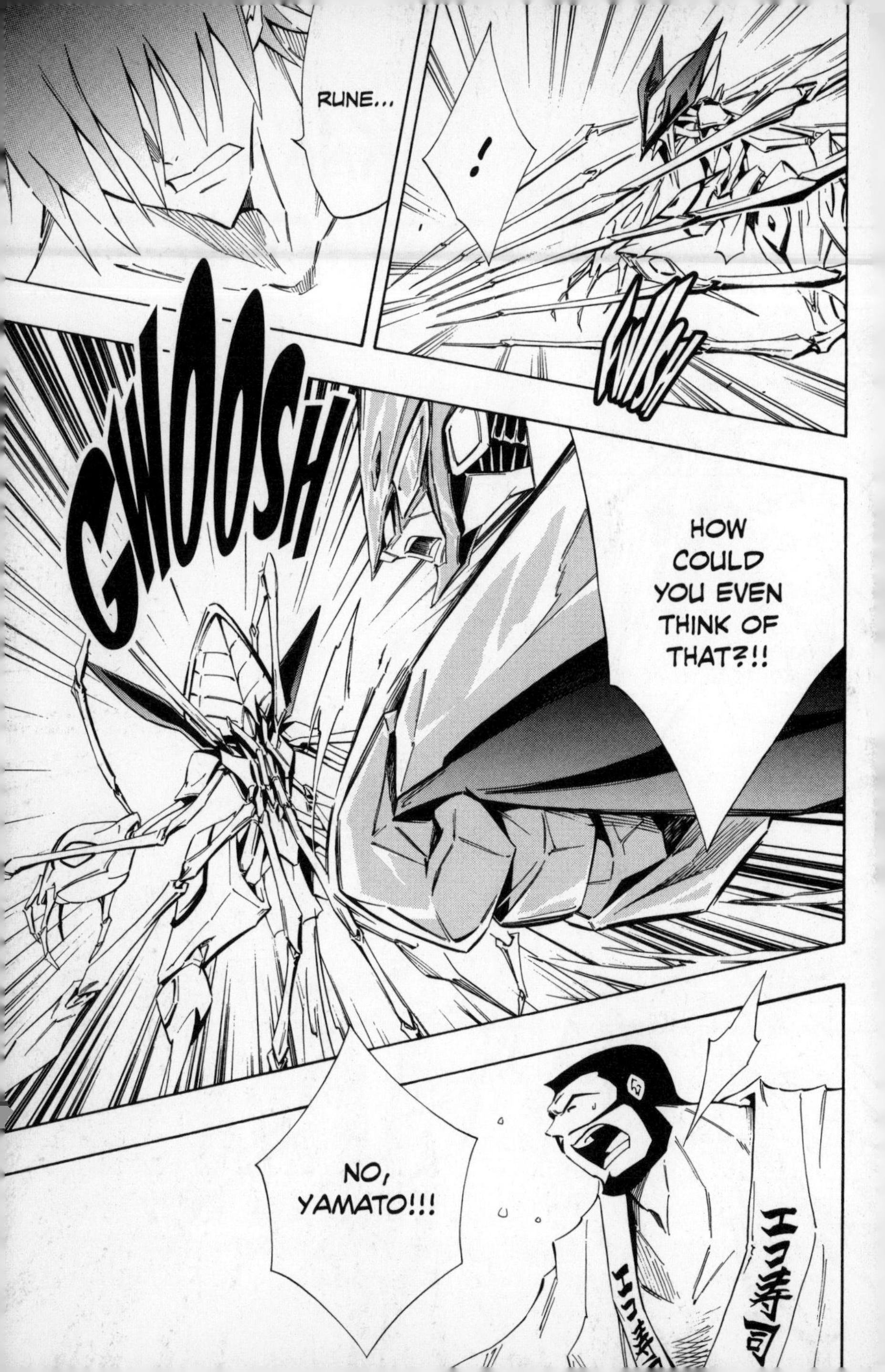
!
RUNE...
GWOOSH
HOW COULD YOU EVEN THINK OF THAT?!!
NO, YAMATO!!!
エコ寿司

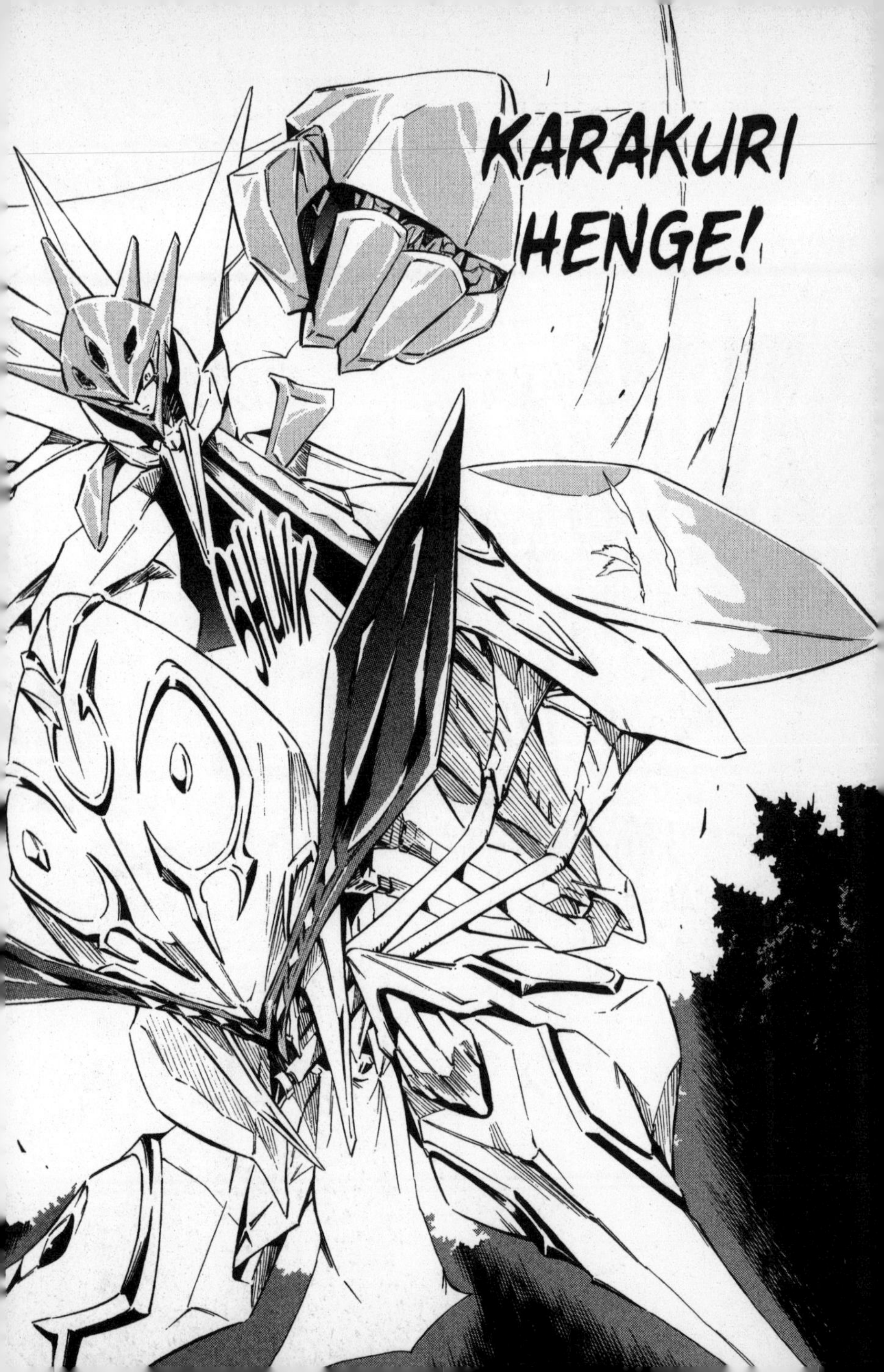
KARAKURI HENGE!
SHUNK

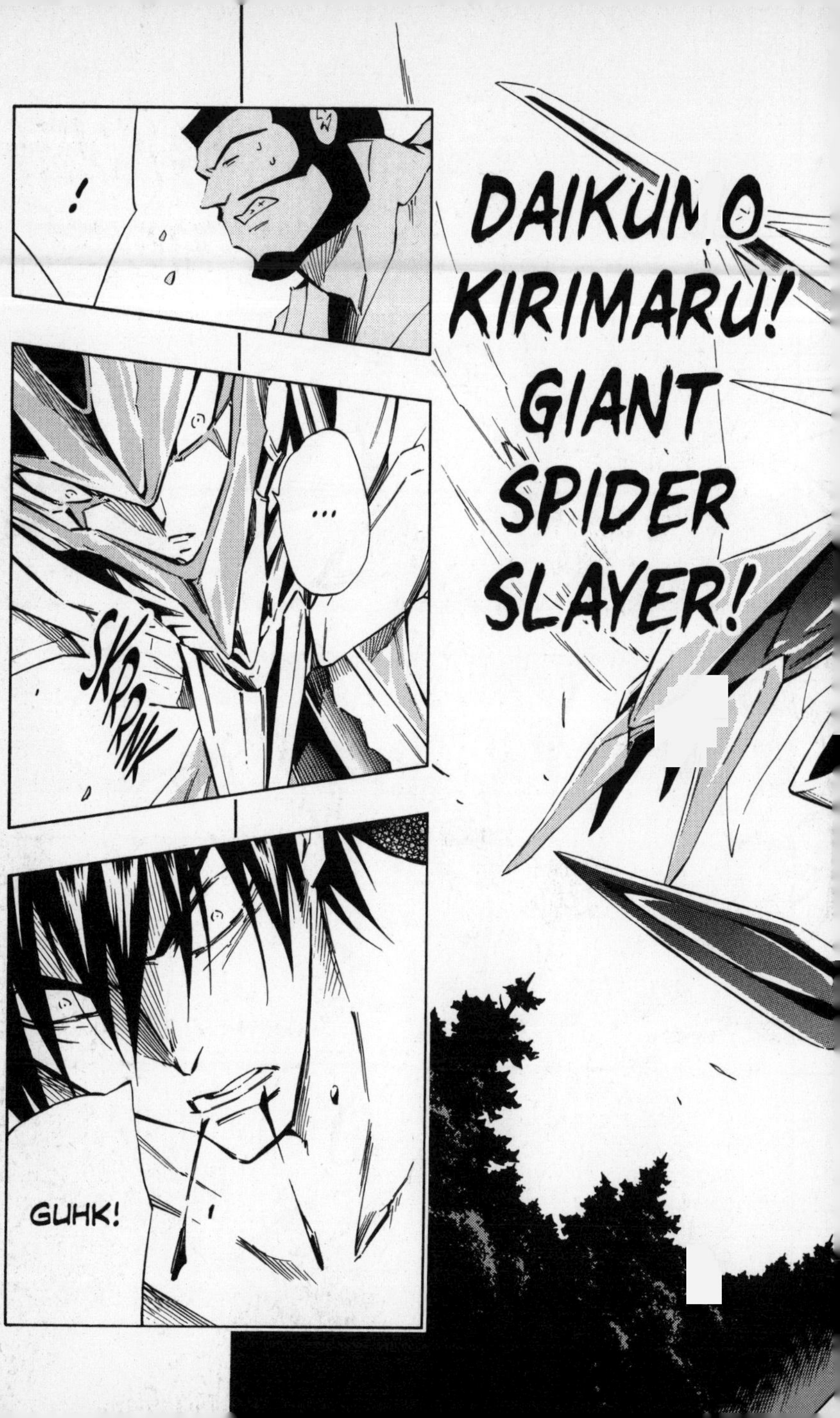
DAIKUMO KIRIMARU! GIANT SPIDER SLAYER!
!
...
SKRRNK
GUHK!

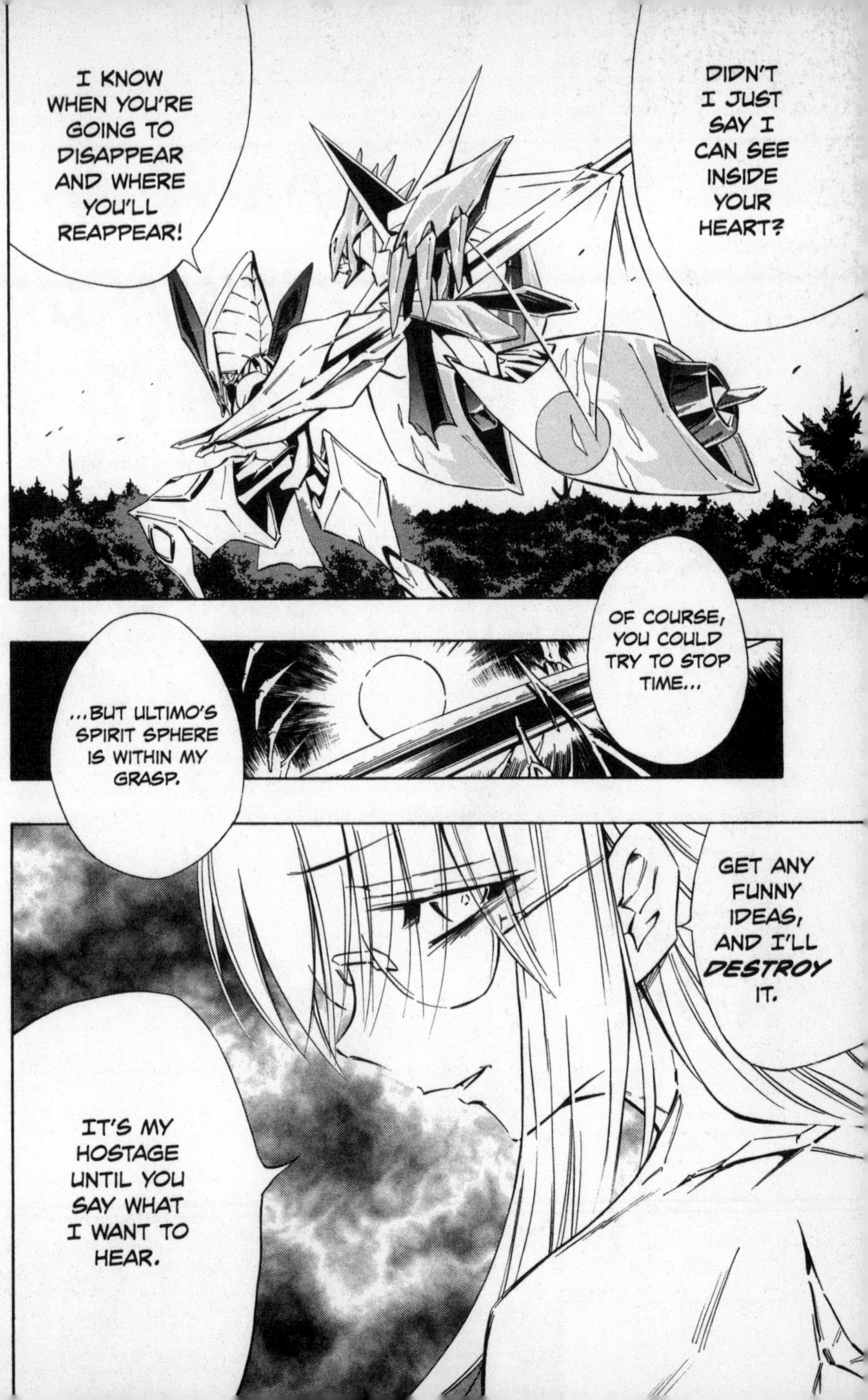
DIDN'T I JUST SAY I CAN SEE INSIDE YOUR HEART?
I KNOW WHEN YOU'RE GOING TO DISAPPEAR AND WHERE YOU'LL REAPPEAR!
OF COURSE, YOU COULD TRY TO STOP TIME...
...BUT ULTIMO'S SPIRIT SPHERE IS WITHIN MY GRASP.
GET ANY FUNNY IDEAS, AND I'LL *DESTROY* IT.
IT'S MY HOSTAGE UNTIL YOU SAY WHAT I WANT TO HEAR.

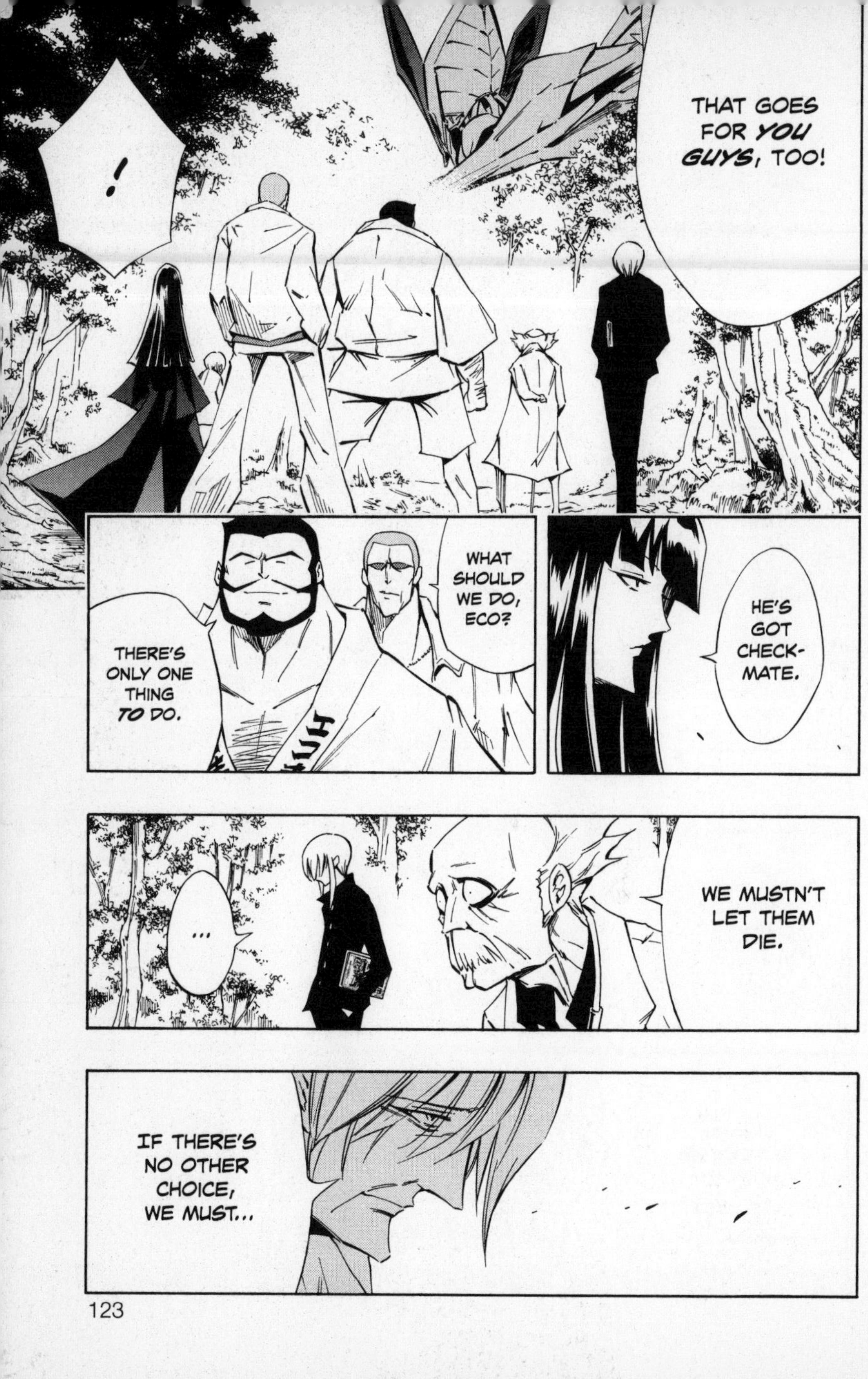
THAT GOES FOR *YOU GUYS*, TOO!
!
HE'S GOT CHECK-MATE.
WHAT SHOULD WE DO, ECO?
THERE'S ONLY ONE THING *TO* DO.
WE MUSTN'T LET THEM DIE.
...
IF THERE'S NO OTHER CHOICE, WE MUST...

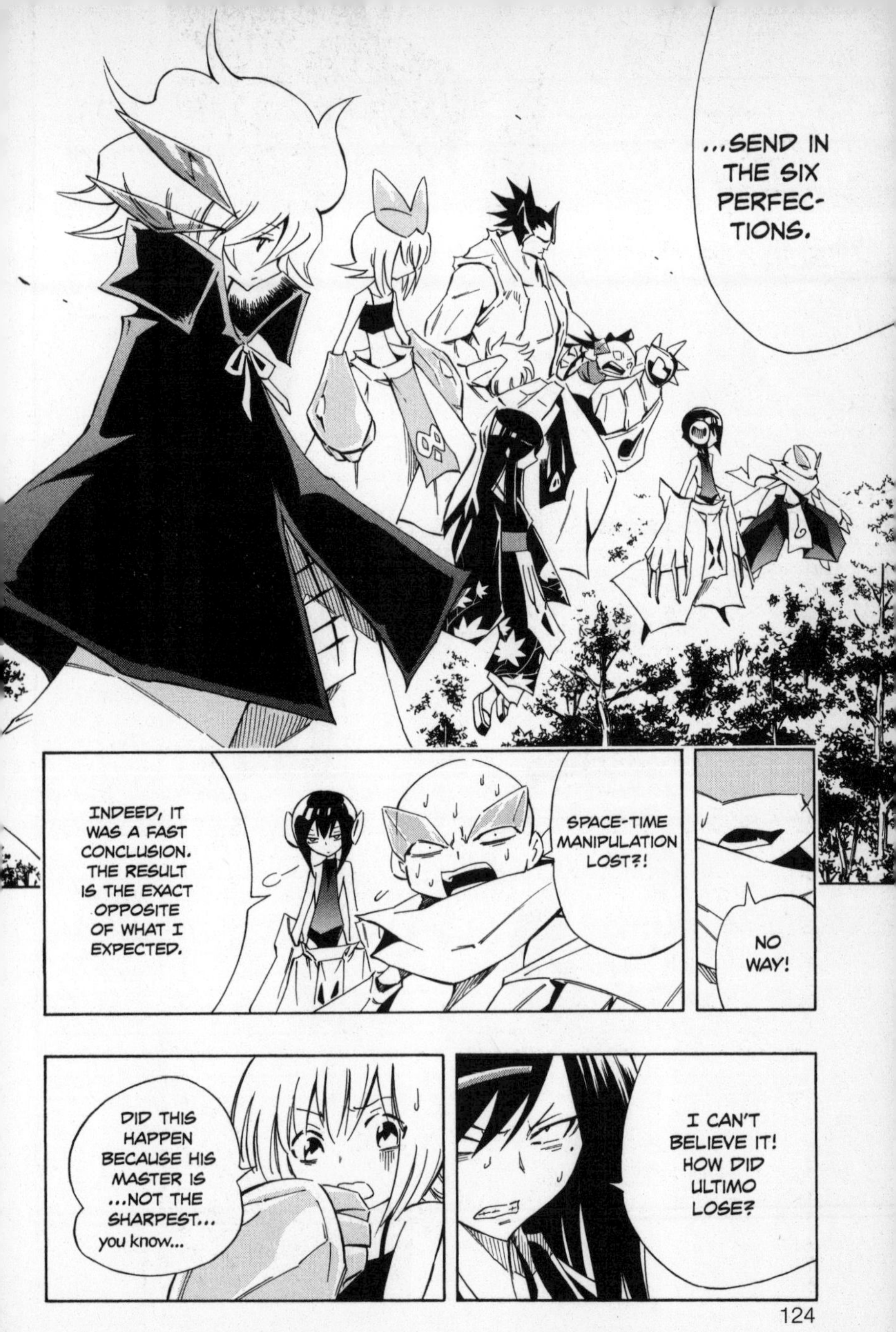
...SEND IN THE SIX PERFECTIONS.
NO WAY!
SPACE-TIME MANIPULATION LOST?!
INDEED, IT WAS A FAST CONCLUSION. THE RESULT IS THE EXACT OPPOSITE OF WHAT I EXPECTED.
I CAN'T BELIEVE IT! HOW DID ULTIMO LOSE?
DID THIS HAPPEN BECAUSE HIS MASTER IS ...NOT THE SHARPEST... you know...

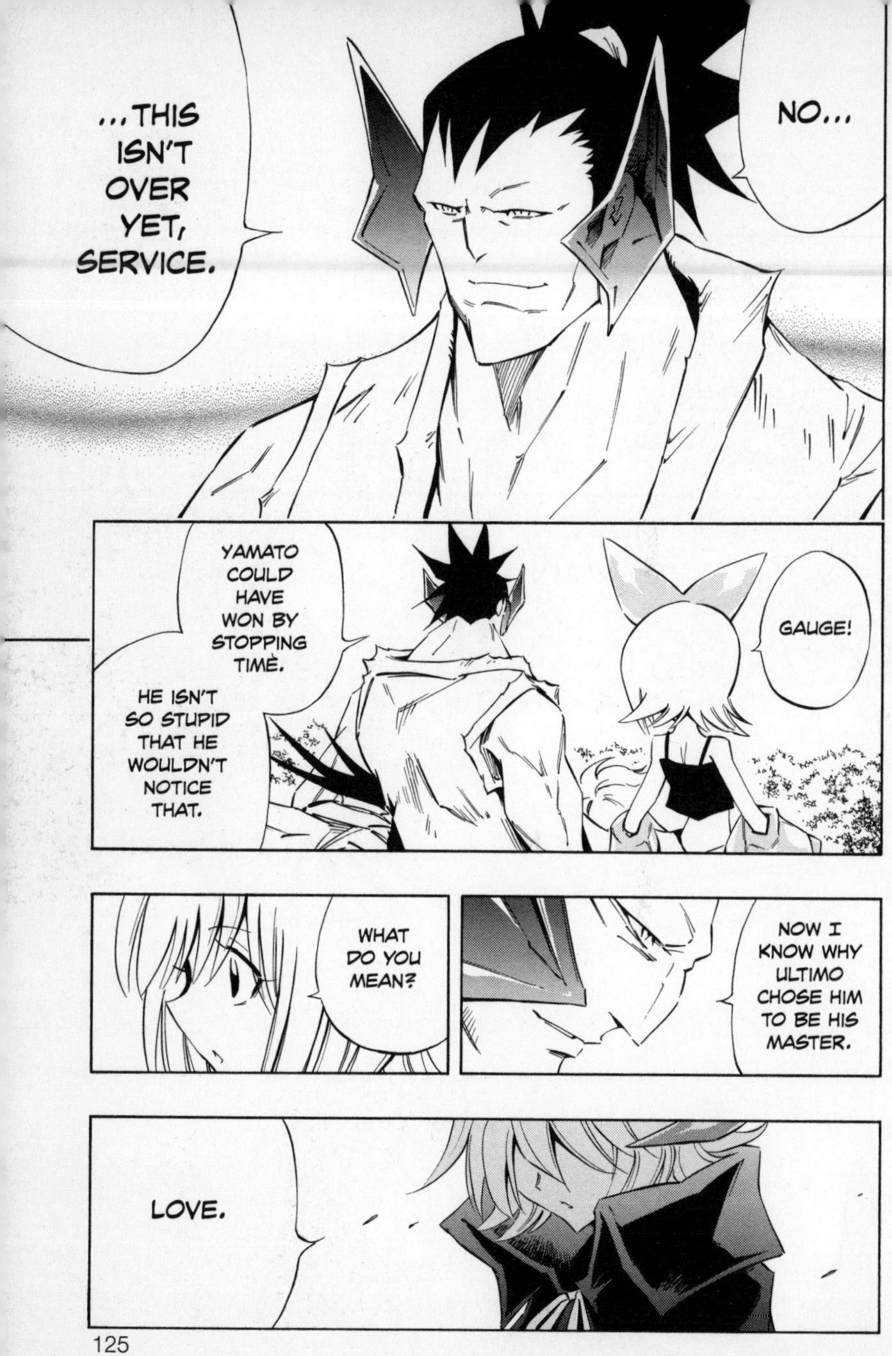
NO...
...THIS ISN'T OVER YET, SERVICE.
GAUGE!
YAMATO COULD HAVE WON BY STOPPING TIME.
HE ISN'T SO STUPID THAT HE WOULDN'T NOTICE THAT.
NOW I KNOW WHY ULTIMO CHOSE HIM TO BE HIS MASTER.
WHAT DO YOU MEAN?
LOVE.

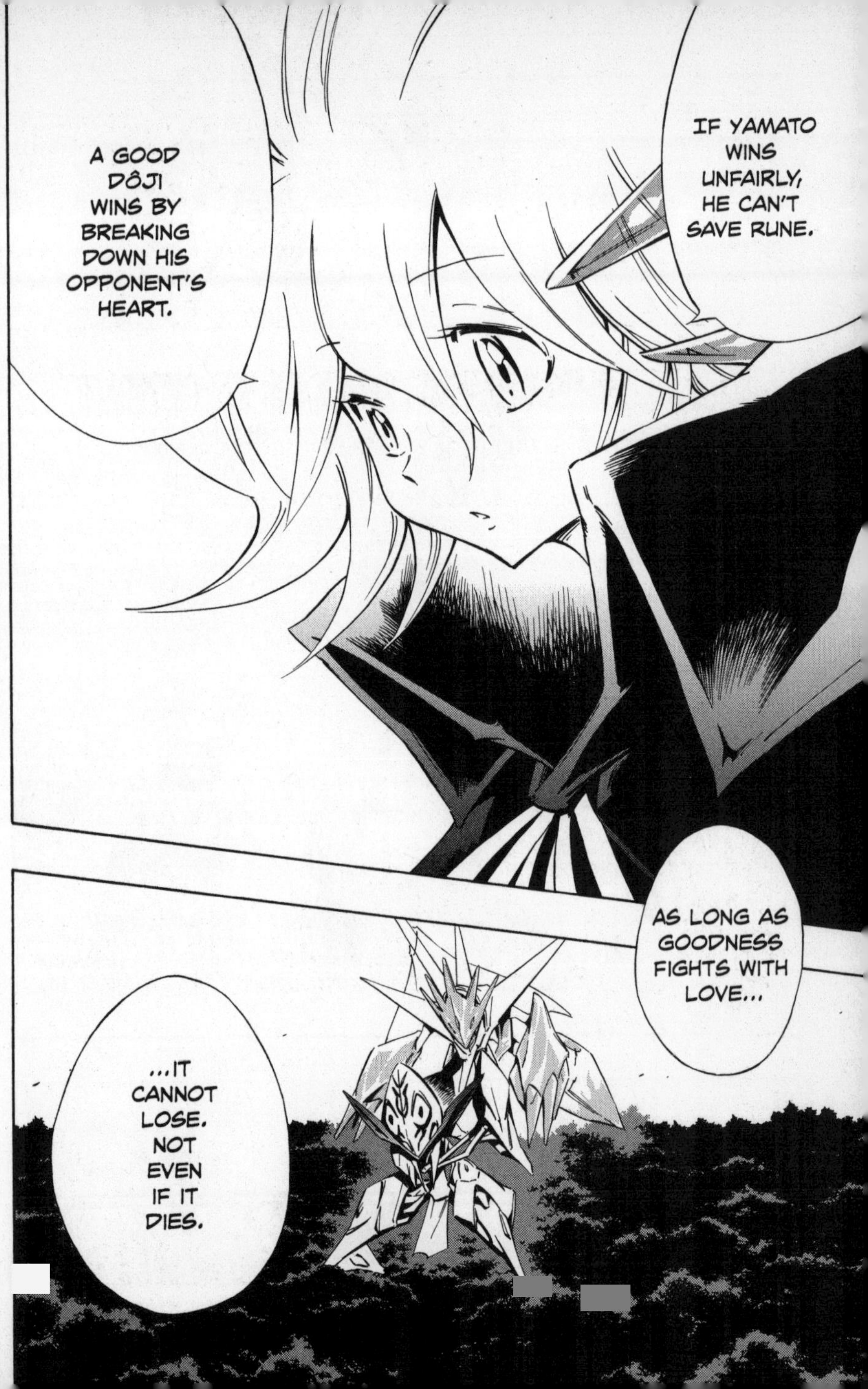
IF YAMATO WINS UNFAIRLY, HE CAN'T SAVE RUNE.
A GOOD DÔJI WINS BY BREAKING DOWN HIS OPPONENT'S HEART.
AS LONG AS GOODNESS FIGHTS WITH LOVE...
...IT CANNOT LOSE. NOT EVEN IF IT DIES.

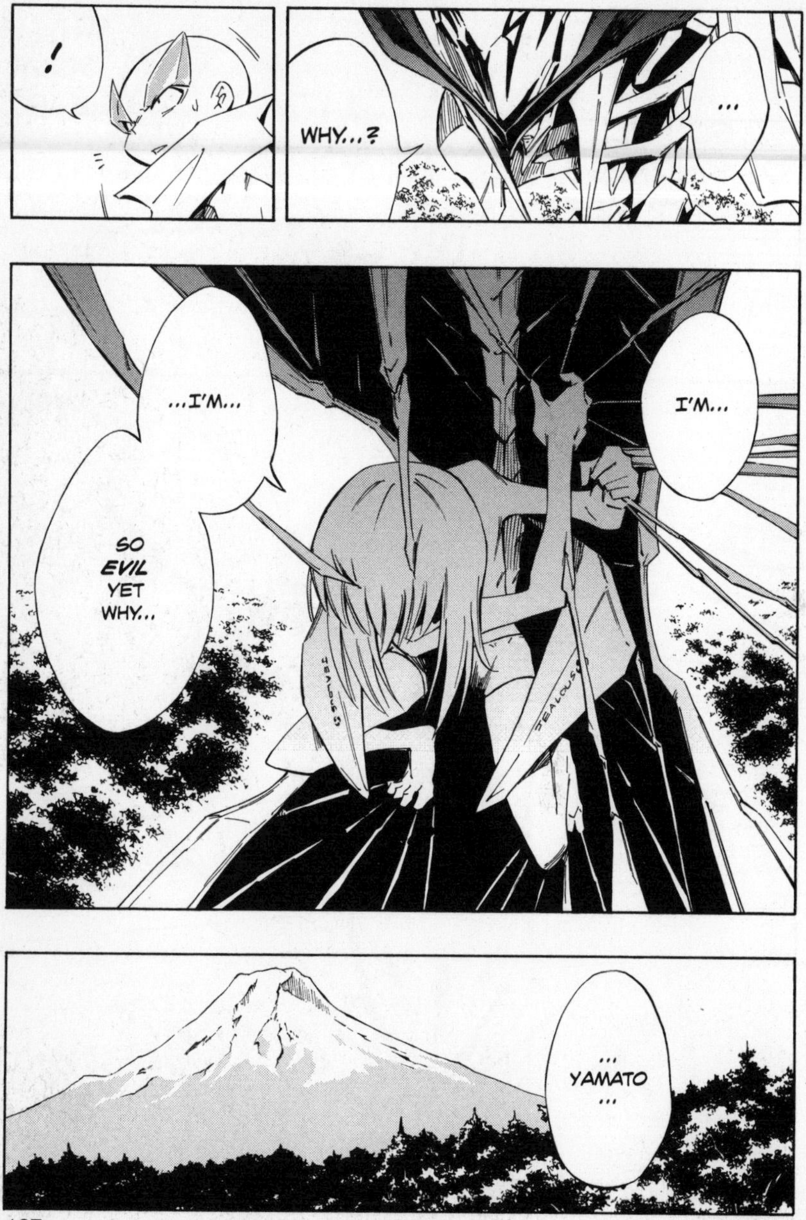
...
WHY...?
!
I'M...
...I'M...
SO EVIL YET WHY...
JEALOUS
JEALOUS
... YAMATO ...

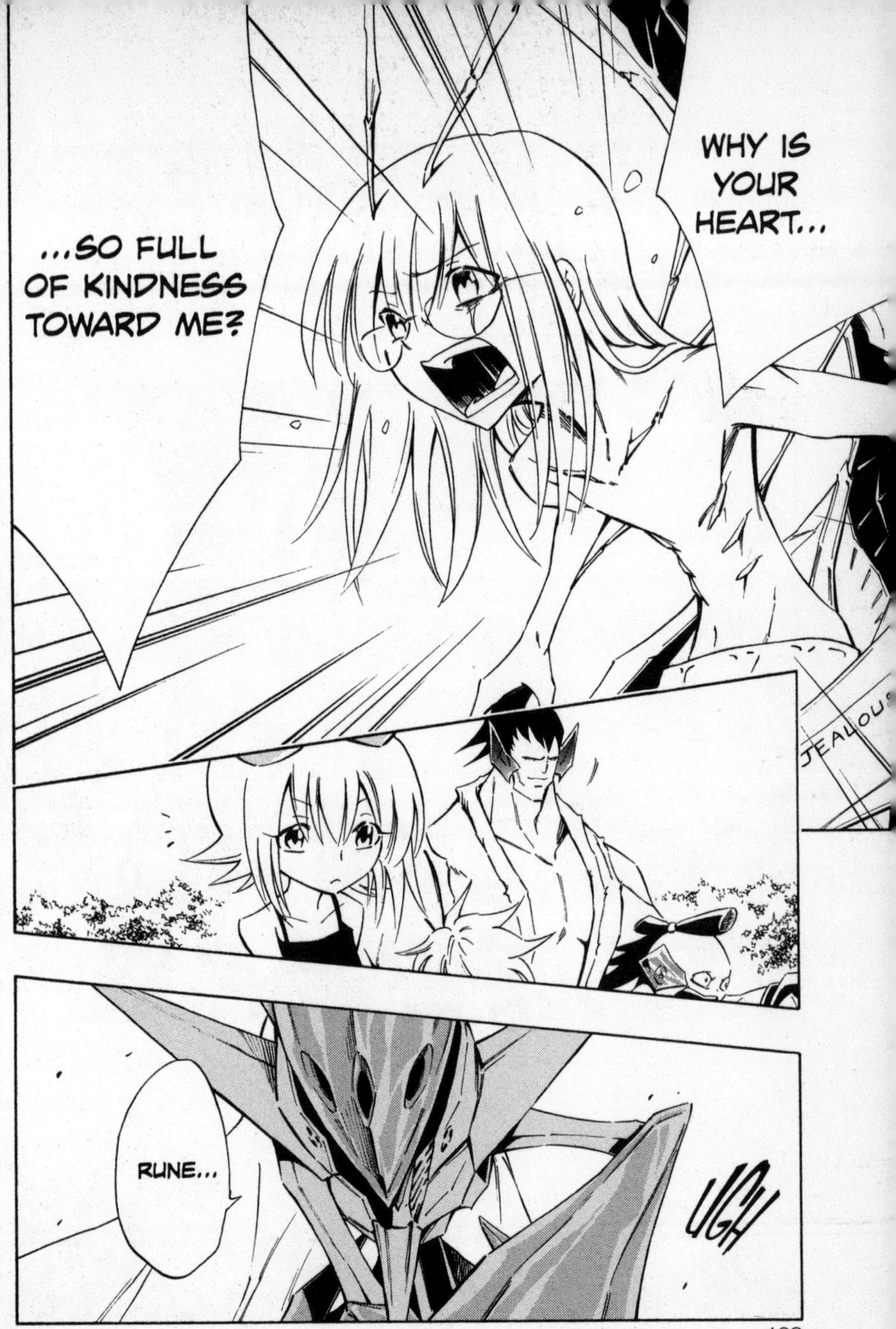
WHY IS YOUR HEART...
...SO FULL OF KINDNESS TOWARD ME?
UGH
RUNE...

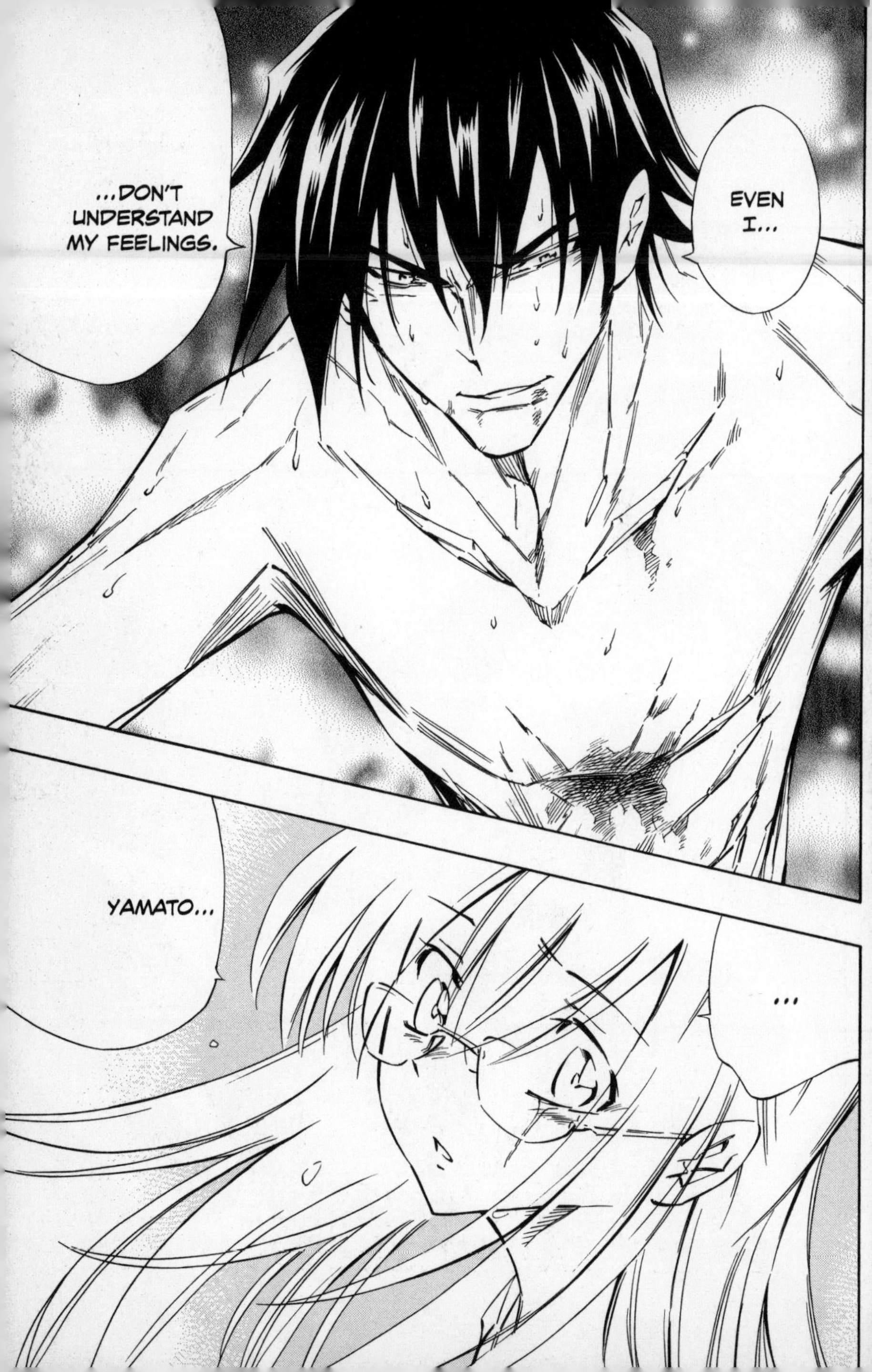
EVEN I...
...DON'T UNDERSTAND MY FEELINGS.
...
YAMATO...

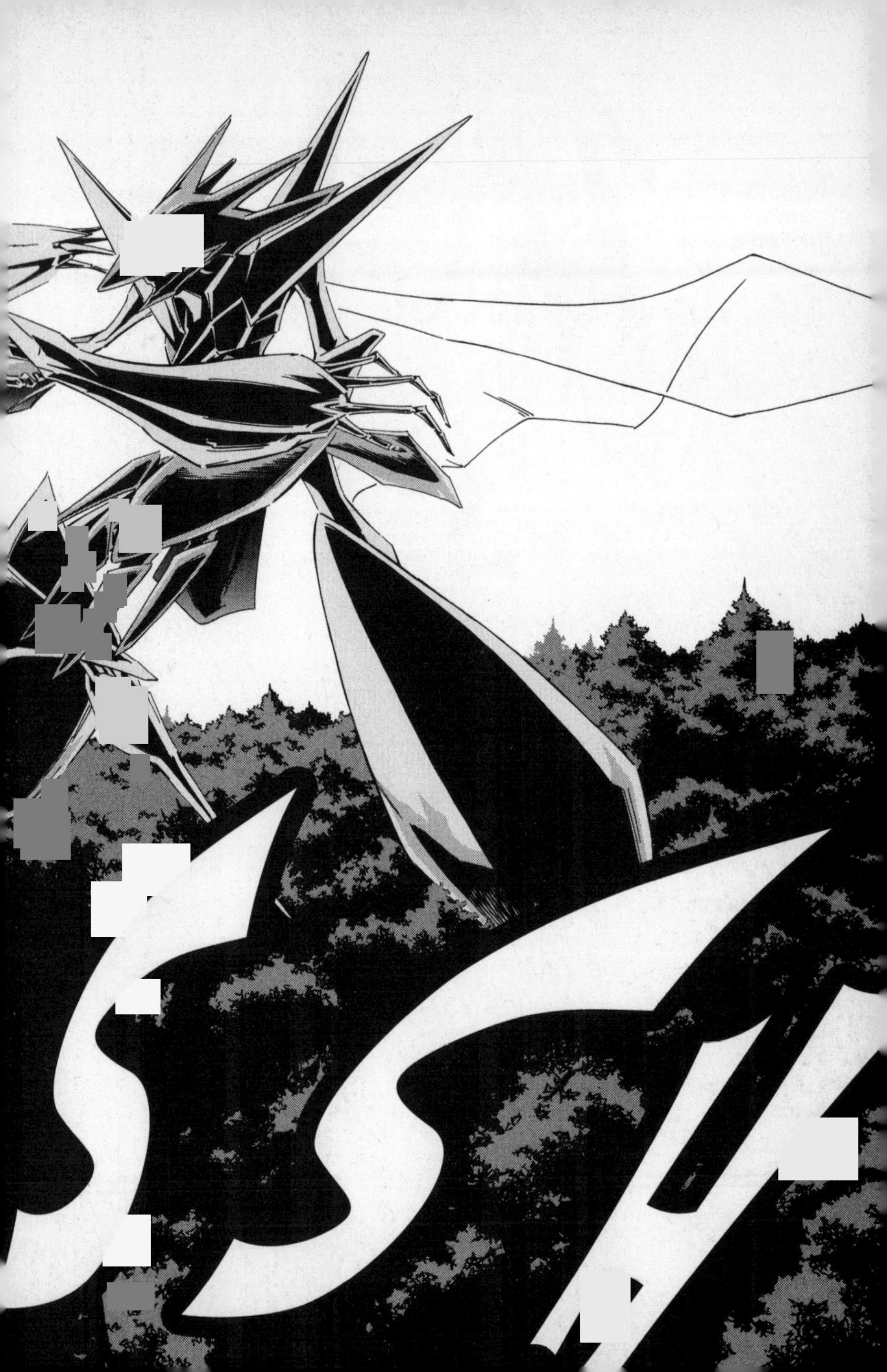

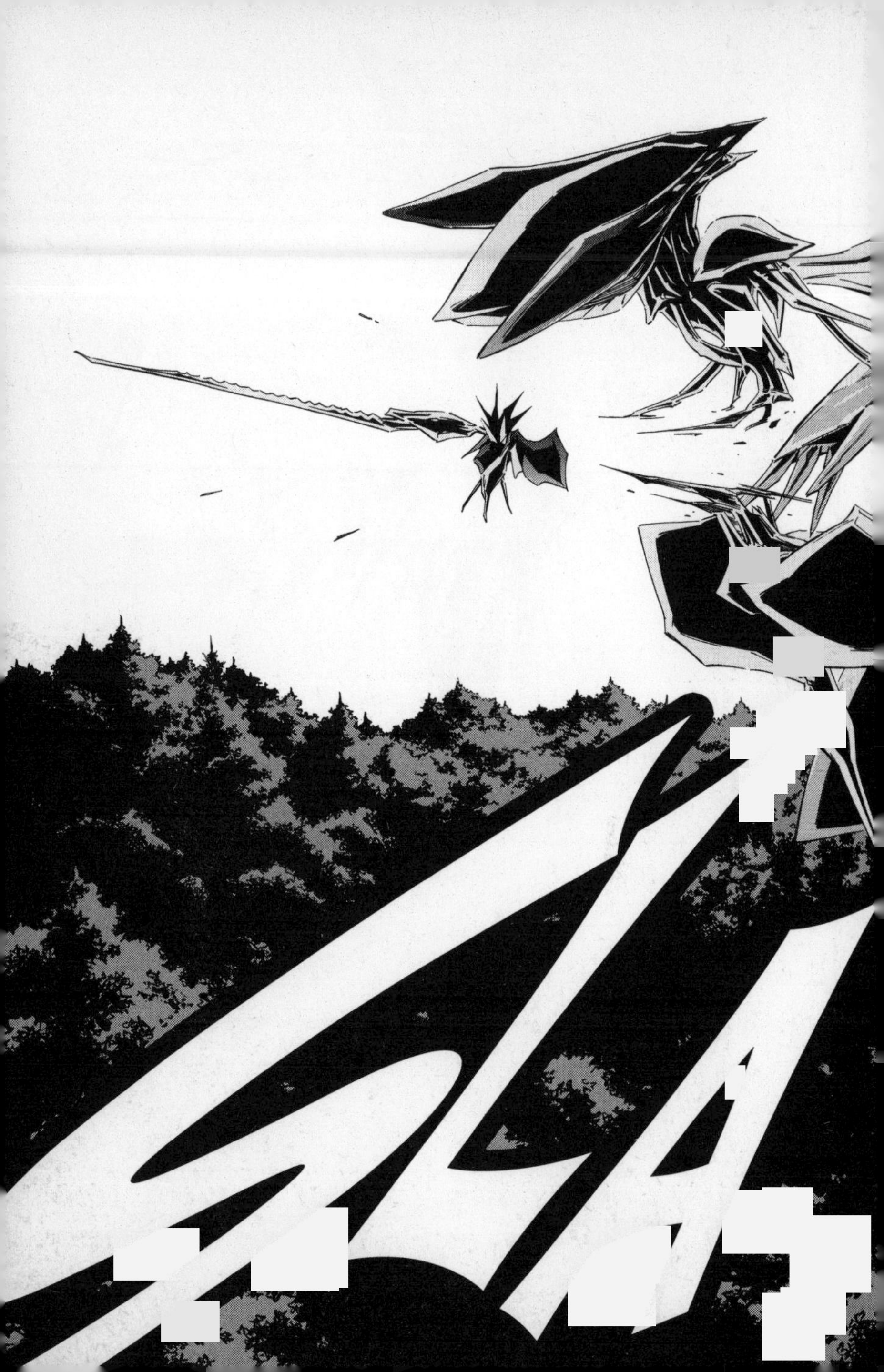

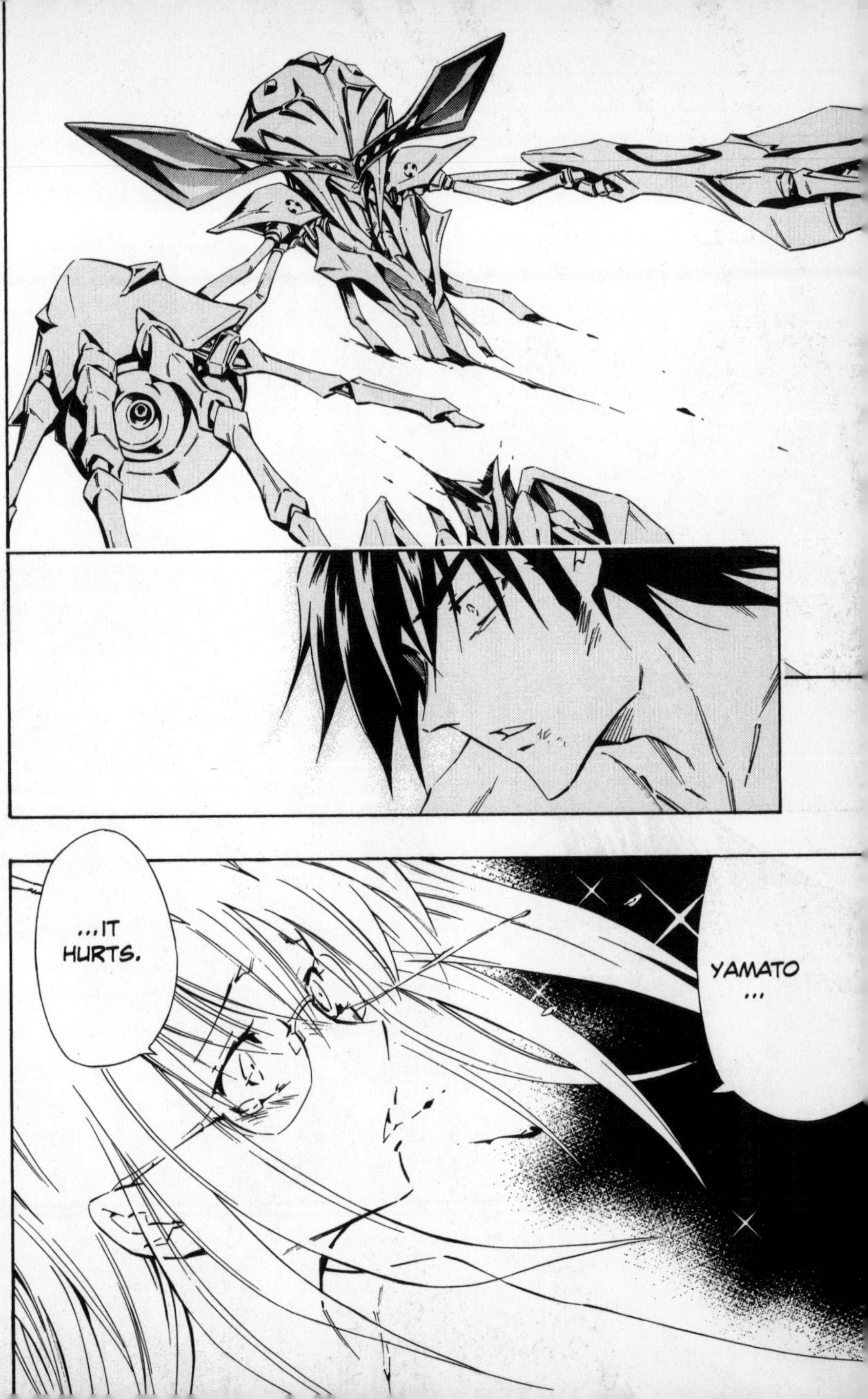
YAMATO ...
...IT HURTS.

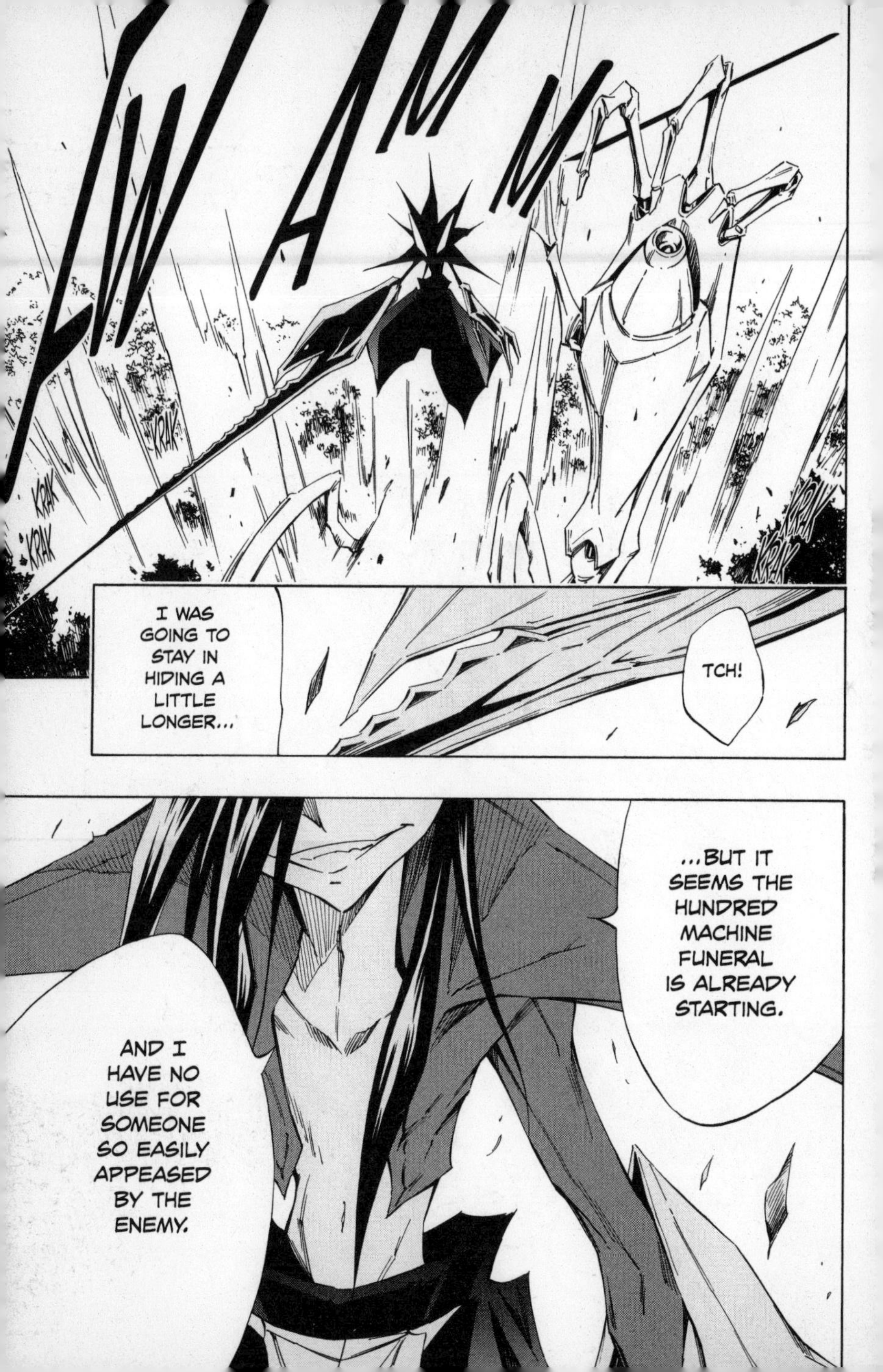
FWAMM
KRAK KRAK
KRAK
KRAK
KRAK
TCH!
I WAS GOING TO STAY IN HIDING A LITTLE LONGER...
...BUT IT SEEMS THE HUNDRED MACHINE FUNERAL IS ALREADY STARTING.
AND I HAVE NO USE FOR SOMEONE SO EASILY APPEASED BY THE ENEMY.

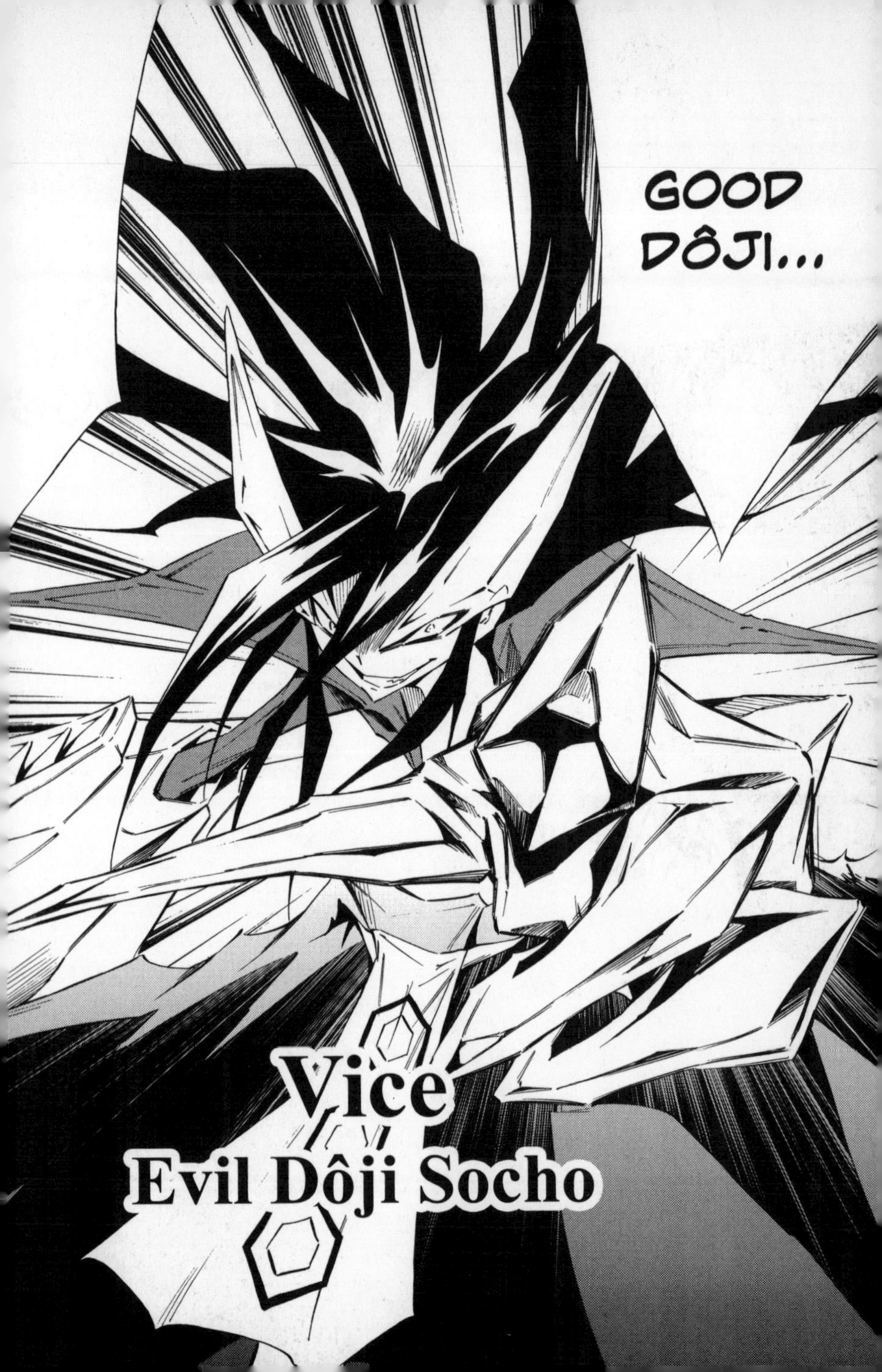
GOOD DÔJI...
Vice
Evil Dôji Socho

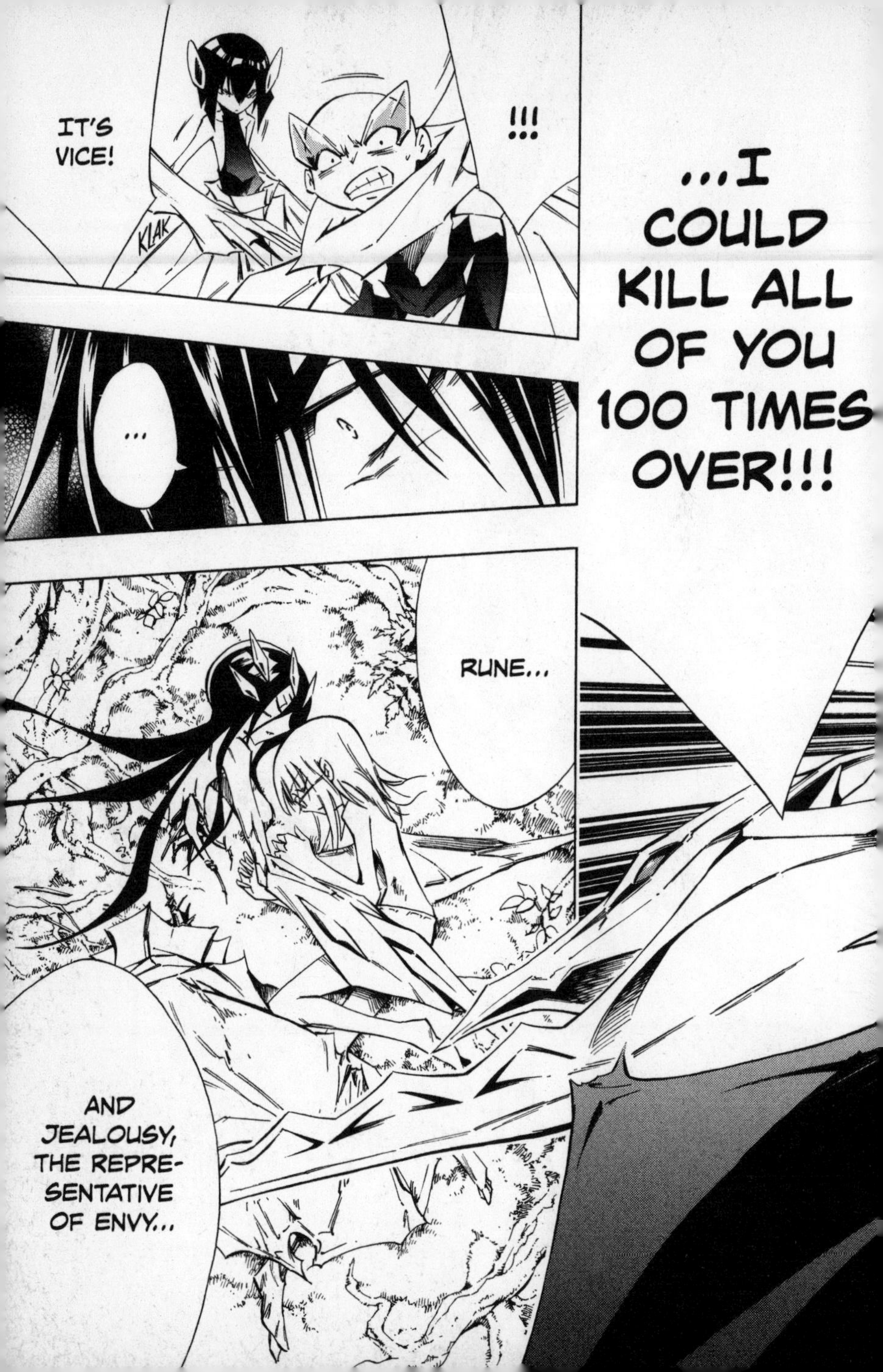
...I COULD KILL ALL OF YOU 100 TIMES OVER!!!
!!!
IT'S VICE!
KLAK
...
RUNE...
AND JEALOUSY, THE REPRE-SENTATIVE OF ENVY...

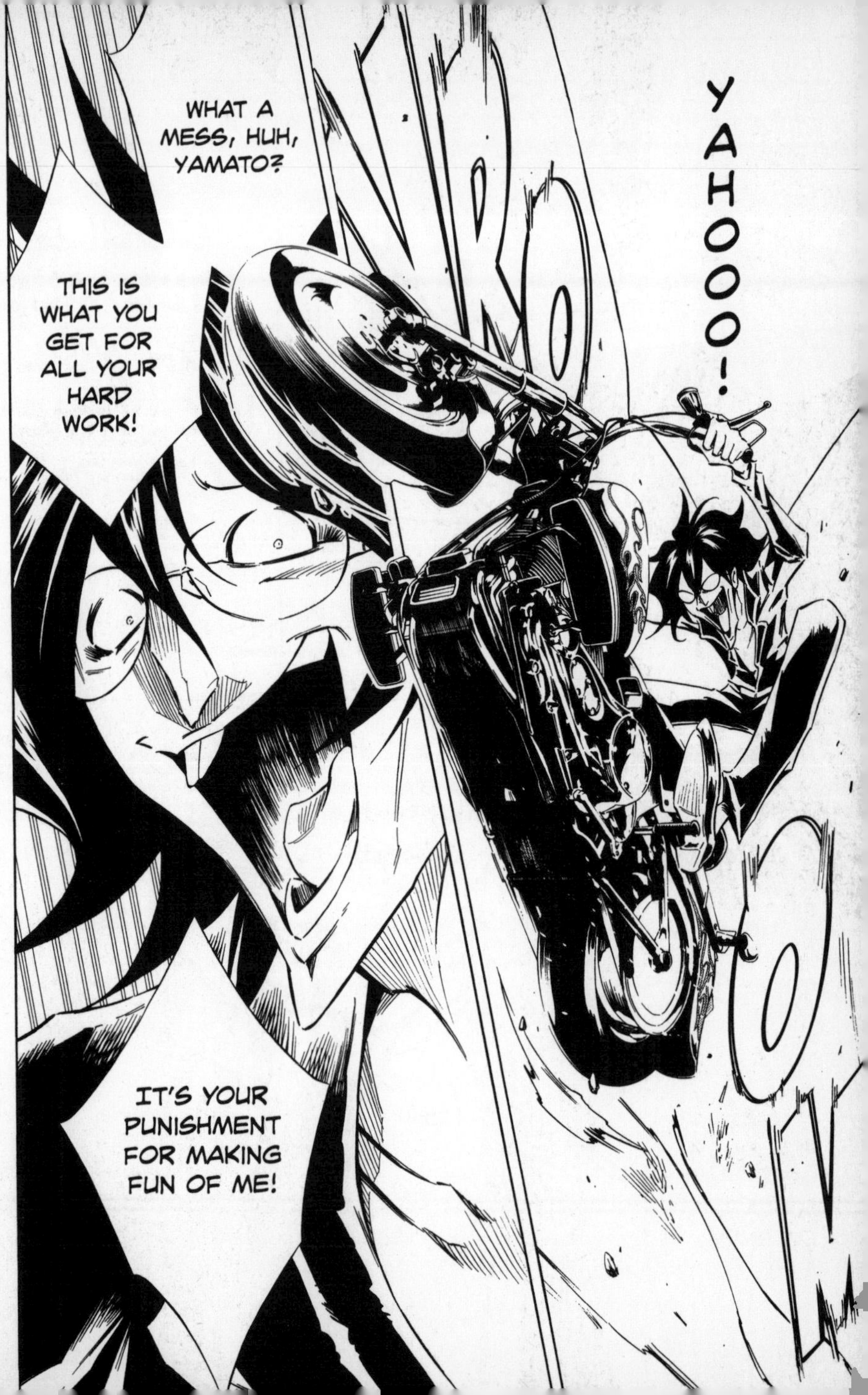
YAHOOOO!
WHAT A MESS, HUH, YAMATO?
THIS IS WHAT YOU GET FOR ALL YOUR HARD WORK!
IT'S YOUR PUNISHMENT FOR MAKING FUN OF ME!

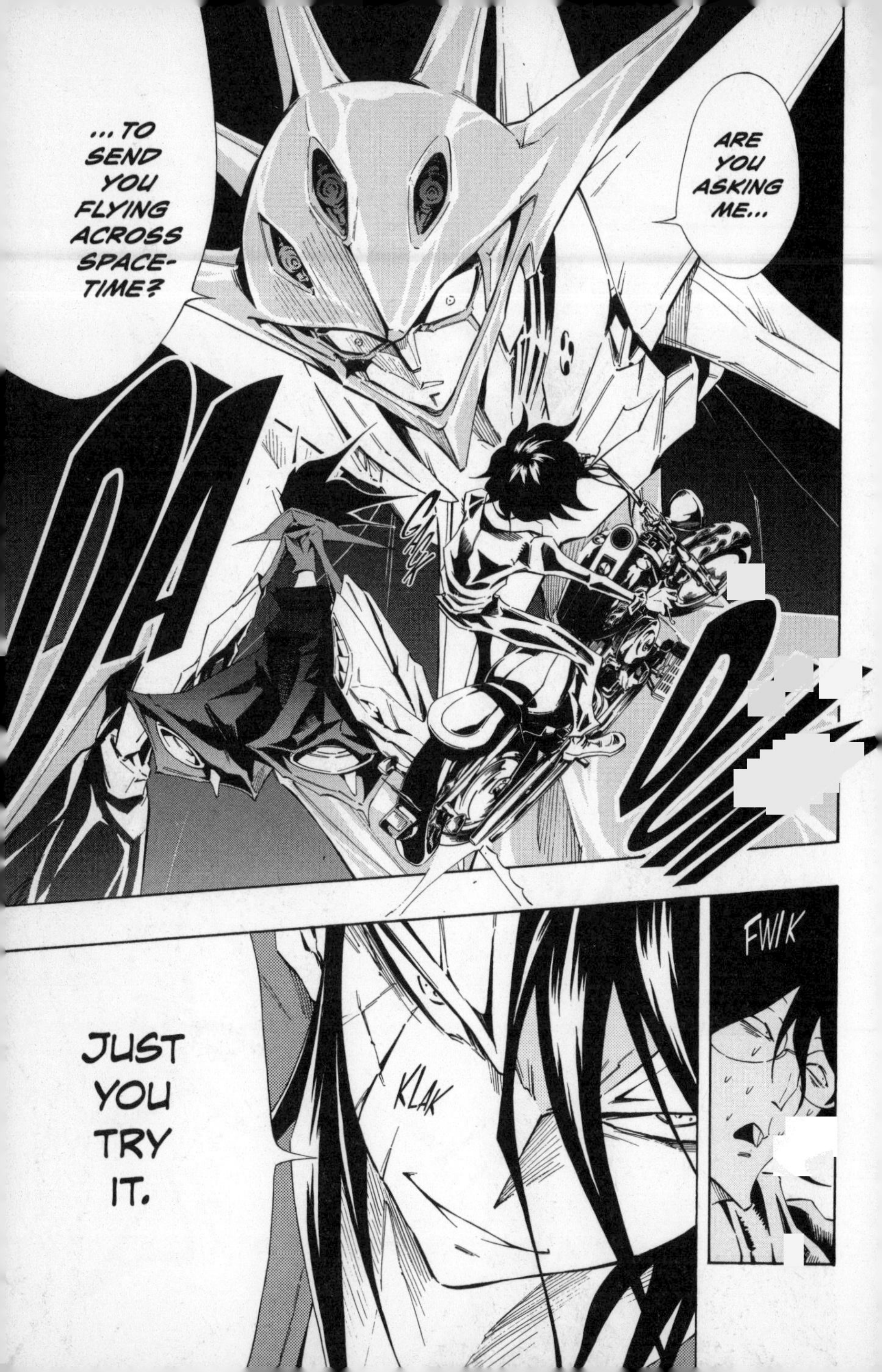
ARE YOU ASKING ME...
...TO SEND YOU FLYING ACROSS SPACE-TIME?
FWIK
KLAK
JUST YOU TRY IT.

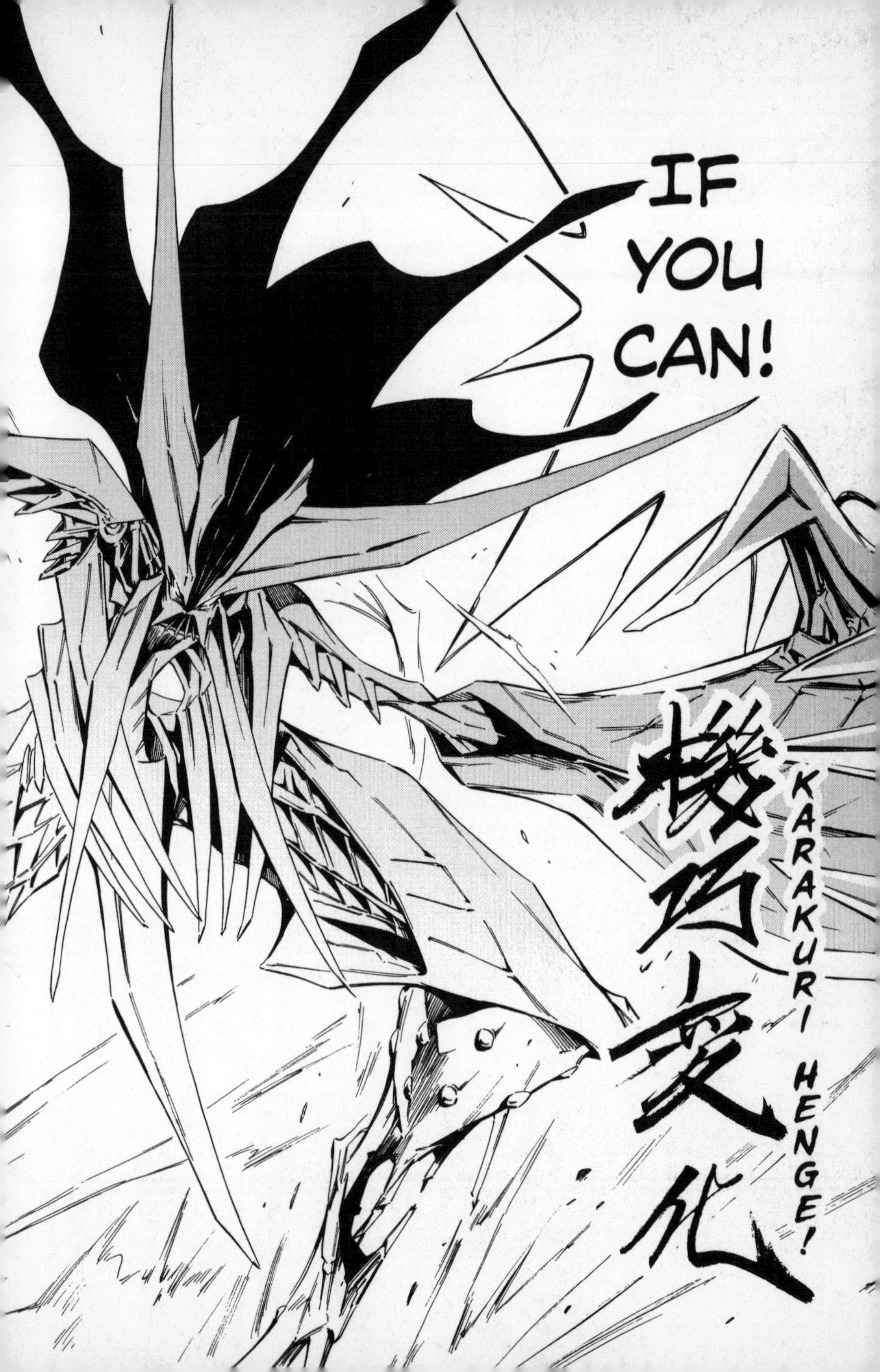
IF YOU CAN!
機巧変化
KARAKURI HENGE!

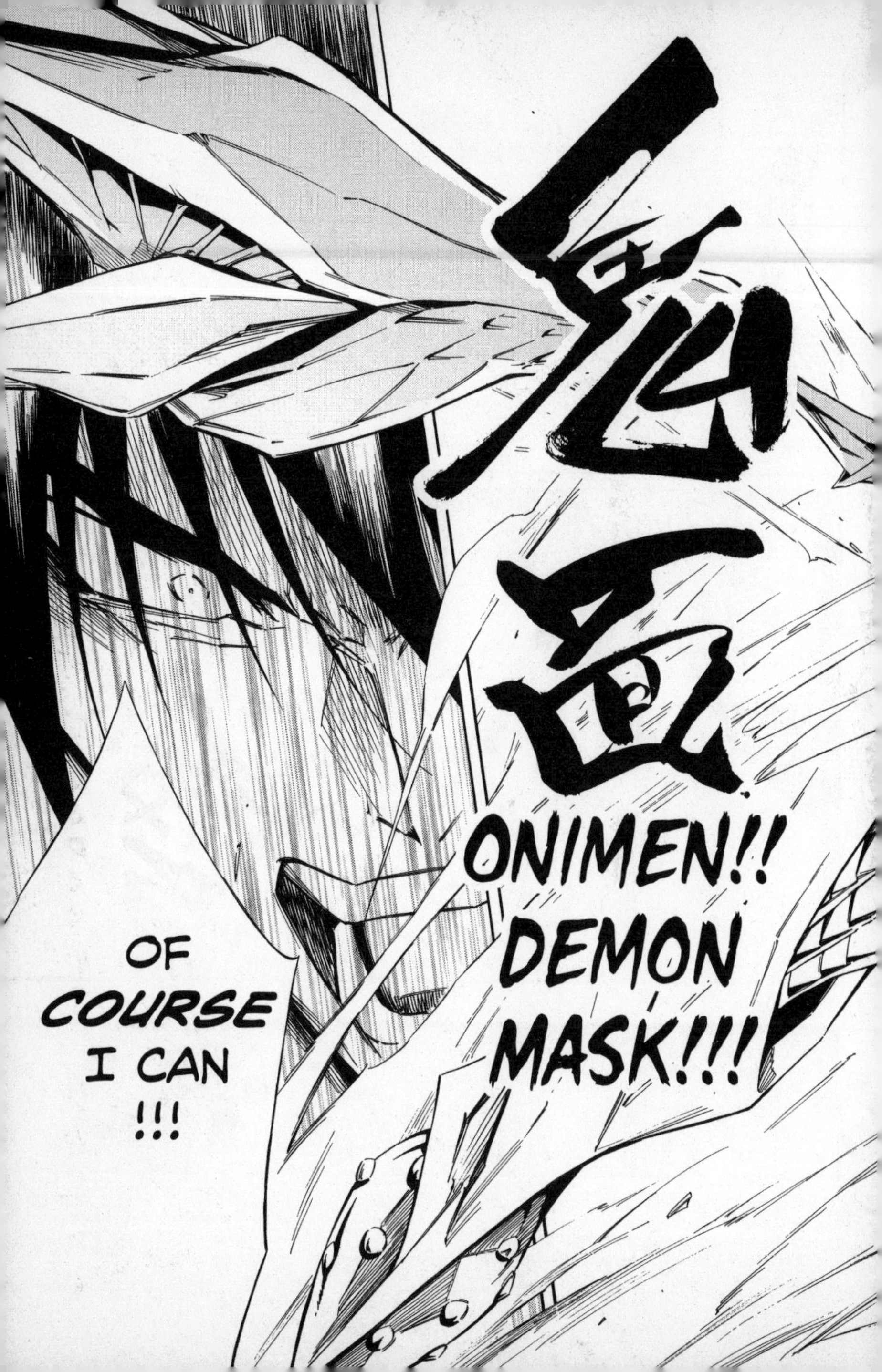
鬼面
ONIMEN!! DEMON MASK!!!
OF COURSE I CAN !!!

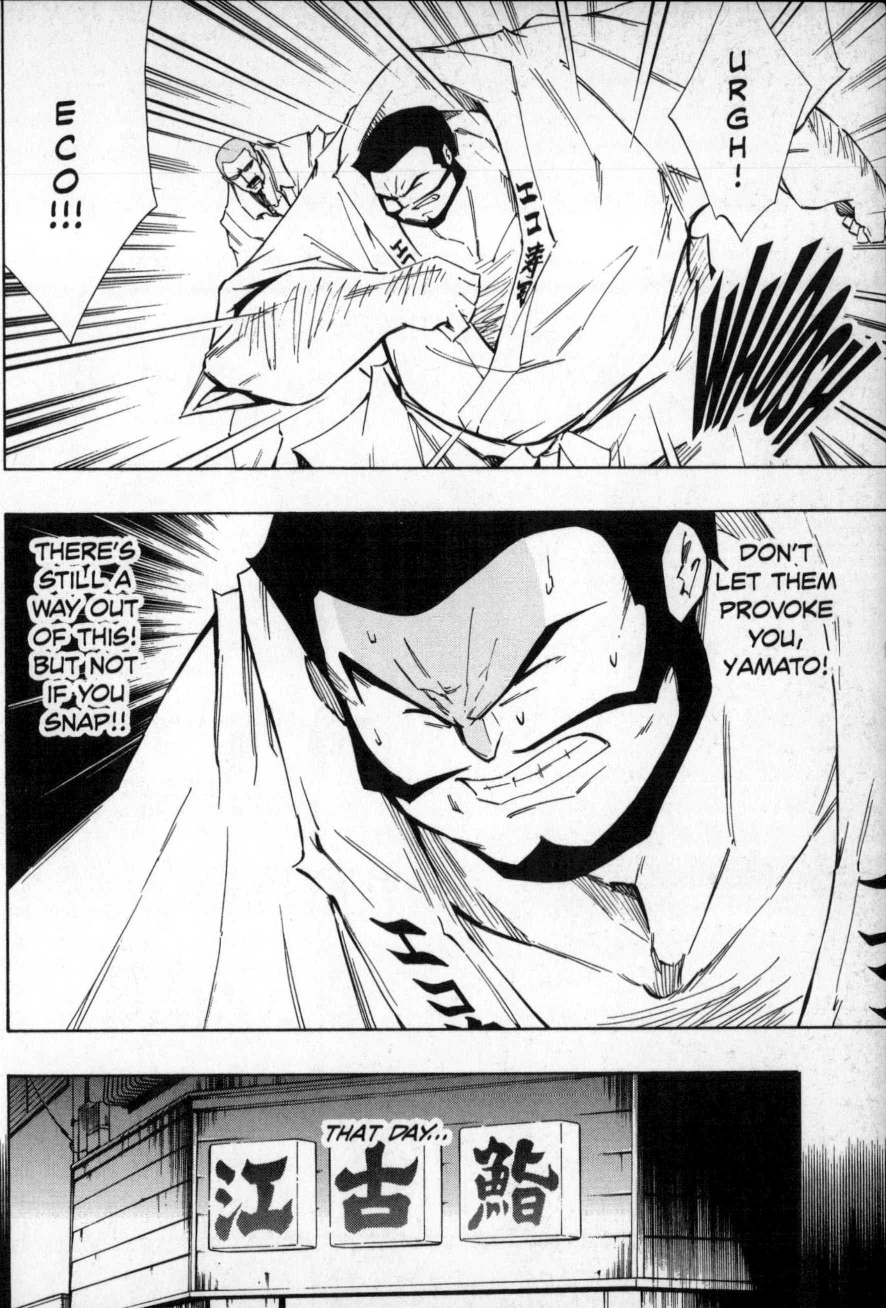
URGH!
ECO!!!
DON'T LET THEM PROVOKE YOU, YAMATO!
THERE'S STILL A WAY OUT OF THIS! BUT NOT IF YOU SNAP!!
THAT DAY...
江古鮨
(ECO SUSHI)

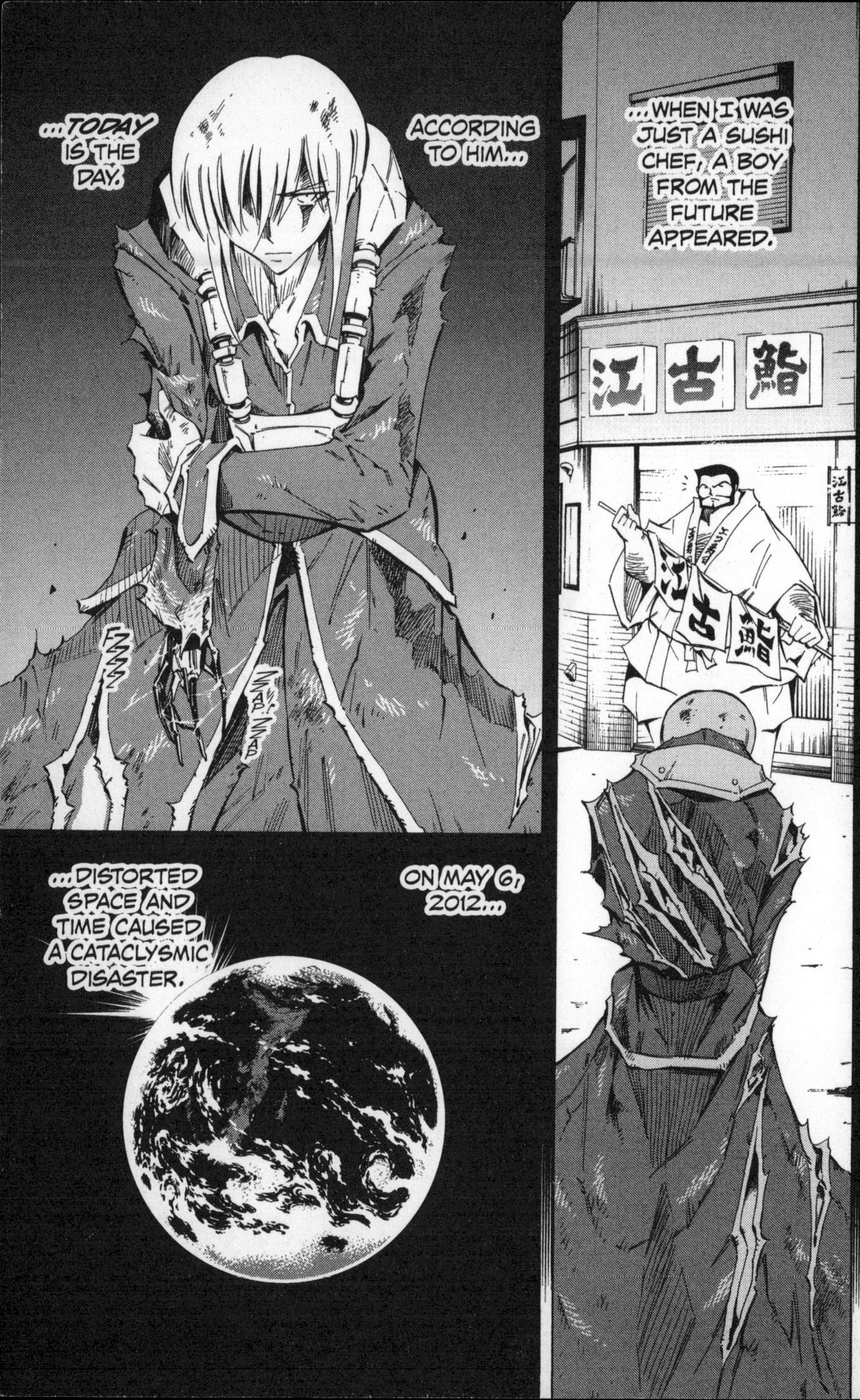
...WHEN I WAS JUST A SUSHI CHEF, A BOY FROM THE FUTURE APPEARED.
江古鮨
江古鮨
ACCORDING TO HIM...
...TODAY IS THE DAY.
FZZZ
ZAP! ZAP
ON MAY 6, 2012...
...DISTORTED SPACE AND TIME CAUSED A CATACLYSMIC DISASTER.

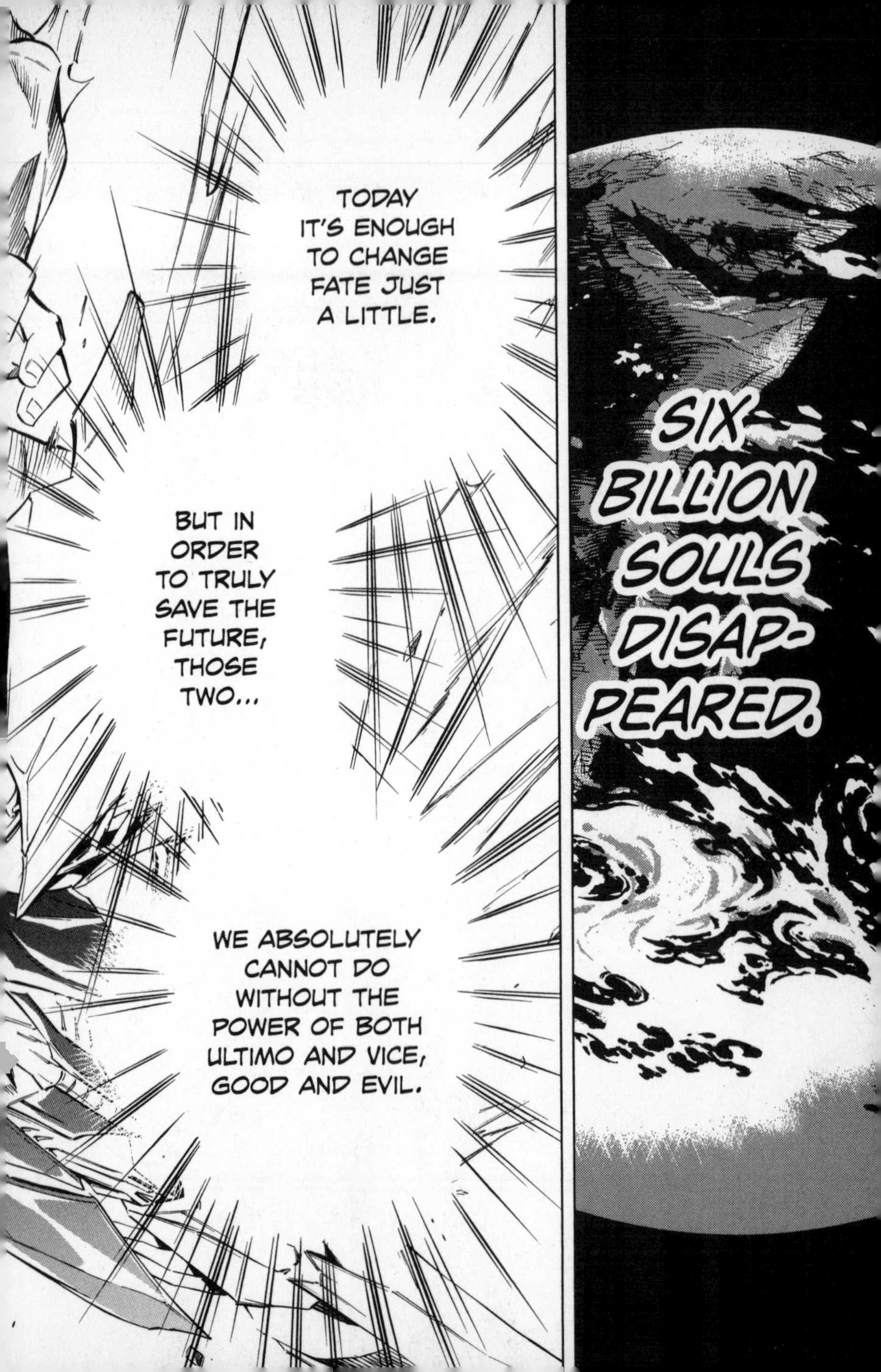
SIX BILLION SOULS DISAP-PEARED.
TODAY IT'S ENOUGH TO CHANGE FATE JUST A LITTLE.
BUT IN ORDER TO TRULY SAVE THE FUTURE, THOSE TWO...
WE ABSOLUTELY CANNOT DO WITHOUT THE POWER OF BOTH ULTIMO AND VICE, GOOD AND EVIL.

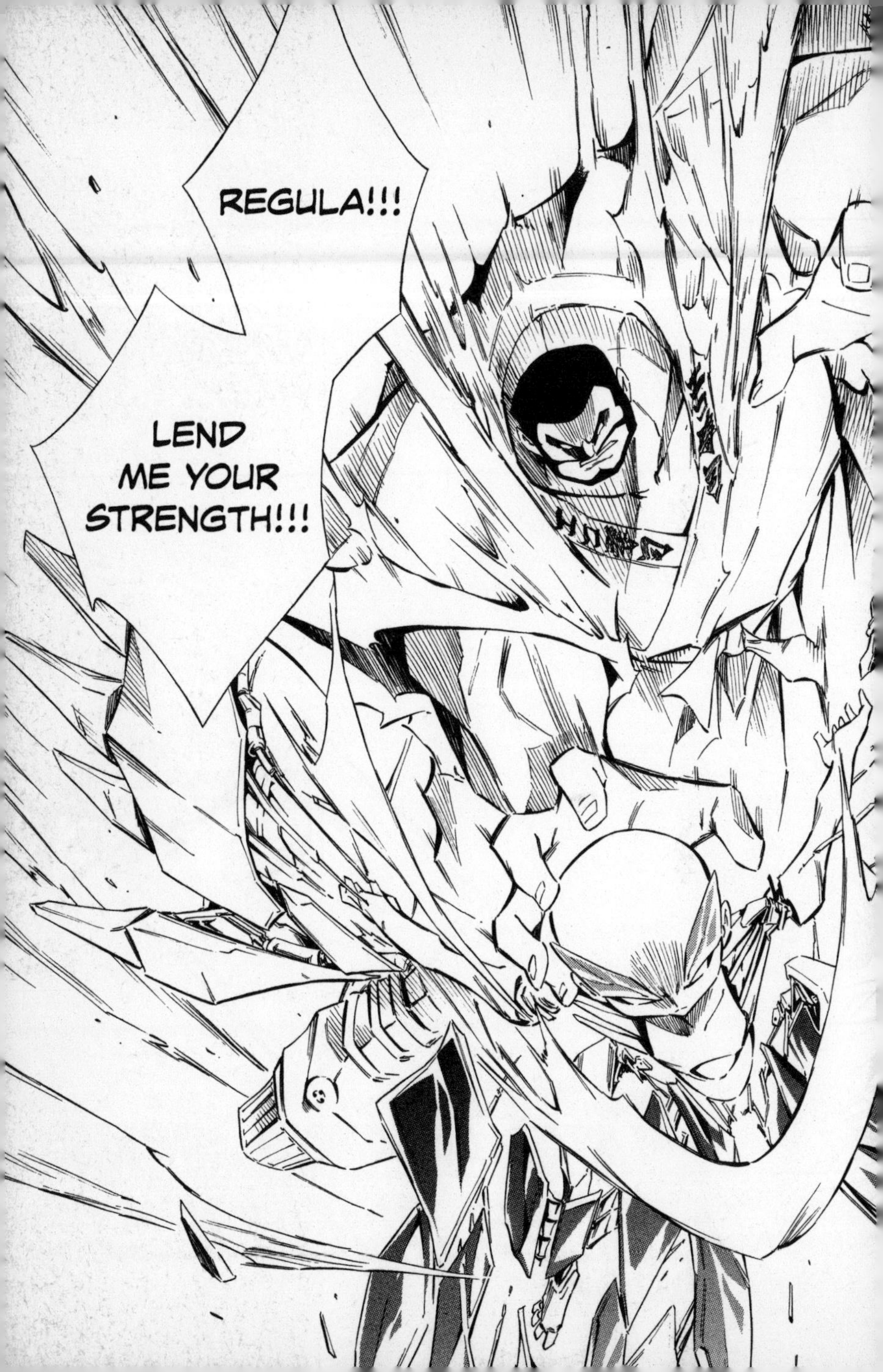
REGULA!!!
LEND ME YOUR STRENGTH!!!

KARAKURIDÔJI
ULTIMO

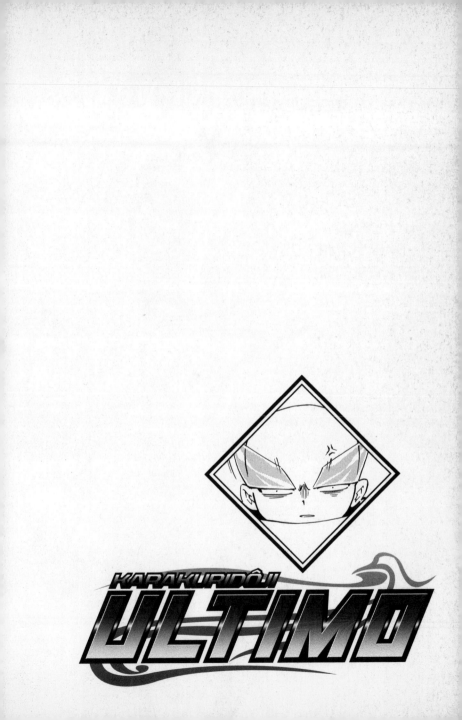

ACT 12
WORLD ANNIHILATIÓN

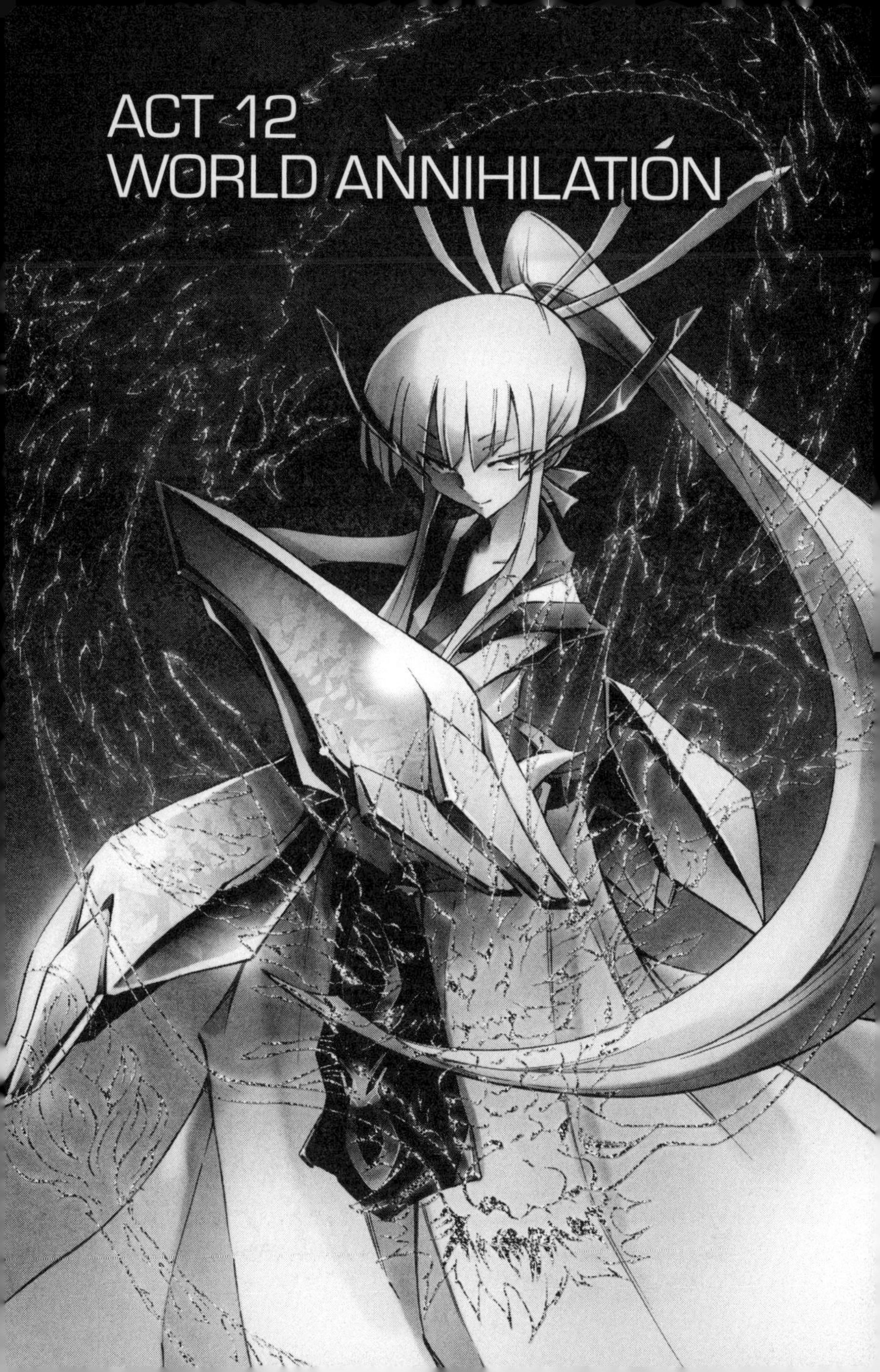

KARAKURIDÔJI
ULTIMO

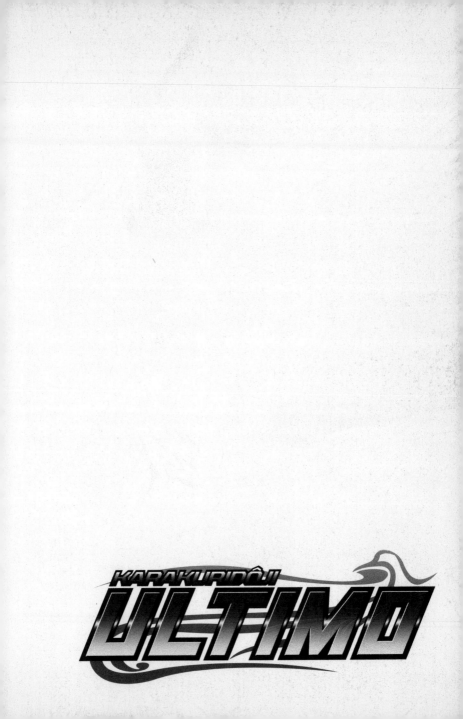

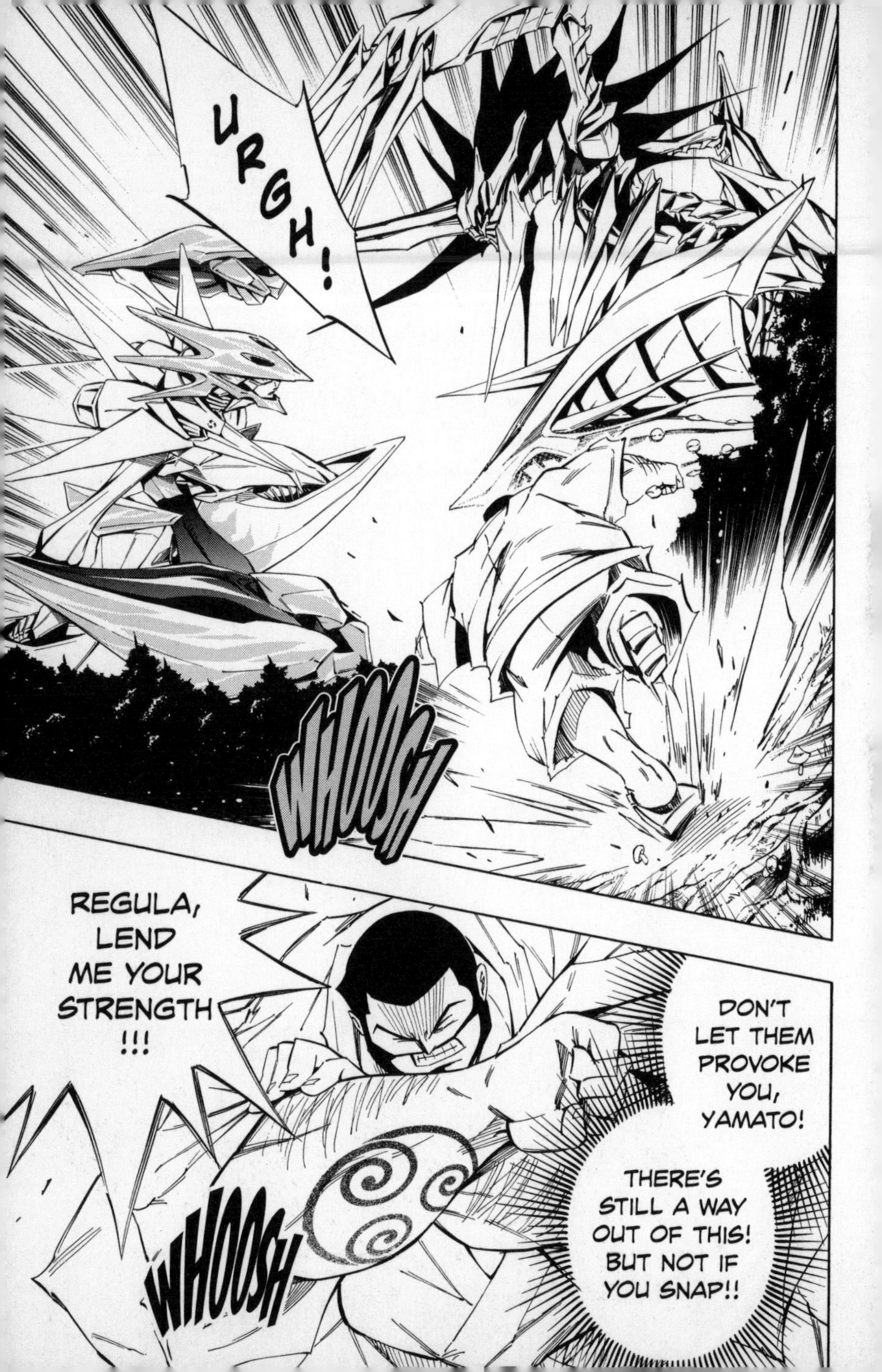
URGH!
WHOOSH
DON'T LET THEM PROVOKE YOU, YAMATO!
THERE'S STILL A WAY OUT OF THIS! BUT NOT IF YOU SNAP!!
REGULA, LEND ME YOUR STRENGTH!!!
WHOOSH

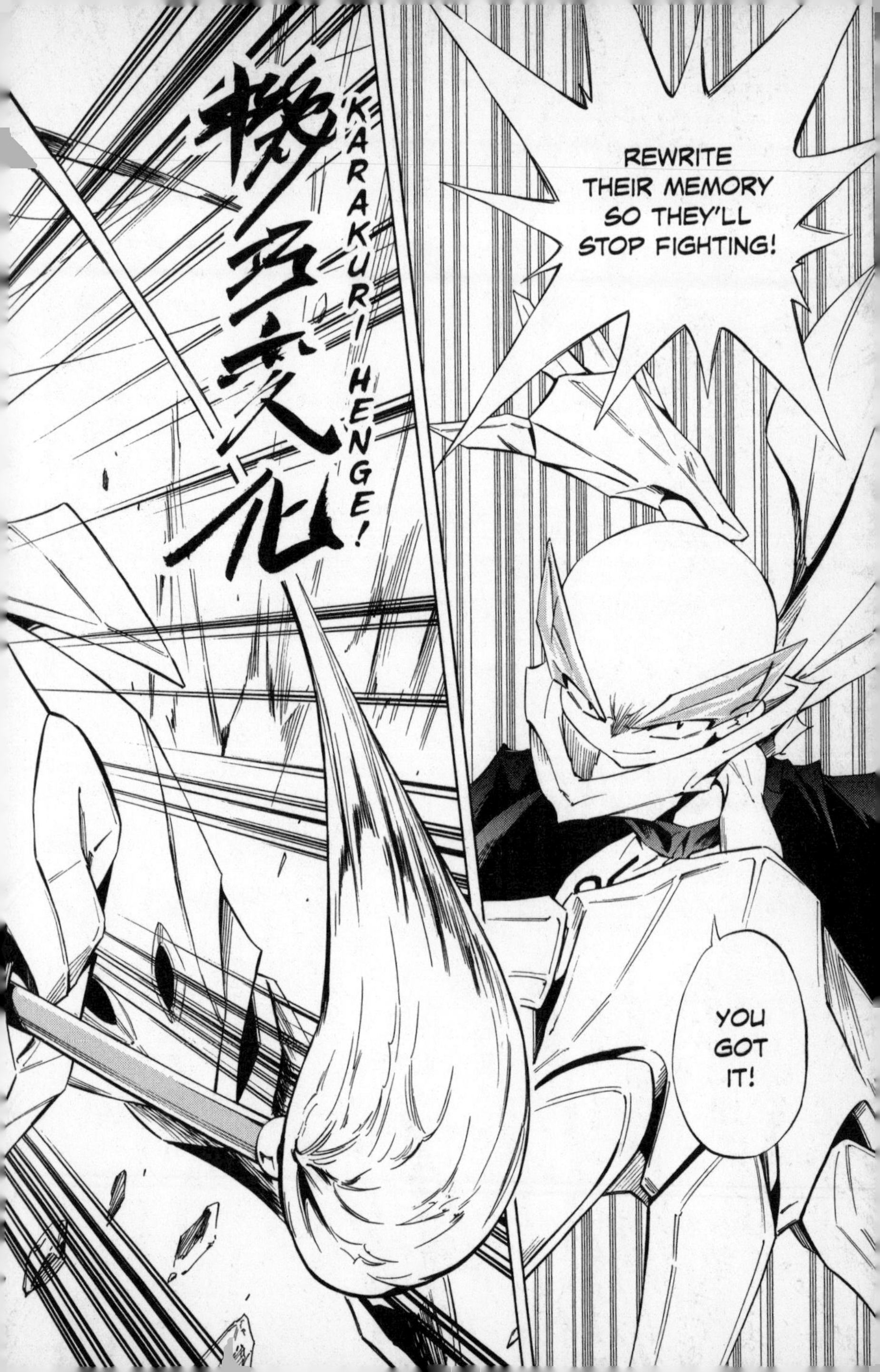
REWRITE THEIR MEMORY SO THEY'LL STOP FIGHTING!
YOU GOT IT!
機巧変化
KARAKURI HENGE!

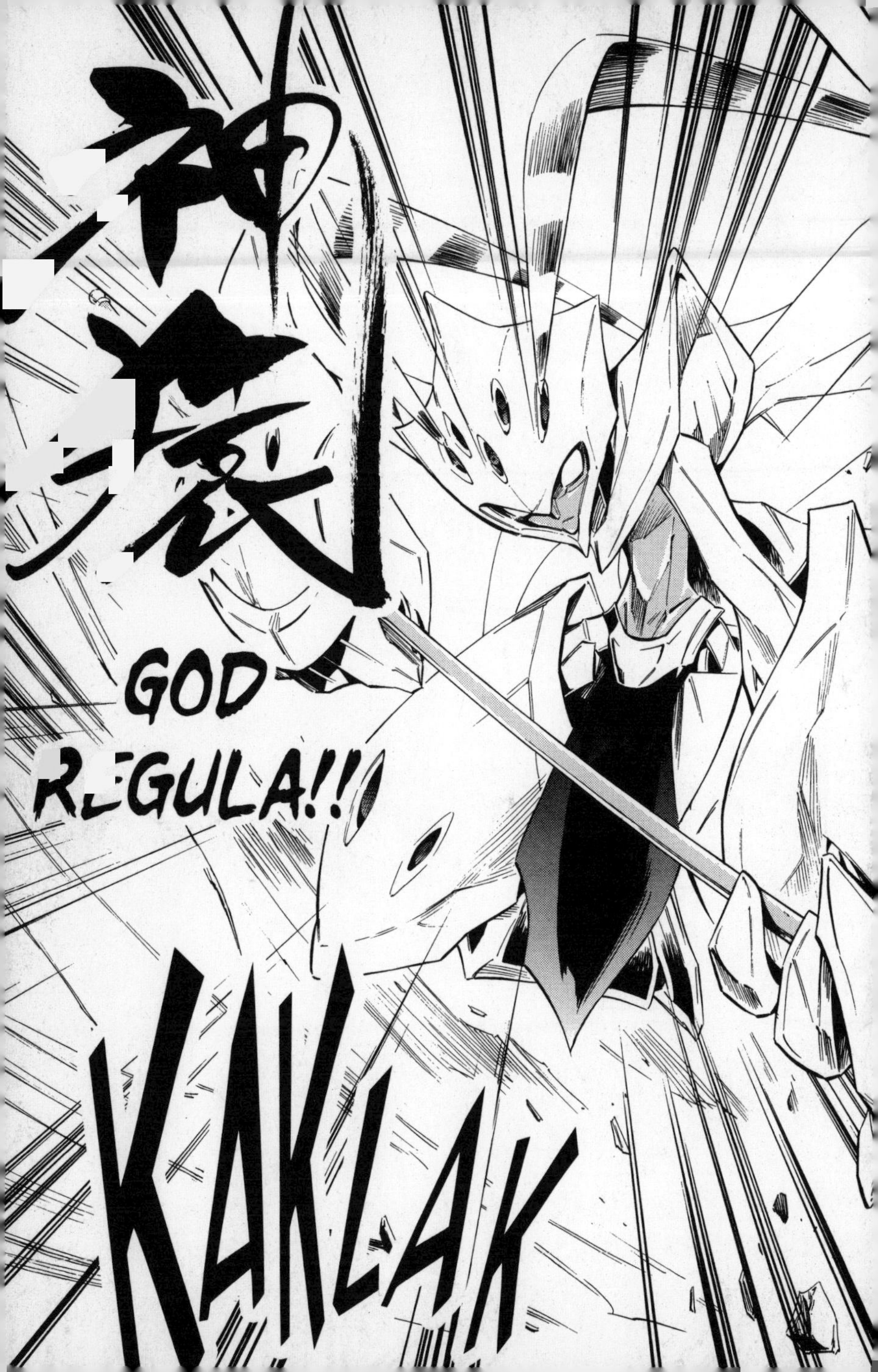
GOD
REGULA!!
KAKLAK

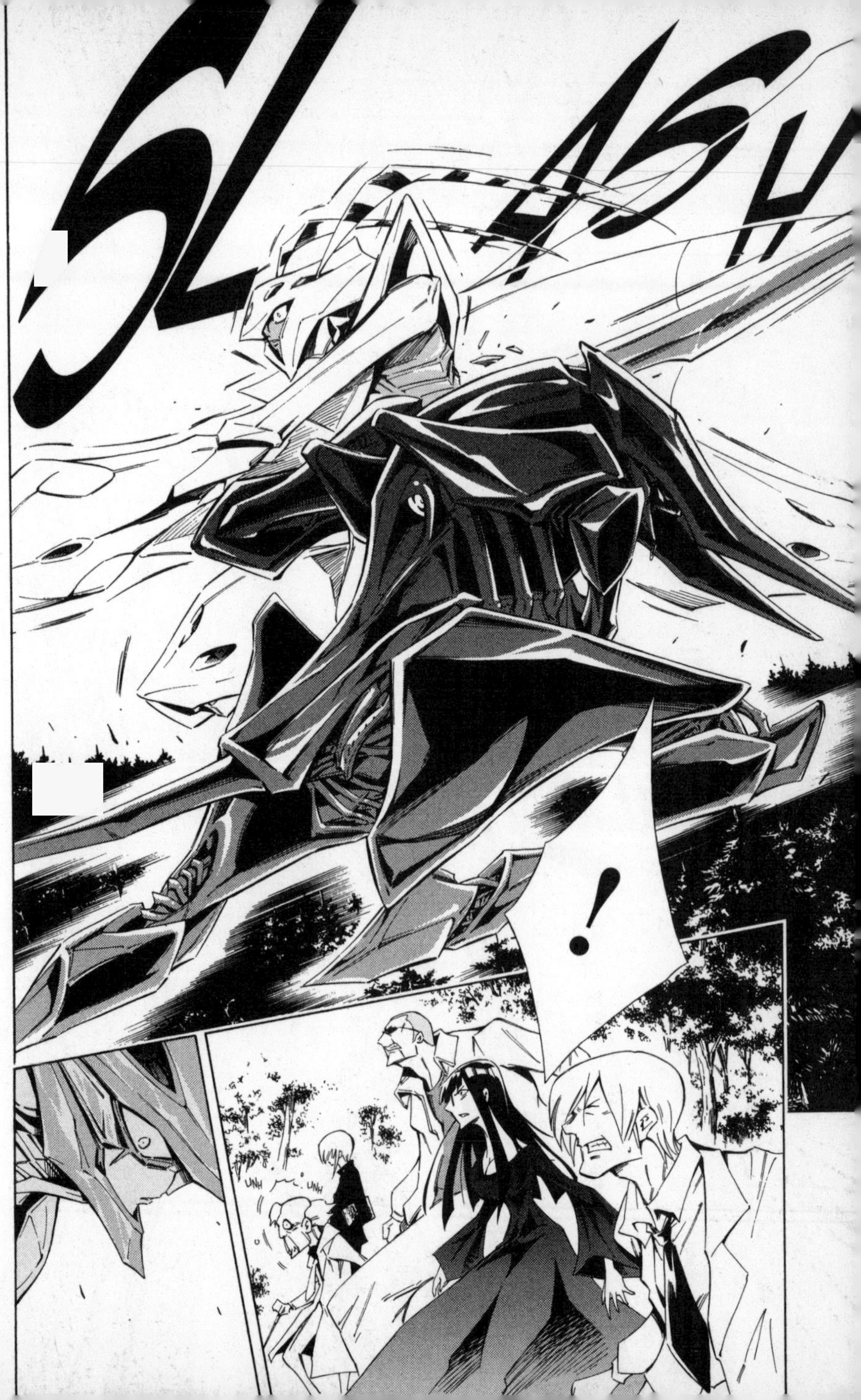
SLASH
!
UNH
UNH

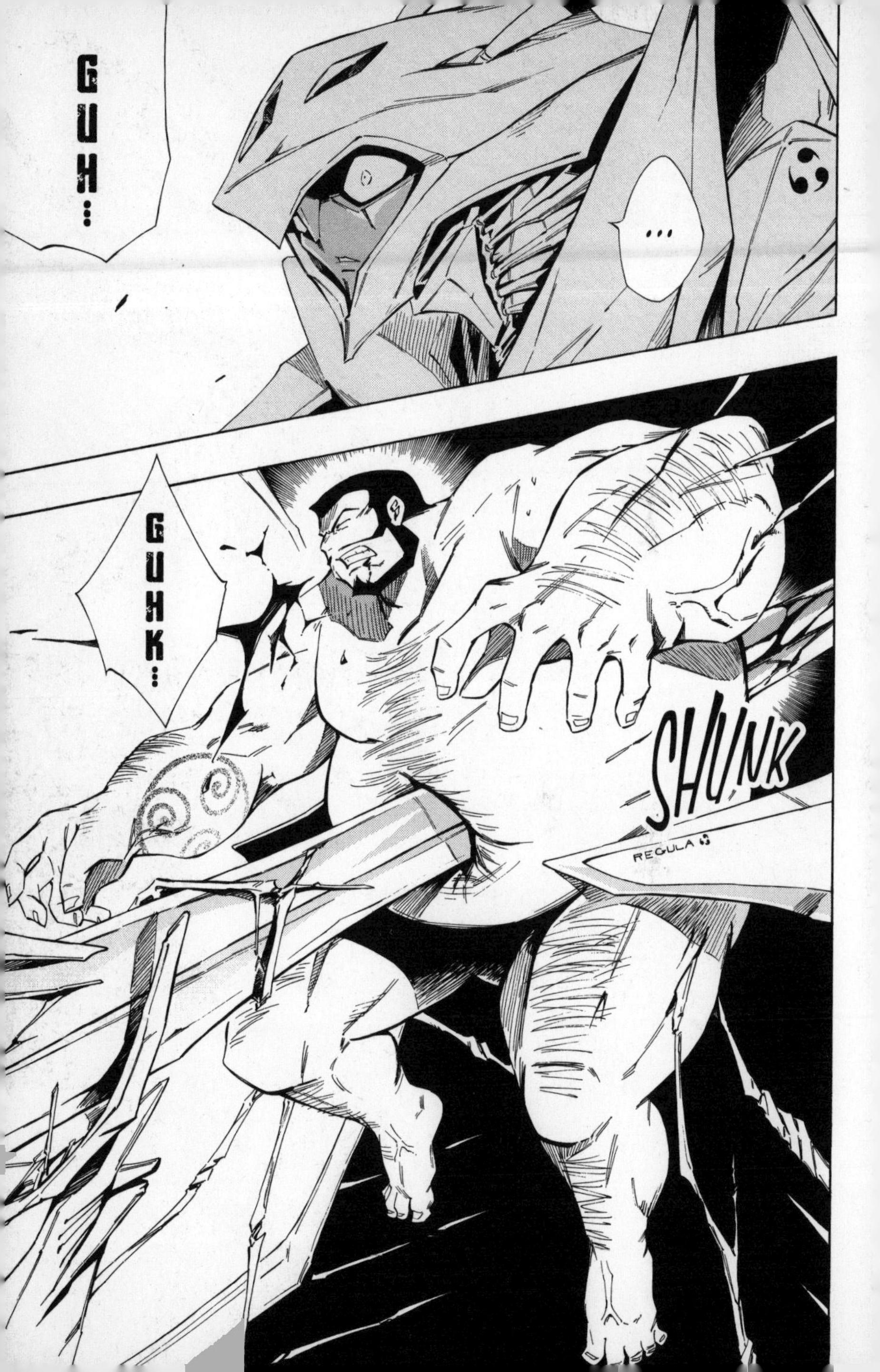
...
GUH..
GUHK..
SHUNK
REGULA

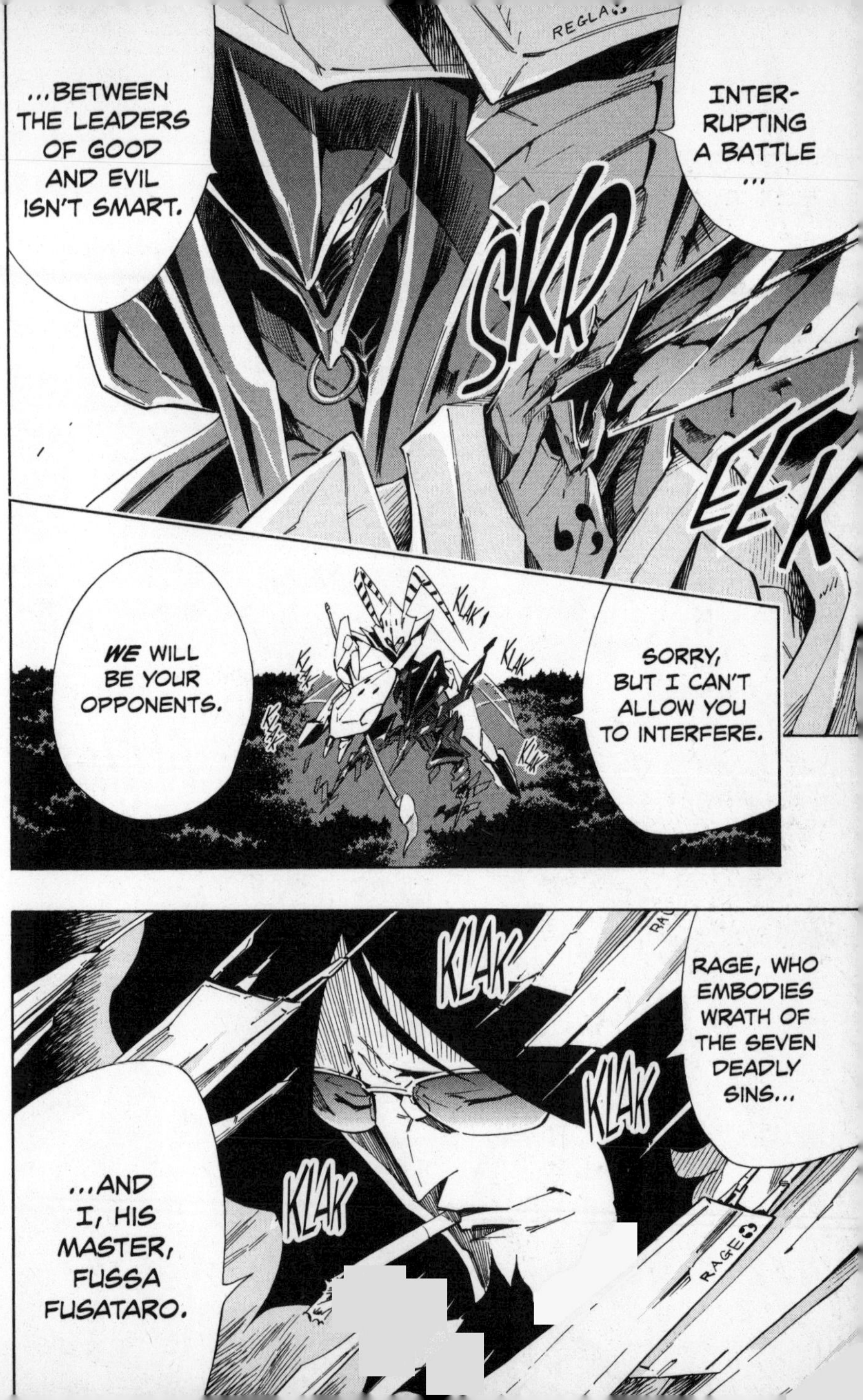
REGLA
INTER-RUPTING A BATTLE ...
SKR
EEEK
...BETWEEN THE LEADERS OF GOOD AND EVIL ISN'T SMART.
SORRY, BUT I CAN'T ALLOW YOU TO INTERFERE.
KLAK
KLAK
KLAK
KLAK
KLAK
KLAK
WE WILL BE YOUR OPPONENTS.
KLAK
RAGE, WHO EMBODIES WRATH OF THE SEVEN DEADLY SINS...
KLAK
RAGE
KLAK
...AND I, HIS MASTER, FUSSA FUSATARO.

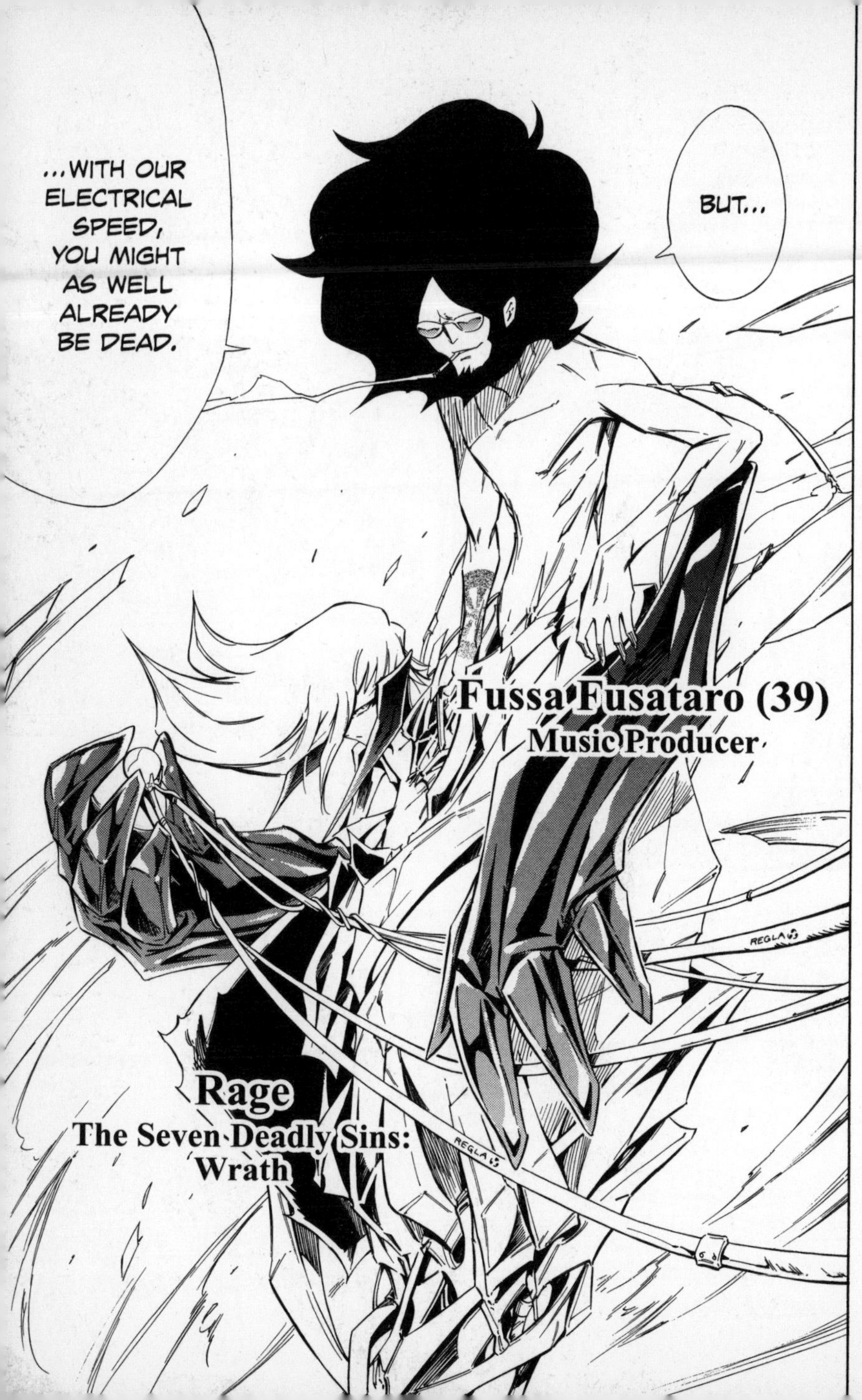
BUT...
...WITH OUR ELECTRICAL SPEED, YOU MIGHT AS WELL ALREADY BE DEAD.
Fussa Fusataro (39)
Music Producer
Rage
The Seven Deadly Sins: Wrath

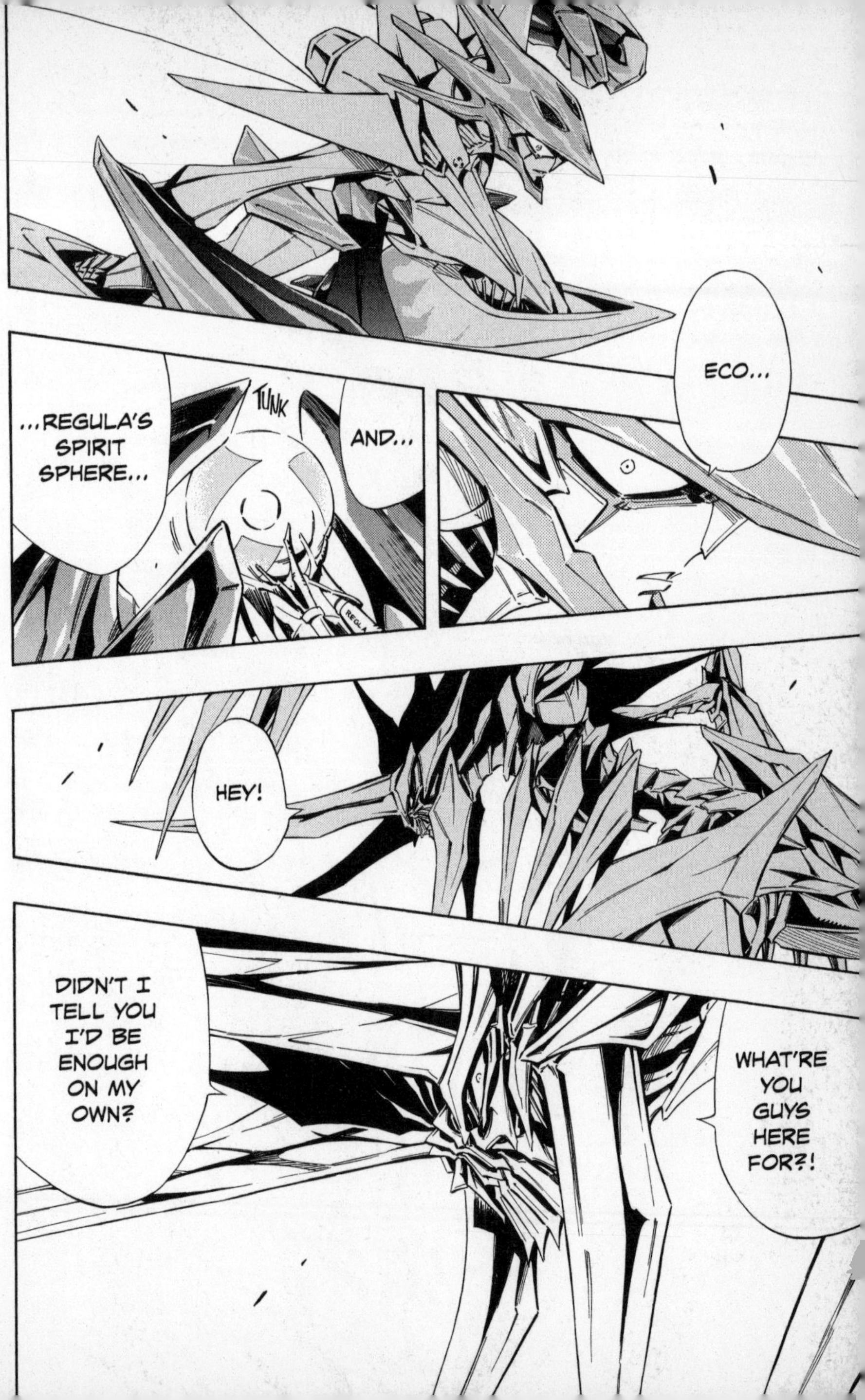
ECO...
AND...
TUNK
...REGULA'S SPIRIT SPHERE...
REGULA
HEY!
WHAT'RE YOU GUYS HERE FOR?!
DIDN'T I TELL YOU I'D BE ENOUGH ON MY OWN?

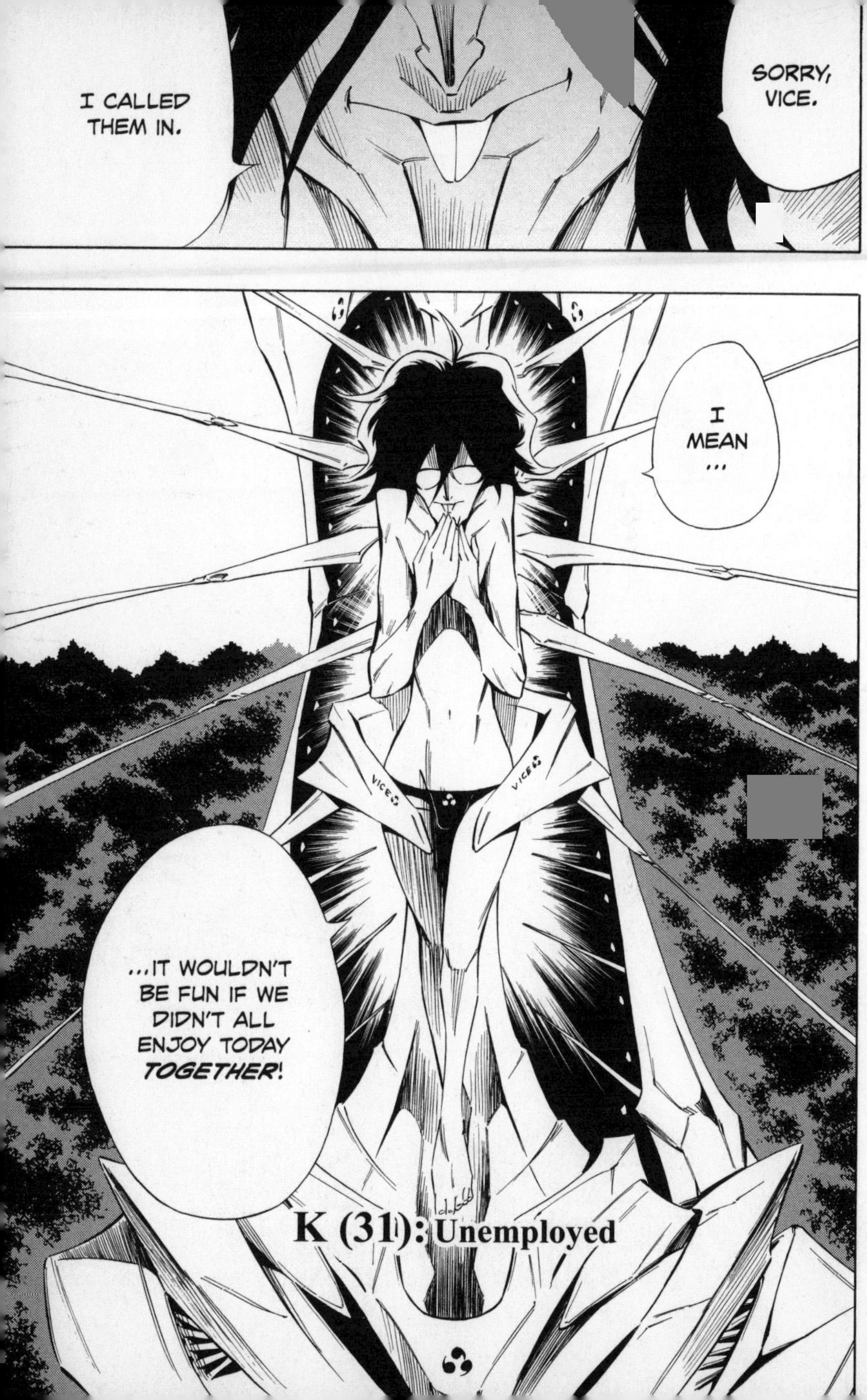
SORRY, VICE.
I CALLED THEM IN.
I MEAN...
...IT WOULDN'T BE FUN IF WE DIDN'T ALL ENJOY TODAY *TOGETHER*!
K (31): Unemployed

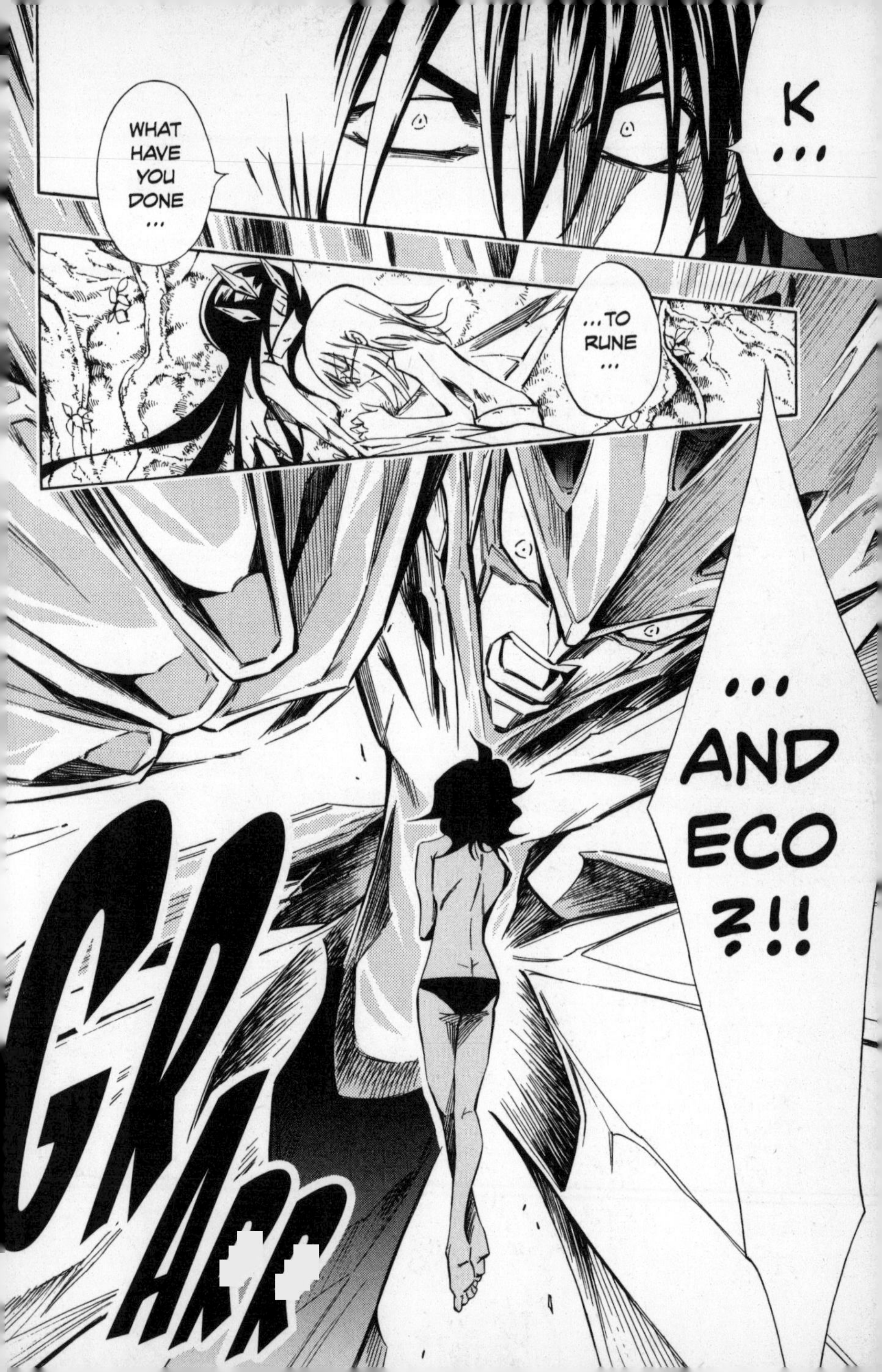
K...
WHAT HAVE YOU DONE...
...TO RUNE...
...AND ECO?!!

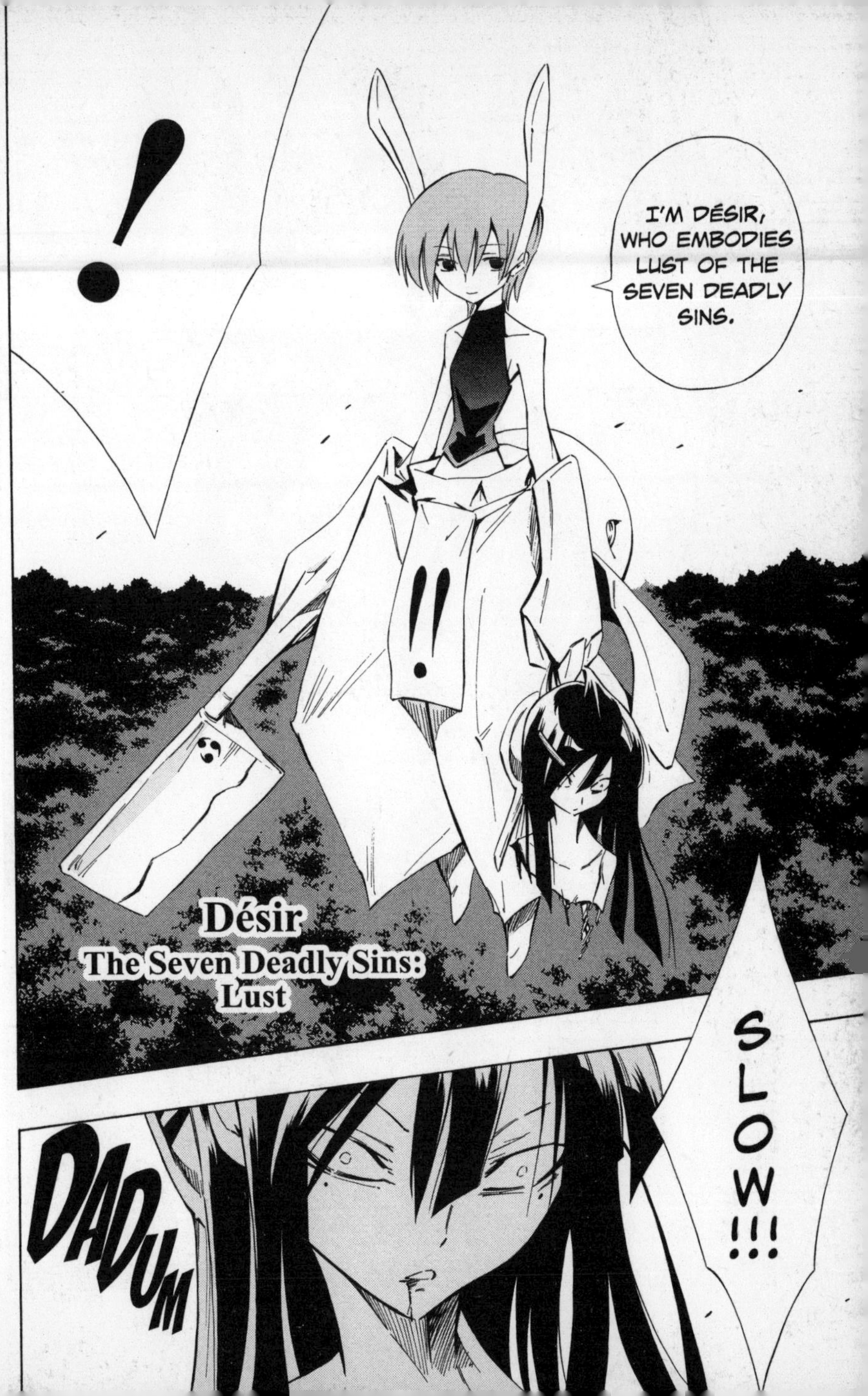
I'M DÉSIR, WHO EMBODIES LUST OF THE SEVEN DEADLY SINS.
!
!!
Désir
The Seven Deadly Sins: Lust
SLOW!!!
DADUM

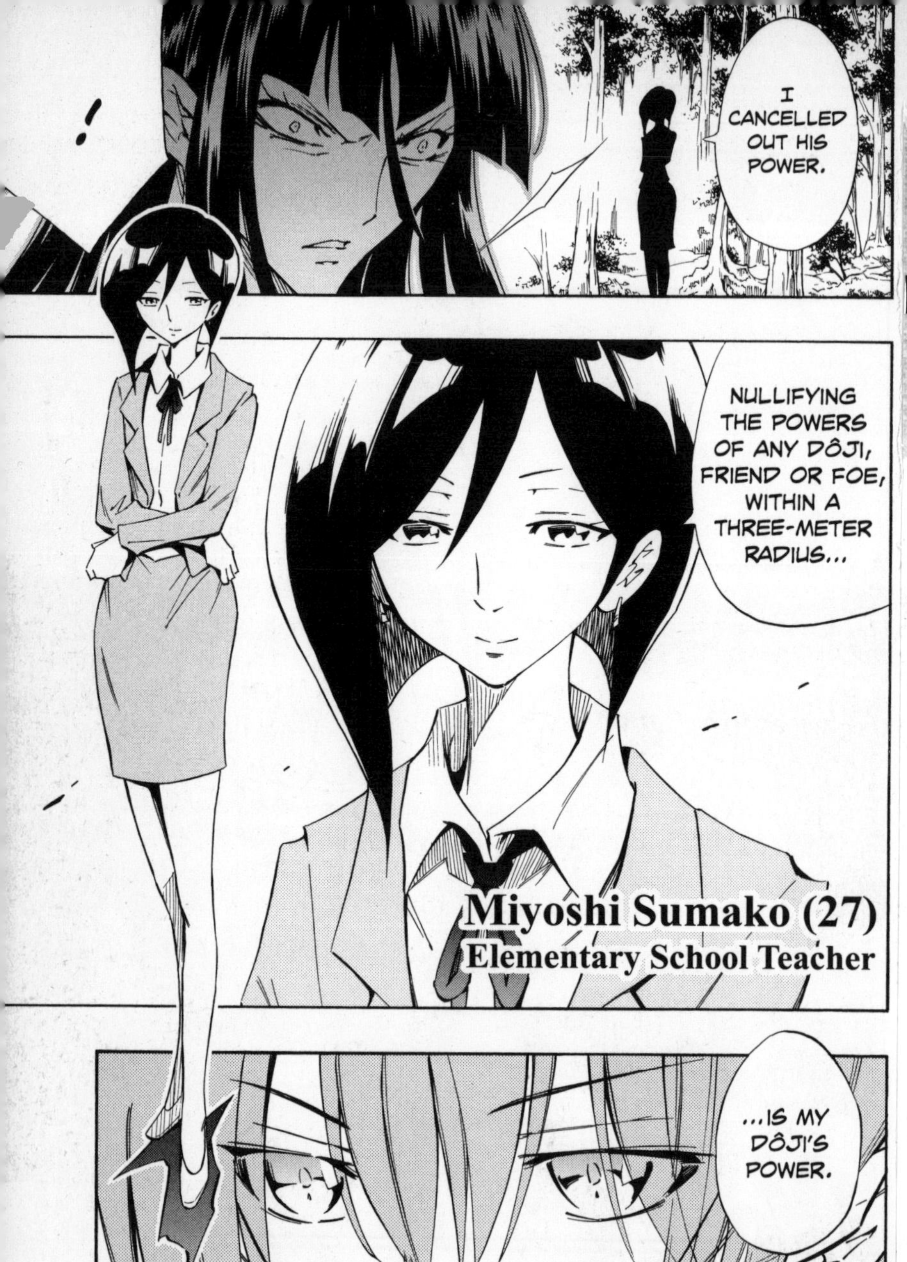
I CANCELLED OUT HIS POWER.
!
NULLIFYING THE POWERS OF ANY DÔJI, FRIEND OR FOE, WITHIN A THREE-METER RADIUS...
Miyoshi Sumako (27)
Elementary School Teacher
...IS MY DÔJI'S POWER.

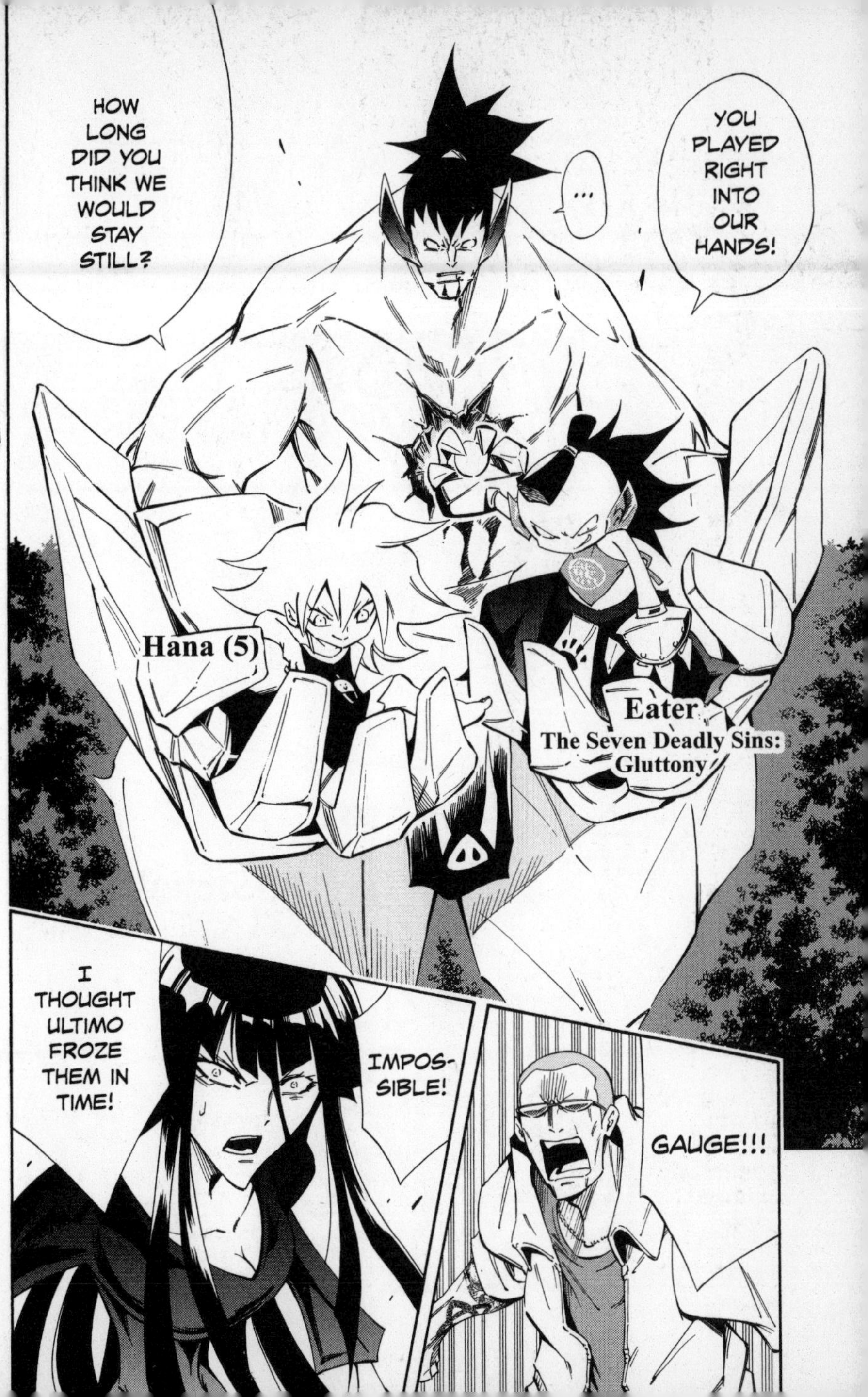
YOU PLAYED RIGHT INTO OUR HANDS!
...
HOW LONG DID YOU THINK WE WOULD STAY STILL?
Eater
The Seven Deadly Sins: Gluttony
Hana (5)
GAUGE!!!
IMPOSSIBLE!
I THOUGHT ULTIMO FROZE THEM IN TIME!

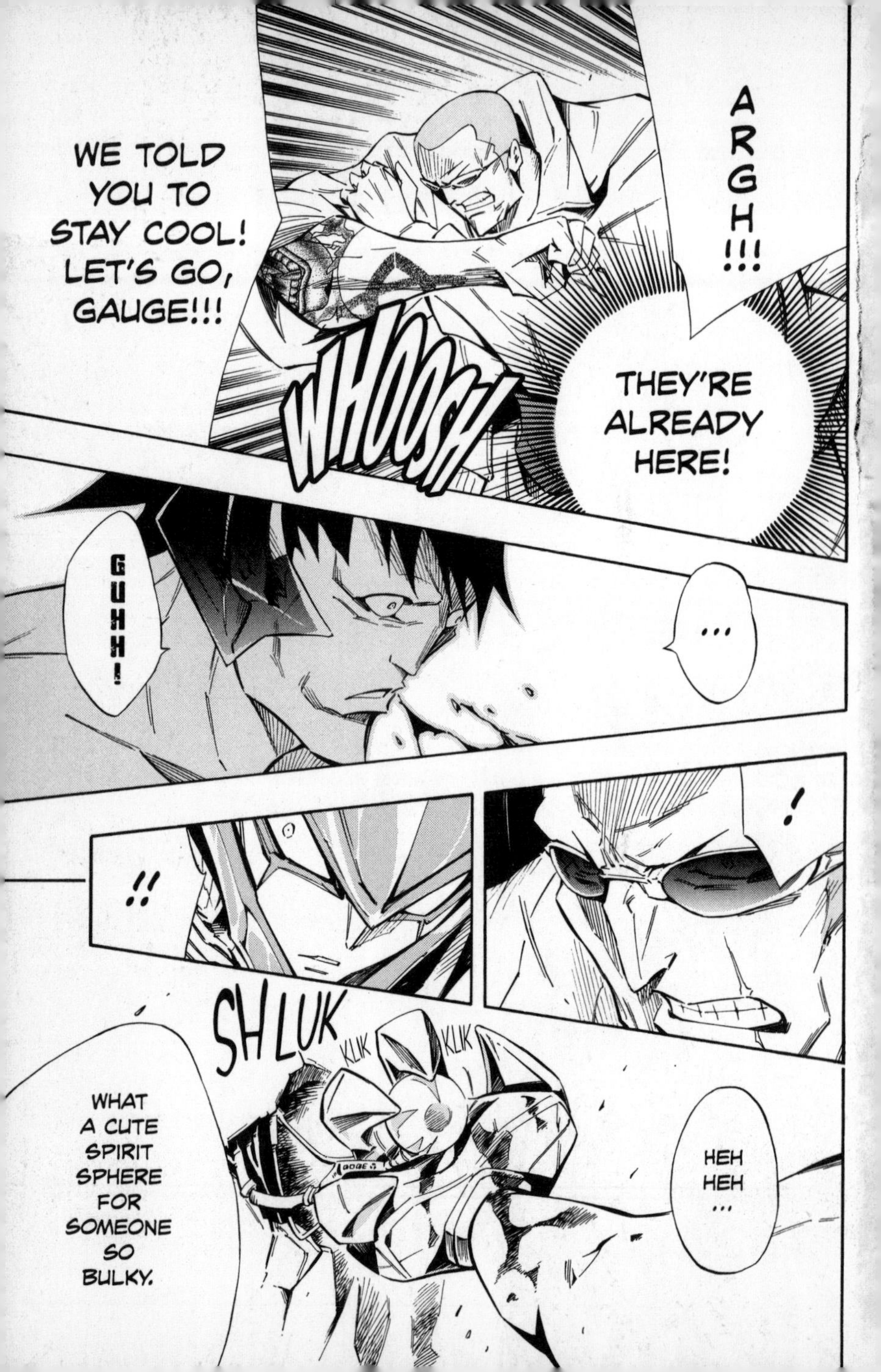
ARGH!!!
THEY'RE ALREADY HERE!
WE TOLD YOU TO STAY COOL! LET'S GO, GAUGE!!!
WHOOSH
...
GUHH!
!
!!
SHLUK
KLIK
KLIK
HEH HEH ...
WHAT A CUTE SPIRIT SPHERE FOR SOMEONE SO BULKY.

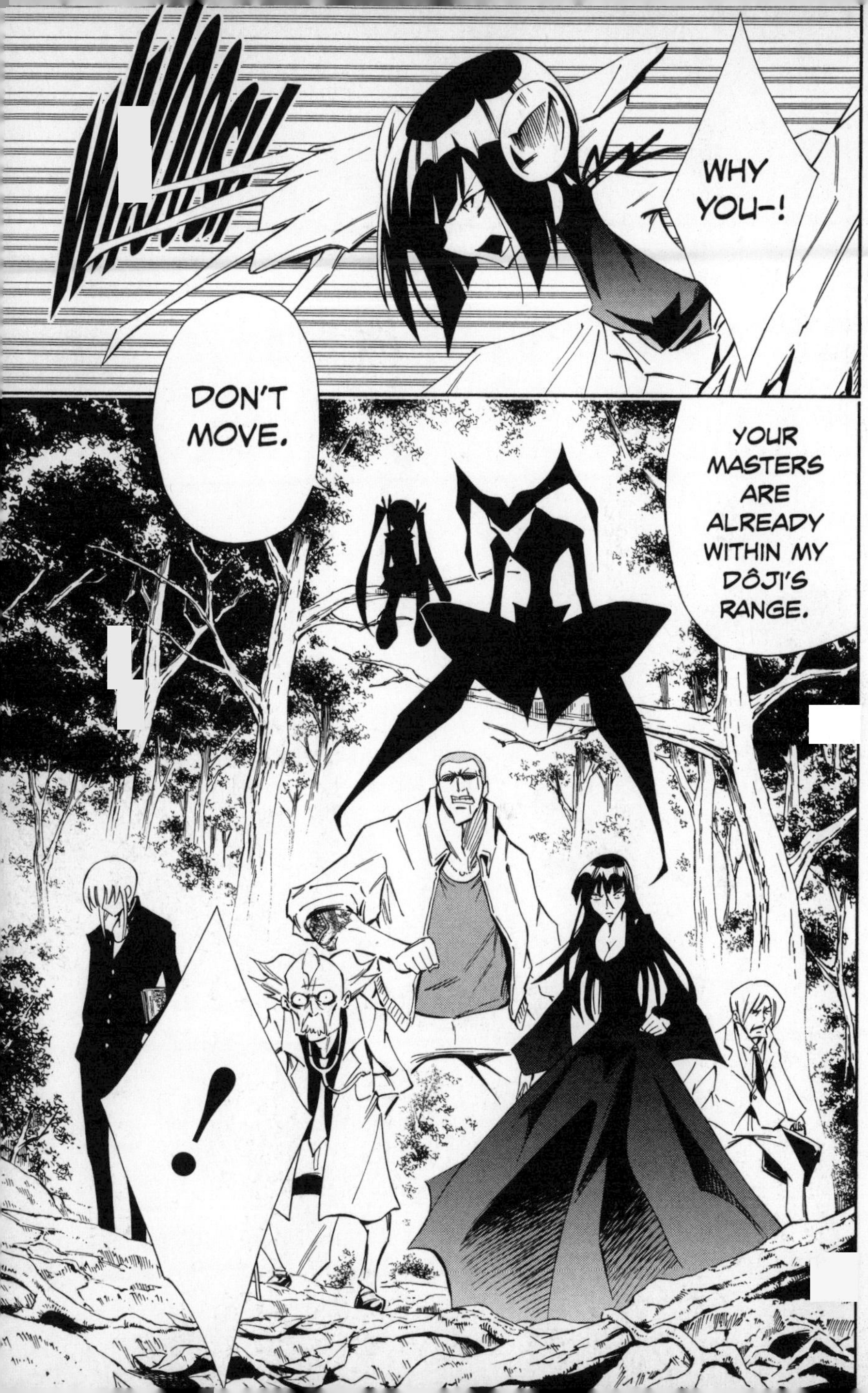
WHY YOU-!
DON'T MOVE.
YOUR MASTERS ARE ALREADY WITHIN MY DÔJI'S RANGE.
!

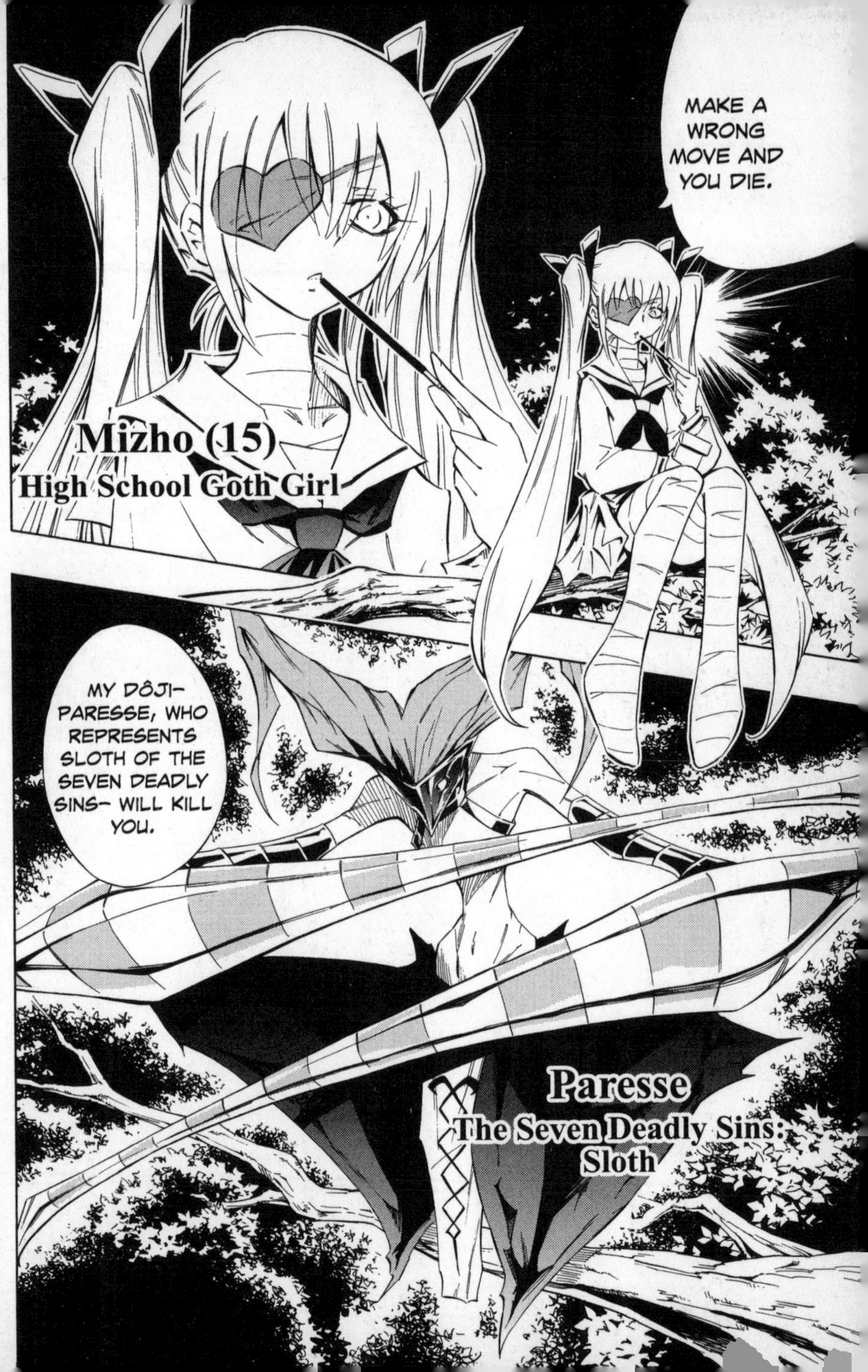
MAKE A WRONG MOVE AND YOU DIE.
Mizho (15)
High School Goth Girl
MY DÔJI- PARESSE, WHO REPRESENTS SLOTH OF THE SEVEN DEADLY SINS- WILL KILL YOU.
Paresse
The Seven Deadly Sins: Sloth

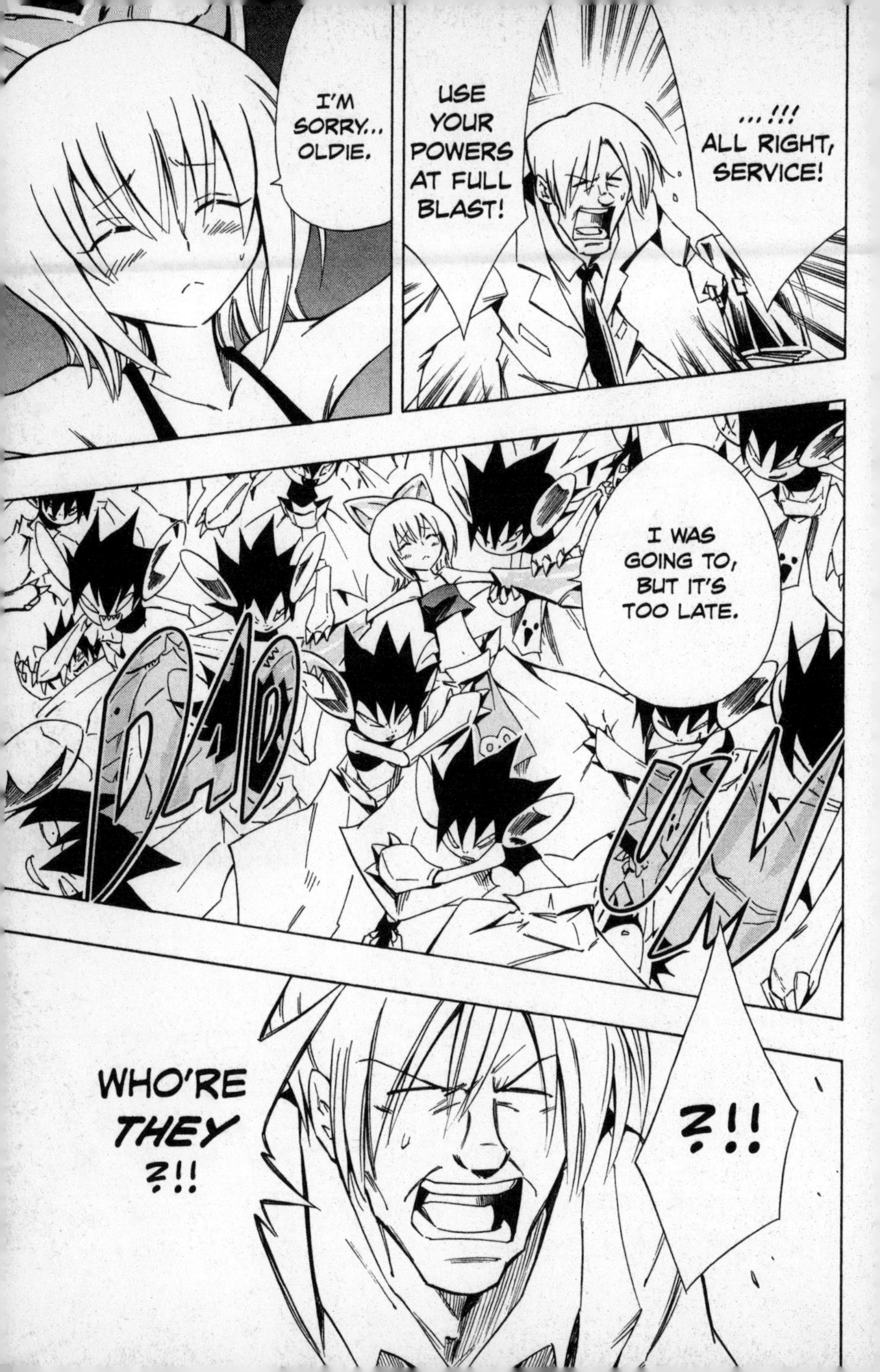
...!!! ALL RIGHT, SERVICE!
USE YOUR POWERS AT FULL BLAST!
I'M SORRY... OLDIE.
I WAS GOING TO, BUT IT'S TOO LATE.
DADOOM
?!!
WHO'RE THEY ?!!

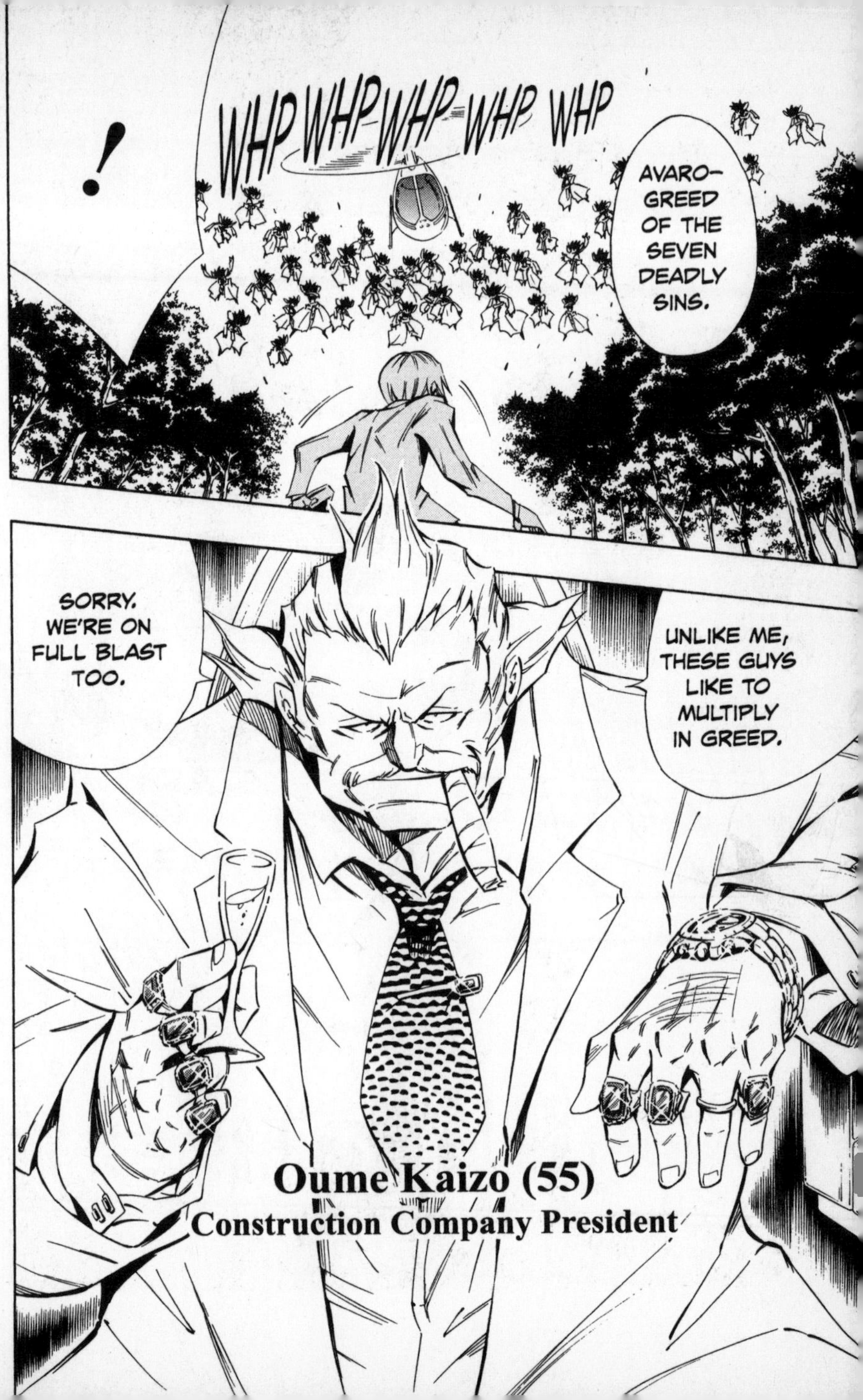
AVARO-GREED OF THE SEVEN DEADLY SINS.
WHP WHP WHP WHP WHP
!
UNLIKE ME, THESE GUYS LIKE TO MULTIPLY IN GREED.
SORRY. WE'RE ON FULL BLAST TOO.
Oume Kaizo (55)
Construction Company President

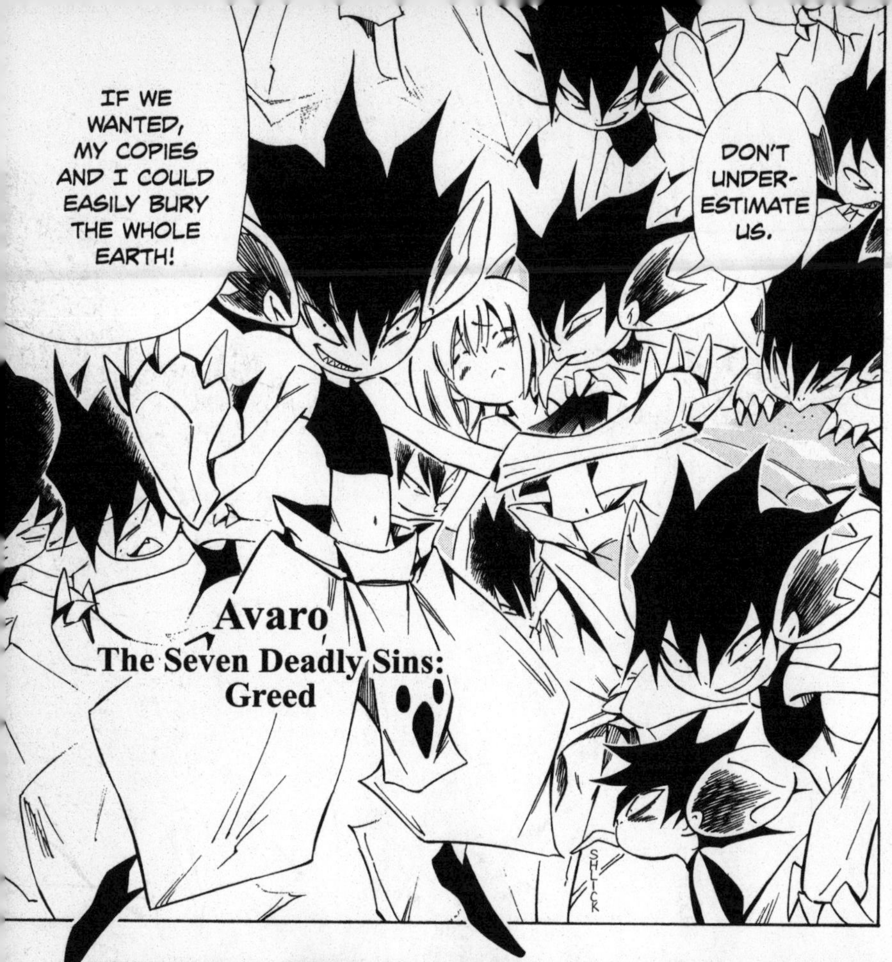
DON'T UNDER-ESTIMATE US.
IF WE WANTED, MY COPIES AND I COULD EASILY BURY THE WHOLE EARTH!
Avaro
The Seven Deadly Sins: Greed
SHLICK

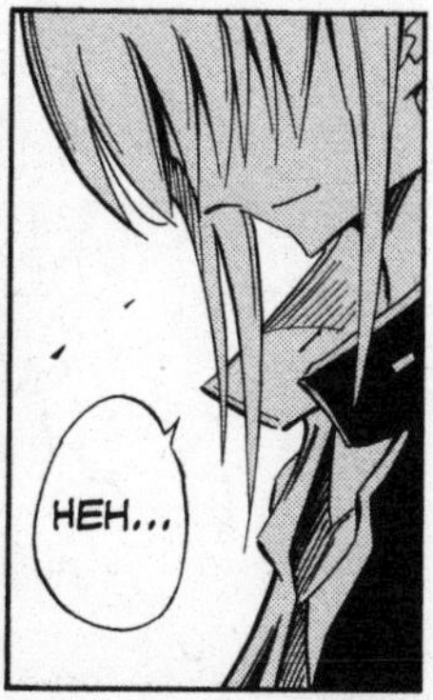
HEH...

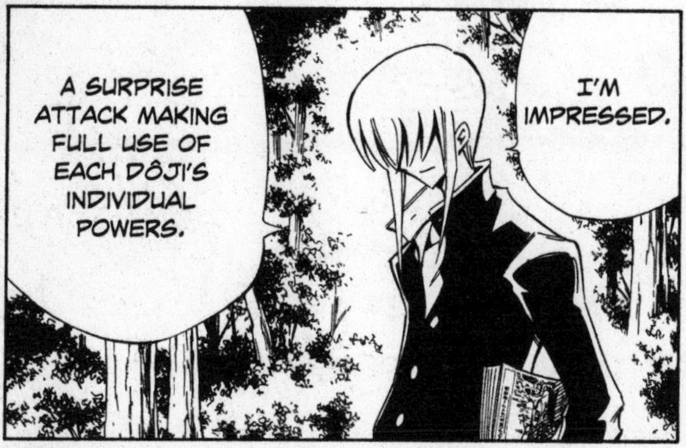
I'M IMPRESSED.
A SURPRISE ATTACK MAKING FULL USE OF EACH DÔJI'S INDIVIDUAL POWERS.

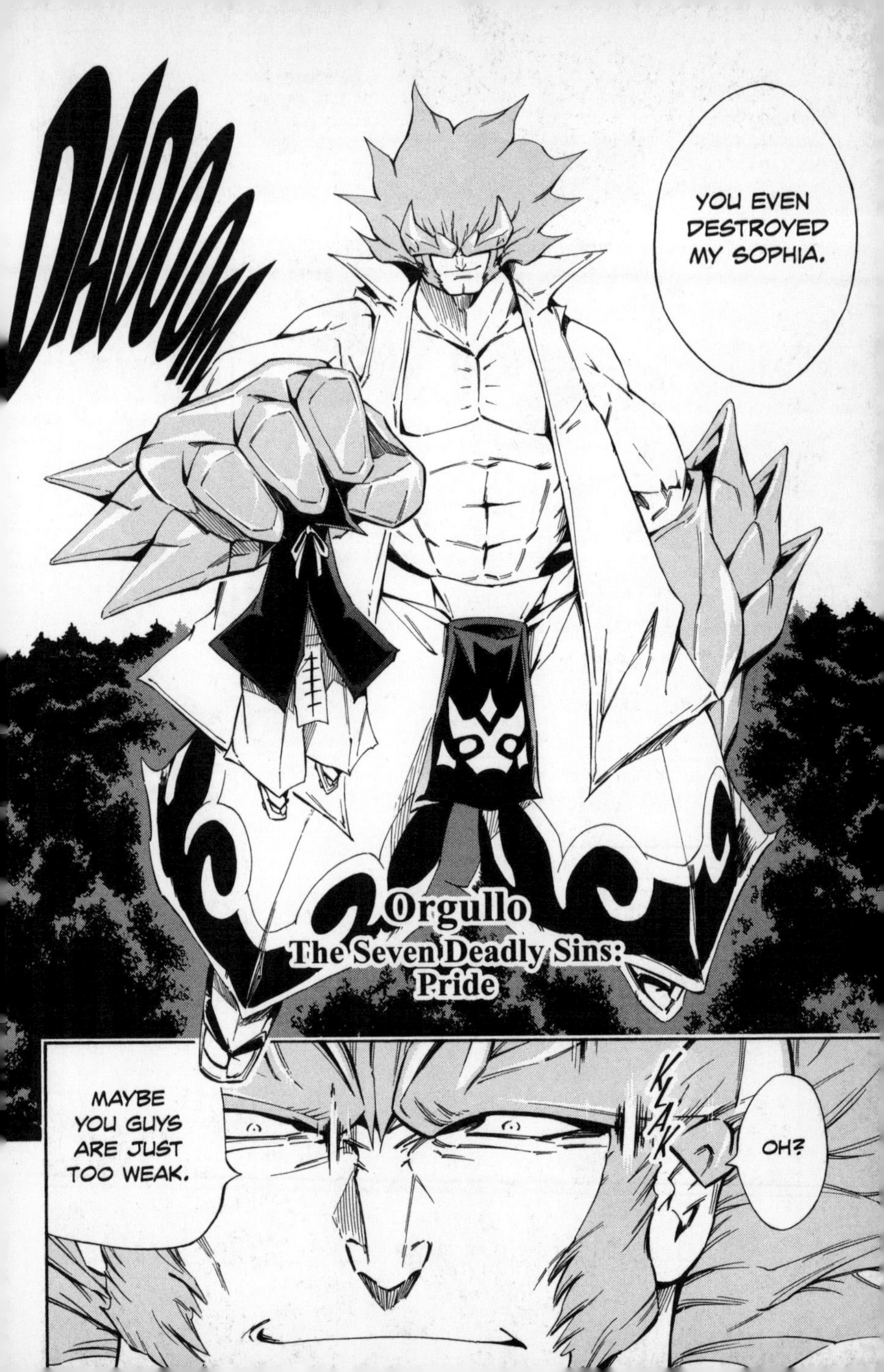
YOU EVEN DESTROYED MY SOPHIA.
DAOOM
Orgullo
The Seven Deadly Sins: Pride
OH?
KLAK
MAYBE YOU GUYS ARE JUST TOO WEAK.

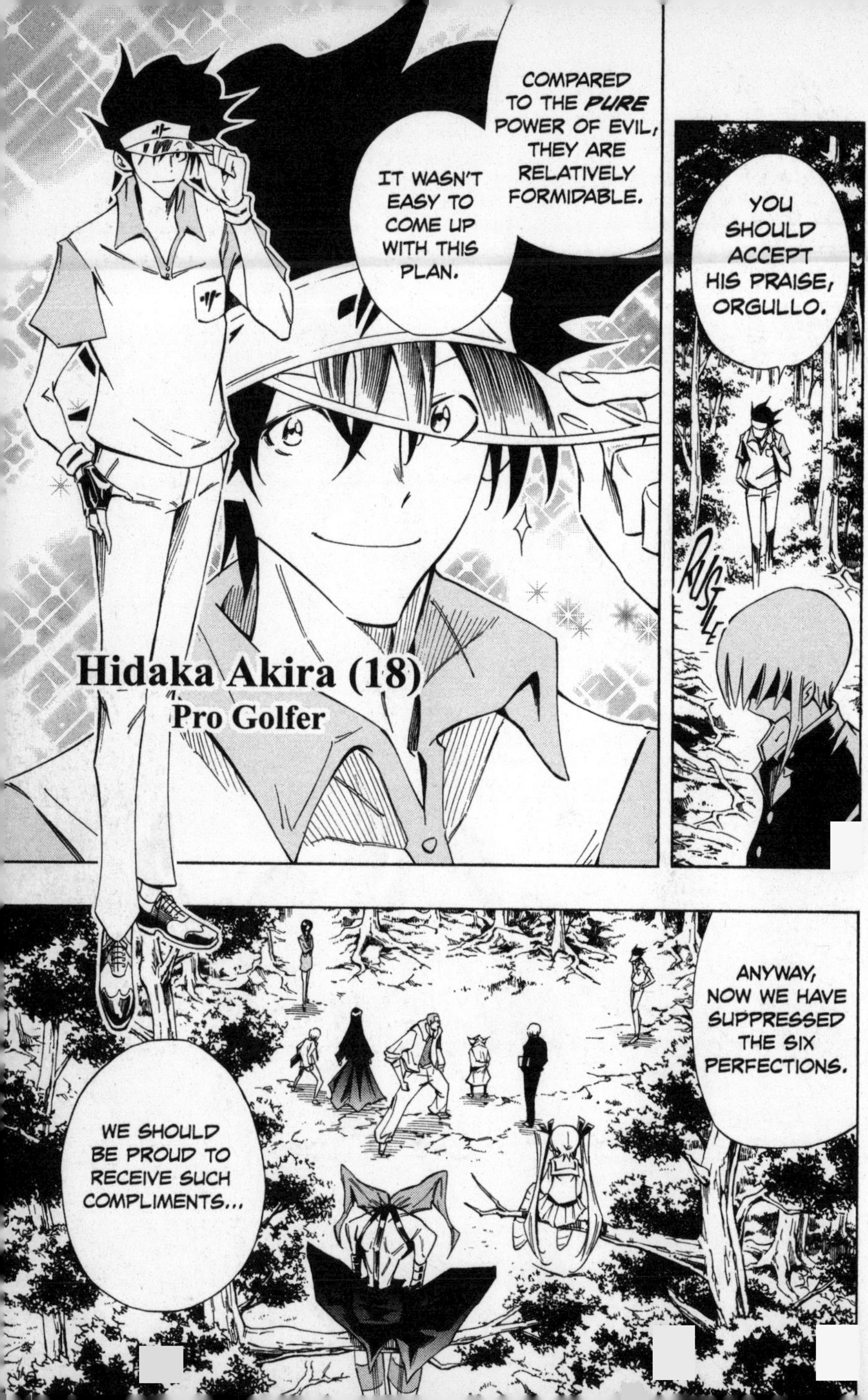
YOU SHOULD ACCEPT HIS PRAISE, ORGULLO.
RUSTLE
COMPARED TO THE *PURE* POWER OF EVIL, THEY ARE RELATIVELY FORMIDABLE.
IT WASN'T EASY TO COME UP WITH THIS PLAN.
Hidaka Akira (18)
Pro Golfer
ANYWAY, NOW WE HAVE SUPPRESSED THE SIX PERFECTIONS.
WE SHOULD BE PROUD TO RECEIVE SUCH COMPLIMENTS...

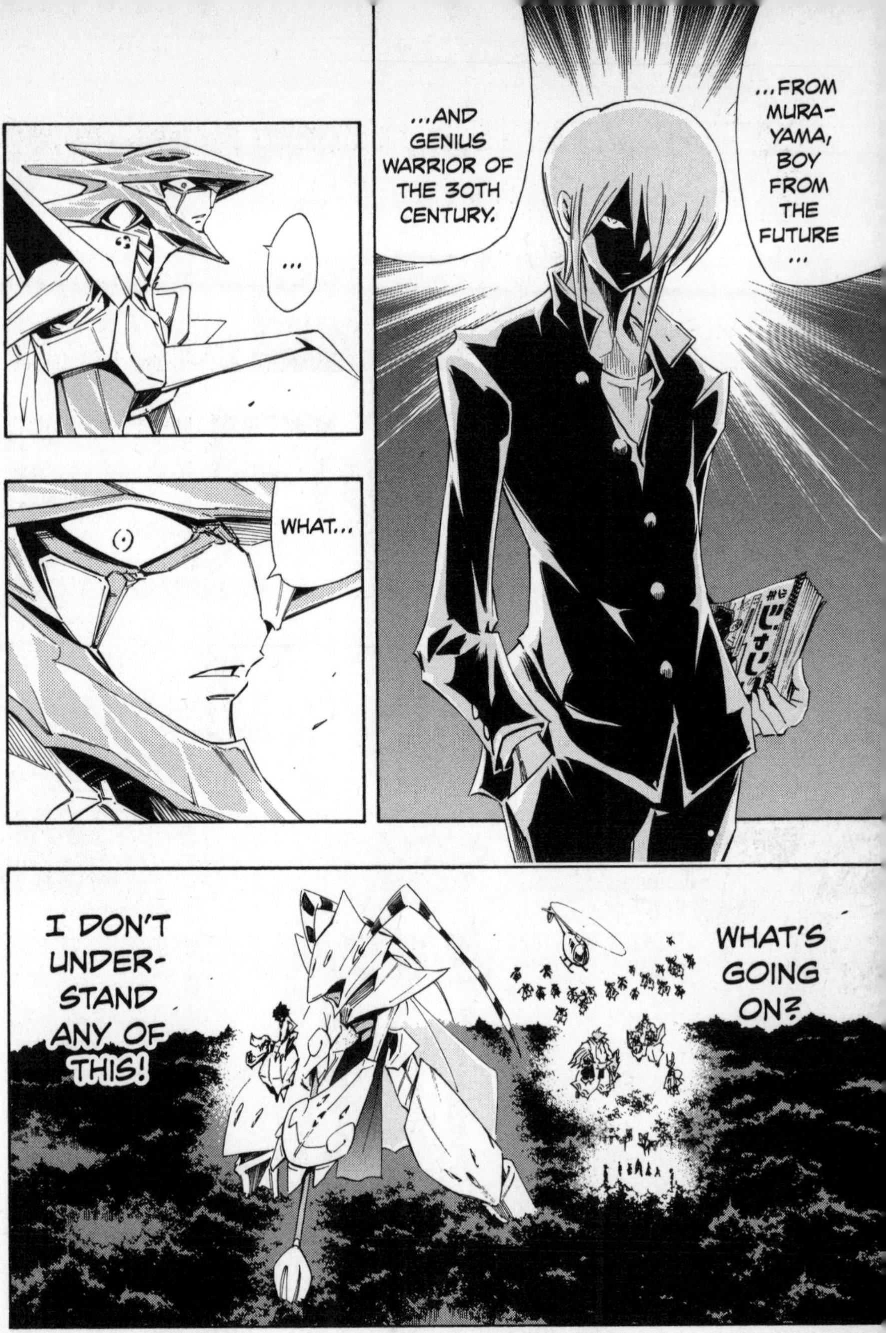
...FROM MURA-YAMA, BOY FROM THE FUTURE ...
...AND GENIUS WARRIOR OF THE 30TH CENTURY.
...
WHAT...
WHAT'S GOING ON?
I DON'T UNDER-STAND ANY OF THIS!

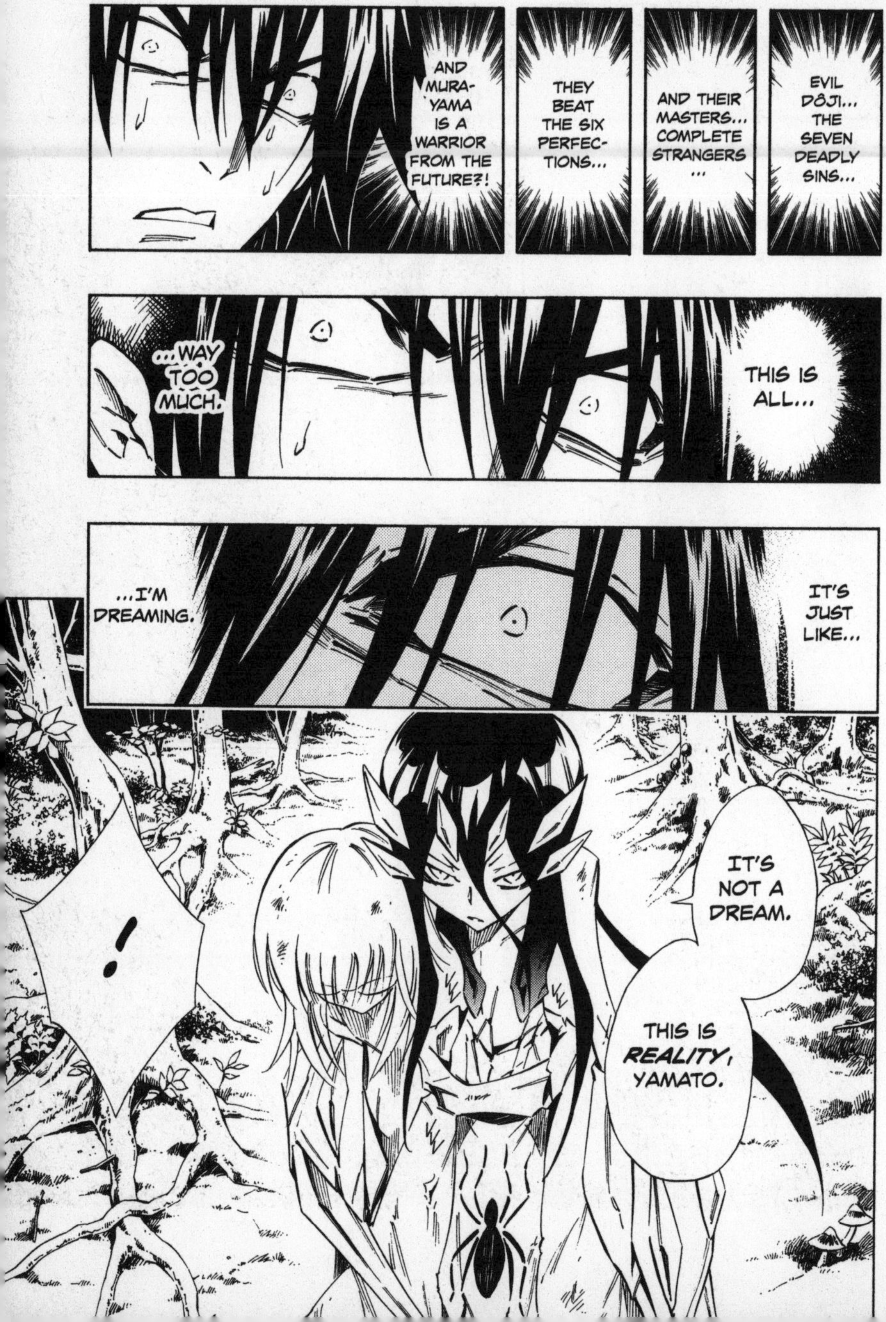
EVIL DŌJI... THE SEVEN DEADLY SINS...
AND THEIR MASTERS... COMPLETE STRANGERS...
THEY BEAT THE SIX PERFECTIONS...
AND MURAYAMA IS A WARRIOR FROM THE FUTURE?!
THIS IS ALL...
...WAY TOO MUCH.
IT'S JUST LIKE...
...I'M DREAMING.
IT'S NOT A DREAM.
THIS IS REALITY, YAMATO.
!

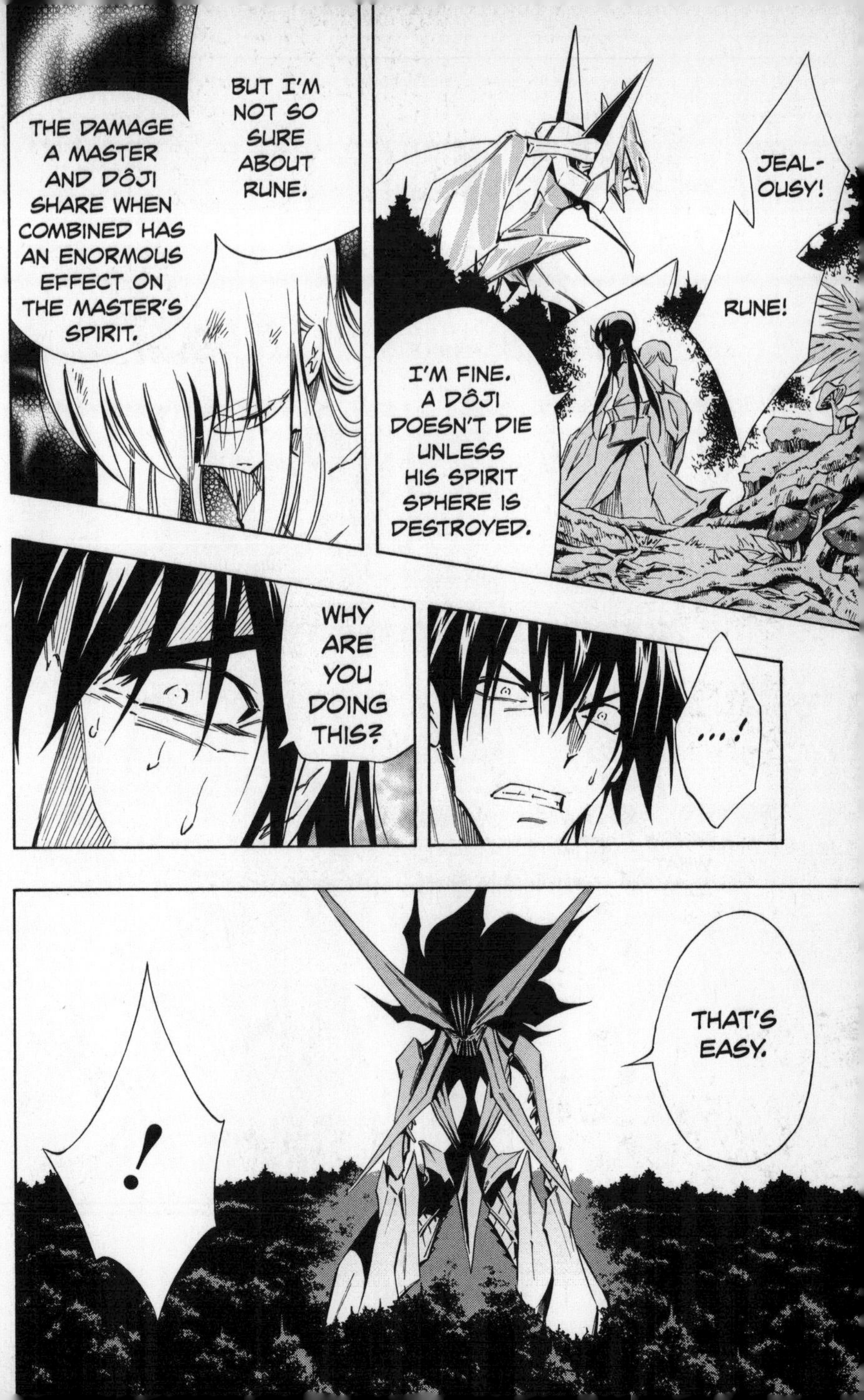
JEAL-OUSY!
RUNE!
I'M FINE. A DÔJI DOESN'T DIE UNLESS HIS SPIRIT SPHERE IS DESTROYED.
THE DAMAGE A MASTER AND DÔJI SHARE WHEN COMBINED HAS AN ENORMOUS EFFECT ON THE MASTER'S SPIRIT.
BUT I'M NOT SO SURE ABOUT RUNE.
...!
WHY ARE YOU DOING THIS?
THAT'S EASY.
!

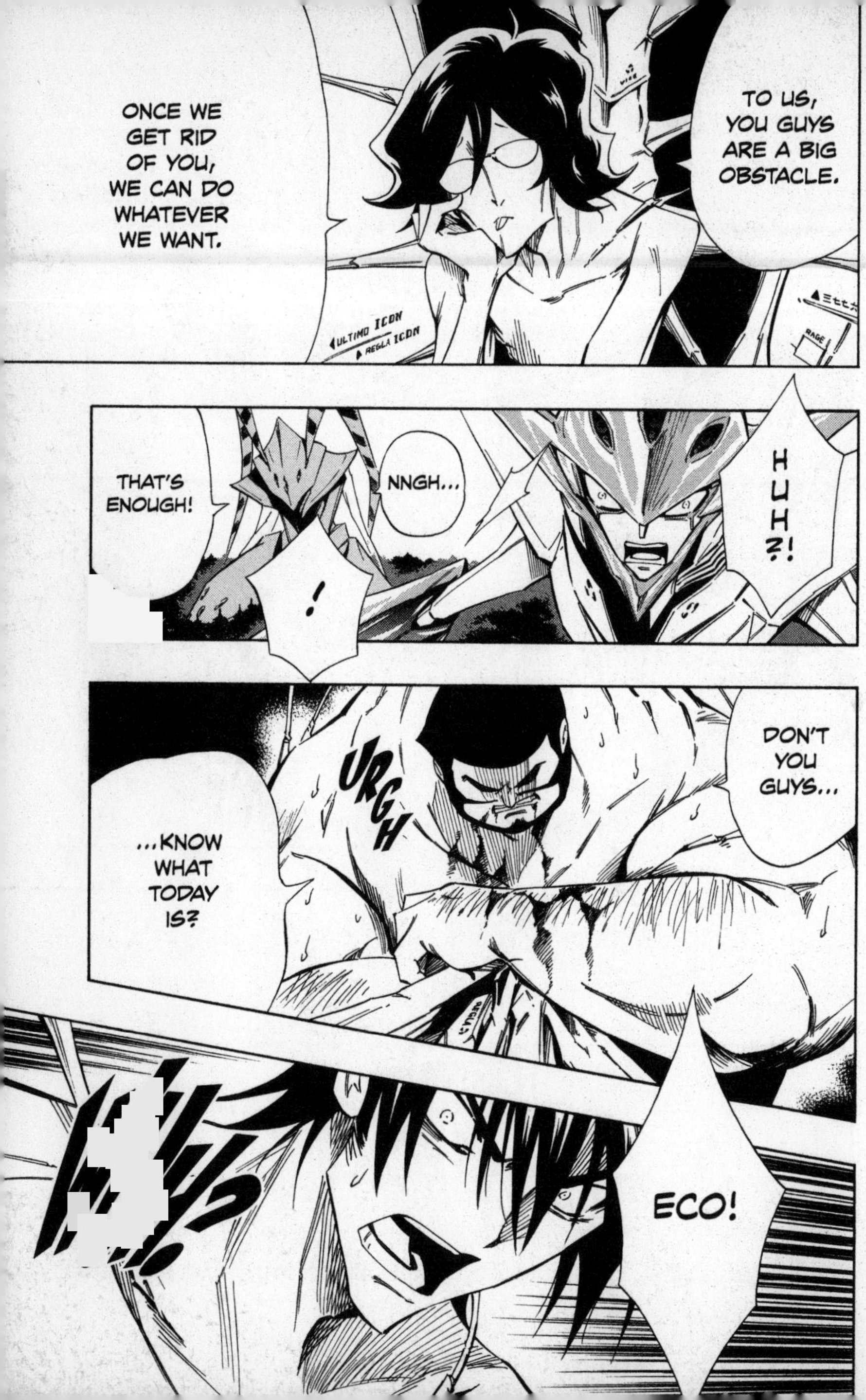
TO US, YOU GUYS ARE A BIG OBSTACLE.
ONCE WE GET RID OF YOU, WE CAN DO WHATEVER WE WANT.
ULTIMO ICON
REGLA ICON
HUH?!
!
NNGH...
THAT'S ENOUGH!
DON'T YOU GUYS...
URGH
...KNOW WHAT TODAY IS?
ECO!

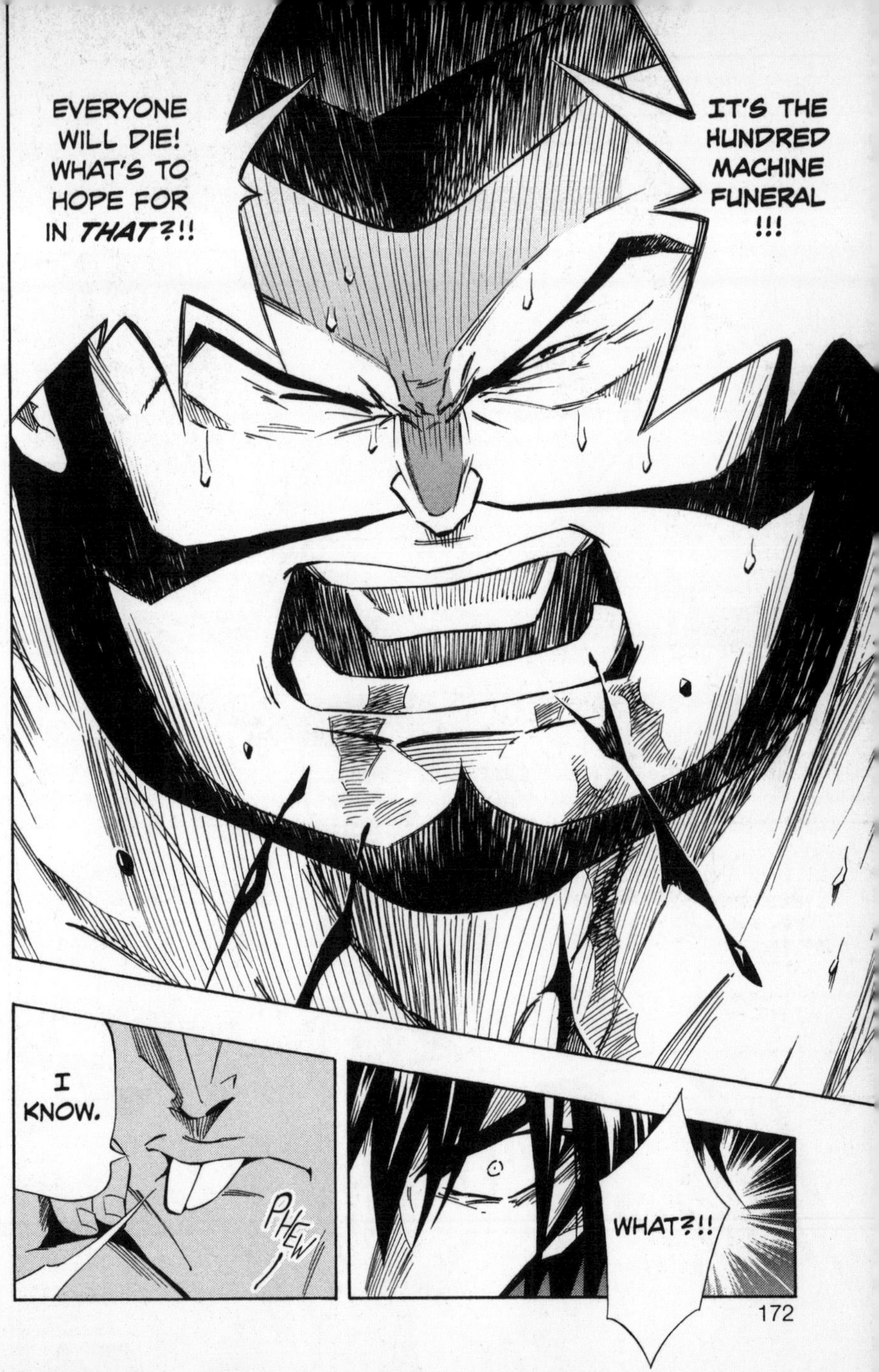
IT'S THE HUNDRED MACHINE FUNERAL!!!
EVERYONE WILL DIE! WHAT'S TO HOPE FOR IN THAT?!!
WHAT?!!
I KNOW.
PHEW

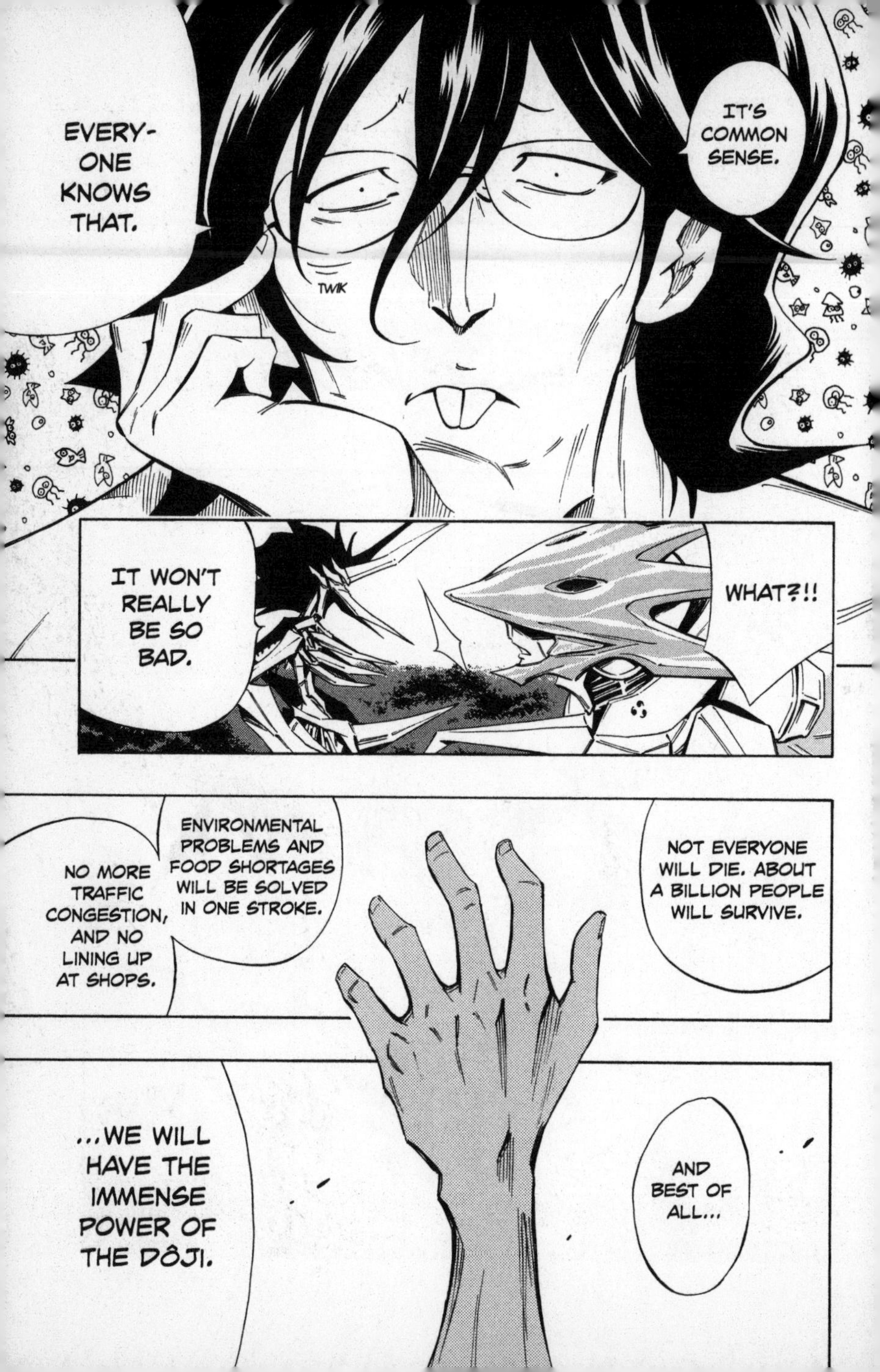

IT'S COMMON SENSE.
EVERY-ONE KNOWS THAT.
TWIK
WHAT?!!
IT WON'T REALLY BE SO BAD.
NOT EVERYONE WILL DIE. ABOUT A BILLION PEOPLE WILL SURVIVE.
ENVIRONMENTAL PROBLEMS AND FOOD SHORTAGES WILL BE SOLVED IN ONE STROKE.
NO MORE TRAFFIC CONGESTION, AND NO LINING UP AT SHOPS.
AND BEST OF ALL...
...WE WILL HAVE THE IMMENSE POWER OF THE DÔJI.

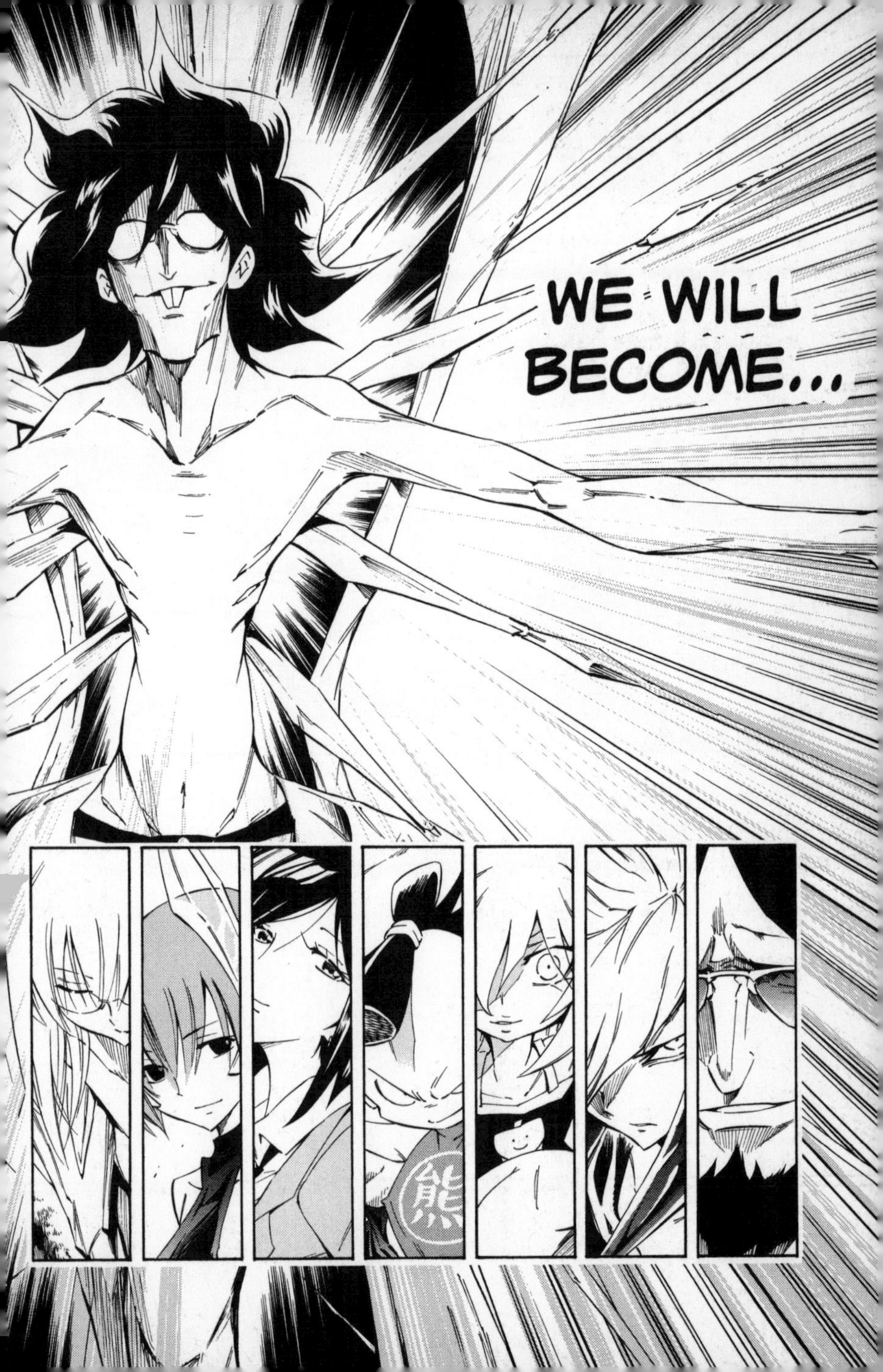
WE WILL BECOME...

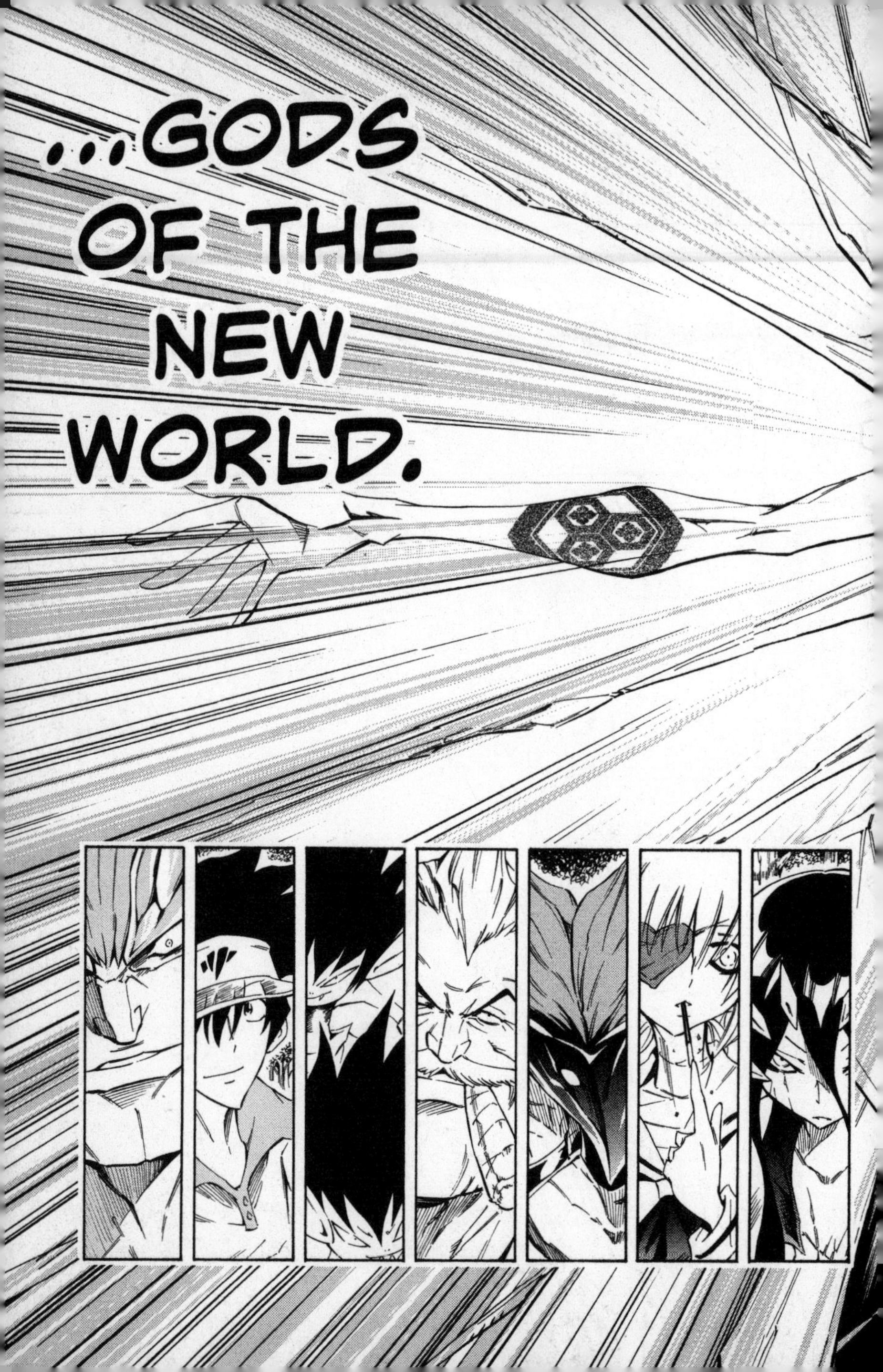
...GODS OF THE NEW WORLD.

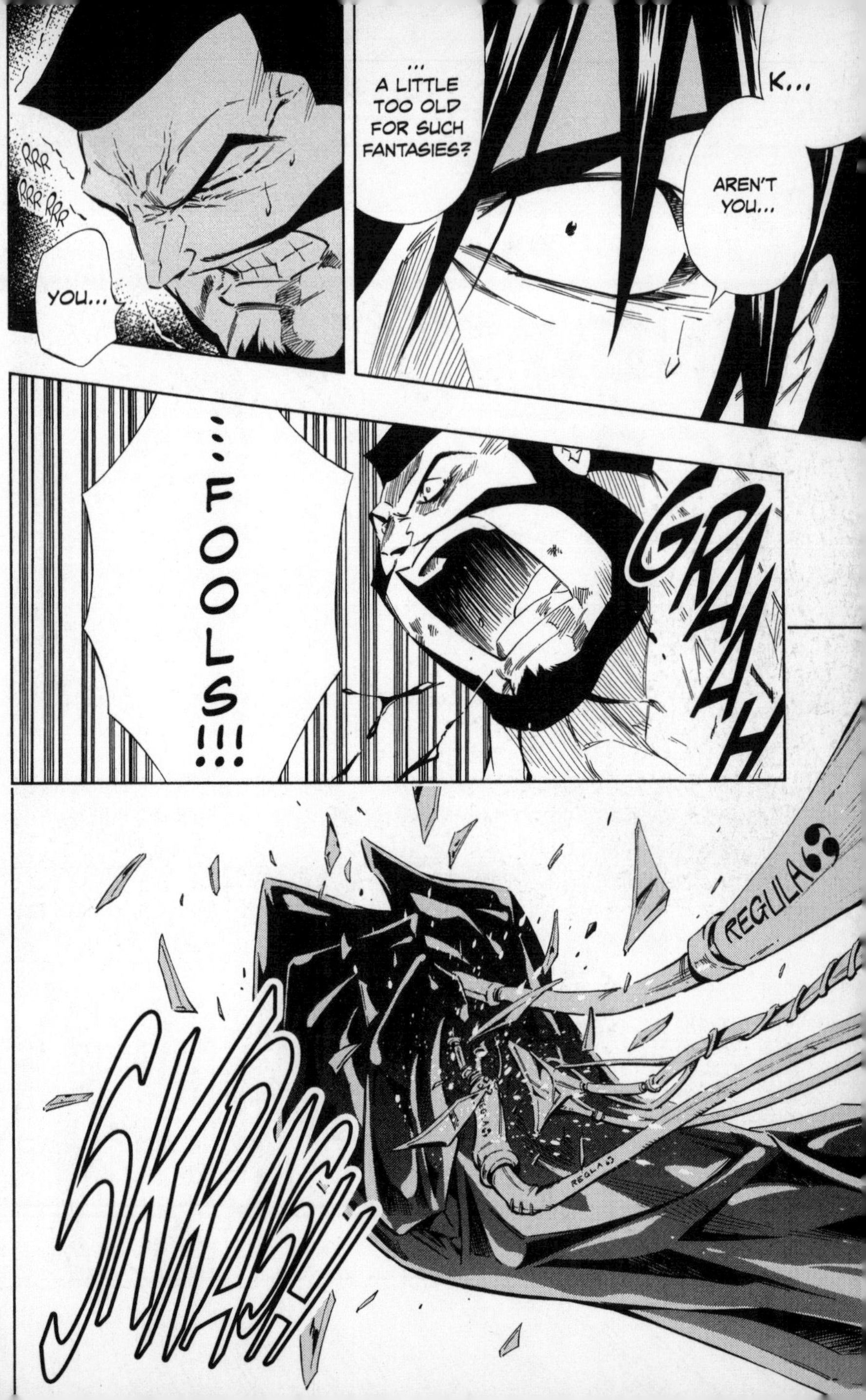
K...
AREN'T YOU...
... A LITTLE TOO OLD FOR SUCH FANTASIES?
RRR RRR RRR
YOU...
GRAAH
...FOOLS!!!
SKRASH!

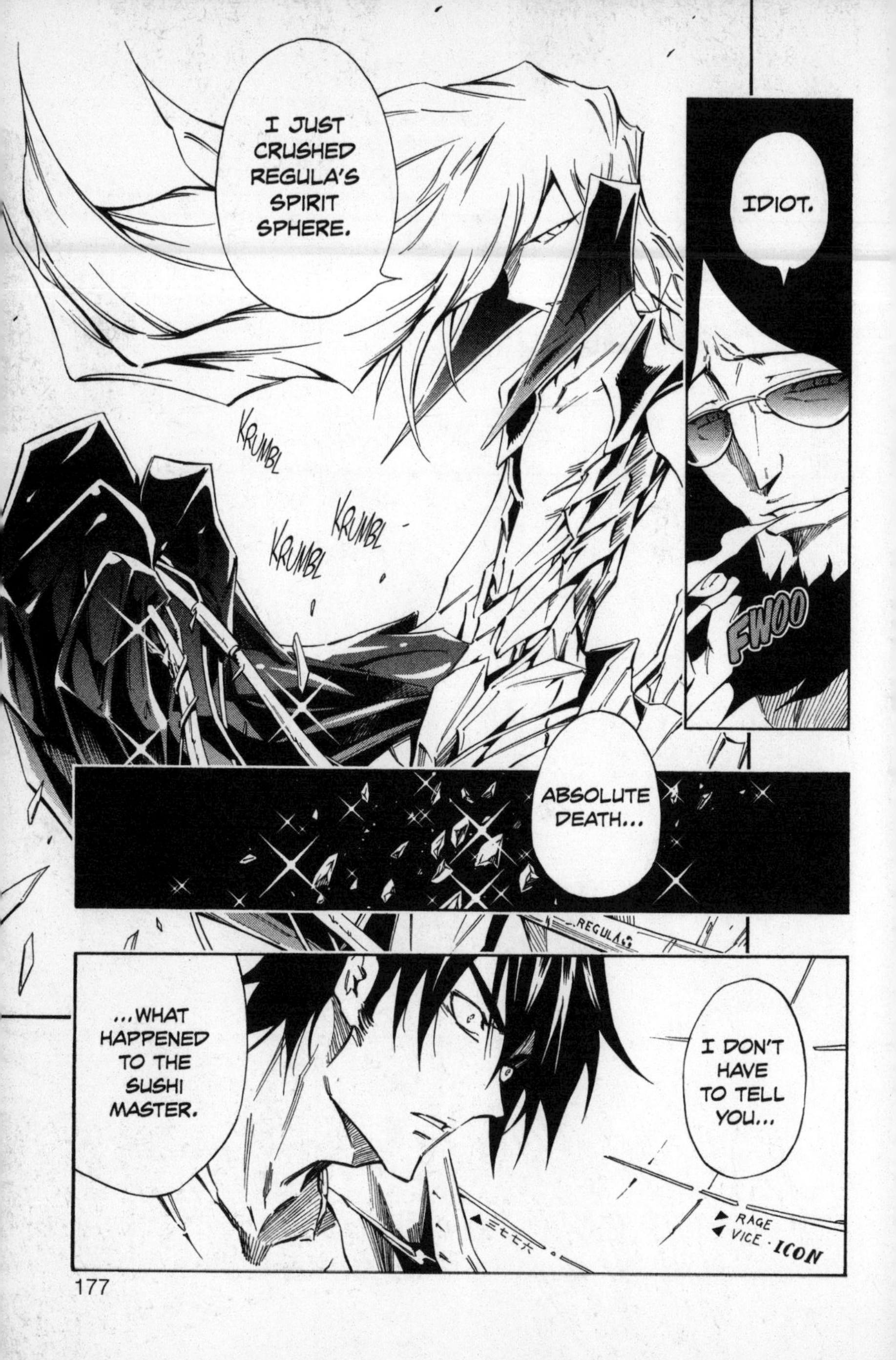
IDIOT.
FWOO
I JUST CRUSHED REGULA'S SPIRIT SPHERE.
KRUMBL
KRUMBL
KRUMBL
ABSOLUTE DEATH...
REGULA
I DON'T HAVE TO TELL YOU...
...WHAT HAPPENED TO THE SUSHI MASTER.
RAGE
VICE · ICON
三七七六

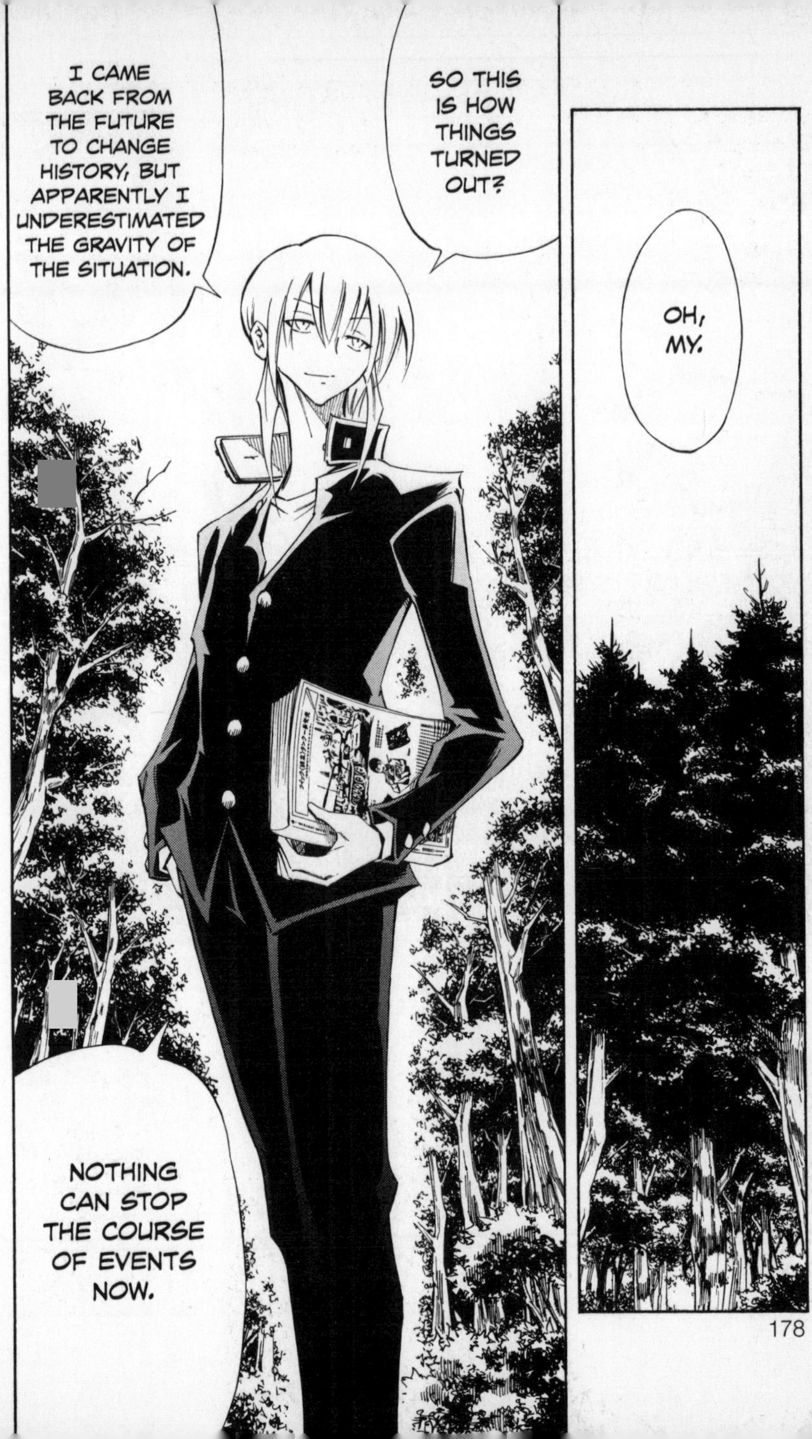
OH, MY.
SO THIS IS HOW THINGS TURNED OUT?
I CAME BACK FROM THE FUTURE TO CHANGE HISTORY, BUT APPARENTLY I UNDERESTIMATED THE GRAVITY OF THE SITUATION.
NOTHING CAN STOP THE COURSE OF EVENTS NOW.

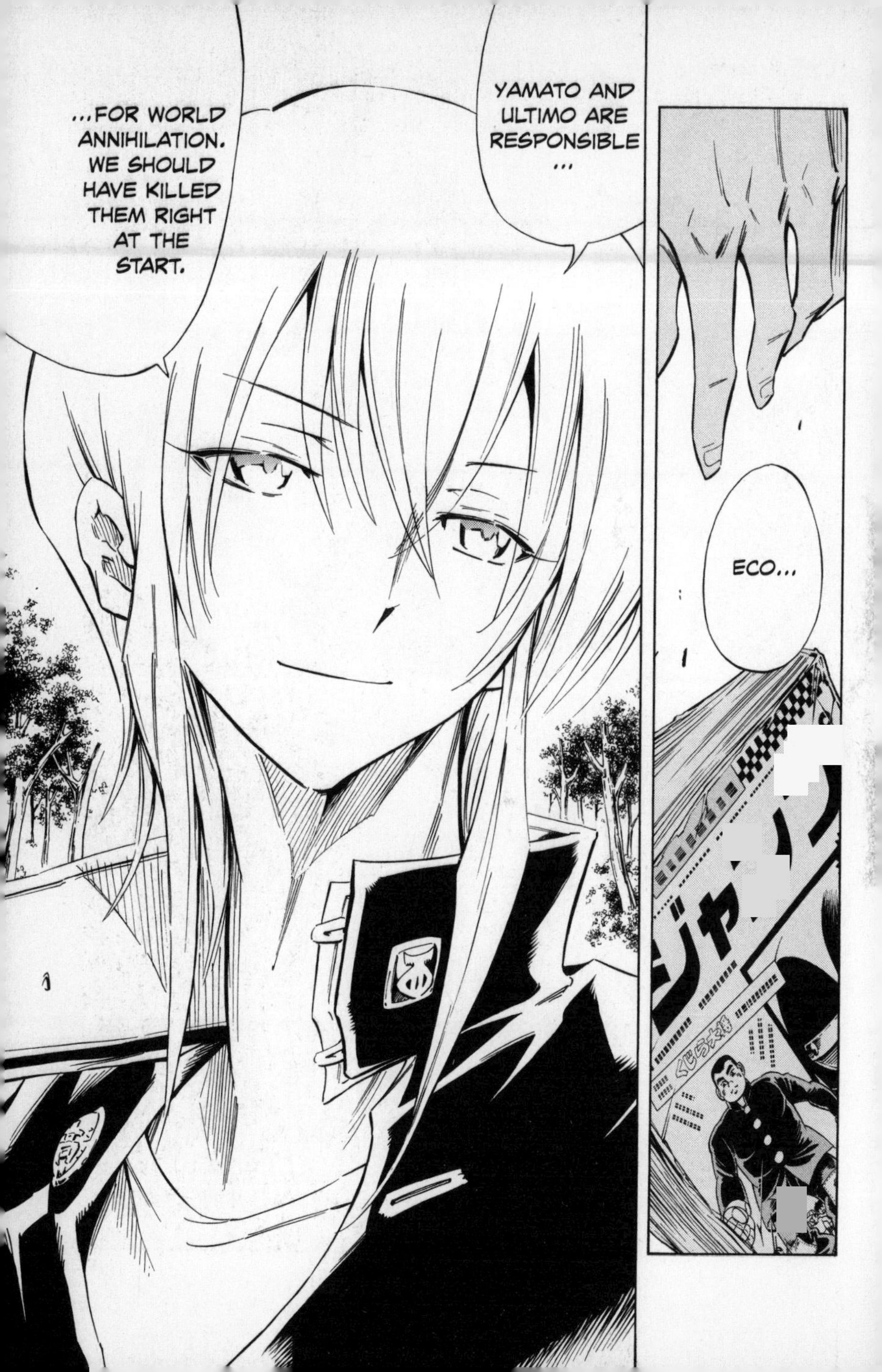
ECO...
YAMATO AND ULTIMO ARE RESPONSIBLE...
...FOR WORLD ANNIHILATION. WE SHOULD HAVE KILLED THEM RIGHT AT THE START.

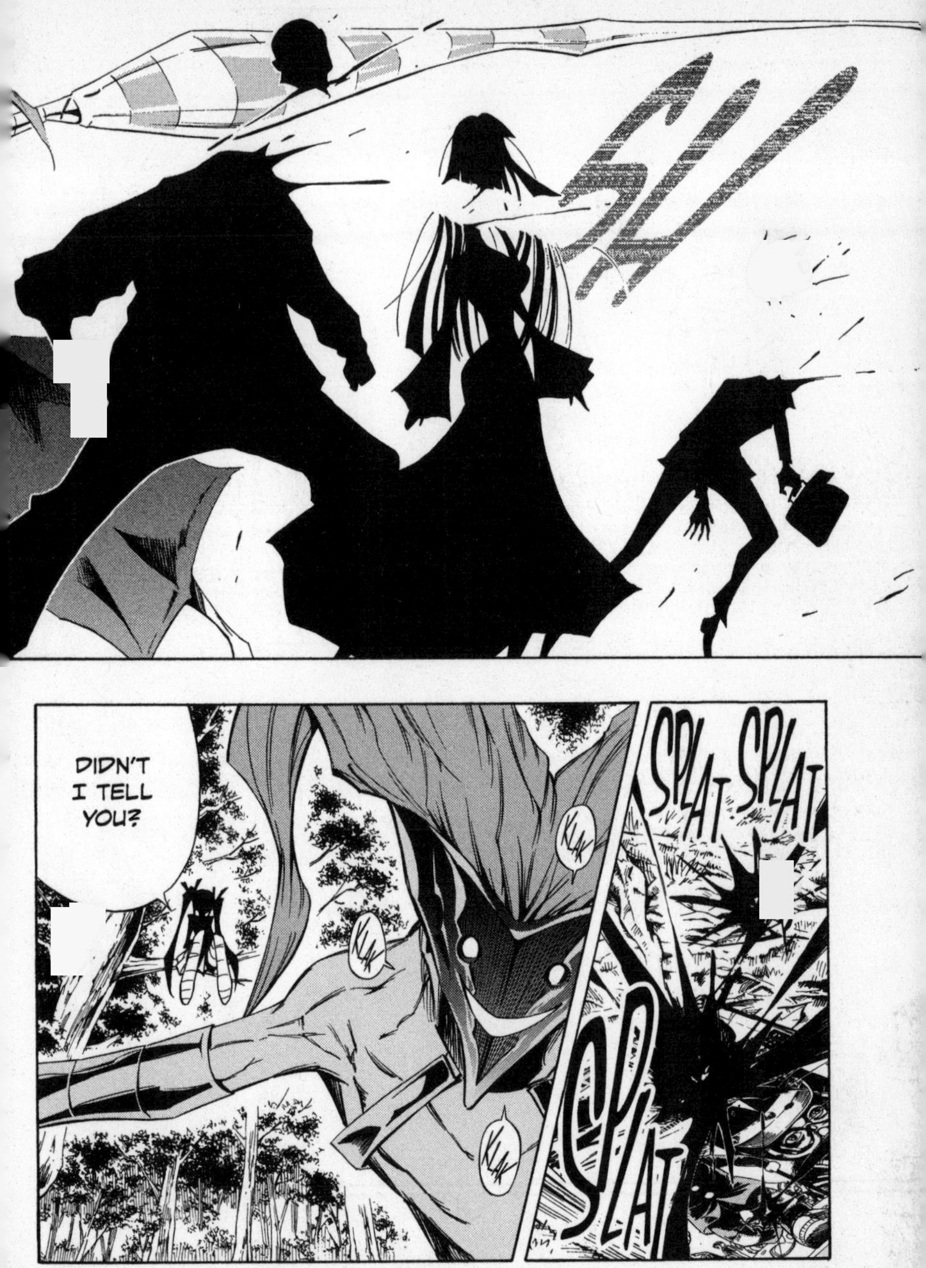
SPLAT SPLAT
SPLAT
DIDN'T I TELL YOU?
KLAK
KLAK
KLAK

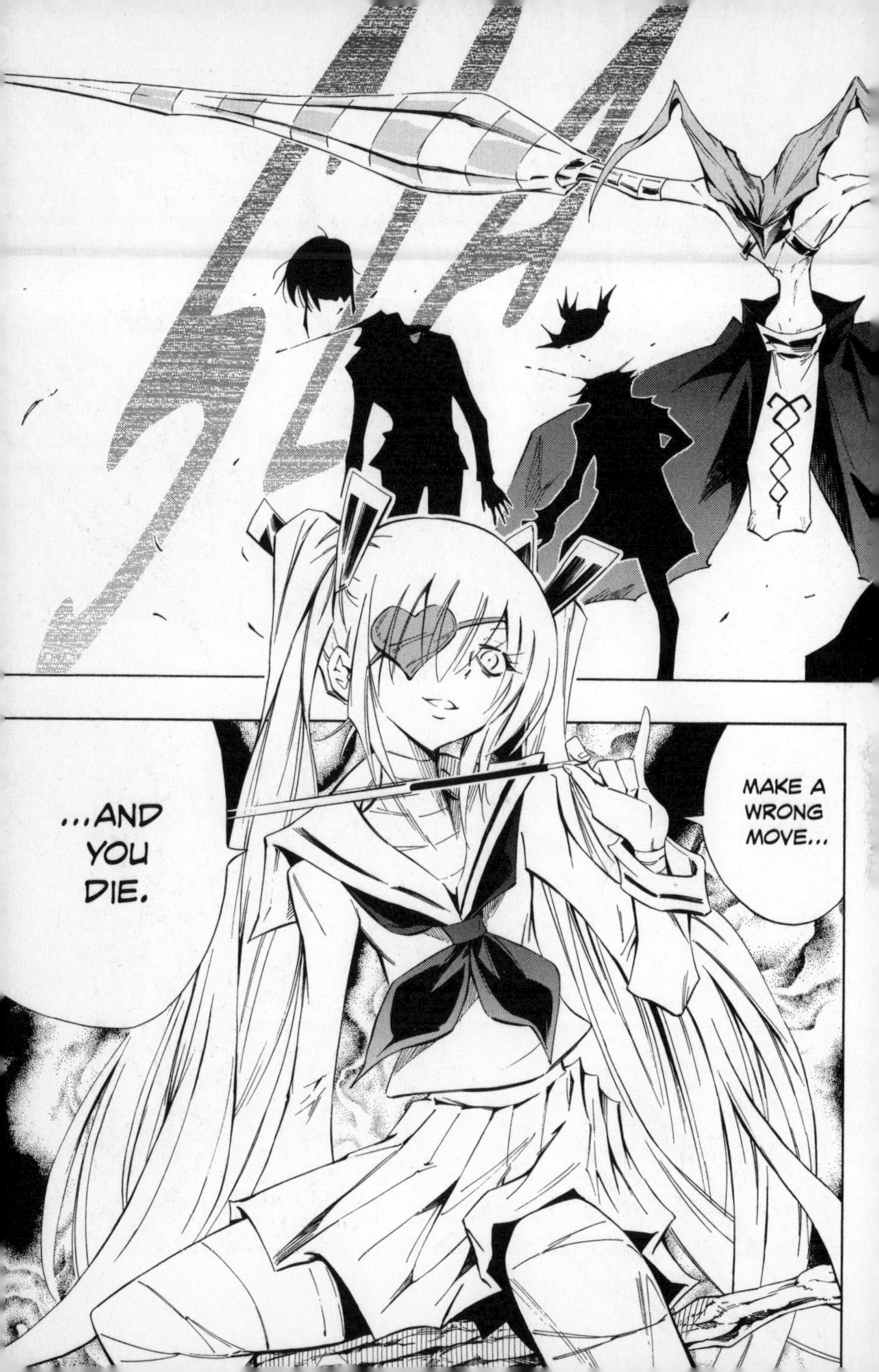
MAKE A WRONG MOVE...
...AND YOU DIE.

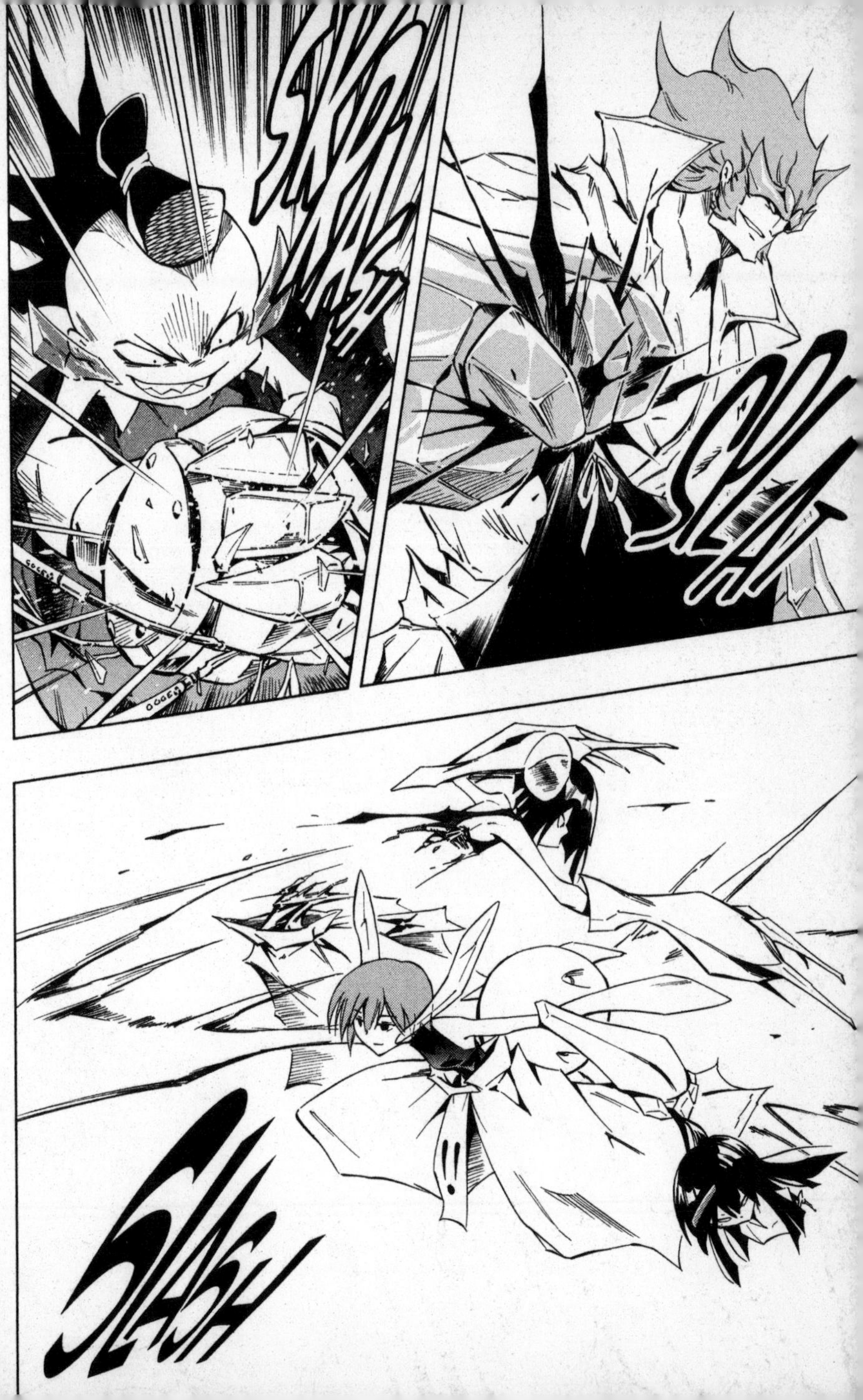
!!
SLASH

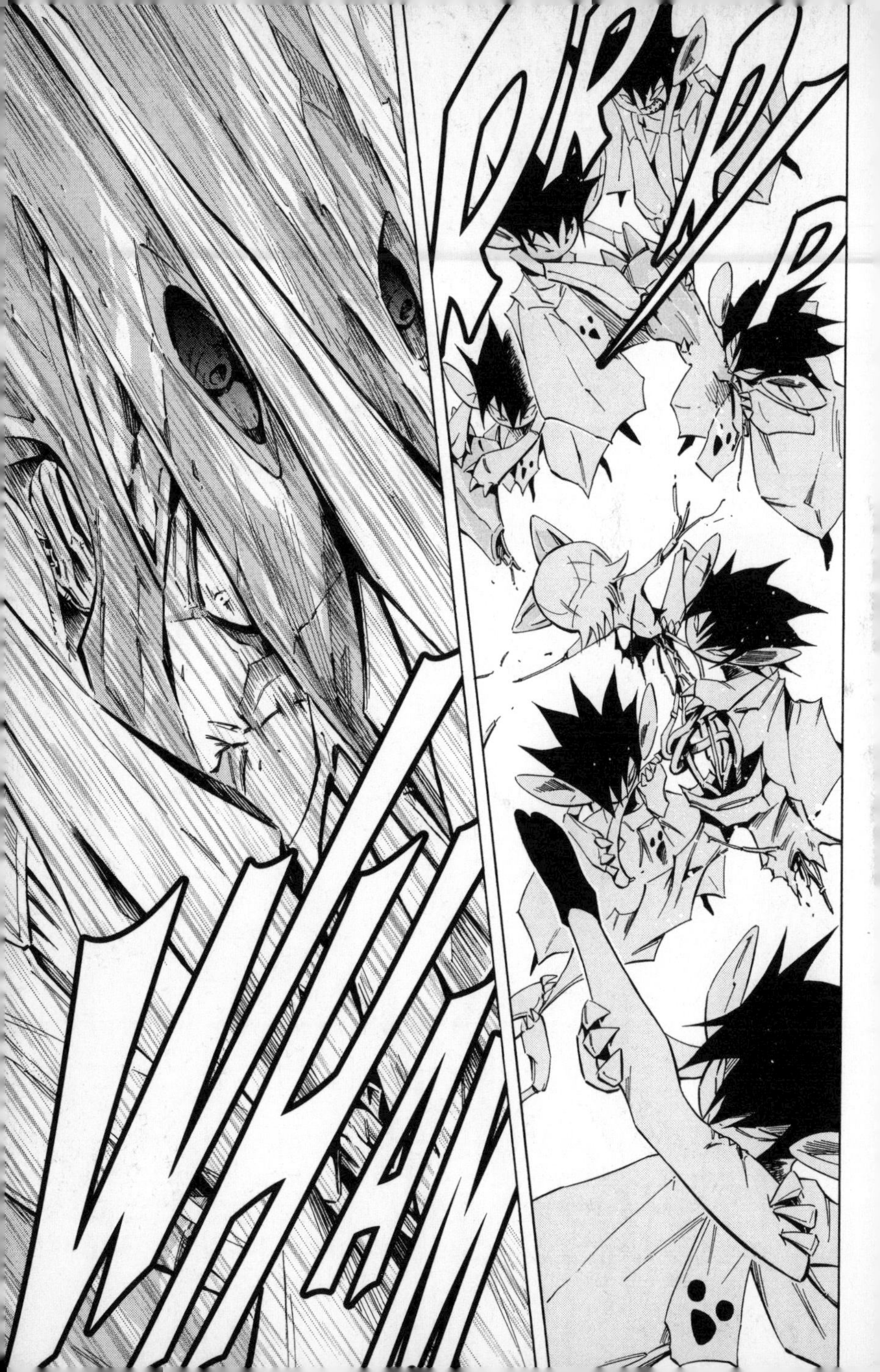
WHAM

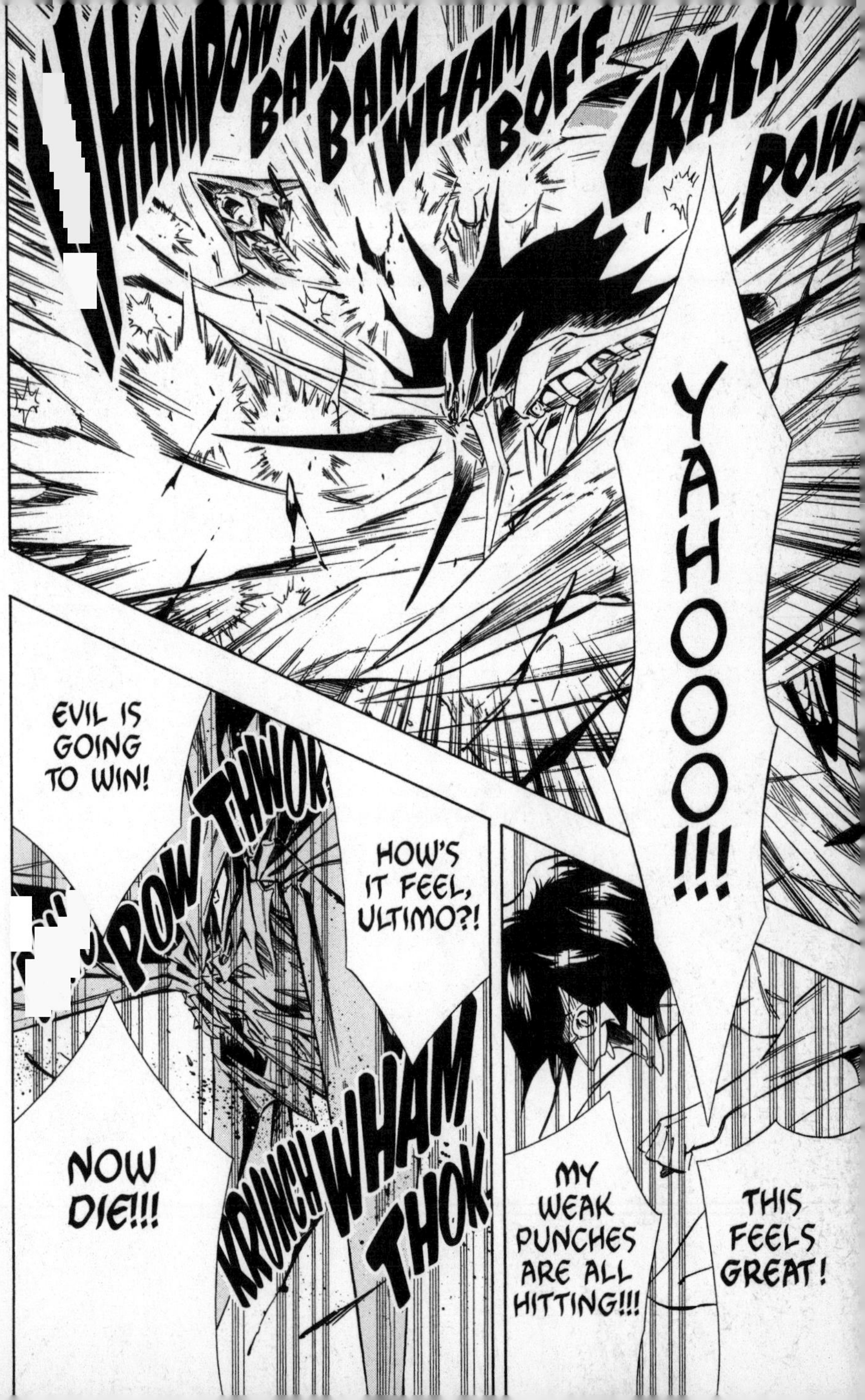

WHAM POW BANG BAM WHAM BOFF CRACK POW
YAHOOO!!!
THIS FEELS GREAT!
MY WEAK PUNCHES ARE ALL HITTING!!!
HOW'S IT FEEL, ULTIMO?!
EVIL IS GOING TO WIN!
POW THWOK
KRUNCH WHAM THOK
NOW DIE!!!

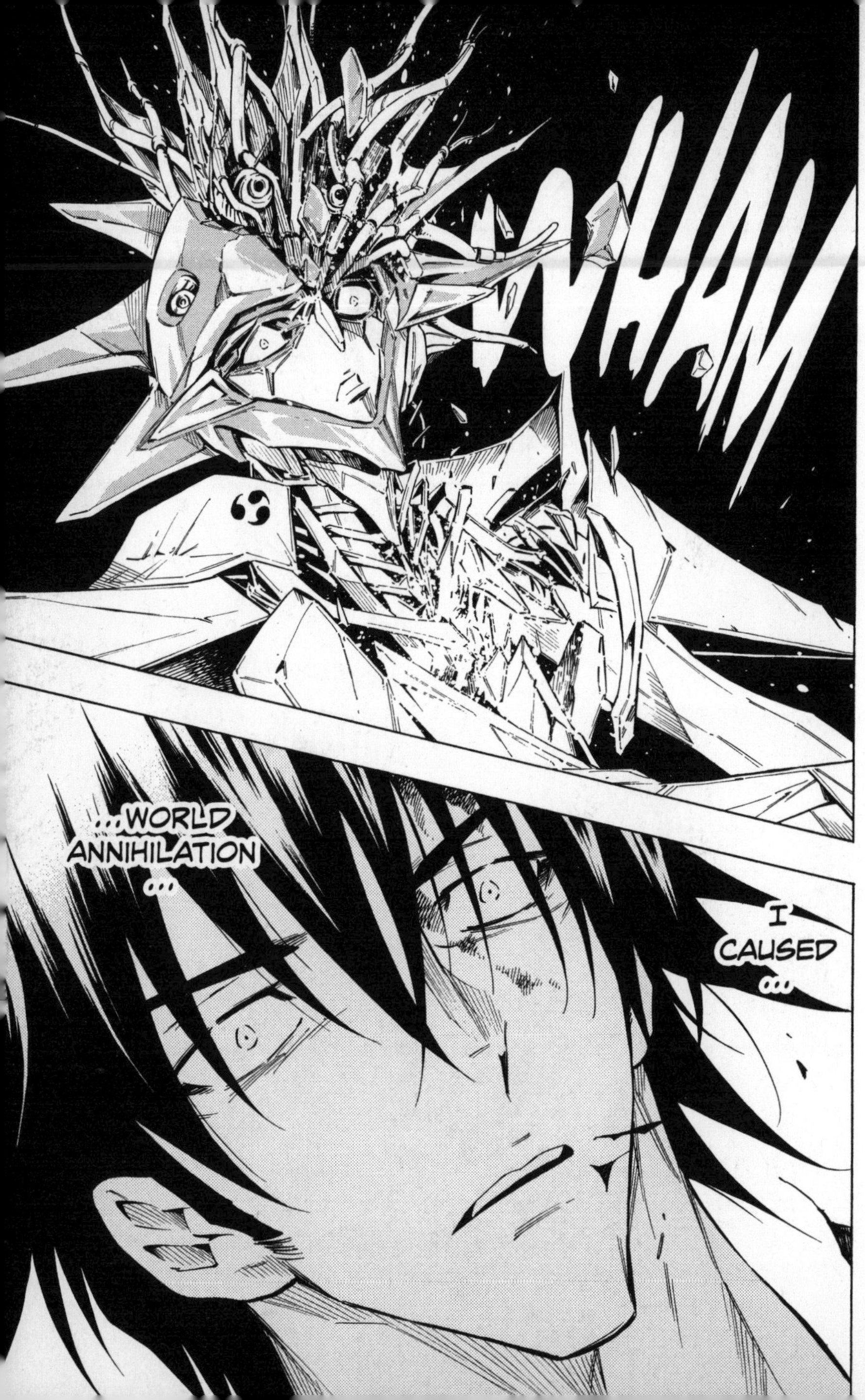
WHAM
I CAUSED ...
...WORLD ANNIHILATION ...

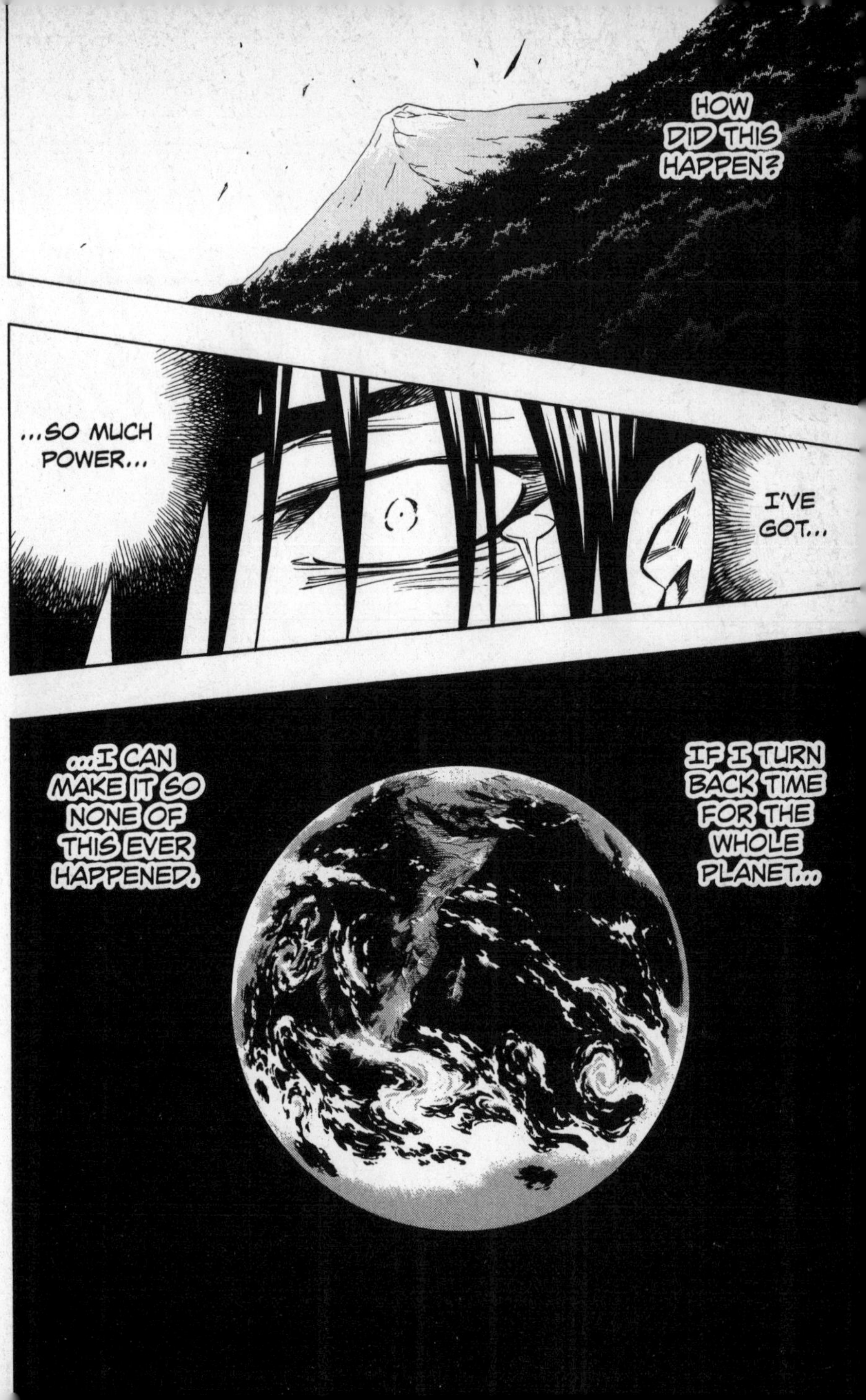
HOW DID THIS HAPPEN?
I'VE GOT...
...SO MUCH POWER...
IF I TURN BACK TIME FOR THE WHOLE PLANET...
...I CAN MAKE IT SO NONE OF THIS EVER HAPPENED.

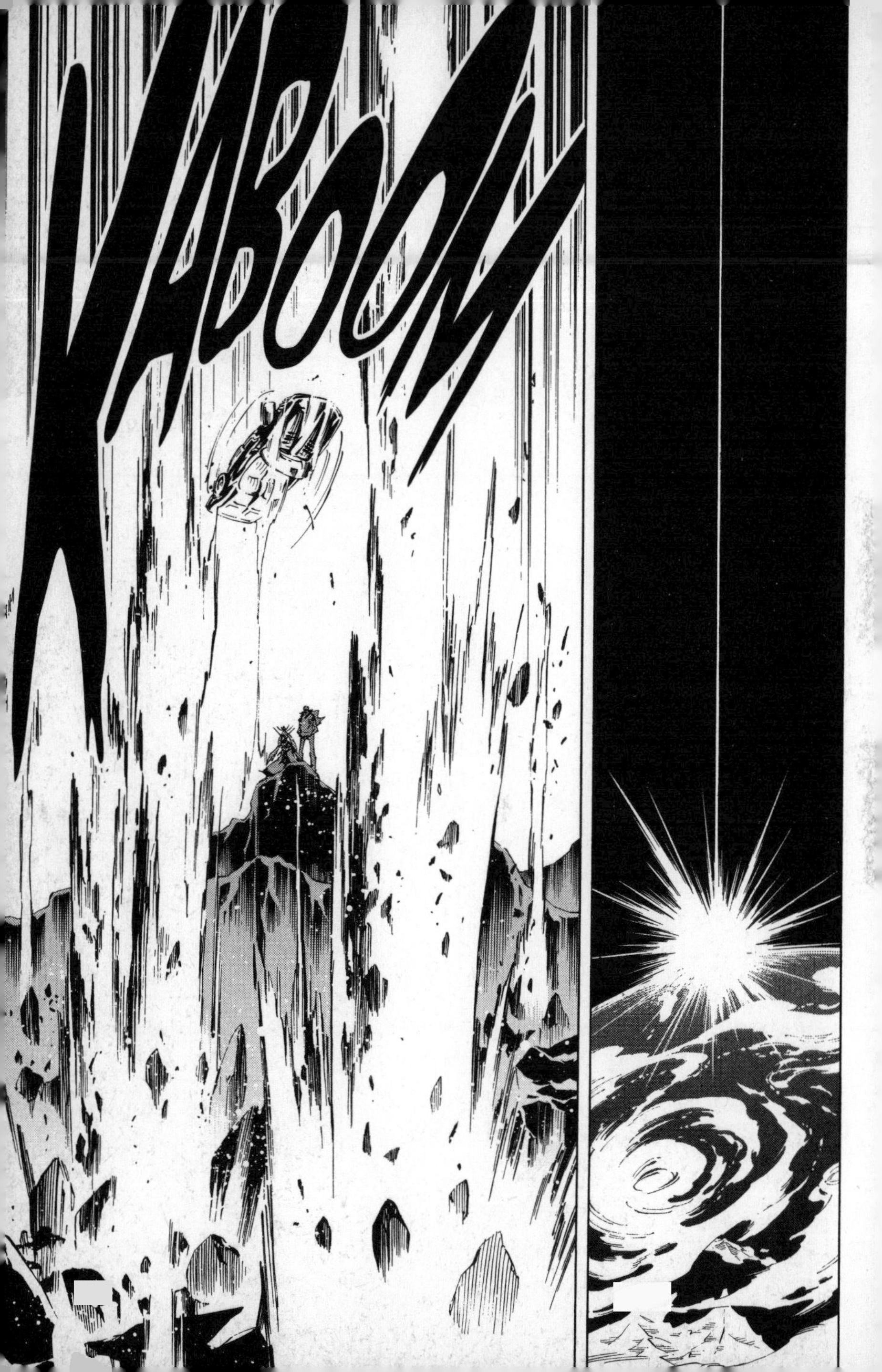
KABOOM

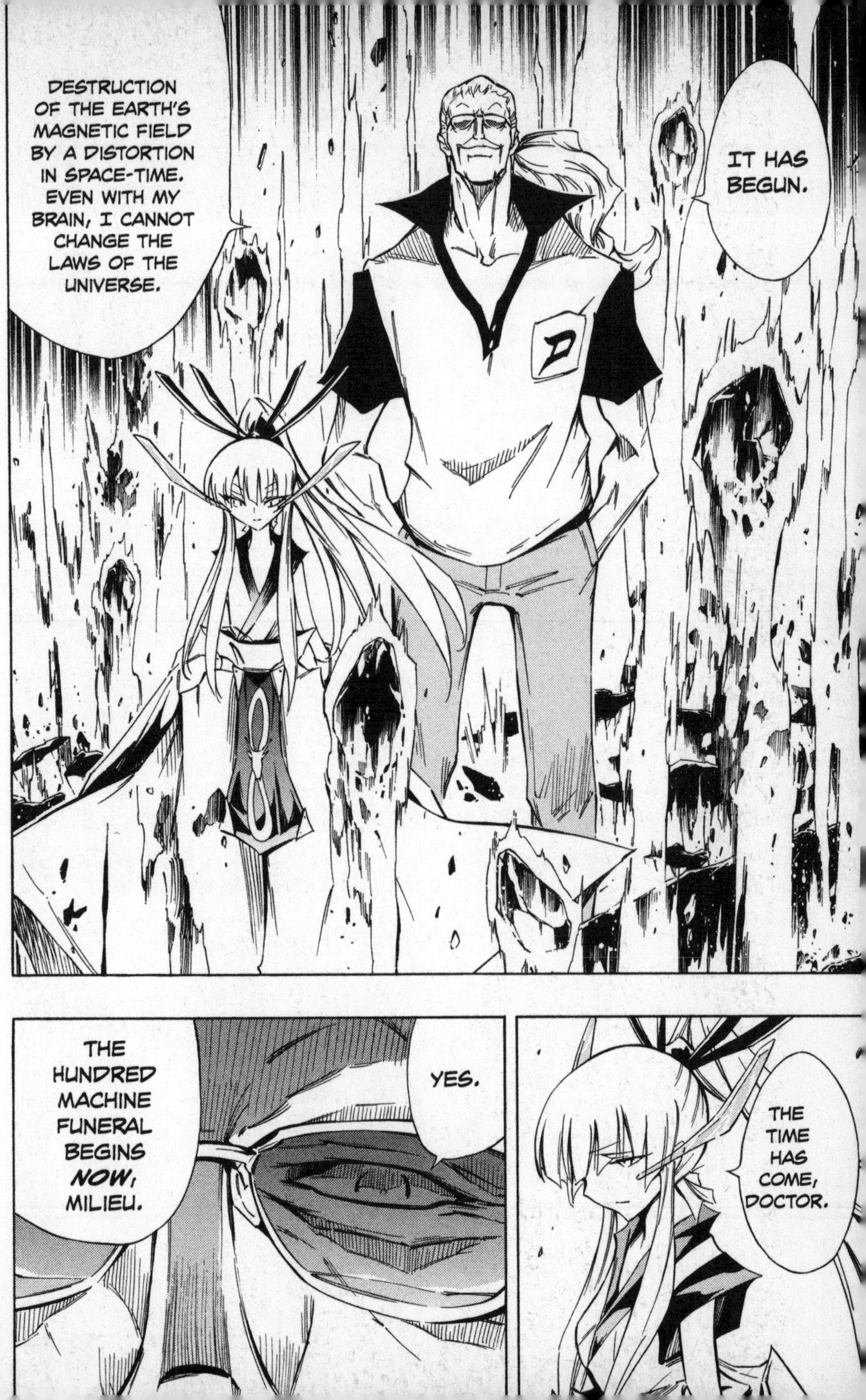
IT HAS BEGUN.
DESTRUCTION OF THE EARTH'S MAGNETIC FIELD BY A DISTORTION IN SPACE-TIME. EVEN WITH MY BRAIN, I CANNOT CHANGE THE LAWS OF THE UNIVERSE.
THE TIME HAS COME, DOCTOR.
YES.
THE HUNDRED MACHINE FUNERAL BEGINS *NOW*, MILIEU.

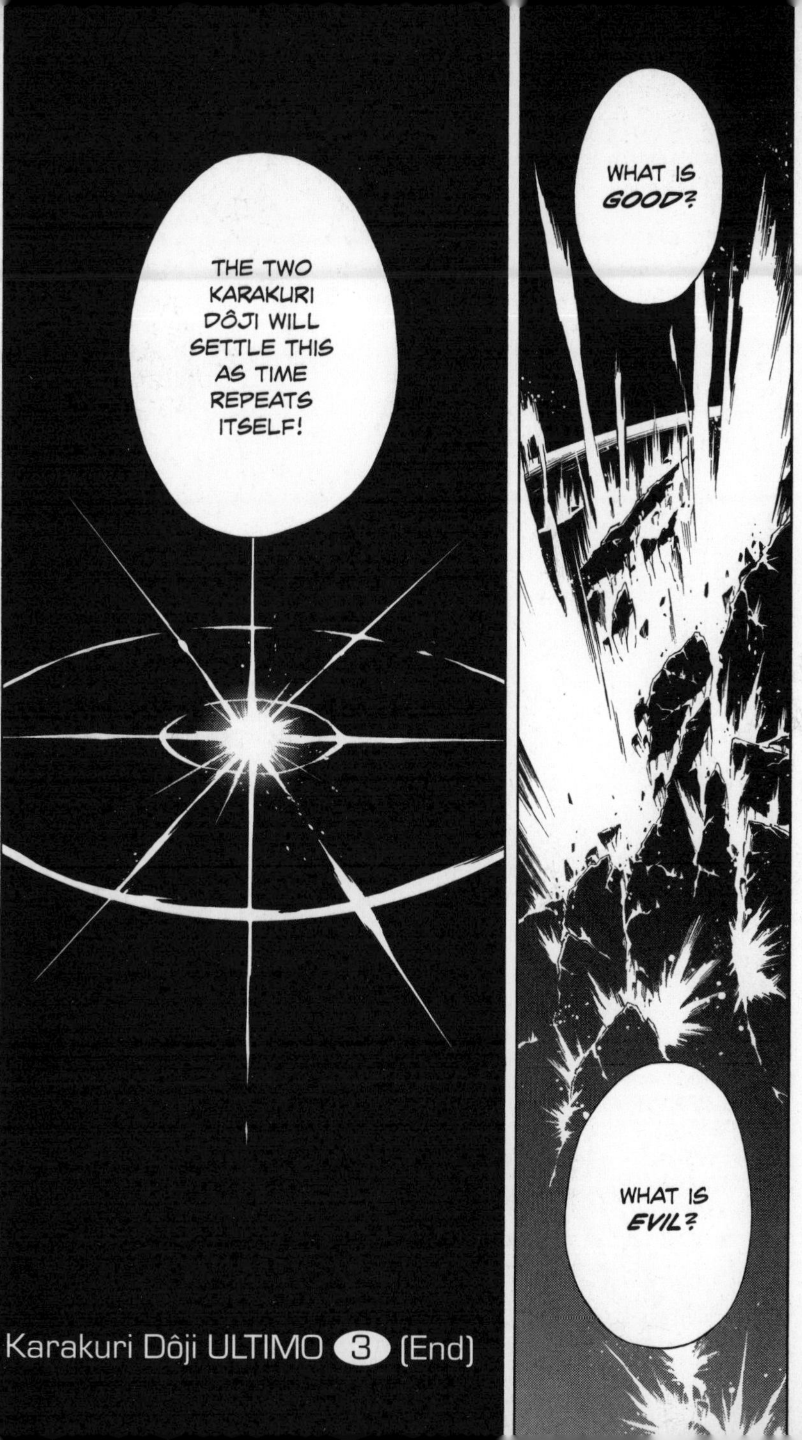
WHAT IS *GOOD?*
WHAT IS *EVIL?*
THE TWO KARAKURI DÔJI WILL SETTLE THIS AS TIME REPEATS ITSELF!
Karakuri Dôji ULTIMO 3 (End)

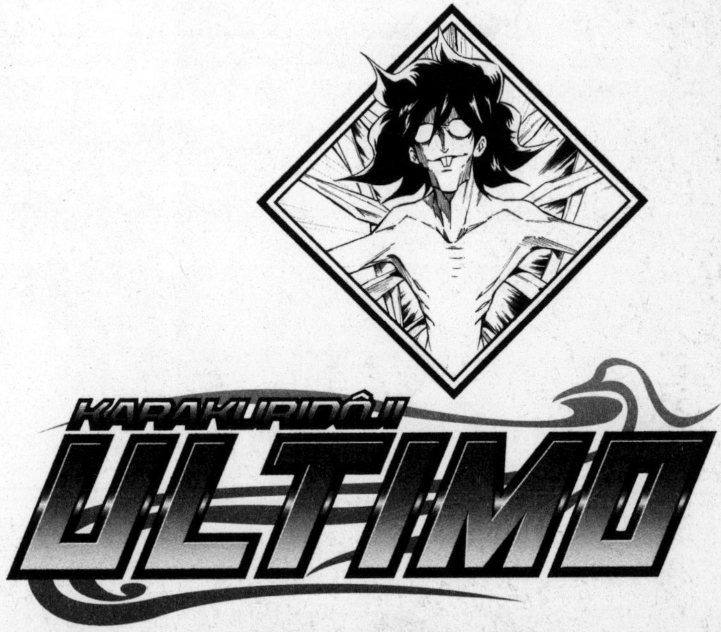

KARAKURIDÔJI
ULTIMO

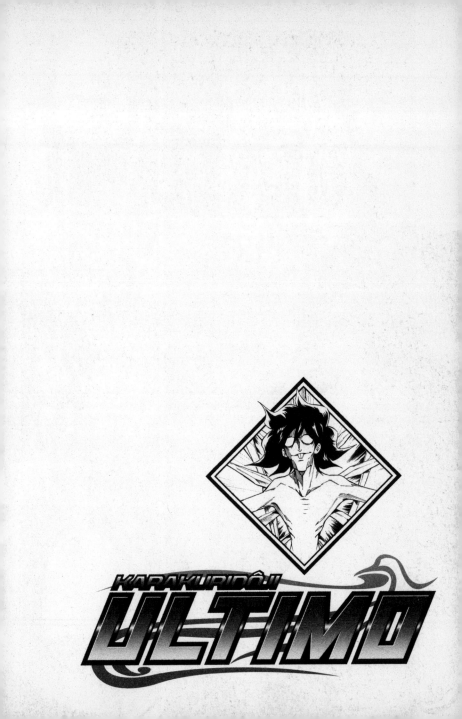

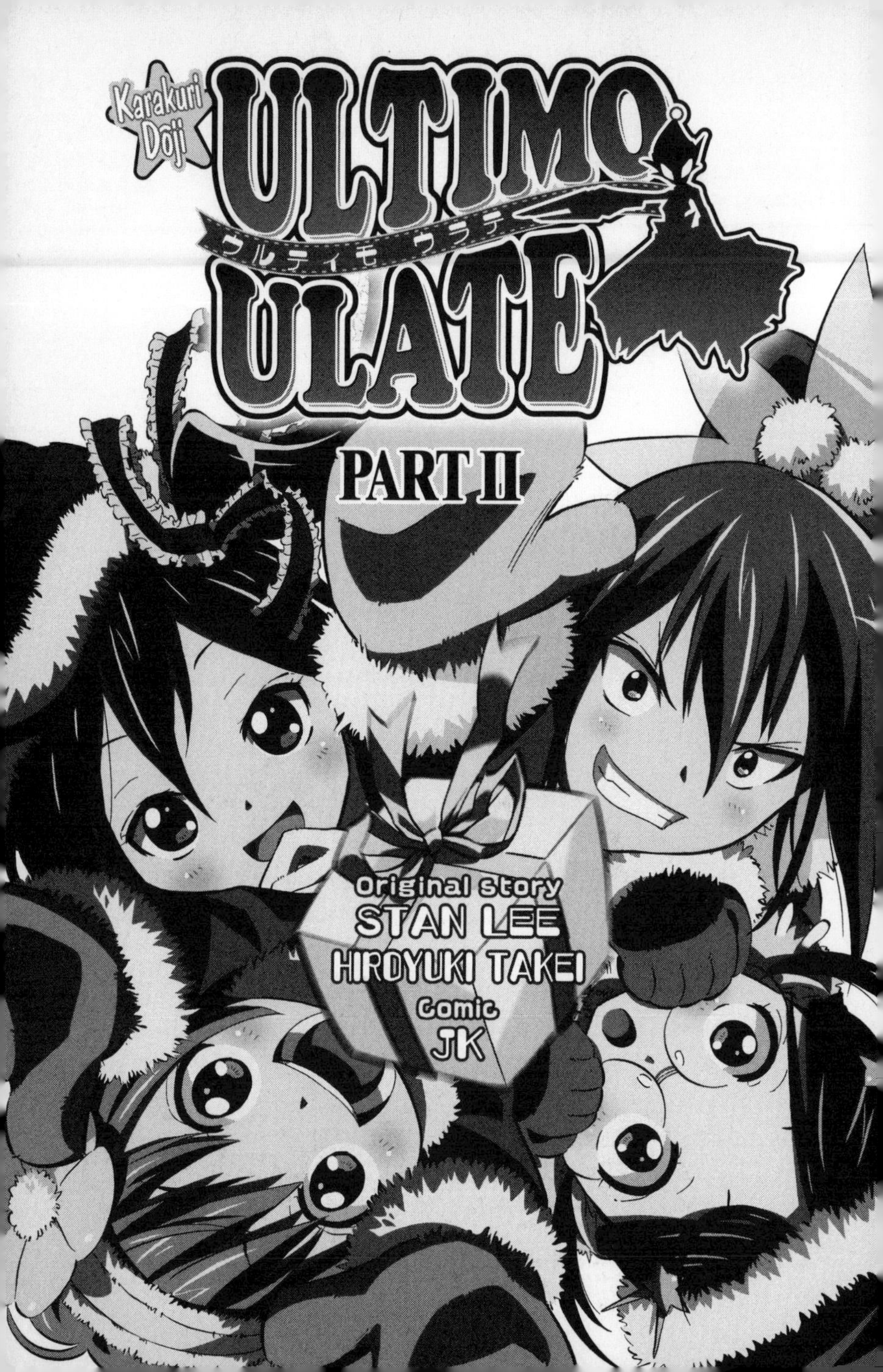
Karakuri Dōji
ULTIMO
ウルティモ ウラテ
ULATE
PART II
Original story
STAN LEE
HIROYUKI TAKEI
Comic
JK

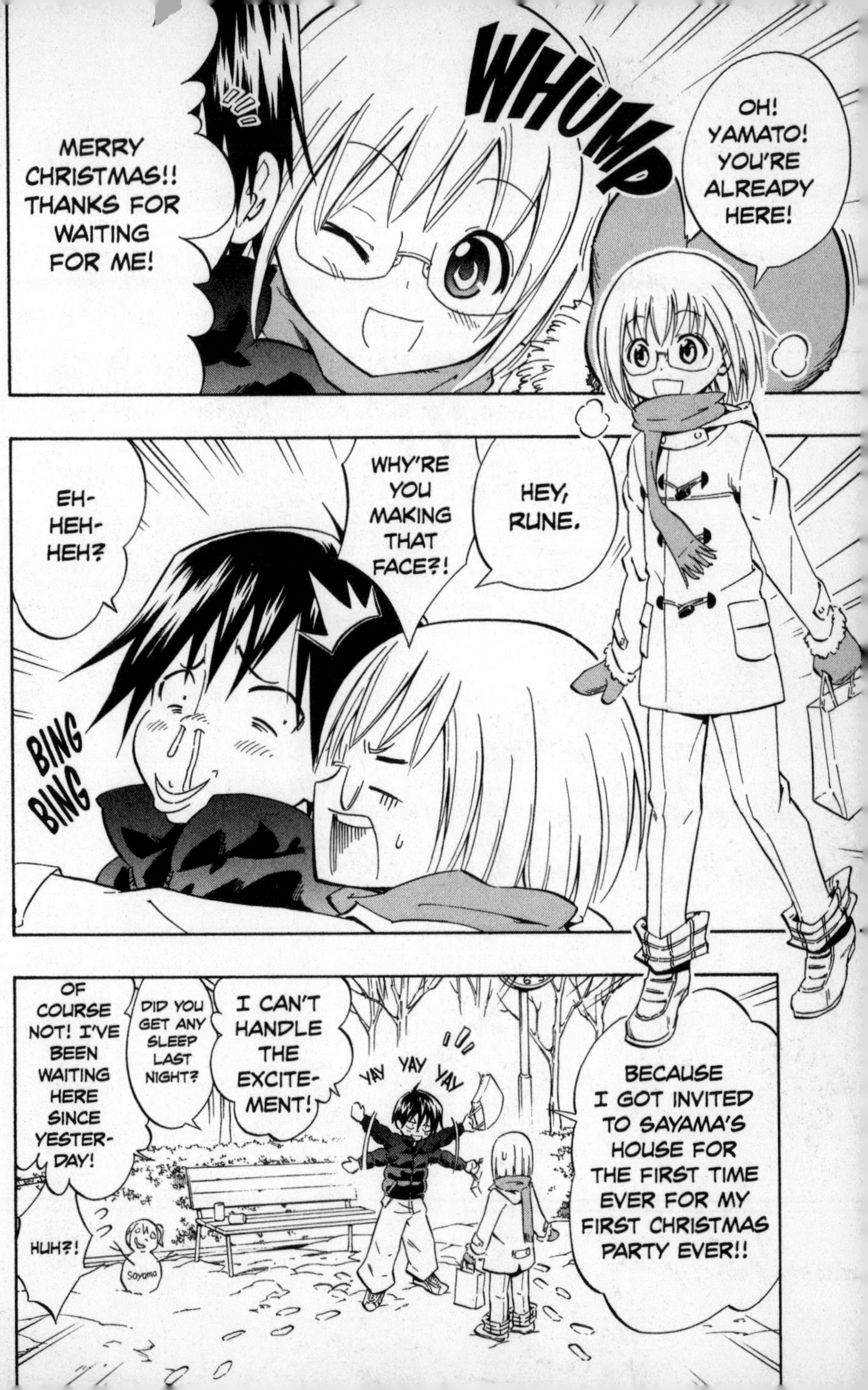
OH! YAMATO! YOU'RE ALREADY HERE!
WHUMP
MERRY CHRISTMAS!! THANKS FOR WAITING FOR ME!
HEY, RUNE.
WHY'RE YOU MAKING THAT FACE?!
EH-HEH-HEH?
BING BING
BECAUSE I GOT INVITED TO SAYAMA'S HOUSE FOR THE FIRST TIME EVER FOR MY FIRST CHRISTMAS PARTY EVER!!
YAY YAY YAY
I CAN'T HANDLE THE EXCITE-MENT!
DID YOU GET ANY SLEEP LAST NIGHT?
OF COURSE NOT! I'VE BEEN WAITING HERE SINCE YESTER-DAY!
HUH?!
Sayama

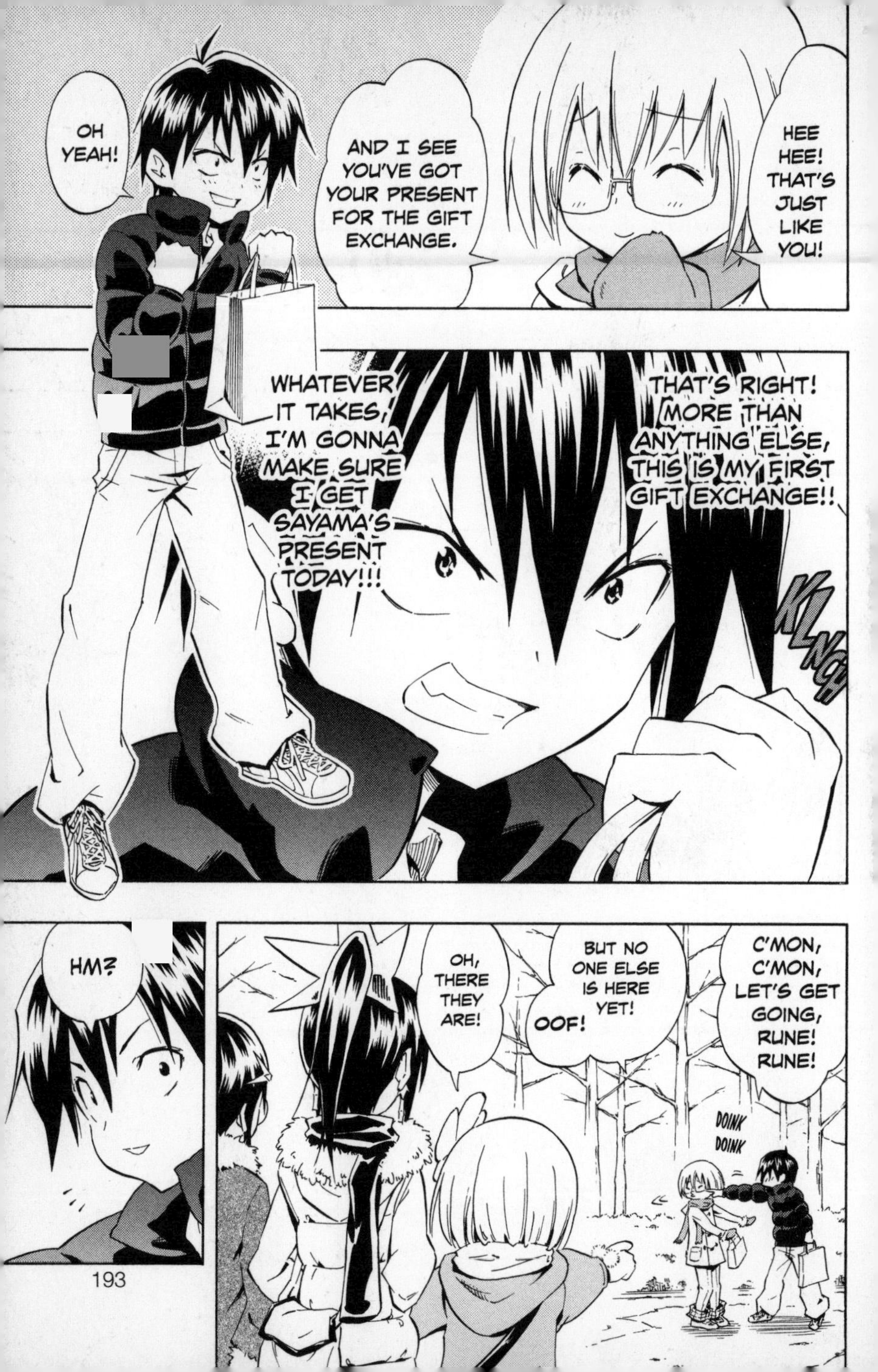
HEE HEE! THAT'S JUST LIKE YOU!
AND I SEE YOU'VE GOT YOUR PRESENT FOR THE GIFT EXCHANGE.
OH YEAH!
THAT'S RIGHT! MORE THAN ANYTHING ELSE, THIS IS MY FIRST GIFT EXCHANGE!!
WHATEVER IT TAKES, I'M GONNA MAKE SURE I GET SAYAMA'S PRESENT TODAY!!!
KLNCH
C'MON, C'MON, LET'S GET GOING, RUNE! RUNE!
DOINK DOINK
BUT NO ONE ELSE IS HERE YET!
OOF!
OH, THERE THEY ARE!
HM?

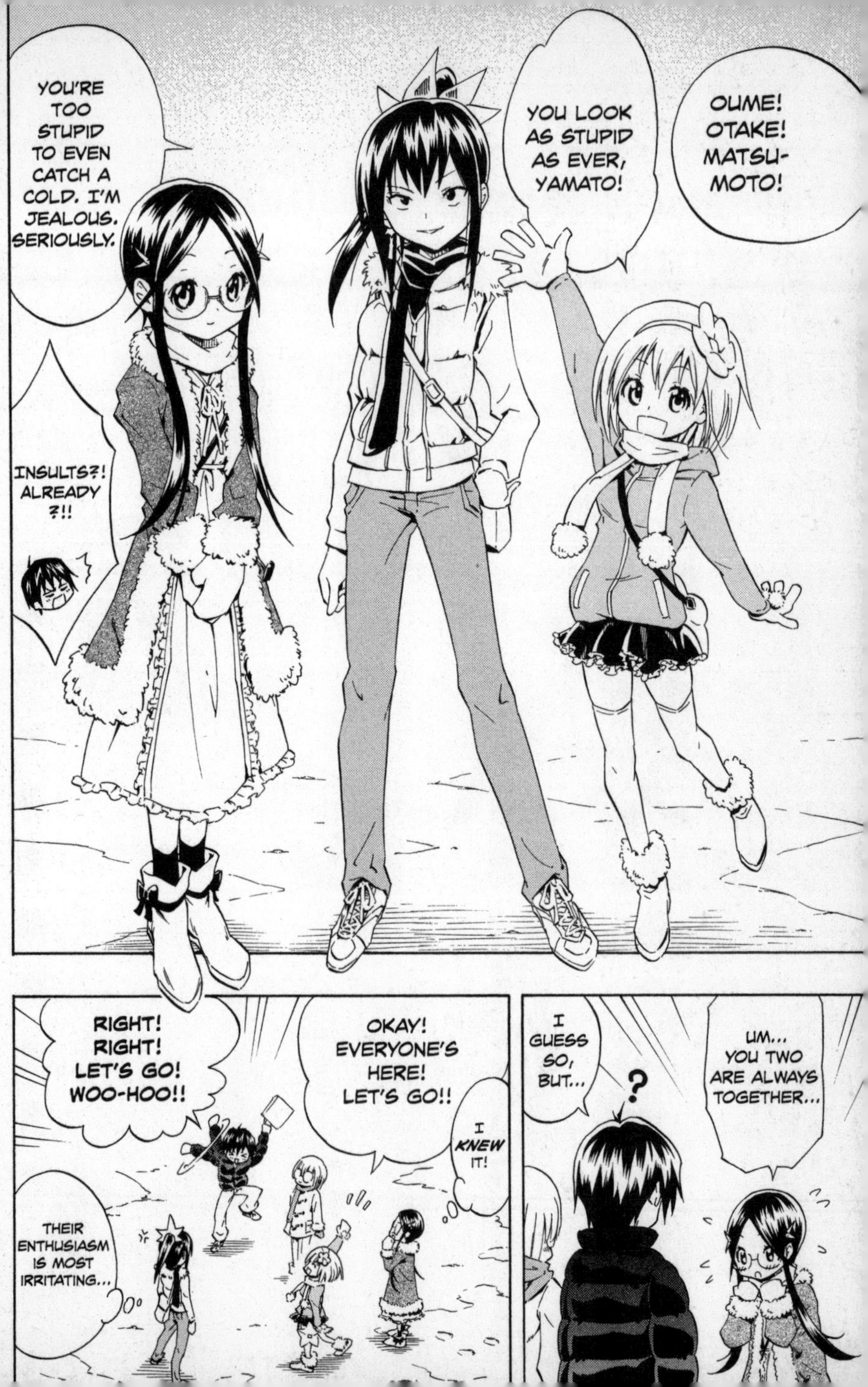
OUME! OTAKE! MATSU-MOTO!
YOU LOOK AS STUPID AS EVER, YAMATO!
YOU'RE TOO STUPID TO EVEN CATCH A COLD. I'M JEALOUS. SERIOUSLY.
INSULTS?! ALREADY?!!
UM... YOU TWO ARE ALWAYS TOGETHER...
I GUESS SO, BUT...
?
OKAY! EVERYONE'S HERE! LET'S GO!!
I KNEW IT!
RIGHT! RIGHT! LET'S GO! WOO-HOO!!
THEIR ENTHUSIASM IS MOST IRRITATING...

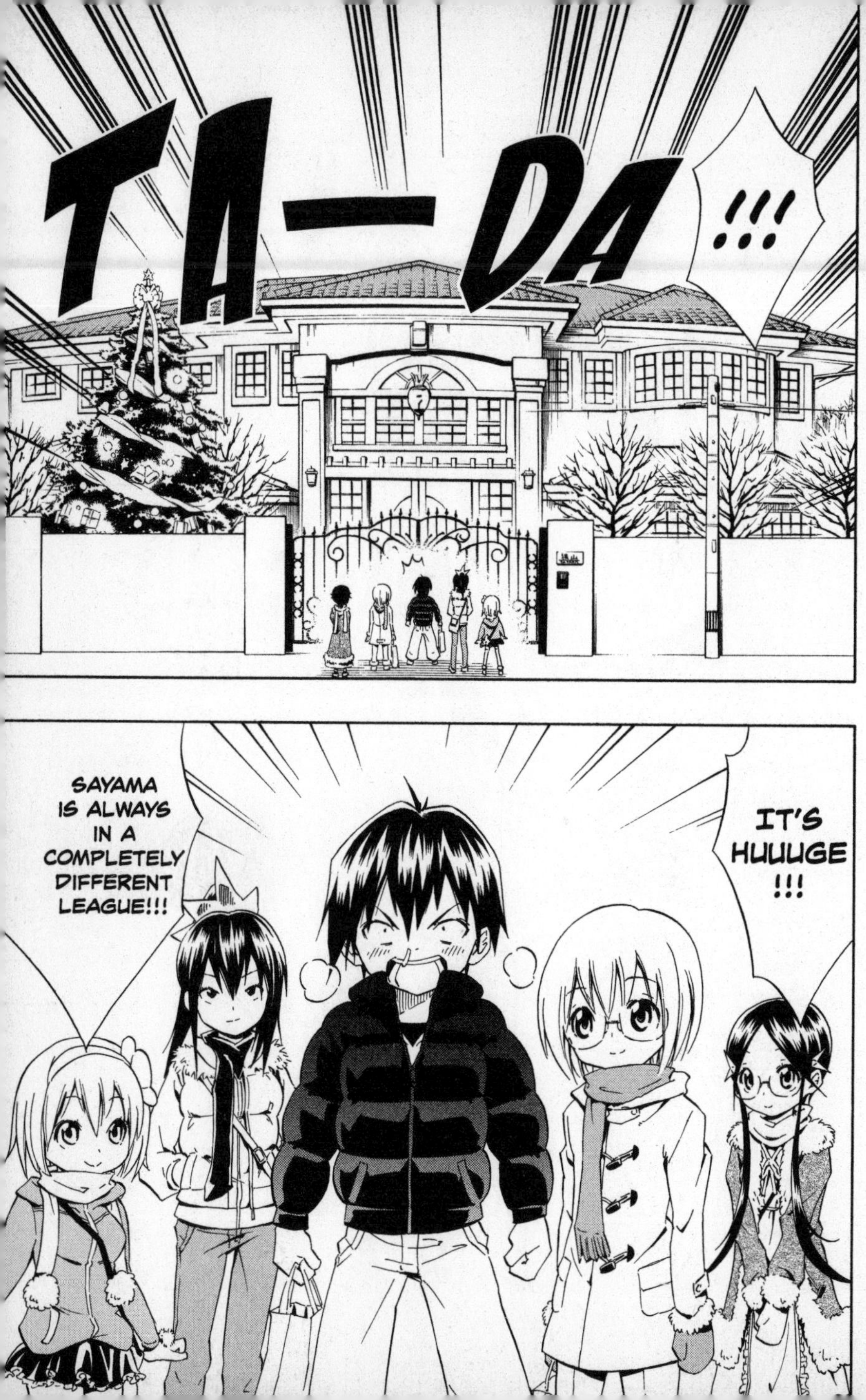
!!!
TA-DA
IT'S HUUUGE!!!
SAYAMA IS ALWAYS IN A COMPLETELY DIFFERENT LEAGUE!!!

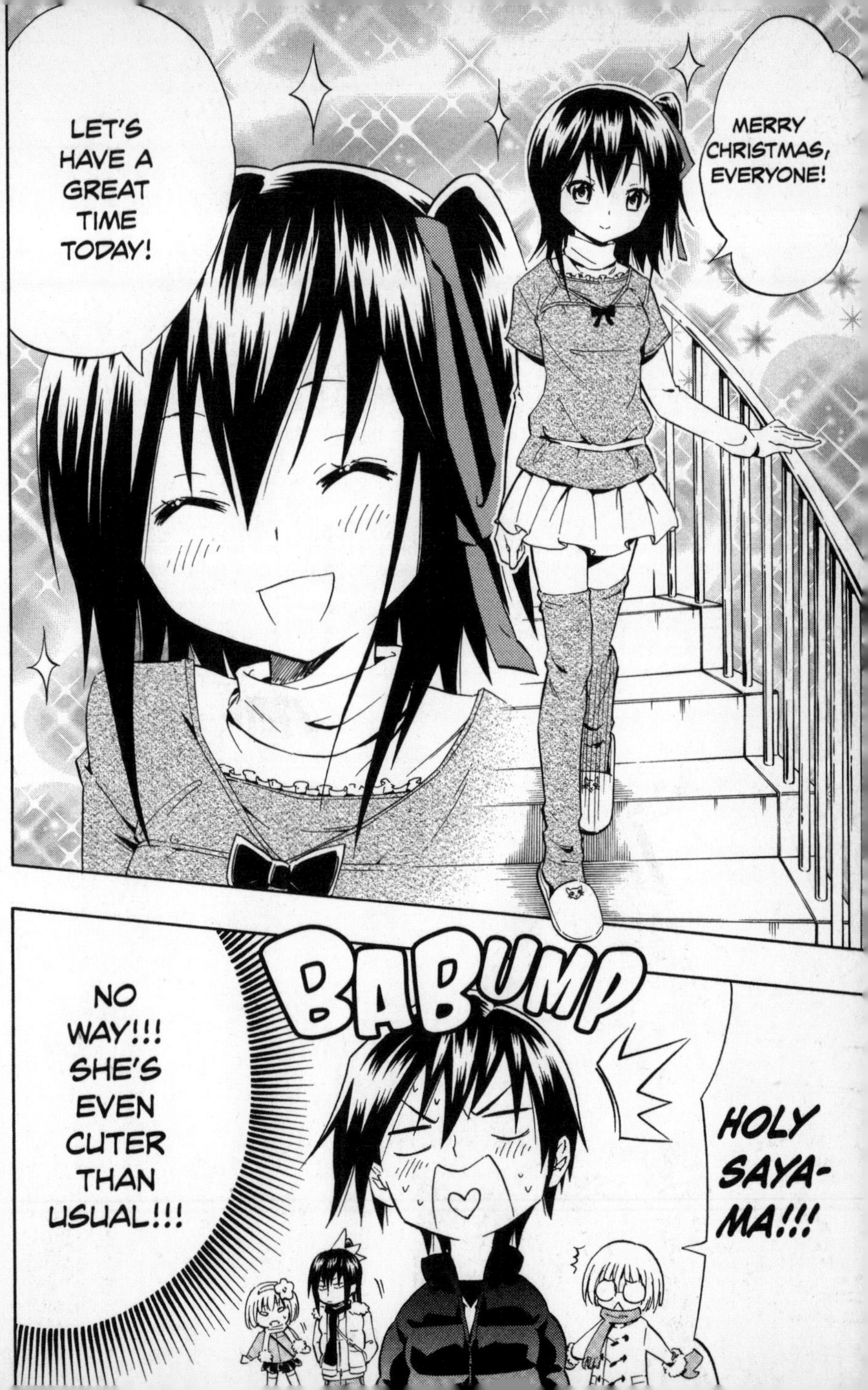
MERRY CHRISTMAS, EVERYONE!
LET'S HAVE A GREAT TIME TODAY!
BABUMP
HOLY SAYA-MA!!!
NO WAY!!! SHE'S EVEN CUTER THAN USUAL!!!

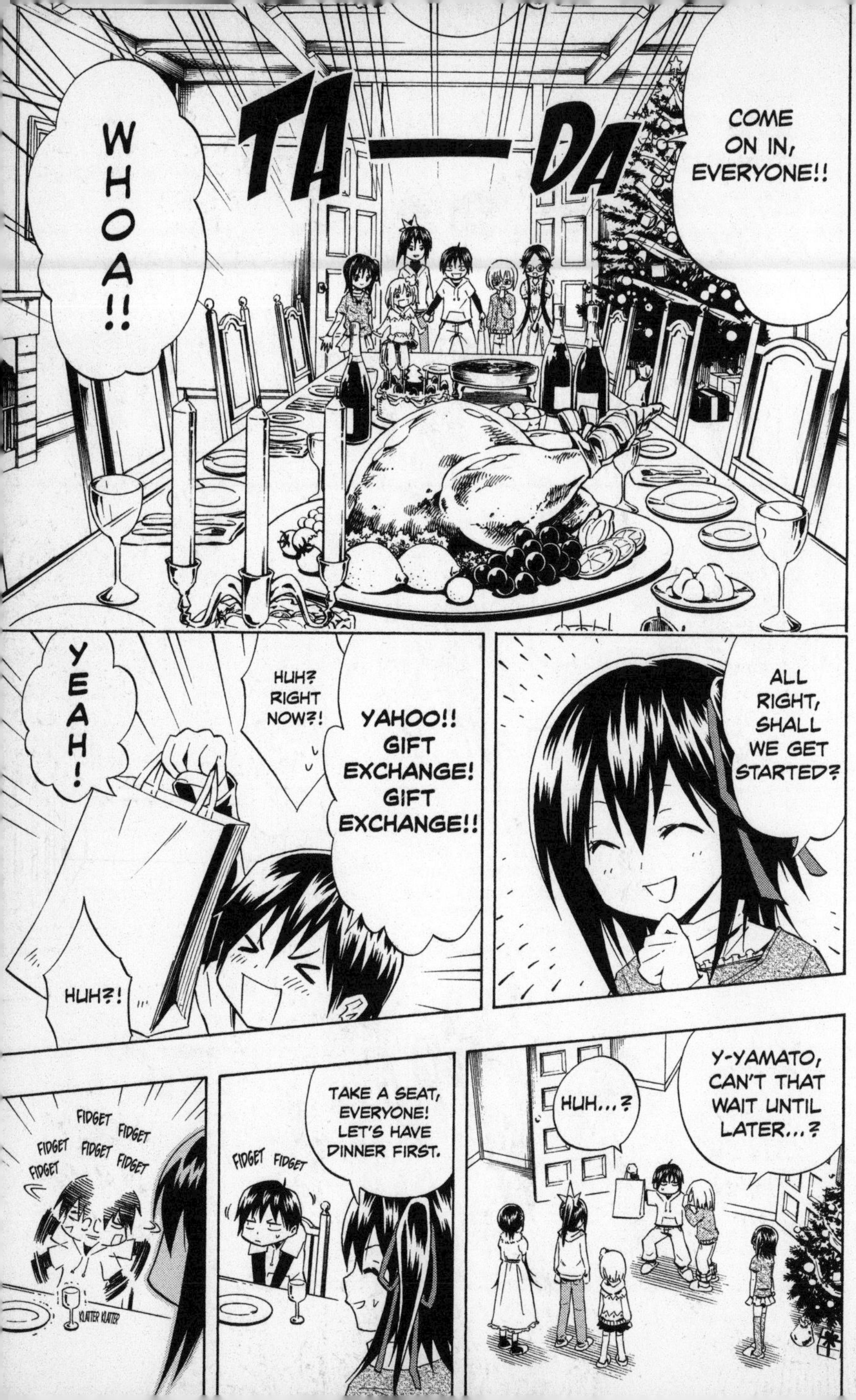
COME ON IN, EVERYONE!!
TA—DA
WHOA!!
ALL RIGHT, SHALL WE GET STARTED?
YAHOO!! GIFT EXCHANGE! GIFT EXCHANGE!!
HUH? RIGHT NOW?!
YEAH!
HUH?!
Y-YAMATO, CAN'T THAT WAIT UNTIL LATER...?
HUH...?
TAKE A SEAT, EVERYONE! LET'S HAVE DINNER FIRST.
FIDGET FIDGET
FIDGET FIDGET
FIDGET FIDGET FIDGET
FIDGET
KLATTER KLATTER

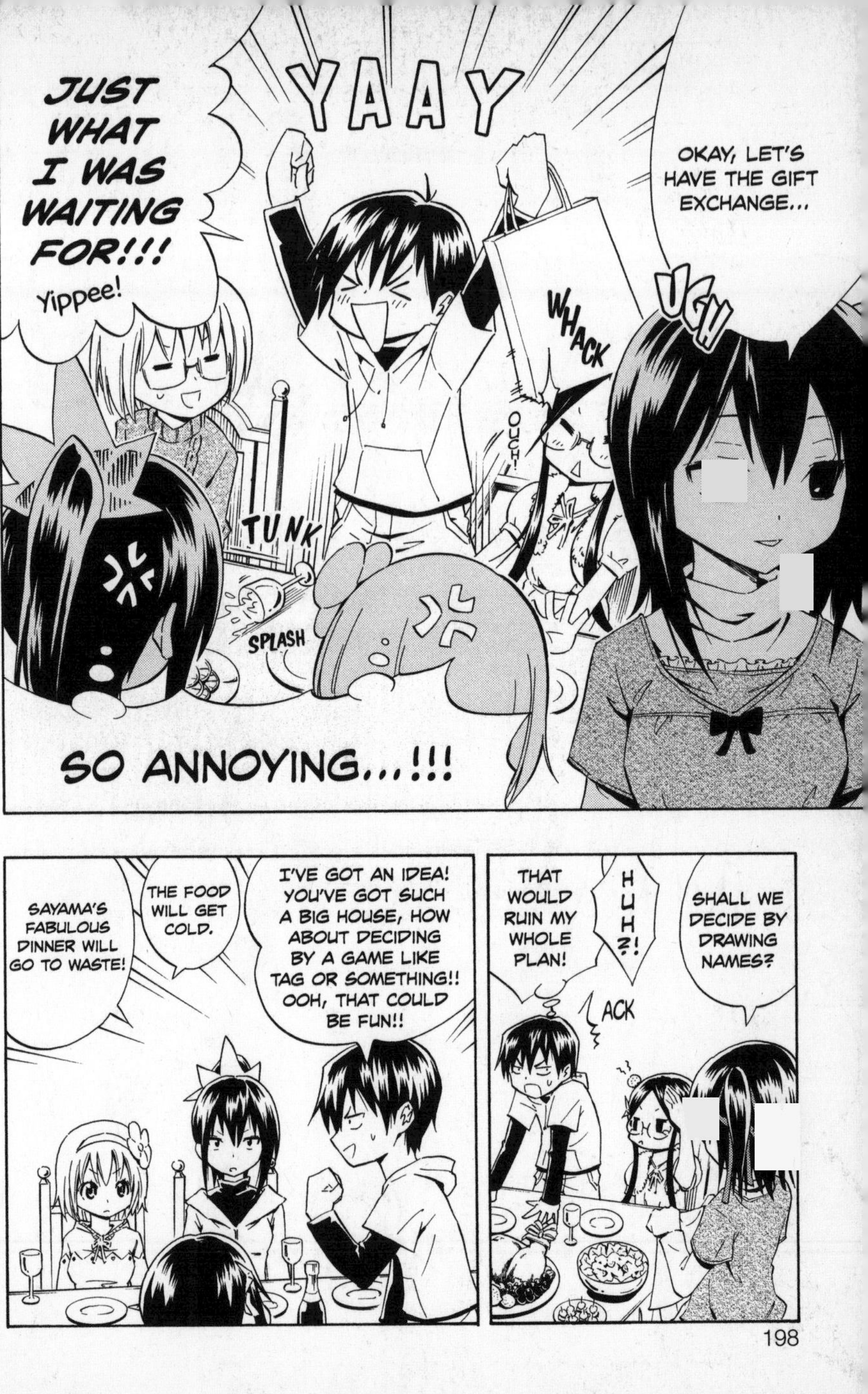
OKAY, LET'S HAVE THE GIFT EXCHANGE...
UGH
WHACK
OUCH!
YAAY
JUST WHAT I WAS WAITING FOR!!!
Yippee!
TUNK
SPLASH
SO ANNOYING...!!!
SHALL WE DECIDE BY DRAWING NAMES?
HUH?!
THAT WOULD RUIN MY WHOLE PLAN!
ACK
I'VE GOT AN IDEA! YOU'VE GOT SUCH A BIG HOUSE, HOW ABOUT DECIDING BY A GAME LIKE TAG OR SOMETHING!! OOH, THAT COULD BE FUN!!
THE FOOD WILL GET COLD.
SAYAMA'S FABULOUS DINNER WILL GO TO WASTE!

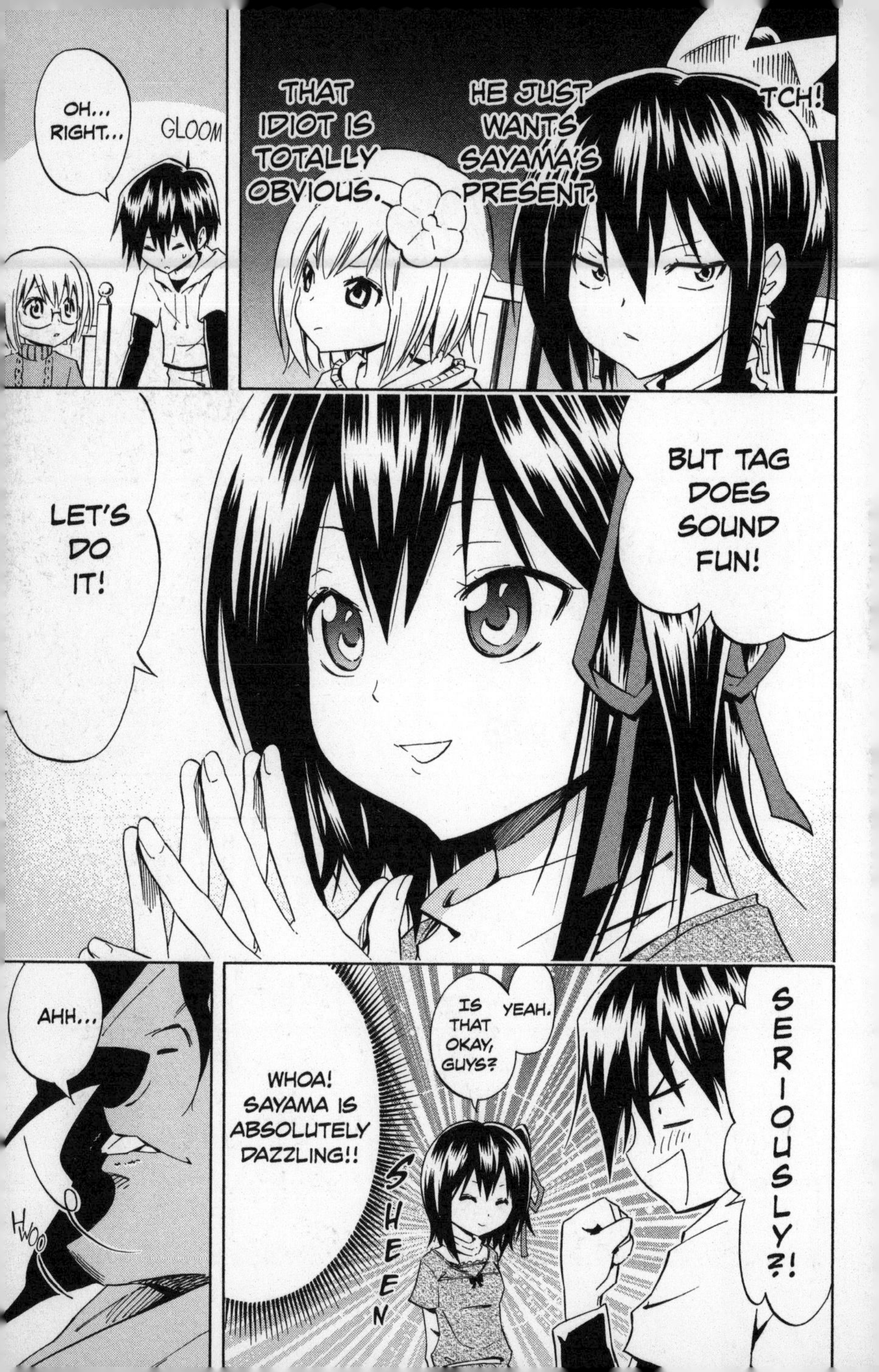
TCH!
HE JUST WANTS SAYAMA'S PRESENT.
THAT IDIOT IS TOTALLY OBVIOUS.
OH... RIGHT...
GLOOM
BUT TAG DOES SOUND FUN!
LET'S DO IT!
SERIOUSLY?!
YEAH.
IS THAT OKAY, GUYS?
WHOA! SAYAMA IS ABSOLUTELY DAZZLING!!
SHEEN
AHH...
HWOO

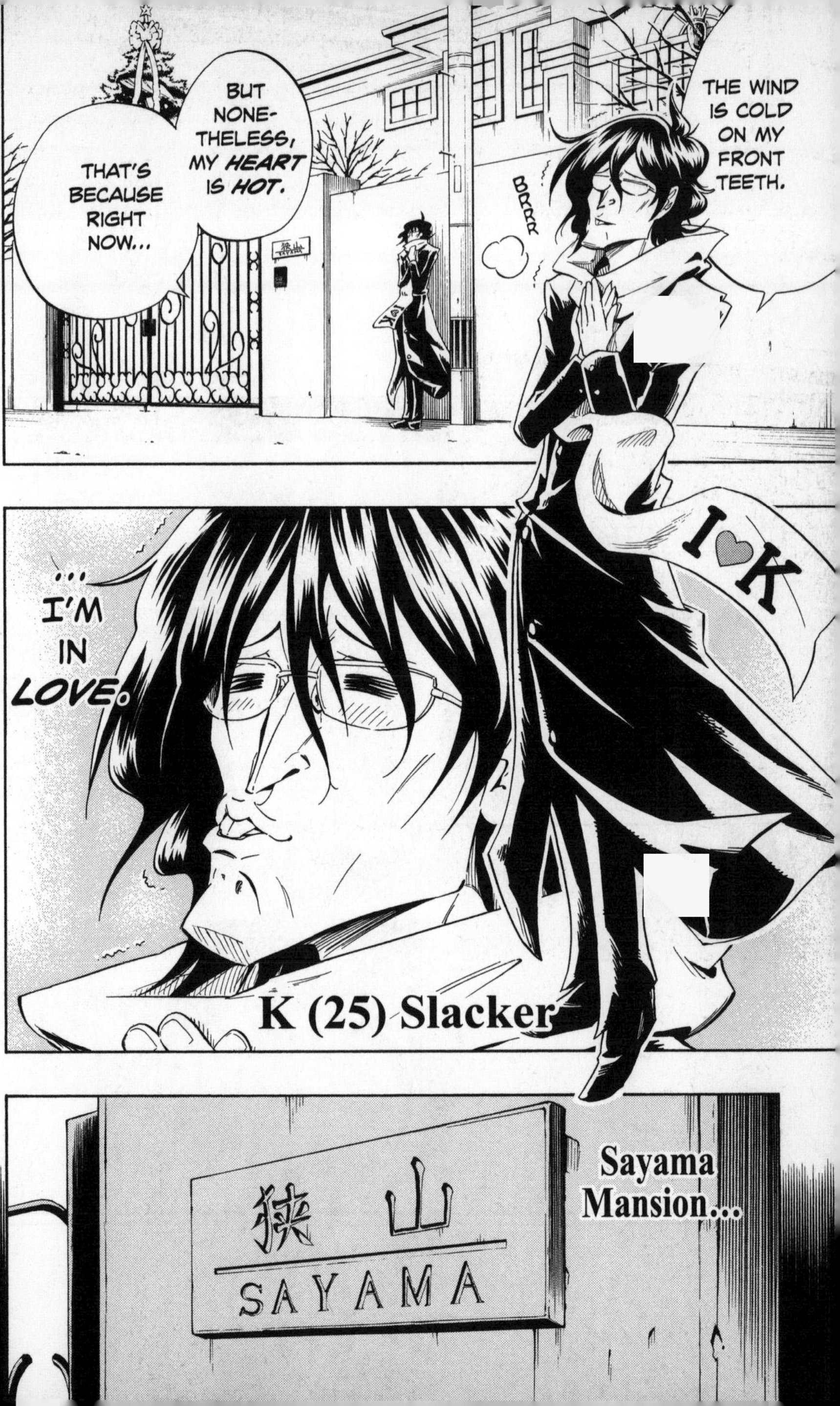
THE WIND IS COLD ON MY FRONT TEETH.
BRRRR
BUT NONE-THELESS, MY HEART IS HOT.
THAT'S BECAUSE RIGHT NOW...
I♥K
...I'M IN LOVE.
K (25) Slacker
Sayama Mansion...
狭山
SAYAMA

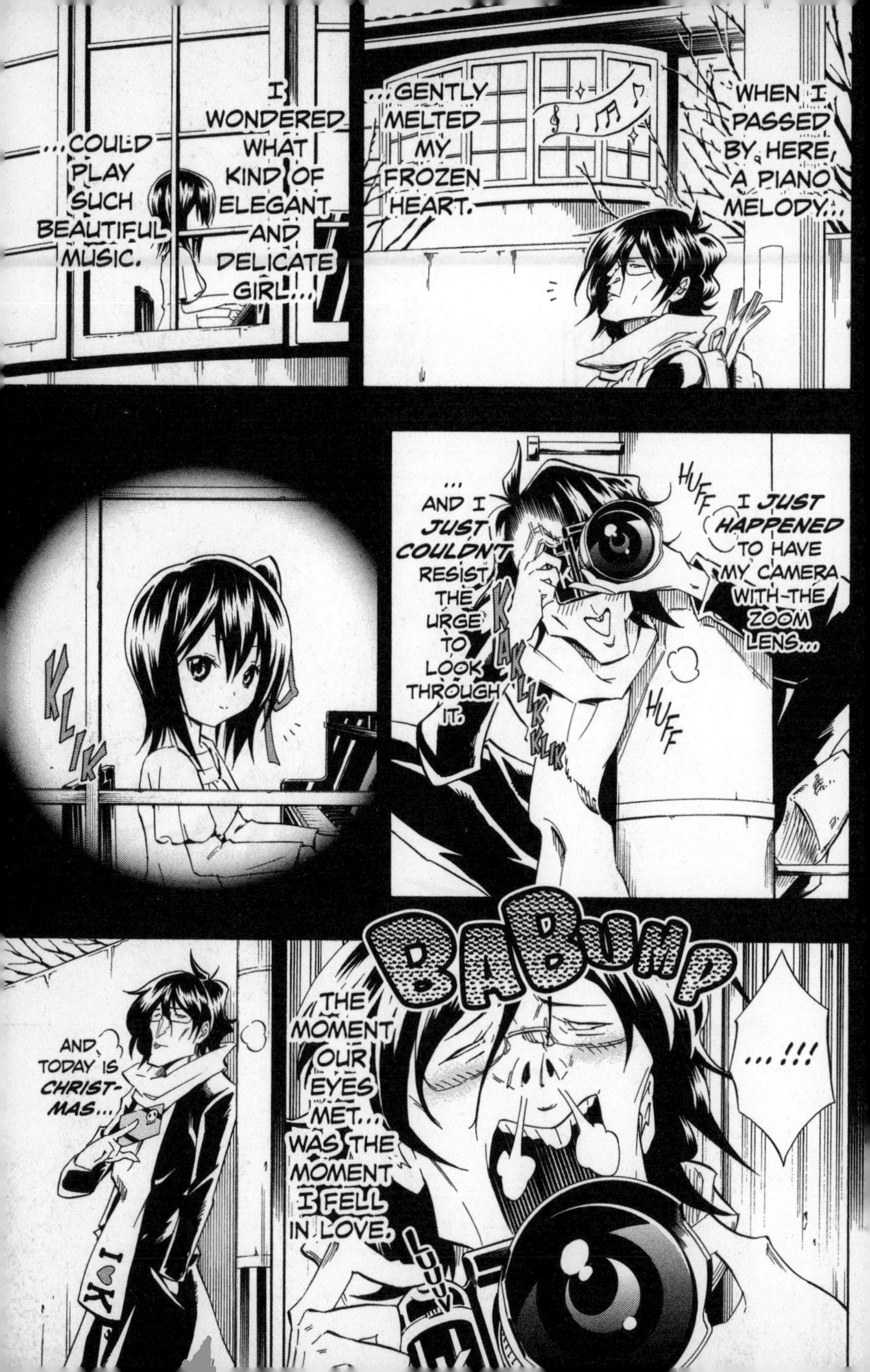
WHEN I PASSED BY HERE, A PIANO MELODY...
...GENTLY MELTED MY FROZEN HEART.
I WONDERED WHAT KIND OF ELEGANT AND DELICATE GIRL...
...COULD PLAY SUCH BEAUTIFUL MUSIC.
HUFF
I *JUST HAPPENED* TO HAVE MY CAMERA WITH THE ZOOM LENS...
HUFF
...AND I *JUST COULDN'T* RESIST THE URGE TO LOOK THROUGH IT.
KLAK KLIK KLIK
KLIK
BABUMP
...!!!
THE MOMENT OUR EYES MET... WAS THE MOMENT I FELL IN LOVE.
LUUV
AND TODAY IS *CHRISTMAS*...
I♥K

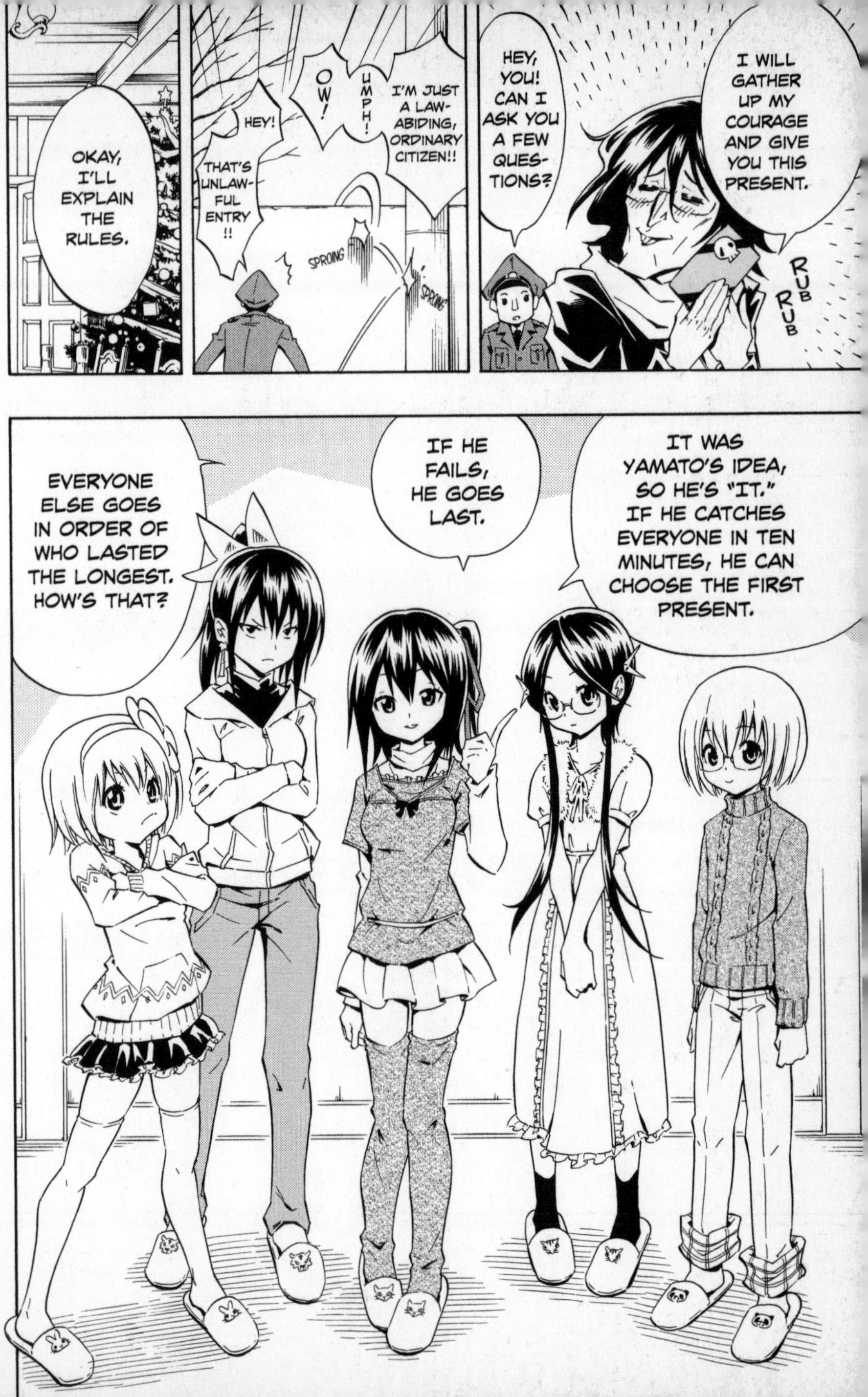
I WILL GATHER UP MY COURAGE AND GIVE YOU THIS PRESENT.
RUB RUB
HEY, YOU! CAN I ASK YOU A FEW QUES-TIONS?
I'M JUST A LAW-ABIDING, ORDINARY CITIZEN!!
UMPH!
OW!
HEY!
THAT'S UNLAW-FUL ENTRY!!
SPROING
SPROING
OKAY, I'LL EXPLAIN THE RULES.
IT WAS YAMATO'S IDEA, SO HE'S "IT." IF HE CATCHES EVERYONE IN TEN MINUTES, HE CAN CHOOSE THE FIRST PRESENT.
IF HE FAILS, HE GOES LAST.
EVERYONE ELSE GOES IN ORDER OF WHO LASTED THE LONGEST. HOW'S THAT?

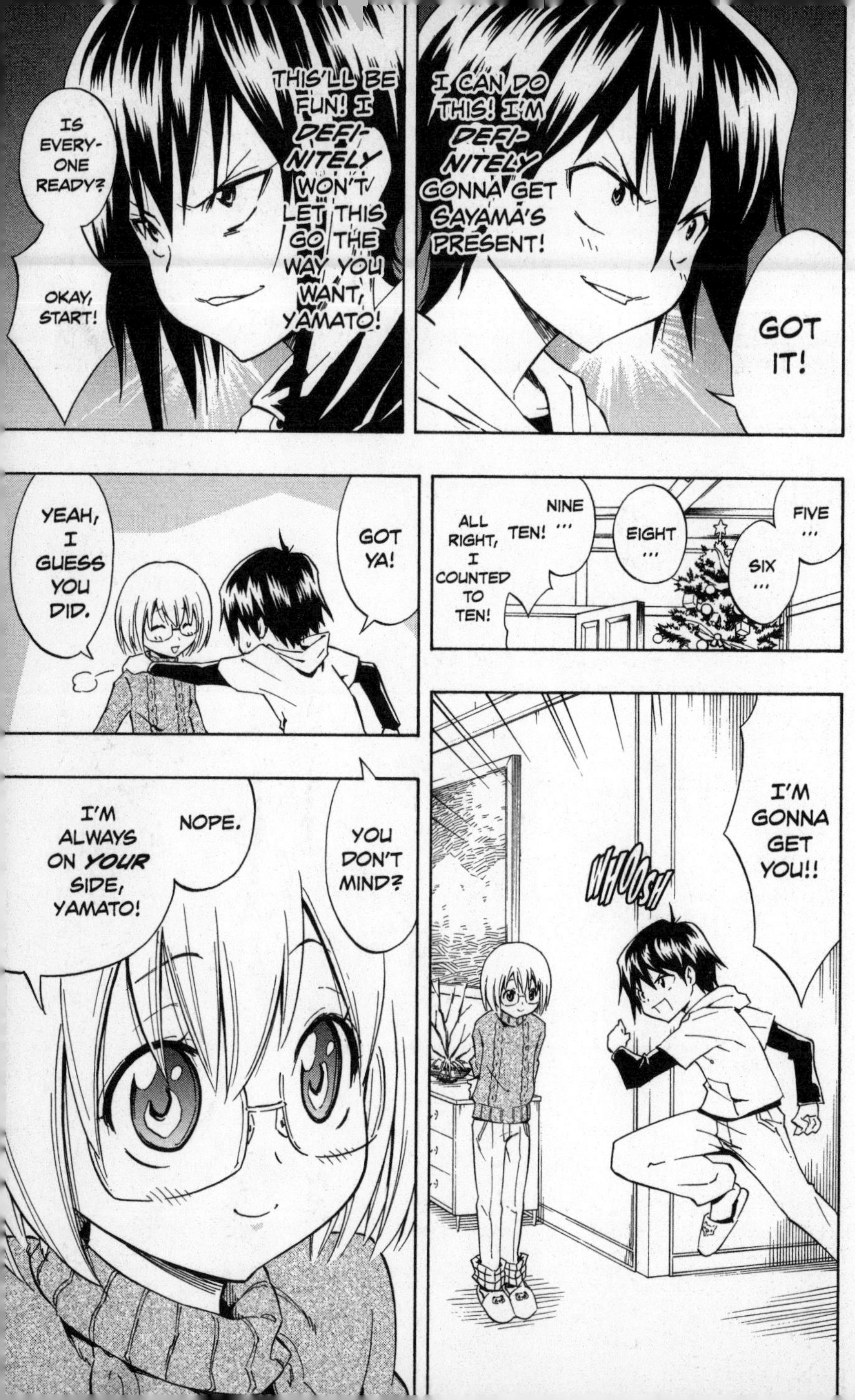
I CAN DO THIS! I'M DEFINITELY GONNA GET SAYAMA'S PRESENT!
GOT IT!
THIS'LL BE FUN! I DEFINITELY WON'T LET THIS GO THE WAY YOU WANT, YAMATO!
IS EVERYONE READY?
OKAY, START!
FIVE...
SIX...
EIGHT...
NINE...
TEN!
ALL RIGHT, I COUNTED TO TEN!
GOT YA!
YEAH, I GUESS YOU DID.
I'M GONNA GET YOU!!
WHOOSH
YOU DON'T MIND?
NOPE.
I'M ALWAYS ON YOUR SIDE, YAMATO!

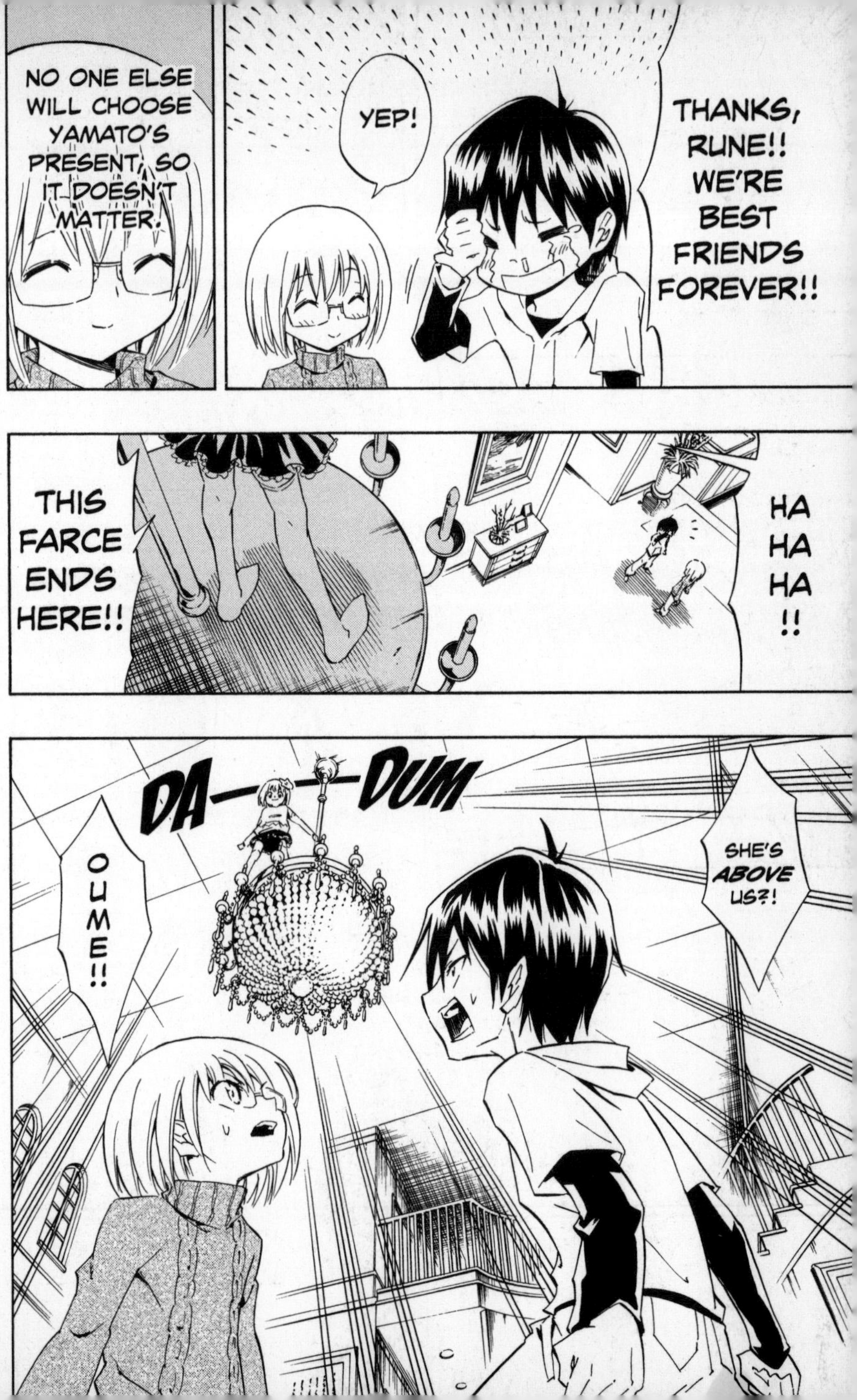
THANKS, RUNE!! WE'RE BEST FRIENDS FOREVER!!
YEP!
NO ONE ELSE WILL CHOOSE YAMATO'S PRESENT, SO IT DOESN'T MATTER.
HA HA HA!!
THIS FARCE ENDS HERE!!
DA—DUM
SHE'S ABOVE US?!
OUME!!

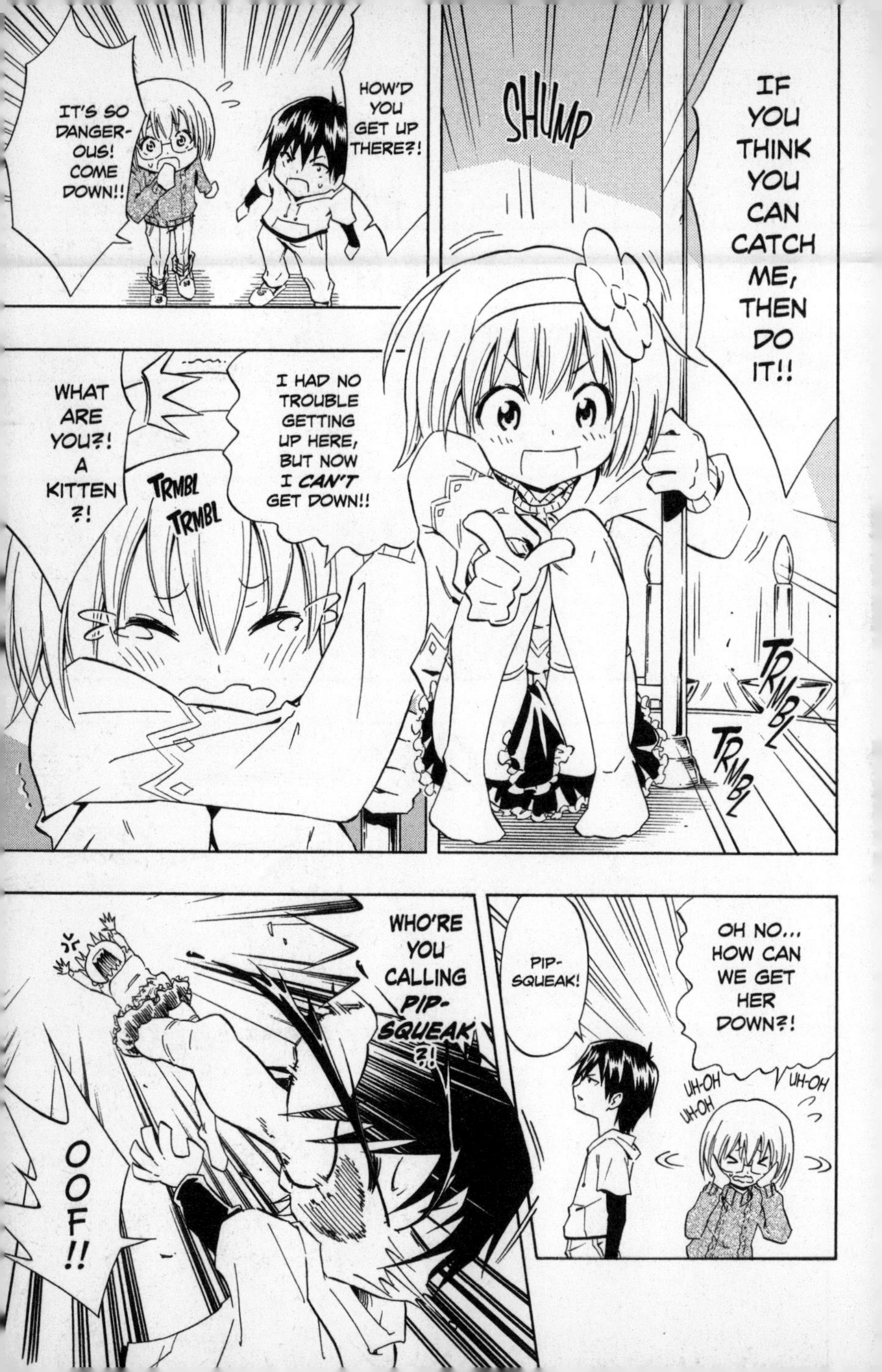
SHUMP
IF YOU THINK YOU CAN CATCH ME, THEN DO IT!!
TRMBL TRMBL
HOW'D YOU GET UP THERE?!
IT'S SO DANGER-OUS! COME DOWN!!
I HAD NO TROUBLE GETTING UP HERE, BUT NOW I *CAN'T* GET DOWN!!
WHAT ARE YOU?! A KITTEN?!
TRMBL TRMBL
OH NO... HOW CAN WE GET HER DOWN?!
UH-OH UH-OH UH-OH
PIP-SQUEAK!
WHO'RE YOU CALLING *PIP-SQUEAK*?!
OOF!!

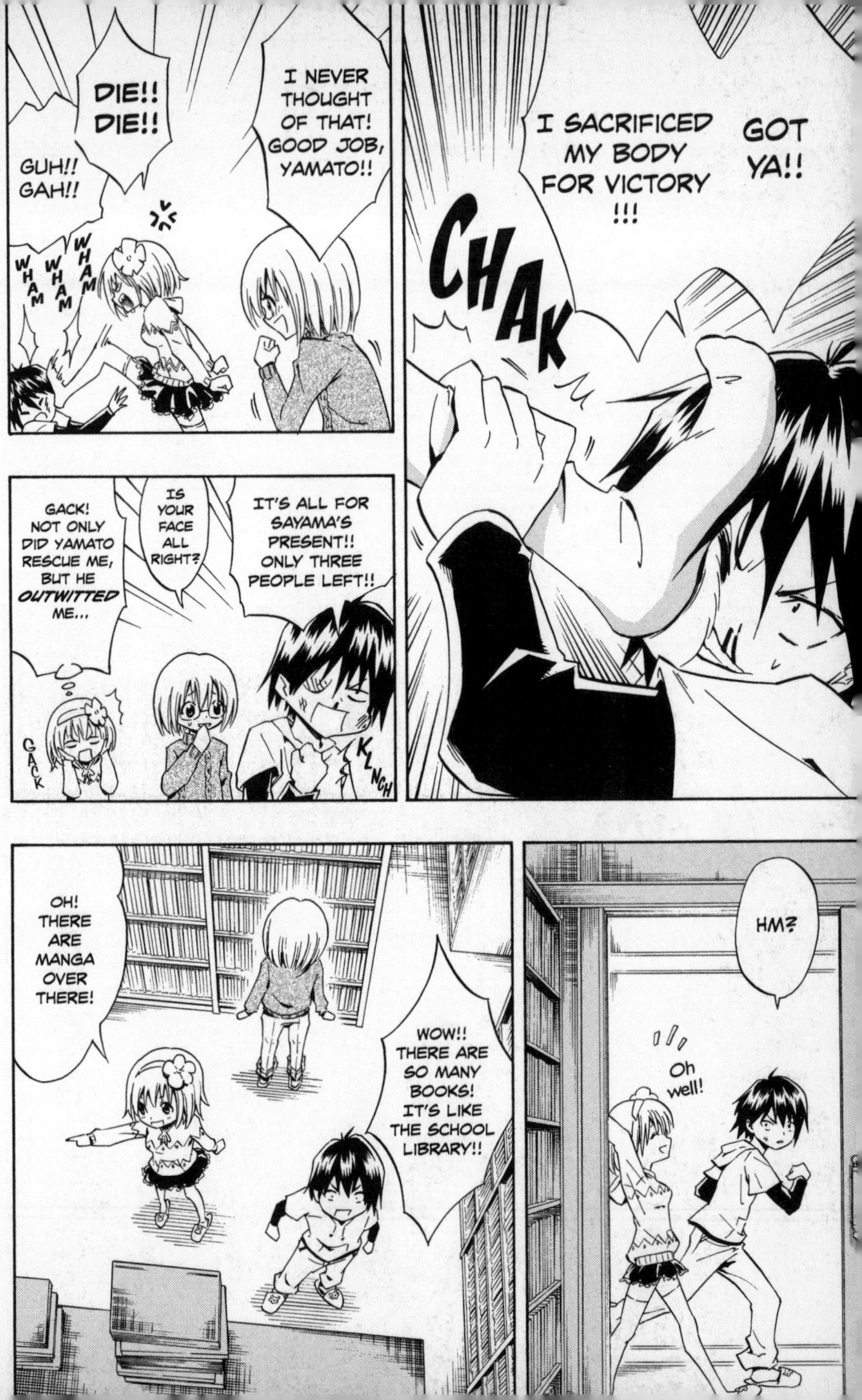
GOT YA!!
I SACRIFICED MY BODY FOR VICTORY!!!
CHAK
I NEVER THOUGHT OF THAT! GOOD JOB, YAMATO!!
DIE!! DIE!!
GUH!! GAH!!
WHAM WHAM WHAM
IT'S ALL FOR SAYAMA'S PRESENT!! ONLY THREE PEOPLE LEFT!!
IS YOUR FACE ALL RIGHT?
GACK! NOT ONLY DID YAMATO RESCUE ME, BUT HE *OUTWITTED* ME...
KLNCH
GACK
HM?
Oh well!
WOW!! THERE ARE SO MANY BOOKS! IT'S LIKE THE SCHOOL LIBRARY!!
OH! THERE ARE MANGA OVER THERE!

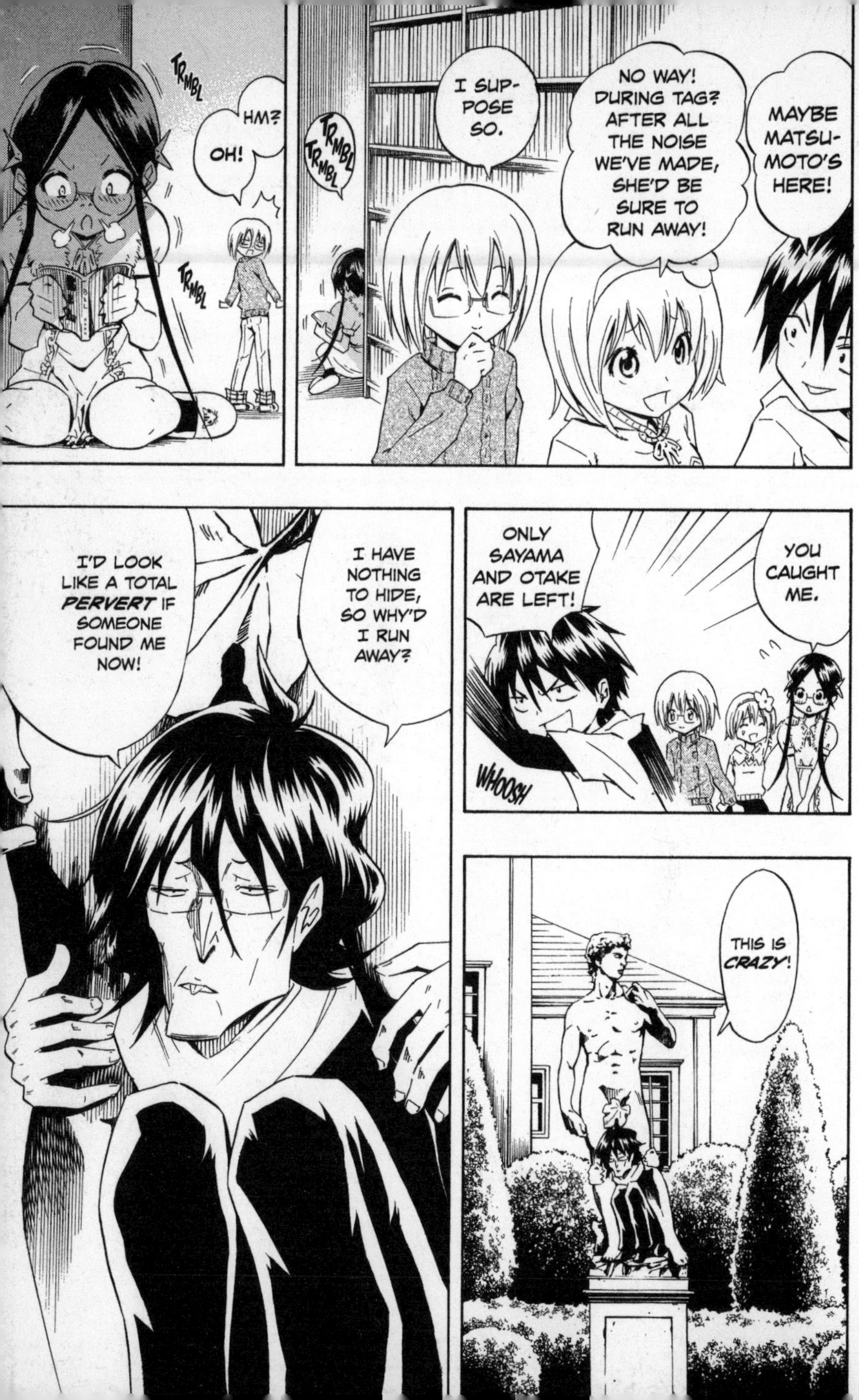
MAYBE MATSU-MOTO'S HERE!
NO WAY! DURING TAG? AFTER ALL THE NOISE WE'VE MADE, SHE'D BE SURE TO RUN AWAY!
I SUP-POSE SO.
TRMBL TRMBL
HM?
OH!
TRMBL
TRMBL
YOU CAUGHT ME.
ONLY SAYAMA AND OTAKE ARE LEFT!
WHOOSH
THIS IS CRAZY!
I HAVE NOTHING TO HIDE, SO WHY'D I RUN AWAY?
I'D LOOK LIKE A TOTAL PERVERT IF SOMEONE FOUND ME NOW!

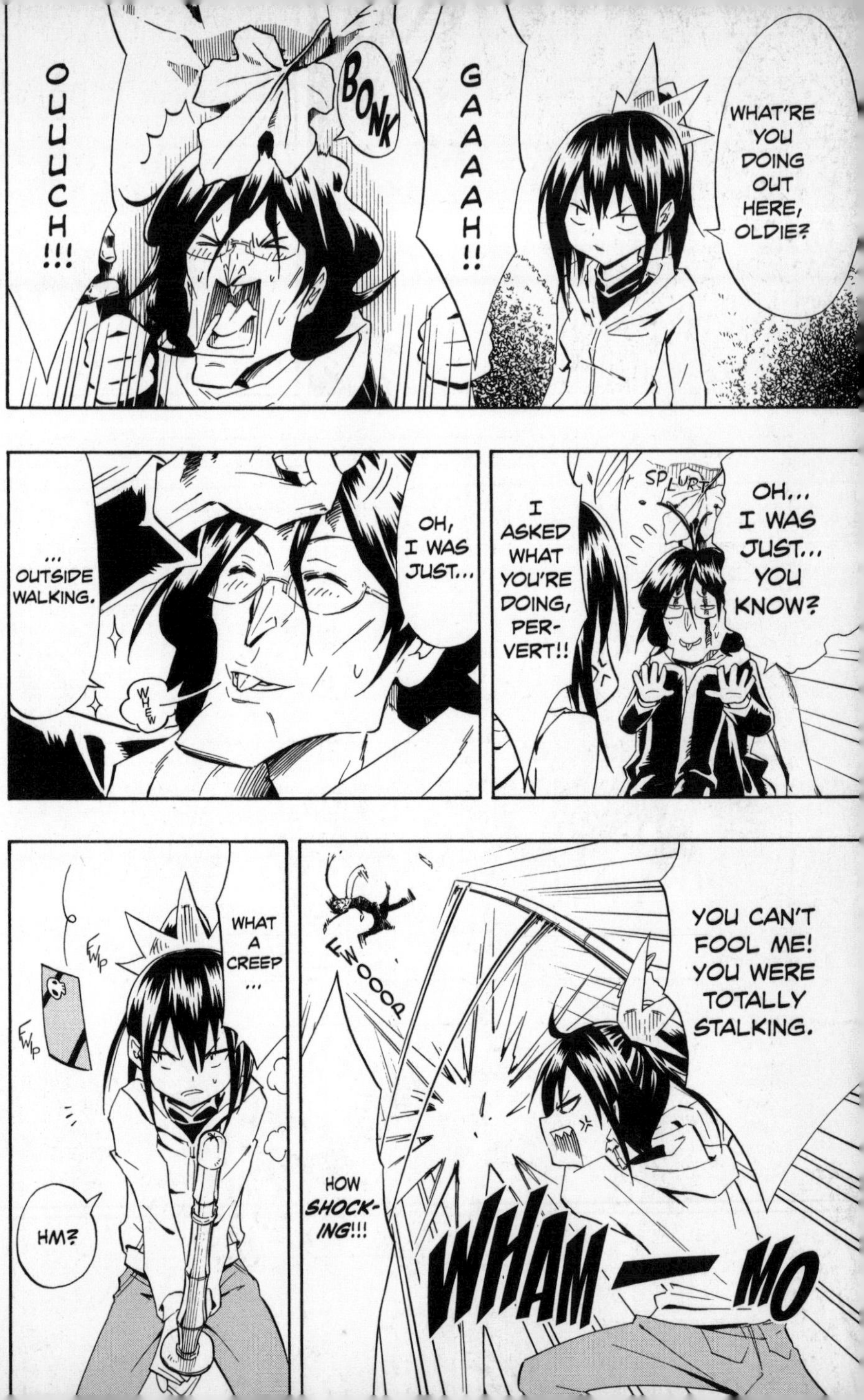
WHAT'RE YOU DOING OUT HERE, OLDIE?
GAAAAAH!!
BONK
OUUUCH!!!
SPLURT
OH... I WAS JUST... YOU KNOW?
I ASKED WHAT YOU'RE DOING, PER-VERT!!
OH, I WAS JUST...
... OUTSIDE WALKING.
WHEW
YOU CAN'T FOOL ME! YOU WERE TOTALLY STALKING.
FWOOOOA
HOW SHOCK-ING!!!
WHAM—MO
WHAT A CREEP ...
FWIP
FWIP
HM?

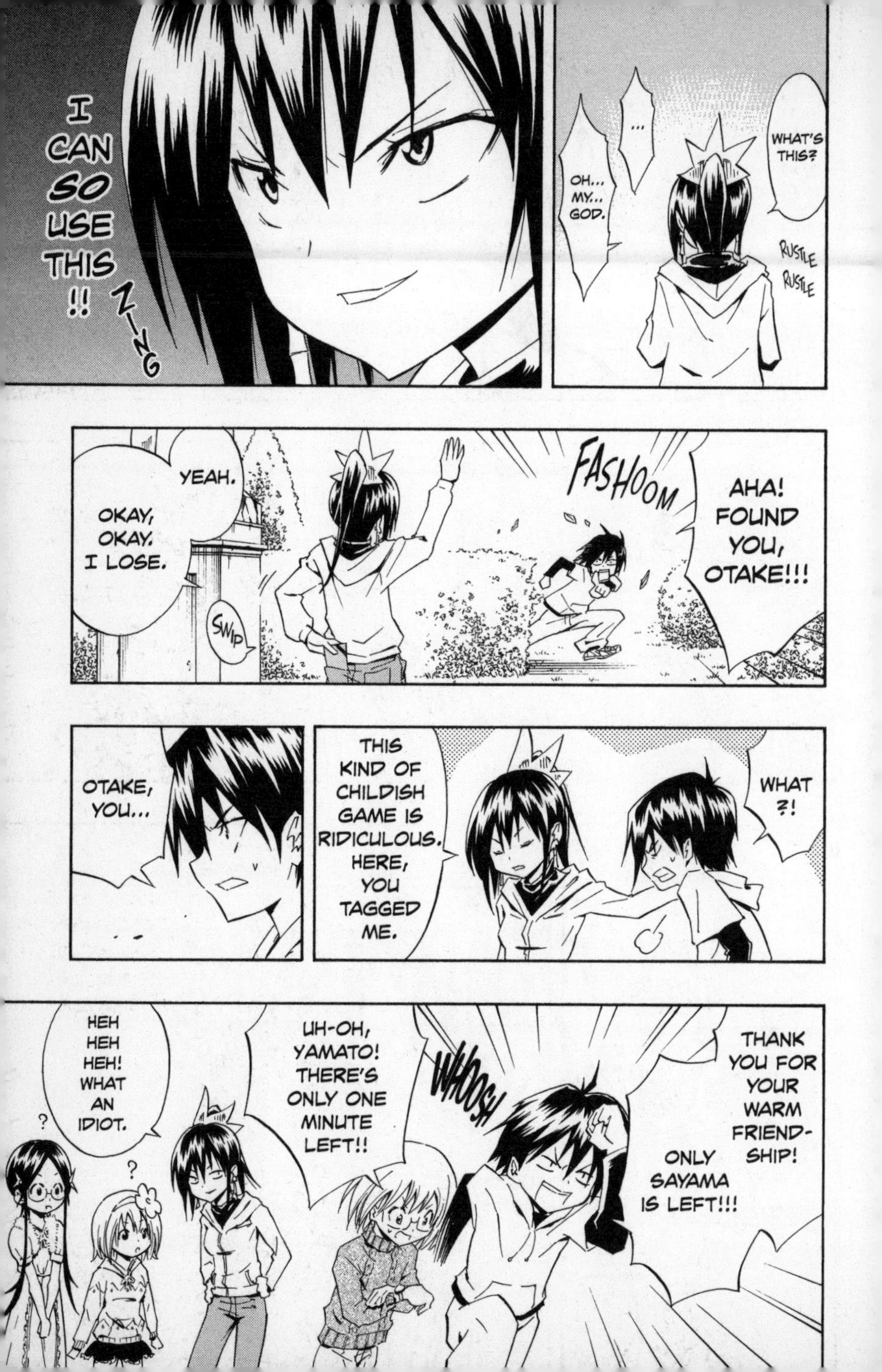

WHAT'S THIS?
RUSTLE RUSTLE
...
OH... MY... GOD.
I CAN SO USE THIS!!
ZING
AHA! FOUND YOU, OTAKE!!!
FASHOOM
YEAH.
OKAY, OKAY. I LOSE.
SWIP
WHAT?!
THIS KIND OF CHILDISH GAME IS RIDICULOUS. HERE, YOU TAGGED ME.
OTAKE, YOU...
THANK YOU FOR YOUR WARM FRIEND-SHIP!
ONLY SAYAMA IS LEFT!!!
WHOOSH
UH-OH, YAMATO! THERE'S ONLY ONE MINUTE LEFT!!
HEH HEH HEH! WHAT AN IDIOT.
?
?

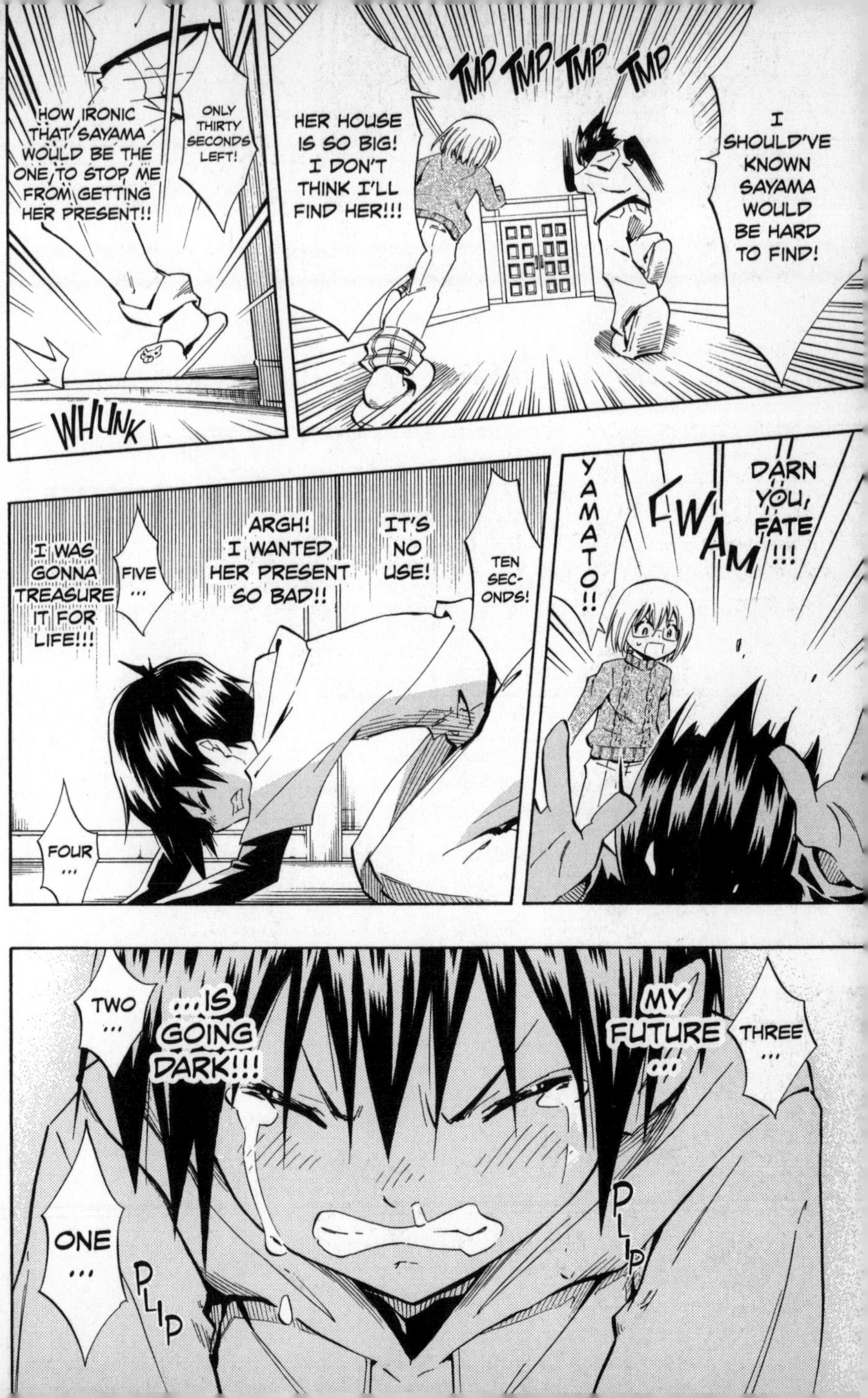
TMP TMP TMP TMP
I SHOULD'VE KNOWN SAYAMA WOULD BE HARD TO FIND!
HER HOUSE IS SO BIG! I DON'T THINK I'LL FIND HER!!!
ONLY THIRTY SECONDS LEFT!
HOW IRONIC THAT SAYAMA WOULD BE THE ONE TO STOP ME FROM GETTING HER PRESENT!!
WHUNK
DARN YOU, FATE!!!
WAM
YAMATO!!
TEN SEC-ONDS!
IT'S NO USE!
ARGH! I WANTED HER PRESENT SO BAD!!
FIVE ...
I WAS GONNA TREASURE IT FOR LIFE!!!
FOUR ...
THREE ...
MY FUTURE ...
...IS GOING DARK!!!
TWO ...
PLIP
ONE ...
PLIP

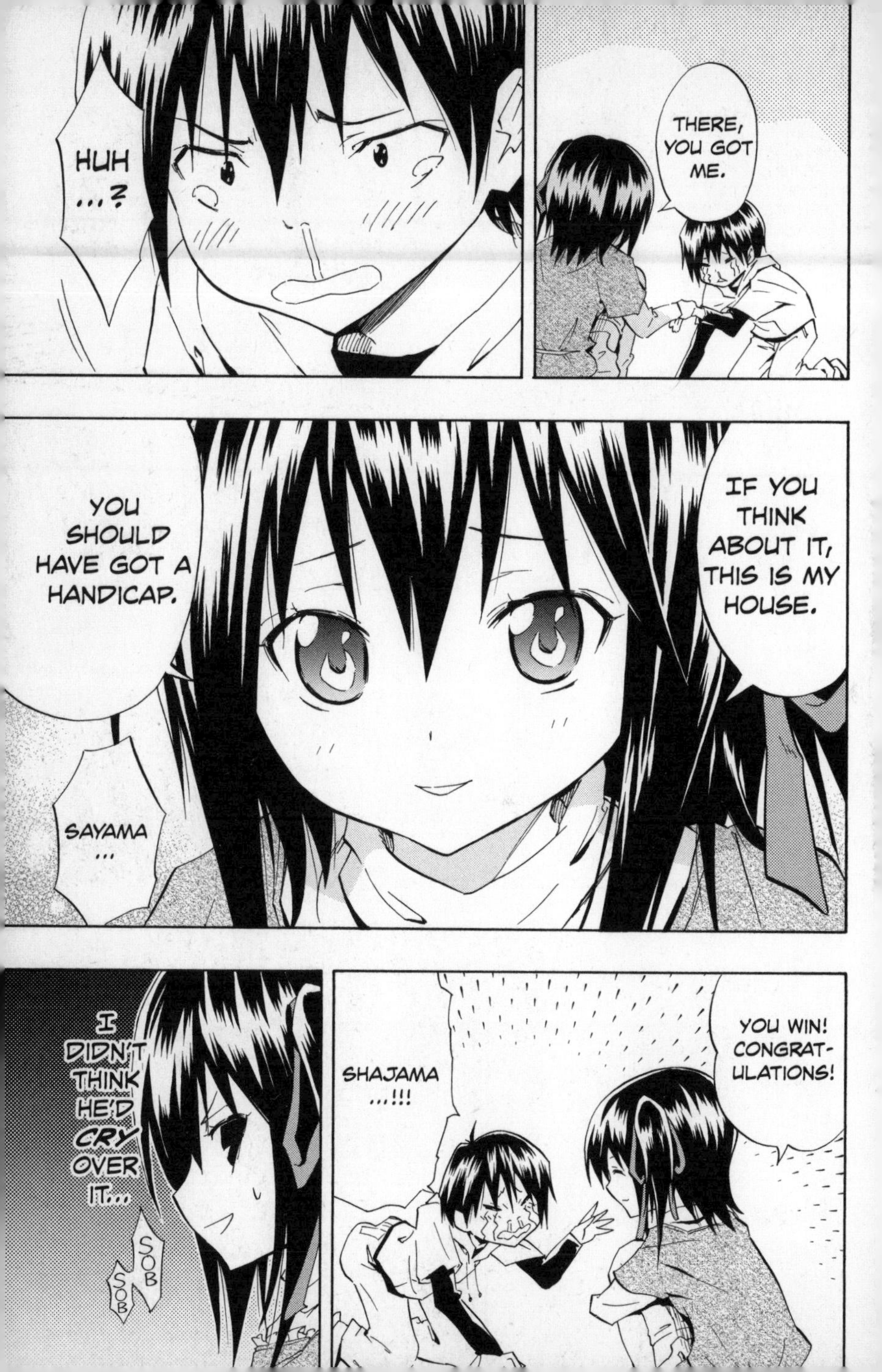
THERE, YOU GOT ME.
HUH ...?
IF YOU THINK ABOUT IT, THIS IS MY HOUSE.
YOU SHOULD HAVE GOT A HANDICAP.
SAYAMA ...
YOU WIN! CONGRAT-ULATIONS!
SHAJAMA ...!!!
I DIDN'T THINK HE'D CRY OVER IT...
SOB
SOB

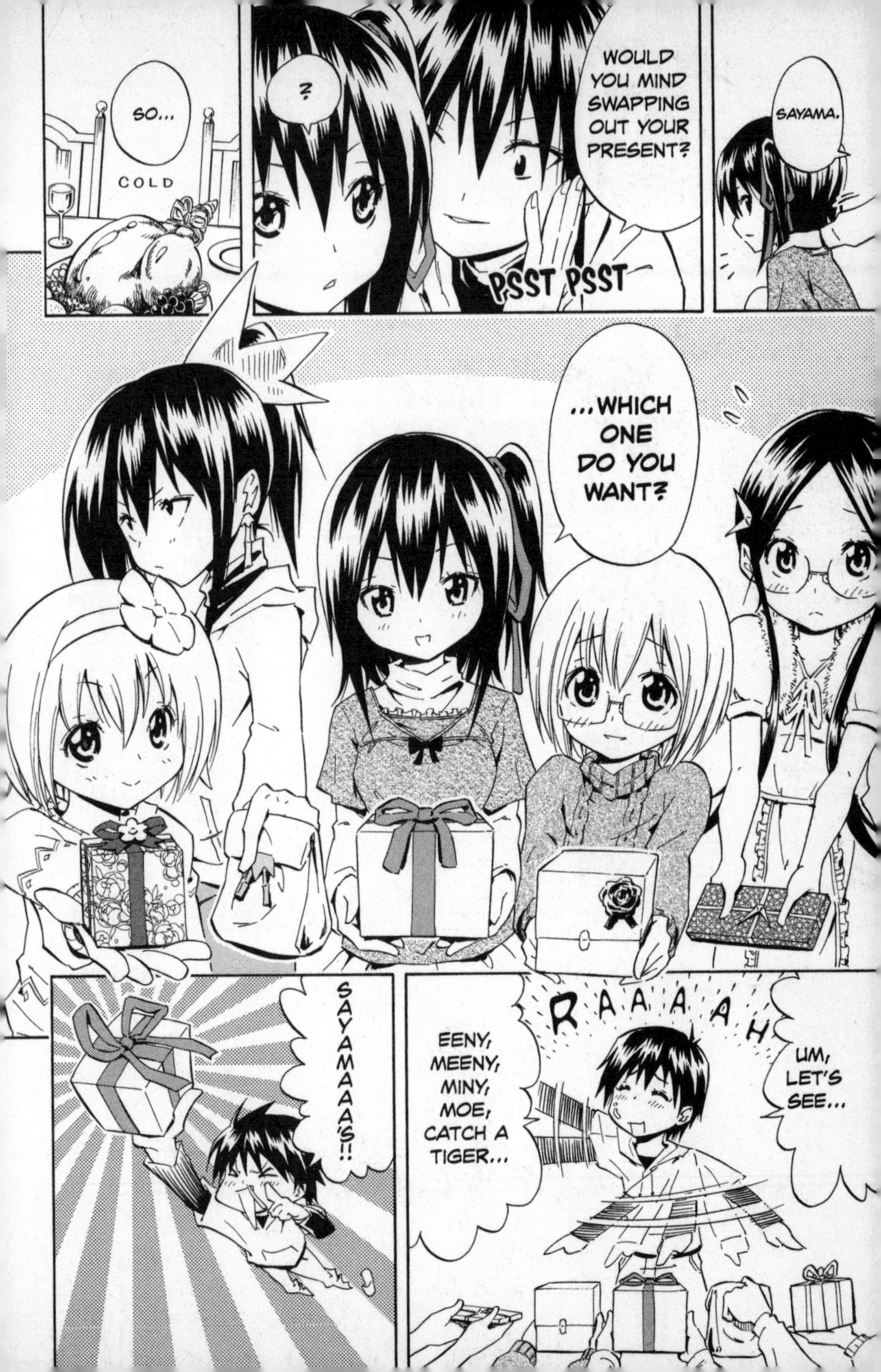
SAYAMA.
WOULD YOU MIND SWAPPING OUT YOUR PRESENT?
?
PSST PSST
SO...
COLD
...WHICH ONE DO YOU WANT?
UM, LET'S SEE...
RAAAAAH
EENY, MEENY, MINY, MOE, CATCH A TIGER...
SAYAMAAAAS!!

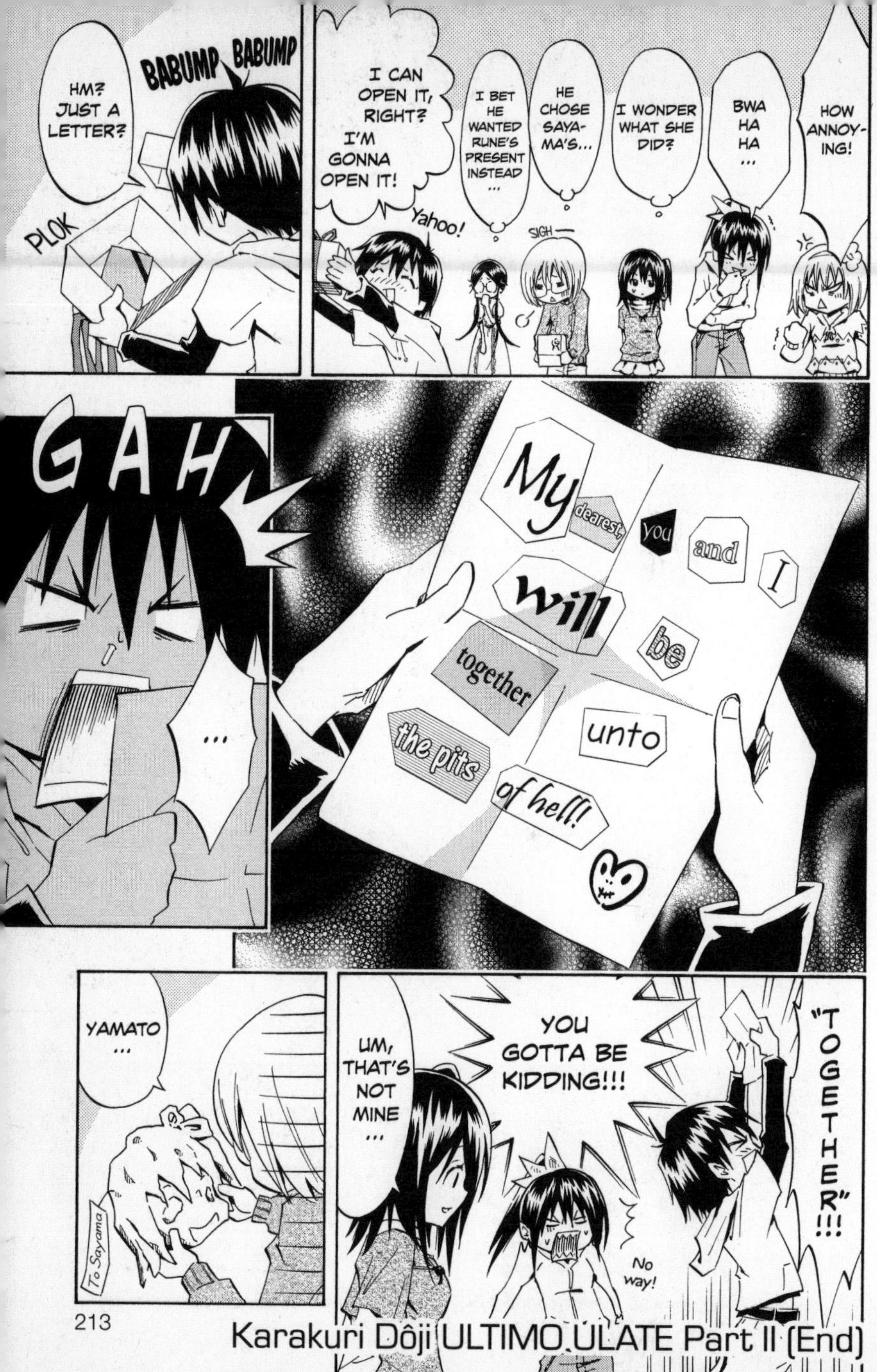
HOW ANNOYING!
BWA HA HA...
I WONDER WHAT SHE DID?
HE CHOSE SAYAMA'S...
I BET HE WANTED RUNE'S PRESENT INSTEAD...
I CAN OPEN IT, RIGHT? I'M GONNA OPEN IT!
SIGH—
Yahoo!
BABUMP BABUMP
HM? JUST A LETTER?
PLOK
My dearest, you and I will be together unto the pits of hell!
GAH
...
"TOGETHER"!!!
YOU GOTTA BE KIDDING!!!
UM, THAT'S NOT MINE...
No way!
YAMATO...
To Sayama

Karakuri Dôji ULTIMO ULATE Part II (End)

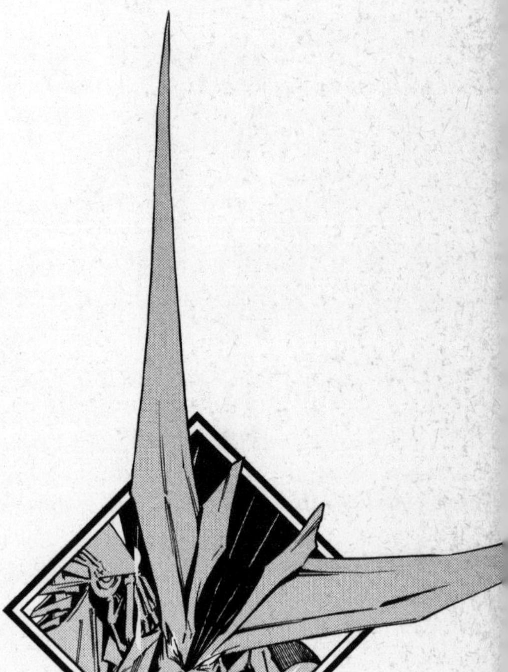

KARAKURIDÔJI
ULTIMO

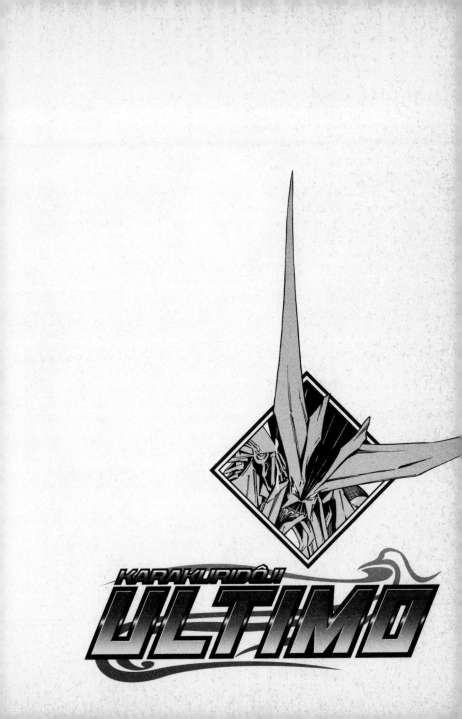

NEXT VOLUME

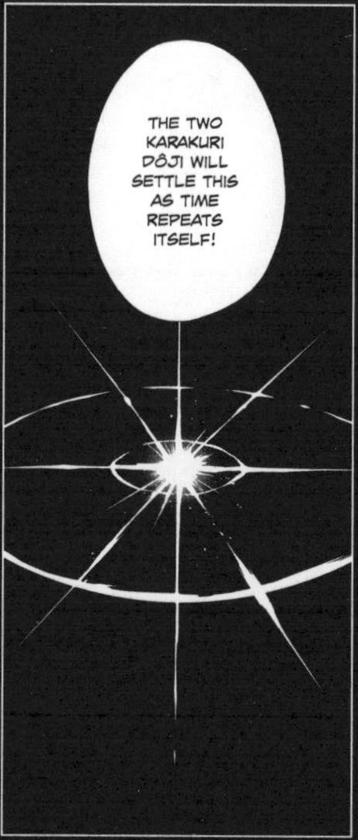
THE TWO KARAKURI DÔJI WILL SETTLE THIS AS TIME REPEATS ITSELF!

The fate of...

...the earth.

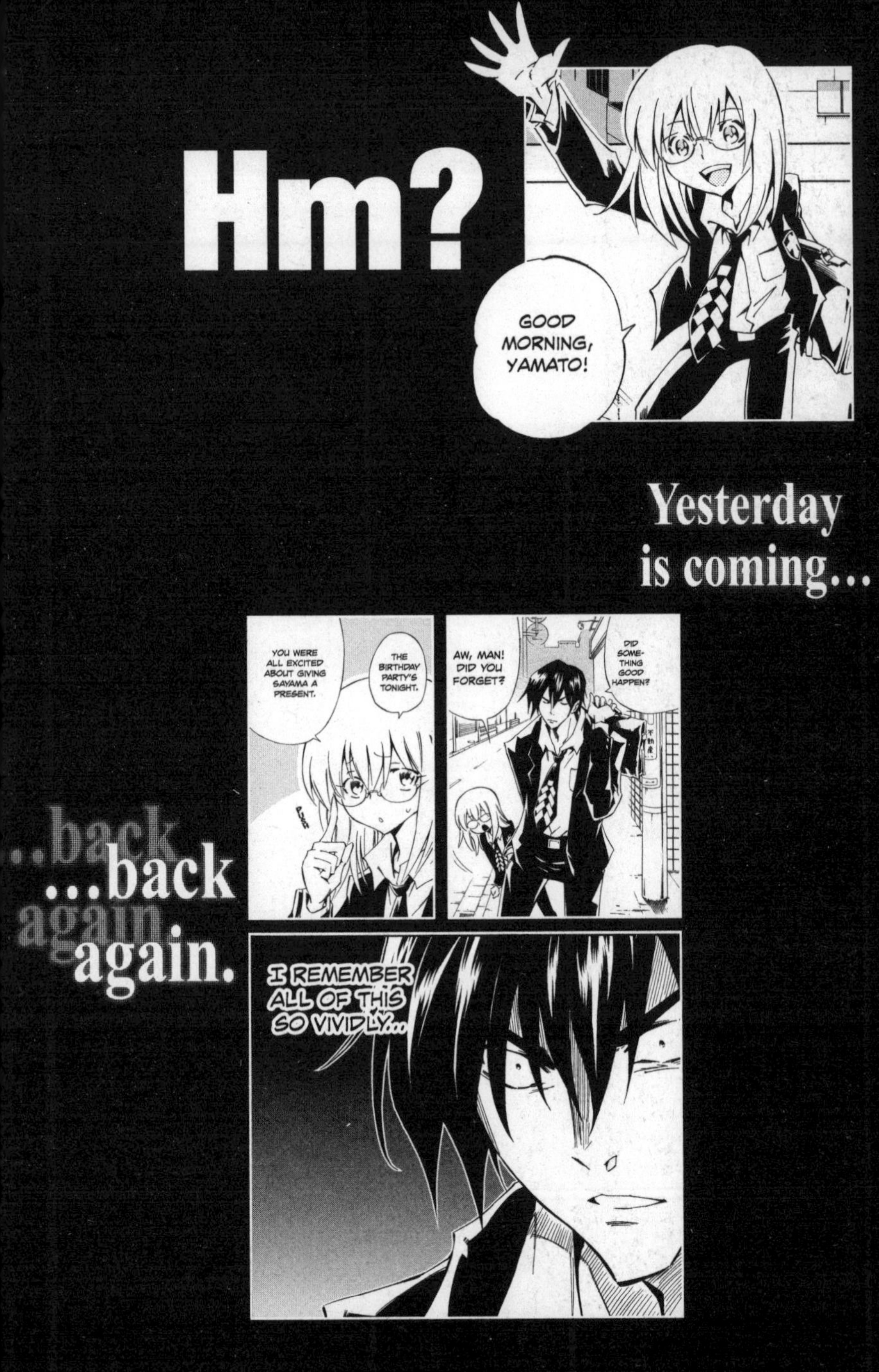
GOOD MORNING, YAMATO!
Hm?
Yesterday is coming...
DID SOMETHING GOOD HAPPEN?
AW, MAN! DID YOU FORGET?
THE BIRTHDAY PARTY'S TONIGHT.
YOU WERE ALL EXCITED ABOUT GIVING SAYAMA A PRESENT.
...back again.
I REMEMBER ALL OF THIS SO VIVIDLY...

And this *yesterday* holds different options.

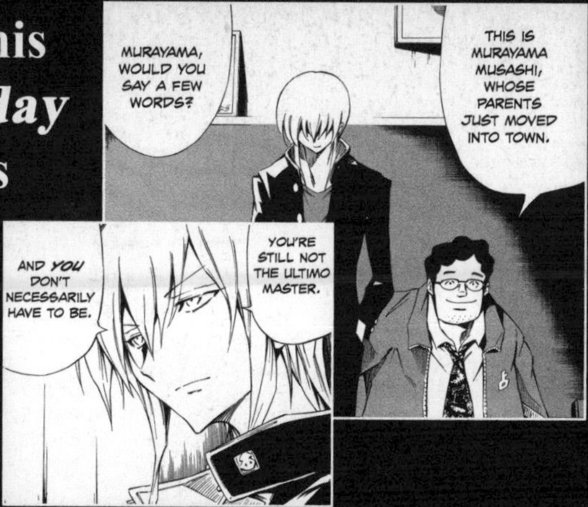
THIS IS MURAYAMA MUSASHI, WHOSE PARENTS JUST MOVED INTO TOWN.
MURAYAMA, WOULD YOU SAY A FEW WORDS?
YOU'RE STILL NOT THE ULTIMO MASTER.
AND *YOU* DON'T NECESSARILY HAVE TO BE.

But there is no escape.

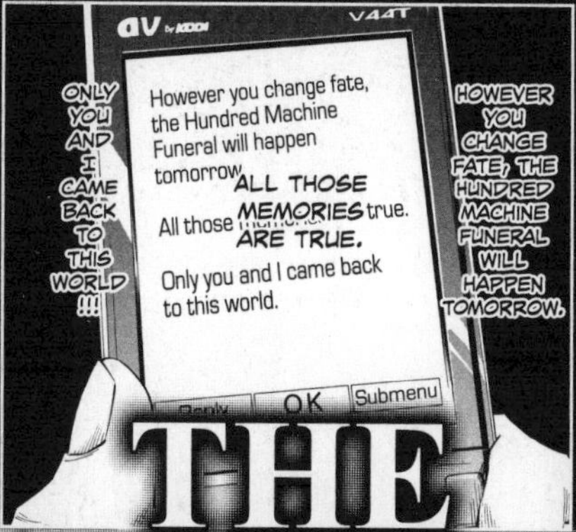
V44T
However you change fate, the Hundred Machine Funeral will happen tomorrow
All those memories true.
Only you and I came back to this world.
OK
Submenu
HOWEVER YOU CHANGE FATE, THE HUNDRED MACHINE FUNERAL WILL HAPPEN TOMORROW.
ALL THOSE MEMORIES ARE TRUE.
ONLY YOU AND I CAME BACK TO THIS WORLD!!!

What will *Yamato* do?!

THE FUTURE

THE HUNDRED MACHINE FUNERAL

KARAKURIDÔJI ULTIMO

VOL. 4

On sale June 2011!!

ULTIMO
Volume 3

Original Concept: Stan Lee
Story and Art by: Hiroyuki Takei

SHONEN JUMP Manga Edition

This graphic novel contains material
that was originally published in English
in SHONEN JUMP #86–90.
Artwork in the magazine may have been
slightly altered from that presented here.

Translation | John Werry
Series Touch-up Art & Lettering | James Gaubatz
Design | Fawn Lau
Series Editor | Joel Enos
Graphic Novel Editor | Megan Bates

Printed in the U.S.A.

Published by VIZ Media, LLC
P.O. Box 77010
San Francisco, CA 94107

10 9 8 7 6 5 4 3 2 1
First printing, December 2010

www.viz.com   www.shonenjump.com

STAN LEE

As a kid, Stanley Martin Lieber spent a lot of time dreaming up wild adventures. By the time he got to high school, he was putting his imagination to work writing stories at Timely, a publishing company that went on to become the legendary Marvel Comics. Starting with the *Fantastic Four*, Lee and his partner Jack Kirby created just about every superhero you can think of, including *Spider-Man*, the *X-Men*, the *Hulk*, *Iron Man*, *Daredevil* and *Thor*. Along the way, he wrote under many pen names, but the one that stuck was Stan Lee.

HIROYUKI TAKEI

Unconventional author/artist Hiroyuki Takei began his career by winning the coveted Hop Step Award (for new manga artists) and the Osamu Tezuka Cultural Prize (named after the famous artist of the same name). After working as an assistant to famed artist Nobuhiro Watsuki, Takei debuted in *Weekly Shonen Jump* in 1997 with *Butsu Zone*, an action series based on Buddhist mythology. His multicultural adventure manga *Shaman King*, which debuted in 1998, became a hit and was adapted into an anime TV series. His new series *Ultimo* (*Karakuri Dôji Ultimo*) is currently being serialized in the U.S. in SHONEN JUMP. Takei lists Osamu Tezuka, American comics and robot anime among his many influences.

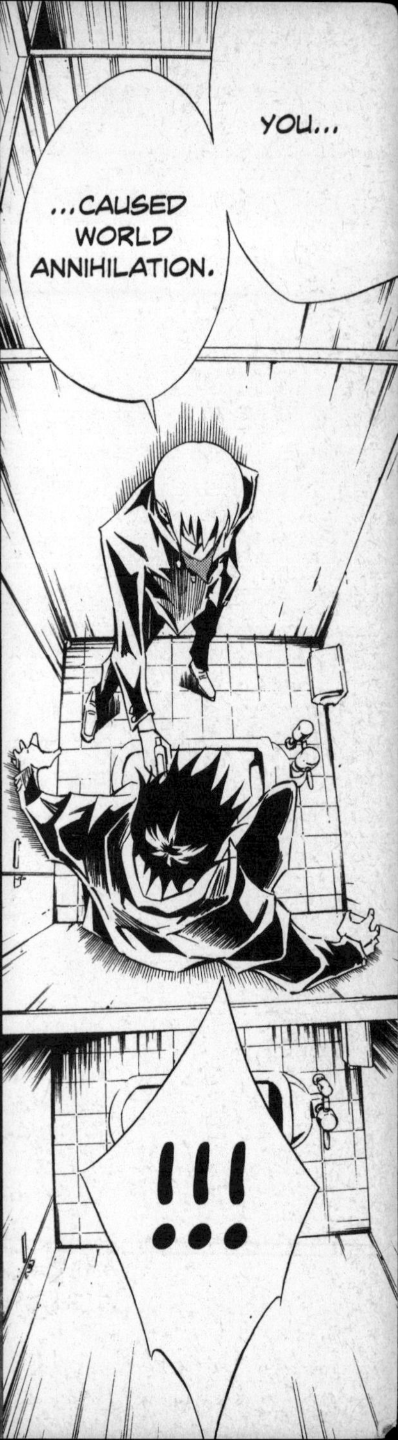
YOU...
...CAUSED WORLD ANNIHILATION.
!!!...

IN THE NEXT VOLUME...

KARAKURI NEW DAWN

Yamato wakes up again on the 21st century day that he first encountered Ultimo, and soon learns that he was sent back in time and it's on him to prevent total world annihilation. But does he really have the ability to stop the apocalypse—and save Ultimo!—in just 24 hours? On a breakneck tour to meet up with all the dôji, Yamato gets into a skirmish with Iruma and Jealousy and must again go back (way back) in time to make things right...

AVAILABLE JUNE 2011!

Read it first in SHONEN JUMP magazine!

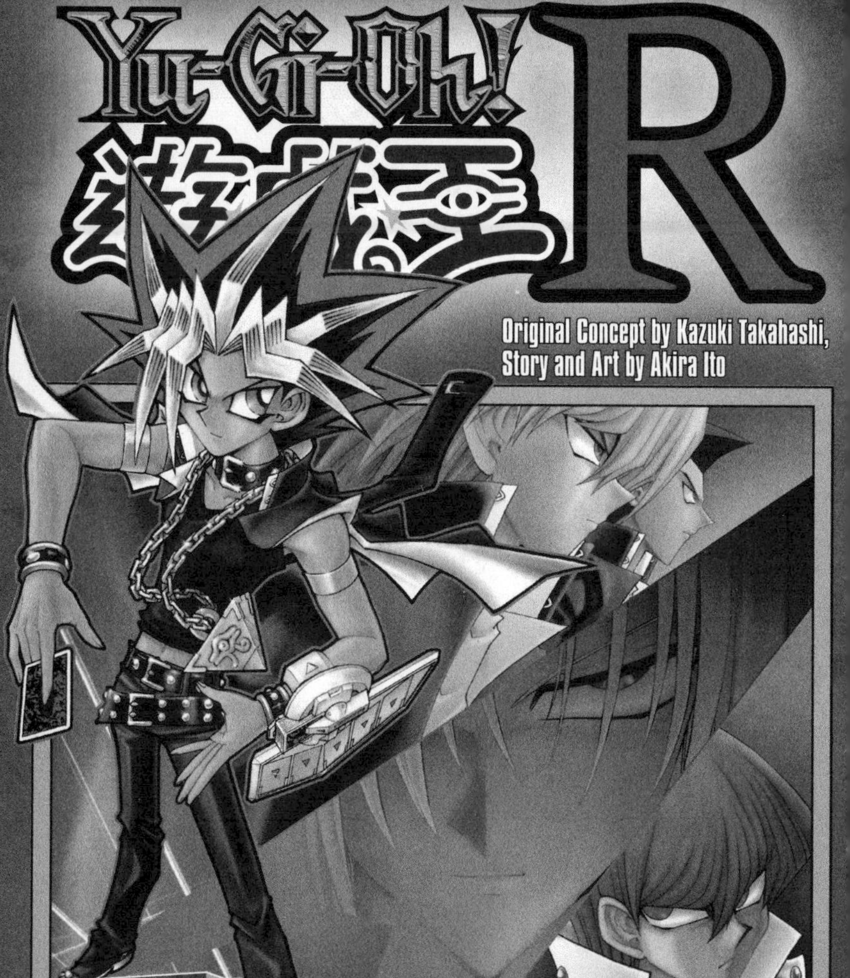
Yu-Gi-Oh!
R

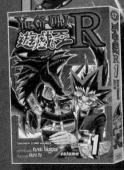

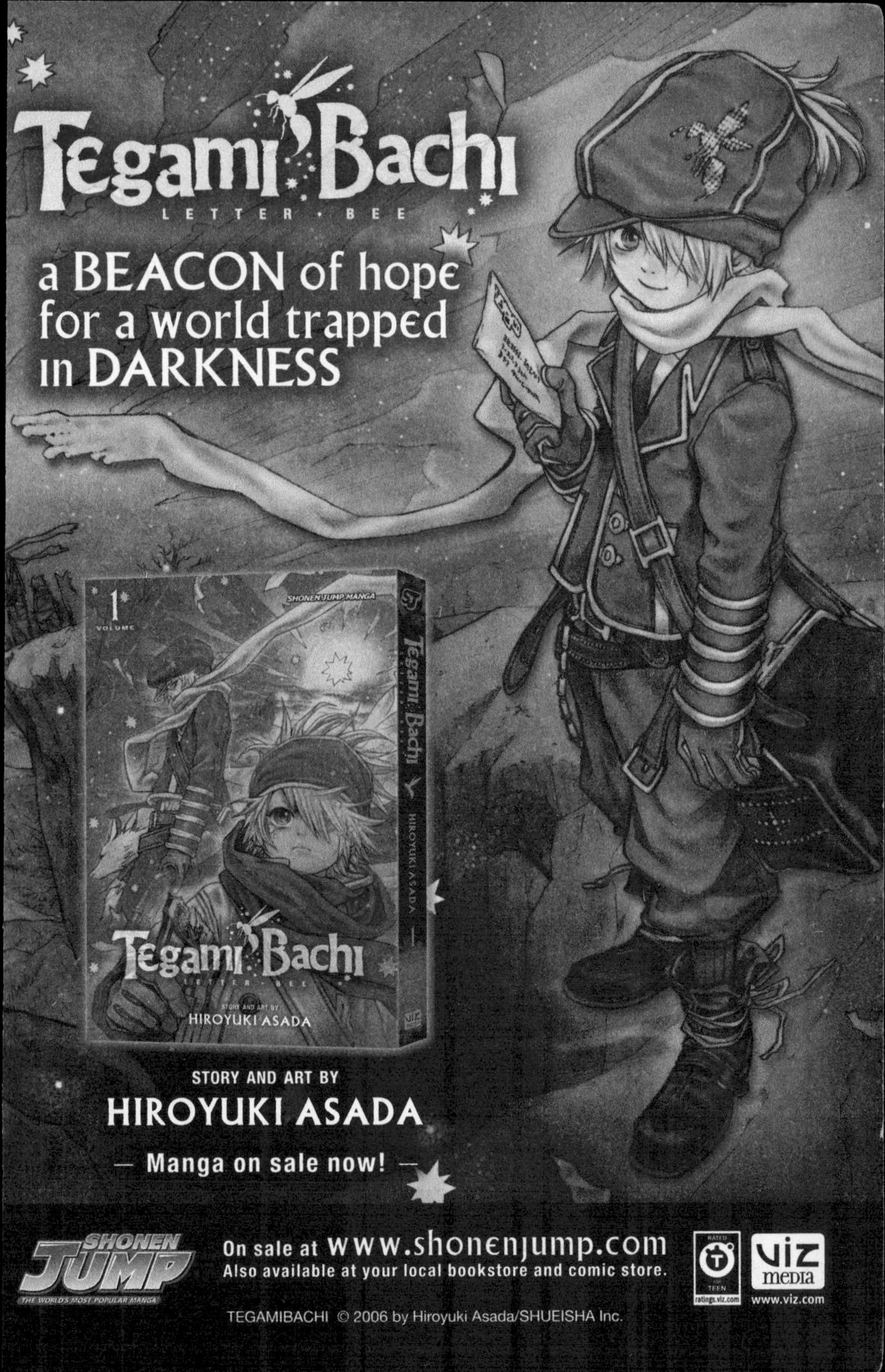
Tegami Bachi
LETTER · BEE
a BEACON of hope for a world trapped in DARKNESS
SHONEN JUMP MANGA
1 VOLUME
Tegami Bachi
LETTER BEE
STORY AND ART BY
HIROYUKI ASADA
STORY AND ART BY
HIROYUKI ASADA
— Manga on sale now! —
SHONEN JUMP
THE WORLD'S MOST POPULAR MANGA
On sale at www.shonenjump.com
Also available at your local bookstore and comic store.
RATED T FOR TEEN
ratings.viz.com
VIZ media
www.viz.com
TEGAMIBACHI © 2006 by Hiroyuki Asada/SHUEISHA Inc.

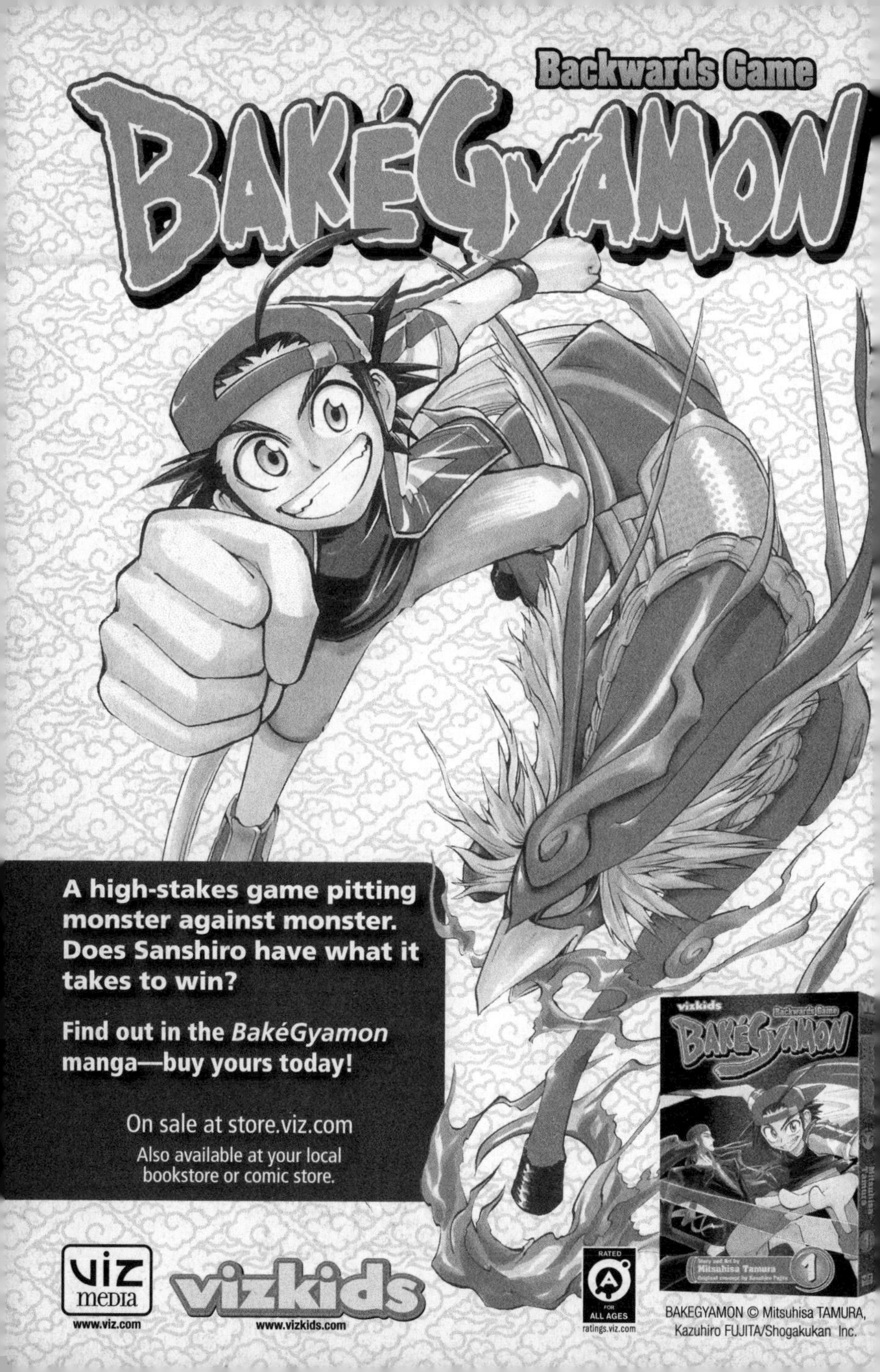
Backwards Game
BAKÉGYAMON
A high-stakes game pitting monster against monster. Does Sanshiro have what it takes to win?
Find out in the *BakéGyamon* manga—buy yours today!
On sale at store.viz.com
Also available at your local bookstore or comic store.
vizkids
Backwards Game
BAKÉGYAMON
1
VIZ media
www.viz.com
vizkids
www.vizkids.com
RATED
A
FOR ALL AGES
ratings.viz.com
BAKEGYAMON © Mitsuhisa TAMURA, Kazuhiro FUJITA/Shogakukan Inc.

SHONEN JUMP

THE WORLD'S MOST POPULAR MANGA

BLEACH

STORY AND ART BY
TITE KUBO

ONE PIECE

STORY AND ART BY
EIICHIRO ODA

Tegami Bachi
LETTER BEE

STORY AND ART BY
HIROYUKI ASADA

JUMP INTO THE ACTION BY TELLING US WHAT YOU LOVE (AND WHAT YOU DON'T)

LET YOUR VOICE BE HEARD!

SHONENJUMP.VIZ.COM/MANGASURVEY

HELP US MAKE MORE OF THE WORLD'S MOST POPULAR MANGA!

3 1901 04989 0330

RATED T FOR TEEN
ratings.viz.com

VIZ media

www.viz.com